THE RECEYT
OF THE
LADIE KATERYNE

EARLY ENGLISH TEXT SOCIETY
No. 296
1990

For Janet

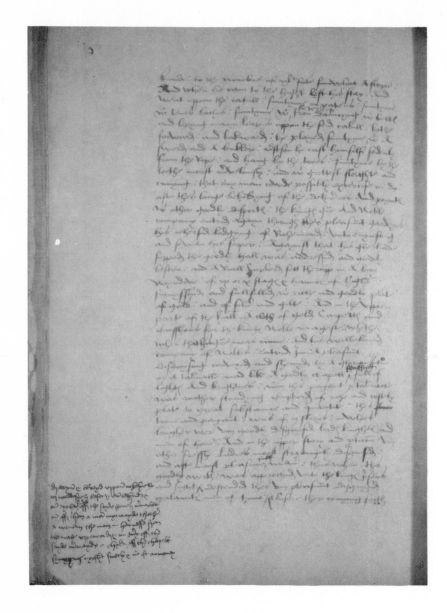

College of Arms, MS 1st M. 13, fol. 64ᵛ
(showing corrections and additions by Scribe C)

THE RECEYT
OF THE
LADIE KATERYNE

EDITED BY

GORDON KIPLING

Published for
THE EARLY ENGLISH TEXT SOCIETY
by the
OXFORD UNIVERSITY PRESS
1990

Oxford University Press, Walton Street, Oxford OX2 6DP

Oxford   New York   Toronto
Delhi   Bombay   Calcutta   Madras   Karachi
Petaling Jaya   Singapore   Hong Kong   Tokyo
Nairobi   Dar es Salaam   Cape Town
Melbourne   Auckland

Associated companied in Beirut   Berlin   Ibadan   Nicosia

Oxford is a trade mark of Oxford University Press

British Library Cataloguing in Publication Data

The Receyt of the Ladie Kateryne.—(Early English Text
Society. Original Series; 296).
I. England. Royal courts. Social life, 1485–1509
I. Kipling, Gordon Lee   II. Series
941.051
ISBN 0–19–722298–6

Set on a Lasercomp at
Oxford University Computing Service
Printed in Great Britain by
Richard Clay (The Chaucer Press) Ltd, Bungay, Suffolk

CONTENTS

PREFACE

Scholars, like spendthrifts, are notorious borrowers; in a sense, scholars are the more desperate debtors because their debts, being those of an intellectual coinage, can never be repaid. Such debts can, however, be gratefully acknowledged, and I have attempted to do so as fully as possible both in the footnotes to the introduction and in the commentary to this edition. I have incurred a number of debts, however, which are either too general or too important to be acknowledged in this way, and I would like to account for them here. First of all, the texts of the *Receyt*, the Buckingham Challenge, and the Tournament score cheque are printed by permission of the College of Arms, whose staff—particularly Sir A. Colin Cole, Garter King of Arms, Mr Walter Chattey, and Mr Robert Yorke, College Archivist—have generously made these and other manuscripts available to me. I am especially grateful to Mr Yorke, who read a draft of the General Introduction at my request, and whose scholarship and thorough knowledge of the College Library saved me from many important errors. The text of the Suffolk Challenge is printed by permission of the Archivo General de Simancas.

A number of other friends and colleagues read versions of this edition and made many important suggestions for improvement. David Bevington, who has followed this project and advised me from its inception, naturally takes pride of place in this regard. But I have also received wise and expert counsel from Charles Batten, Norman Blake, John N. King, Arthur Kinney, Alan Nelson, and Meg Twycross. Mr R.R. Stratton, Assistant Librarian, Worcester Cathedral Library, very kindly examined both the Cathedral archives and the records of the Worcester County Record Office in an attempt to settle some important matters of fact for me. I owe particular gratitude to my research assistant, Dr Victor Scherb, who has laboured long and carefully over the glossary and proofreading. Mrs Jeannette Gilkison has expertly both typed and wordprocessed various drafts of the introduction, commentary, and glossary. All remaining errors of fact and opinion are my own.

My various particular acknowledgements in the Introduction and Commentary cannot adequately account for my indebtedness to the work of Sydney Anglo and Glynne Wickham. This is true even when, as I sometimes do, I differ significantly in matters of interpretation from one or the other of these two scholars who have done so much to demonstrate the crucial importance of the pageantry and revels described in the *Receyt* to the history of drama, politics, and ideas in the Tudor period.

Research and preparation of this edition has been aided by a generous grant from the UCLA Committee on Research. Finally, I am especially grateful to the Council of the Early English Text Society, particularly Dr Pamela Gradon (former Editorial Secretary) and Dr M.R. Godden (present Editorial Secretary), for supporting this edition and shepherding me through its publication.

The frontispiece is reproduced by permission of the College of Arms.

ABBREVIATIONS

The following abbreviations appear frequently throughout the Introduction, Textual Notes, and Commentary.

A	British Library, MS Additional 45131
Antiquarian Repertory	Francis Grose and Thomas Astle, *The Antiquarian Repertory*, 4 vols (London, 1807–09)
C	British Library, MS Cotton Vitellius A. XVI (ed. C.L. Kingsford, in *Chronicles of London* (Oxford, 1905))
Collectanea	John Leland, *De Rebus Britannicis Collectanea*, ed. Thomas Hearne (London, 1770)
G	Guildhall MS 3313 (ed. A.H. Thomas and I.D. Thornley, *The Great Chronicle of London* (London, 1938))
BC	The Buckingham Challenge, Appendix, pp.97–102
H	British Library, MS Harley 69
I.3	College of Arms, MS I. 3
I.9	College of Arms, MS I. 9
M	College of Arms, MS 1st M. 13
M.3	College of Arms, MS M. 3
R	College of Arms, MS 1st M. 13, fols 27–75 (originally a separate MS, now a part of *M*)
SC	The Suffolk Challenge, Appendix, pp.103–7
Sp	Archives of Simancas, MS P.R. 54–14
St	Staffordshire County Record Office, MS D.1721/1/1
V	British Library, MS Cotton Vitellius C. XI
V25	College of Arms, MS Vincent 25

HISTORICAL RECORDS

Although the *Receyt of the Ladie Kateryne* provides the best single source of information about the Tudor festival it describes, the event is also well-documented in a number of other sources. The following are those most frequently cited in the Introduction and Commentary.

I. Much of the diplomatic correspondence detailing the negotiations for the marriage of Katharine and Arthur has been extensively calendared in G.A. Bergenroth, ed., *Calendar of State Papers, Spanish*, i (London, 1862) and *Supplement to I and II* (London, 1868). Some important matters of detail have been overlooked in Bergenroth's usually admirable summaries, however, and original sources should often be consulted (e.g., Ambassador de Puebla's report on the Calais conference, Archives of Simancas, MS P.R. 54–14, and the correspondence of Jean de Houppelines, Henry VII's French Secretary at Calais, British Library MS 46455).

II. The Tudor court's extensive planning for the wedding festival can be traced through a series of Privy Council orders. 1) The earliest version of these Orders dates from the spring of 1500 and is represented by two fragmentary texts: *The traduction & mariage of the princesse* (London: Richard Pynson, [1500]) and British Library MS Cotton Vitellius C. XI, fols 112ᵛ–113ᵛ. Pynson's printed version (unique copy in British Library) is the longer fragment, but the manuscript version contains several passages missing from the print. The manuscript version has been printed in J. Gairdner, ed., *Letters and Papers Illustrative of the Reigns of Richard III and Henry VII* (London, 1861–3), ii, 103–05. 2) These orders were revised a year later to suit the altered circumstances of the summer of 1501. The resulting version of the Privy Council Orders is represented by College of Arms, MS 1st M. 13, fols 1–11. British Library, MS Harley 69, fols 39ʳ–44ʳ, is a seventeenth-century transcript; the Harley version has been printed in P. Yorke, second Earl of Hardwicke, *Miscellaneous State Papers* (London, 1778), i, 1–20. 3) A final version of the Orders was compiled in early October 1501 when Katharine unexpectedly arrived in Plymouth instead of Southampton, and the Council had to revise correspondingly.

Numerous alterations to the previous version of the Orders represent the Council's planning upon the very eve of the festival. This version appears uniquely in British Library, MS Cotton Vespasian C. XIV, fols 94^r–103^v, and has been printed by Gardiner (*Letters and Papers*) i, 404–17. For the dating of these various texts, see Gordon Kipling, *Triumph of Honour* (The Hague, 1977), pp.173–4.

III. Two London chronicles report the events of the festival from a civic, rather than a court, point of view. As a consequence, they provide relatively detailed accounts of the 'public' events of the festival (the royal entry, the tournaments), but only cursory reports—or no report at all—of the 'courtly' events (the disguisings, the state banquets, the trip to Richmond). Both of the extant chronicles are abridged versions of the lost 'Main City Chronicle'. Of the two versions, Guildhall MS 3313, fols 275^r–92^v, has been edited by A.H. Thomas and I.D. Thornley, *The Great Chronicle of London* (London, 1938), pp.296–316. The other chronicle, though briefer, occasionally supplies details missing from the Guildhall chronicle: British Library, MS Cotton Vitellius A. XVI, fols 183^v–201^v. It has been edited by C.L. Kingsford, *Chronicles of London* (Oxford, 1905), pp.234–55.

IV. These sources can be supplemented by a series of court and civic financial records. The court's extensive financing of the various events of the festival appear in the Account Books of John Heron, Treasurer of the Chamber. The volume covering the wedding festival is PRO, E. 101/415/3. Sydney Anglo has printed a helpful selection of Heron's entries in 'The Court Festivals of Henry VII', *Bulletin of the John Rylands Library*, xliv (1960–1), 12–45. For Arthur's funeral, Heron's accounts should be supplemented by PRO, LC 2/1, which details the expenses for all of the royal funerals of Henry VII's reign. Details of the civic financing of the royal entry pageantry appear in two manuscripts in the Corporation of London Record Office: *Journals*, x, fols 187, 190, 235, 238, 276 and *Rental of the Bridge House*, fols 224^v, 227^v.

GENERAL INTRODUCTION

In October and November of 1501, the Tudor court devised a festival to celebrate the marriage of Henry VII's eldest son, Prince Arthur, to Katharine of Aragon, daughter of the Spanish monarchs, Ferdinand and Isabella. Such festivals, as Huizinga reminds us in *The Waning of the Middle Ages*, 'still preserved something of the meaning they have in primitive societies, that of the supreme expression of their culture, the highest mode of collective enjoyment and an assertion of solidarity.'[1] Since the festival was unusually significant to Henry, representing as it did the successful culmination of his dynastic and political ambitions, it was designed from the first as a lavish celebration of the Tudor dynasty. Richmond Palace was built and inaugurated for the festival. Artists were summoned to provide it with paintings, poetry, tapestries, a triumphal procession, a costumed tournament, court masques, and plays.

That contemporary Englishmen felt the festival to be especially important is demonstrated by the detailed account of the event which one writer compiled, probably as an official memorial. *The Receyt of the Ladie Kateryne*[2] chronicles Katharine of Aragon's arrival in England, her triumphant entry into London, her marriage to Prince Arthur, the disguisings and tournament held in honour of that marriage, and Prince Arthur's funeral in Ludlow and Worcester a few months thereafter. Divided into books and chapters, it attempts to cast its historical materials into the form of a medieval romance, occasionally borrowing prose cadences from Malory or Lord Berners to describe the actions of Katharine, Arthur, and Henry VII.

No other contemporary source preserves such a full and vivid account of the social history, visual arts, and drama in England at the opening of the sixteenth century. While almost every serious study of early Tudor history and society in the past century is also

1. Tr. F. Hopman (London, 1924), 229–30.
2. If the narrative ever had a title, it was lost when the original vellum covering was discarded (see pp.xxxii–iii below). Supposing the text had a title, I supply 'The Receyt of the Ladie Kateryne', a phrase borrowed from the first lines of the prologue to the text.

indebted to the *Receyt*,[1] the manuscript has proven especially
indispensable for historians of the drama. Glynne Wickham, for
one, regards the manuscript in which this narrative is found to be
'unquestionably the most important extant document relative to
the dramatic records of the early Tudor period'.[2] The *Receyt*, in
fact, provides detailed accounts of three of the age's most
important forms of courtly and spectacular drama at a time when
such accounts are otherwise impossible to find. First, its account
of the magnificent dramatic pageantry for Katharine of Aragon's
triumphal entry into London is unrivaled for its detail in the
history of these shows. Second, the similarly detailed accounts of
the four disguisings held at Westminster and Richmond are of
necessity cited by every scholar of the English masque from
Chambers, Reyher, and Welsford to Anglo, Orgel, and
Wickham.[3] Third, its descriptions of the mimetic tournament,
with its anticipation of Artesia's tournament in the *Arcadia* and of
the Elizabethan Accession Day jousts, constitutes one of the
landmarks of Tudor allegory and chivalry.[4] With the single
exception of the interlude, which is well documented by a number
of texts, the *Receyt* thus provides a complete picture of the state of
English court drama at a crucial point in its development.

THE CIVIC TRIUMPH

Katharine of Aragon's royal entry into London has been called
'the supreme masterpiece of English civic pageantry'.[5] It is
certainly the most literary and erudite, at least until Ben Jonson's
essay in the same form a century later. To begin with, the devisor
of the pageantry conceived of the show largely in dramatic terms.

1. In addition to those works mentioned in note 3 below, see W. Busch, *King
Henry VII*, tr. A.M. Todd (London, 1895); G. Mattingly, *Catherine of Aragon*
(Boston, 1941); and S.B. Chrimes, *Henry VII* (London, 1972).
2. MS 'Calendar of contents' dated 1949 and appended to College of Arms, MS
1st M. 13.
3. Cf. E.K. Chambers, *The Mediaeval Stage*, 2 vols (Oxford, 1903) and *The
Elizabethan Stage*, 4 vols (Oxford, 1923); P. Reyher, *Les Masques Anglais* (Paris,
1909); E. Welsford, *The Court Masque* (Cambridge, 1927); S. Anglo, *Spectacle,
Pageantry and Early Tudor Policy* (Oxford, 1969); G. Wickham, *Early English
Stages*, i (London, 1959); S. Orgel, *The Jonsonian Masque* (Cambridge, Mass., 1965).
All these works make extensive use of the descriptions in the *Receyt*, sometimes
as in Reyher printing long extracts from one or another of the derivative
manuscripts.
4. G. Kipling, *The Triumph of Honour: Burgundian Origins of the Elizabethan
Renaissance* (The Hague, 1977), 116–36, cited hereafter as *Triumph of Honour*.
5. Anglo, *Spectacle*, 97.

By a careful structuring of the Princess's encounters with the actors on the six pageant stages, he arranges for Katharine to travel from earth, through the spheres of the cosmos, to an apotheosis upon the Throne of Honour in heaven. At the first pageant on London Bridge, Saints Katharine and Ursula descend from the 'Courte Celestiall' to announce that the Princess will be 'conveyed ... to Honour' in the heavens, where she is to become the star Hesperus set among the 'sterres bright' (2/60–119). The rest of the pageants fulfill this prophecy as Katharine makes her 'ascent' to her stellar home. She therefore climbs from the earthly Castle Policy (pageant two), to the sphere of the moon (pageant three), to the sphere of the sun (pageant four), to the Throne of God the Father (pageant five). At each station, she acquires the virtues she will need for the next stage of her ascent. Finally, she is invited to take a throne beside Honour himself, a throne fixed upon the eternal foundation of the seven virtues and set above the cosmos (pageant six).

Nor is Katharine allowed to be a merely passive witness to this drama. She is both audience and protagonist of the show. Indeed, the pageant designer so contrives the Princess's encounters with the pageant actors that she seems to play an active part. Her approach to the second pageant thus miraculously causes the gates of Castle Policy to swing open. 'Who openyd these gatis?' enquires the captain of the castle; 'what, opened they alone?' Then, searching the skies, he discovers the reason:

> The bright sterre of Spayne, Hesperus, on them shone,
> Whoes goodly beames hath persid mightily
> Thorugh this castell to bring this good lady,
> Whoes prosperous comyng shall right joyefull be.
>
> (2/188–91)

As Elizabeth I would discover later in the century, the pageantry of the civic triumph had transformed the city into 'a stage wherein was shewed the wonderfull spectacle, of a noble hearted princesse toward her most louing people'.[1]

This civic triumph, perhaps more than any other in the history of the form, is distinguished by its erudition as well as its dramatic form. The devisor drew his plot, characters, and pageant designs from a number of varied sources, ranging from courtly elegy, to patristic commentary, to scholastic allegory, to popular

---

1. Richard Mulcaster, *The Passage of our most drad Soueraigne Lady Quene Elyzabeth through the citie of London to westminster the daye before her coronacion* (London, 1558), fol. Aii[v].

legend.[1] Perhaps the most important of these sources was Jean Molinet's *Le Trosne d'Honneur*, an elegy on the death of Philip the Good, Duke of Burgundy, composed for the Duke's son, Charles the Bold. In its vision of the apotheosis of Duke Philip, the poem provided the pageant designer with his plot, some characters, and the design of the final pageant. Just as Duke Philip ascends the planetary spheres of the cosmos to reach the Throne of Honour, so Katharine makes the same journey through the streets of London. Just as each sphere of the cosmos represents one of Philip's virtues, so Katharine must ascend a 'stair of virtues' to reach the Throne. Several of Molinet's characters step out of the poem onto the pageant stages of London: Noblesse, Virtue, Honour himself. Molinet even places King Arthur 'en chaiere royale' upon one of the spheres of the cosmos, thus providing one important inspiration for the fourth pageant's vision of King Arthur riding a golden triumphal chariot through the sphere of the sun. Finally, the last pageant of the series carefully imitates Molinet's description of the Throne of Honour above the cosmos. Like Charles the Bold before her, Katharine sees a vision of Honour's throne flanked by two empty chairs. One of these has already been awarded to Arthur; the other is reserved for Katharine when she marries her Tudor prince.

The pageant master found still other elements of his plot and characterization in 'the most successful textbook ever written', Martianus Capella's *Marriage of Philologia and Mercury*.[2] In Capella's allegory of the marriage of a mortal to a star-god, the pageant designer found a metaphor at once both patriotic and allegorical for Katharine in the role of the mortal Philologia whom the gods make immortal so that she can marry Mercury. Mercury, in the pageant designer's imagination, however, becomes Arcturus, at once both Prince Arthur and seven-starred constellation. Arthur, a Tudor star-god, awaits Katharine, a Spanish mortal, from his stellar home in the heavens. Katharine, who aspires to ascend to her own stellar home in the evening star, Hesperus, struggles to join him. Once she reaches that destination, the marriage of Arthur and Katharine will seem to mortals like the astrological conjunction of Arcturus and Hesperus. Even so, it will be a joining of unequals, a constellation with a planet.

---

1. The following discussion of the devisor's use of Molinet, Capella, and popular legend follows Chapter 4 of *Triumph of Honour*, where fuller explanations will be found.

2. P.R. Cole, *Later Roman Education* (New York, 1909), 16; E.R. Curtius, *European Literature and the Latin Middle Ages*, tr. W.R. Trask (New York, 1953), 38–9.

By identifying Arthur with Arcturus, the pageant designer draws upon yet a third source of imagery, this time from popular legend. Since the mid-fifteenth century, English writers had occasionally postulated King Arthur's ascension to Arcturus as a more Christian alternative to his final voyage to Avalon. Lydgate, for example, interprets the journey to Avalon as a poetic metaphor for Arthur's translation to 'the rich, starry, bright castle which Astronomers call Arthur's Constellation', where he lives in Christian glory.[1] A century and a half later, Jonson and Davies are still imagining Arthur 'translated to a star' in the constellation Arcturus.[2] The idea behind this widespread and enduring tradition, of course, ultimately derives from the *Timaeus*, where Plato imagines the stars to be the proper dwellings of human souls. From the stars we descend to our incarnations on earth, and to them, if we are successful, we return again after death.[3] Henry VII's court poets, indeed, made much of this imagery at Prince Arthur's birth. Noting that the Tudor child had been born 'under' the star Arcturus, they imagined that the soul of King Arthur had descended again from the star to be reborn.[4] The pageant devisor carries this theme of the second coming of King Arthur further; he imagines Prince Arthur riding his constellation, Arcturus, like a chariot through the heavens, waiting for Princess Katharine to ascend to her own native star.

Much of the individual pageant imagery, meanwhile, draws heavily from patristic and scholastic sources. As Sydney Anglo has shown, the pageant devisor draws extensively from Gregory the Great's *Moralia in libros beati Job* for the various allegorical explications of Arcturus which Katharine learns as she travels from pageant to pageant.[5] The seven stars of his constellation are thus successively identified with the seven gifts of the Holy Spirit,

1. *Fall of Princes*, viii, 3095–3108.
2. Ben Jonson, *The Speeches at Prince Henry's Barriers*, in *Works*, ed. C.H. Herford and Percy and Evelyn Simpson (Oxford, 1925–52), vii, 325. *The Poems of Sir John Davies*, ed. R. Krueger (Oxford, 1975), 231–2.
3. J.A. Stewart, *The Myths of Plato*, ed. G.R. Levy, 2nd ed. (Fontwell, Sussex, 1960), 252–80. See also Boethius, *De consolatione philosophiae*, iv, met. 1; Macrobius, *Commentary on the Dream of Scipio*, ed. and tr. W.H. Stahl (New York, 1952), 142–6; Chaucer, *Works*, ed. F.N. Robinson, 2nd ed. (Boston, 1957), 287 for medieval literary uses of this platonic idea.
4. See the contemporary poems on Arthur's birth by Bernard André and Giovanni Gigli (J. Gairdner, ed., *Memorials of King Henry VII* (London, 1858), lx, 44–6) and by Pietro Carmeliano (H.A. Kelly, *Divine Providence in the England of Shakespeare's Histories* (Cambridge, Mass., 1970), 323–4).
5. The following discussion of the devisor's use of Gregory the Great and Boethius follows, in the main, Anglo, *Spectacle*, 56–97, where fuller explanation will be found.

the seven-branched candlestick of the Apocalypse, the seven pieces of spiritual armour worn by the Christian knight, and with the seven angels who watch over the seven churches of Asia. He also made good use of Boethius, particularly in pageants three and four, which owe a good deal to Book One, Metre Five of the *Consolation of Philosophy*. Boethius himself appears in the first of these pageants to read the Princess's fortune from a 'volvell'. The following pageant then virtually recreates Metre Five with its turning, cosmic wheel and its references to the star Arcturus and to the dimming of Hesperus before the rising sun. The same pageant draws further inspiration from Book Four, Metre Five, which explains that the star Arcturus turns close to the pole and never sets while the other stars (such as Hesperus) do, and from Book Four, Metre One, which outlines the Platonic idea of souls being translated to stars.

The success of this civic triumph, however, lies not so much in its dramatic form or its use of varied and erudite sources. Rather, the pageant devisor moulds these materials into a complex and richly allegorical work of medieval art. He thus shapes his materials according to the four-fold allegorical method. Literally, Katharine celebrates a triumphal reception in the streets of London. Tropologically, this triumph represents the search on the part of the just ruler for honour. Allegorically, the astrological conjunction of Arcturus and Hesperus mirrors the political union of England and Spain. Anagogically, Katharine's triumph stands for the just soul's translation from earth to its native star in heaven.[1] Further, in its allegorical method, the show even takes on something of the form of a medieval dream vision. The pageants transform the streets of London into the geography of the heavens, and Katharine is allowed to see, as if in a dream, a vision of the honour she may achieve both for herself and for England. At the same time, she catches a glimpse of her husband's true, spiritual nature.

The creator of this extraordinary civic triumph unfortunately remains a mystery. He receives no payment for his labours in either the civic or court account books. As Sydney Anglo rightly observers, the tradition that Bishop Fox devised the show 'stems from no more ancient a source than Warton', who based his conclusion upon a misreading of Francis Bacon's description of the wedding festivities.[2] Yet, as a consideration of the literary sources of the pageantry suggests, the devisor must have been

---

1. H. Caplan, 'The Four Senses of Scriptural Interpretation', in *Of Eloquence* (Ithaca, 1970), 93–104.
2. Anglo, *Spectacle*, 58.

someone very much like Fox. Thoroughly familiar with patristic and scholastic texts (Gregory the Great, Boethius, Martianus Capella), he must have been a cleric with academic credentials; he almost certainly went to a university. At the same time, he was familiar with Molinet's elegy, a circumstance which suggests that he may have spent some time at the Burgundian court, since the poem was otherwise unknown in England at this time.[1] He was also familiar with one of the main themes of Tudor panegyric— the identification of King Arthur, the star Arcturus, and Prince Arthur. He also wrote English verse in competent, if sometimes wooden, rhyme royal stanzas, even though the Princess Katharine could not understand that language. He thus conceived of his audience as English rather than Spanish, a circumstance which suggests that he saw himself primarily as a Tudor apologist. These traits certainly describe Fox, who was university educated, a bishop, an envoy upon occasion to the court of Burgundy, a man of literary leanings, a Tudor apologist, and a writer of competent if undistinguished English. They also describe a good many other Englishmen at the Tudor court, however, and can hardly serve to identify Bishop Fox as the devisor of the show. In the end, we shall have to remain content with Bacon's observation: 'whoever had these toys in compiling, they were not altogether pedantical'.[2]

THE DISGUISINGS

At the court of Henry VII, disguisings were usually a collaboration between a 'master of the revels', who superintended the construction of the costumes and pageants, and the personnel of the Chapel Royal, who probably devised them and certainly acted in them. The master of the revels was almost invariably drawn from among the more prosaic offices of the royal household. Never a playwright or poet, he was rather a bookkeeper and purchasing agent; for the rest of his duties, he might be found buying silks, delivering messages, mending roads, constructing forts, keeping accounts, and finding houses for visiting dignitaries.[3] By contrast, the Gentlemen and Children of the

1. But see *Triumph of Honour*, 74–5, for one possible route by which a copy of Molinet's poem may have reached England in the year 1500.
2. *King Henry the Seventh*, ed. R. Lockyer (London, 1971), 204.
3. For John Holt's account of the origin of his office, circa Henry VII, which he wrote later in the century, see E.K. Chambers, *Notes on the History of the Revels Office Under the Tudors* (London, 1906), where it is reprinted in full. Holt's contention that these 'seasonal' masters of the revels were actually called by that title is borne out in Henry VII's revels accounts, where Harry Wentworth, one of

Chapel Royal actually perform in these annual Christmas shows, both as dancers and as singers. Chief among these performers and devisors was William Cornish, Gentleman of the Chapel Royal, whom we find acting in a disguising as early as 1494 and who was to dominate the form for the next three decades. Such a collaboration led, during Henry's reign, to a distinctively Tudor marriage of spectacle and drama, the former provided by the artisans of the household and the latter by the creative genius of Cornish and his colleagues. Together, these two groups transformed what had been a costumed dance into a spectacular drama.[1]

In this development, the disguisings devised for Prince Arthur's wedding played a central role. In 1501 for the first time, the Tudor disguising adopted Continental pageant cars as an essential medium of dramatic production. Such pageant cars had long been familiar in the Franco-Burgundian *entremet*, but they had yet to make much of an impression upon English courtly entertainment. Walter Alwyn, Henry VII's 'master of the revels' in 1493/4, provided a 'Terryble & huge Rede dragun, The which in Sundry placys of the halle as he passed spytt ffyre at his mowth' for a disguising in which William Cornish played St George.[2] But this spectacle represented little more than an especially elaborate costume for one or two men who played St George's reptilian antagonist. By contrast, real pageant cars appear at the wedding revels in 1501—large pageants in the shape of ships, arbours, lanterns, castles, mountains, and two-storey thrones. 'Right cunnyngly devysid, sett uppon certayn whelys and drawen in to the seid hall of iiijor great bestis with cheynys of golde' (4/156–8), these large structures were capable of bearing not only a few actors to perform a skit, but also eight, twelve, or even twenty-four dancers. The dancers, however, did not use the pageant-cars as part of the disguising itself. Rather, the actors entered upon them, performed a kind of dramatic prologue in conjunction with them, and then only after they were rolled out of the hall did the performance of the dance—the disguising proper—begin.

As a consequence, the Tudor disguising consisted of a two-part performance: an elaborate and spectacular prologue preceded a costumed dance. The end of the prologue and the beginning of

Henry VII's revels masters, bears the title 'Master of the Revels' as early as 1509 (Public Record Office, MS E 36/217, fol. 5ʳ).
1. For this collaboration, see G. Kipling, 'Henry VII and the Origins of Tudor Patronage', in *Patronage in the Renaissance*, ed. G.F. Lytle and S. Orgel (Princeton, 1982), 155–9.
2. *Great Chronicle*, 251.

the dance might even be signalled by a complete change of performers. Thus Cornish and a 'king's daughter' led Walter Alwyn's fire-spitting dragon on stage in 1494, but only after they had spoken their lines, sung their anthem, and departed did the dancers enter, each gentleman leading his lady by a 'kerchief of pleasance'.[1]

The introduction of pageant-cars in 1501 thus allowed Cornish and his colleagues to define their dramatic dances with more spectacular visual imagery than they had yet been able to employ. All of the pageants, indeed, consist of little more than visualizations of conventional courtly love imagery: the Knights of the Mount of Love attack a Castle of Ladies, thus acting out a familiar metaphor for courtship, before resolving their discord in a matrimonial dance.[2] Other lovers enter the hall on pageants designed to represent the symbolic locales made familiar by Lydgate's *Temple of Glass* and *The Complaint of the Black Knight*: brilliantly shining palace and romantic arbour.[3] In their symbolic vocabulary, the pageant-cars contribute fully to what Rosemond Tuve calls 'that rather decadent literalizing of metaphors ... the bleeding heart separated from the body' that we find in so much late medieval romance.[4]

After this wedding festival, the masque's future as an essentially spectacular entertainment was assured. Pageants were henceforth used increasingly in the disguising hall, often in multiples: a castle, ship, and mount to allegorize a courtship; a castle, tree, and mount to symbolize an alliance, and so on. Since the enlargement and multiplication of pageantry made these shows ever more expensive, they could not have been performed without the active encouragement of the King, whose wishes must therefore have been central to the form. Indeed, we have abundant evidence to suggest that Henry VII took a keen interest in these increasingly spectacular and expensive shows. So that the King might examine and approve his work in progress, for example, Harry Wentworth, master of the revels in 1508/09, was obliged to pack up his costumes and pageantry, ship them from London to Richmond 'to thentent he [the King] myght se the disguising stuff', then ship it back from Richmond to London again so that the work could be completed.[5] By the end of Henry

1. *Great Chronicle*, 251–2; *Triumph of Honour*, 101–2.
2. R.S. Loomis, 'The Allegorical Siege', *Am. Jour. of Arch.*, 2nd ser., xxiii, 255–9; *Triumph of Honour*, 102–5.
3. *Triumph of Honour*, 107–9.
4. *Allegorical Imagery* (Princeton, 1966), 387.
5. Public Record Office, MS LC 9/50, fol. 152ᵛ.

VII's reign, in any case, these sophisticated scenic devices had transformed the disguising into a danced and enacted emblem, and it was this tradition that Inigo Jones and Ben Jonson inherited.

In the spring of 1500, the Privy Council commissioned Jacques Hault and William Pawne to prepare disguisings for the royal wedding. Hault had already served as Henry VII's master of the revels for six successive years, and Pawne, a mender of highways and purveyor of materials for the royal household, was another of Henry VII's efficient servants attached to the 'below stairs' side of the royal establishment.[1] By August 1501, however, court account books show that yet another member of the 'below stairs' household, John Atkinson, had succeeded Hault and Pawne as superintendent of the diguisings while William Cornish had become the devisor of the disguisings.[2] The nature of the entries in the household account books clearly suggests this division of labour. Atkinson, a senior official in the household, is always paid specifically for 'certain stuff' or 'upon his book' or upon presentation 'of his rekoning'. Cornish, however, is always paid in even amounts and never for specified materials or upon presentation of an account book. In other words, he is almost certainly being paid for his artistic labours according to the indenture system. He therefore draws an initial payment of £10 'for a disguising' on 6 August, and then as the work proceeds he draws three further payments of £10 each at approximately two-week intervals. Finally, upon completion of the work, he draws a final payment of £20 on 3 November 'for his three pageants'. John English, master of the King's Players, entered into partnership with Cornish late in August, when it became apparent that the work would be too much for one man alone. English draws three equal payments of ten marks each, receiving his final instalment 'for his pageant' on 3 November, the same day Cornish drew his last payment. Evidently, the court budgeted £20 for each of its four disguisings, and of these four, Cornish designed three, receiving a total of £60 in three equal instalments. The work was

---

1. 'Item that Jacques Hault and William Pawne ... devise and prepare disguisings and some morisks after the best manner they can' (M, fol. 11ʳ). Pawne went on to oversee the arrangements for the housing and expenses of the Scots ambassadors who arrived during Prince Arthur's wedding (Public Record Office, MS E 101/415/3, 14 Nov. 1501, 31 Dec. 1501, 31 March 1502). For the 'above stairs' and 'below stairs' divisions of the royal household, see Myers, 13–29.

2. 'Item deliuered to cornysh for a disguysing ... £10' (Public Record Office, MS E 101/415/3, 6 August 1501). For Atkinson, a clerk of the ordinance, see 30 June, 16 July, 23 July, 31 July, and 18 August entries.

completed by 3 November, when the court treasurer paid each devisor for his 'pageants' or disguisings and closed his books.

The descriptions of the disguisings and the account-book entries, moreover, allow a reasonable identification of Cornish's and English's shares of the work. Both the first and the fourth disguisings, for example, make use of the Chapel Children as singing performers for the first time in the history of the revels. As a past teacher of the singing boys at Westminster Abbey and future Master of the Children of the Chapel, Cornish was more likely to have made this important innovation. The third disguising also depends upon the professional musical talents of its participants. As the twelve gentlemen and ladies roll into the hall aboard two heraldic mountains, they play a rich variety of instruments so well that the author of the *Receyt* thought it the best music he had ever heard (4/626–8). And when the twelve ladies began to sing, even a sober Scots humanist like Walter Ogilvie thought that he had heard 'almost angelic voices'.[1] Certainly a musician with a dramatic flair like Cornish would most likely devise disguisings like these.

Even more compelling circumstances link John English with the second of the four disguisings, which was built around a pair of spectacular lantern and arbour pageants. The performance of an interlude by the King's Players immediately prefaced the entry of the pageant cars and disguisers in this case only. Perhaps English used his own company of players as a further dramatic setting for the disguising. But the disguising's lantern pageant provides the strongest evidence of English's authorship. This round, lantern-shaped pageant, 'fenestered' with fine linen and brilliantly shining with over a hundred 'great lights' so pleased the King that it earned a revival three months later when it formed the basis of a new disguising to celebrate the betrothal of Princess Margaret to the King of Scots. Since the account books show that English created this betrothal disguising,[2] we can reasonably assume that he modified his earlier pageant to suit the requirements of a new disguising, and that the court treasurer's payment of ten marks 'to John English for his pageant' refers to the second of the four wedding disguisings.[3]

1. National Library of Scotland, MS 33.2.24, p. 36.
2. *Collectanea*, iv, 263; Public Record Office, MS E 101/415/3, 18 Feb. 1502.
3. Throughout this discussion, I assume that the court accountant uses 'pageant' to mean 'disguising', so that Cornish's 'three pageants' can be taken to refer to three disguisings. This is consistent with his customary practice in other places in the manuscript. S. Anglo, 'William Cornish in a Play, Pageants, Prison, and Politics', *Review of English Studies*, n.s. x (1959), 350–3, equates 'pageant' with 'pageant car' and thus assigns only the first of the disguisings to Cornish.

THE TOURNAMENTS

To judge from the surviving records, English tournaments in the
fifteenth century were little influenced by Continental fashions in
fanciful costumes, pageant cars, and elaborate stage settings
erected on the tilting field. There is little in England to match the
pageantry of such famous Burgundian tournaments as the *Pas de
l'Arbre d'Or*, in which knights entered the lists in pageant cars,
emerged in costumes, and fought against the background of an
elaborate *mise en scène* dominated by a Golden Tree hung with
shields and presided over by the Dame de l'Ile Celée. Occasionally, we hear of a single knight such as the Earl Rivers who enters
an English tilt in a pageant car, but the experiment seems not to
have caught on generally.[1] For these reasons, the fifteenth-
century tournament was a far less spectacular affair in England
than it had been at the fourteenth-century courts of Edward III
and Richard II.

For the wedding tournaments, however, Henry's court made a
determined effort to catch up with Continental fashions. Two
groups of Henry's courtiers—one headed by the Marquis of
Dorset, the other by the Duke of Buckingham—entered the lists
in a variety of pageant cars and costumes and engaged in
deliberate chivalric playacting. On one occasion, for example, the
Marquis of Dorset, adopting the persona of a hermit knight,
entered in a pageant hermitage preceded by thirty beadsmen
dressed in black; on the same day, the Earl of Devonshire entered
within a red dragon pageant car that was led at the end of a green
and white leash by a giant wildman. On another day, an entire
team of knights 'sailed' on to the lists aboard a full-rigged ship
'with all maner of taclynges and marinurs in her' (4/452–3), its
guns booming out volleys at the waiting defenders. In some of the
individual 'acts' of this long tournament, the knights clearly made
their martial sport subservient to the 'literary' demands of a
romantic scenario. On one day, the Marquis of Dorset and his
companions accordingly entered the lists as henchmen to a
triumphal chariot in which rode 'a faire yong lady'. After circling
the field, they stopped before the royal box, bowed to their lady,
and helped her to a seat among the Court party. Then they fought
their day's tournament, collected their lady again after having
defended her beauty against all comers, and rode off as they came.

This solution, however, leaves the rest of the disguisings unaccounted for in the
household books.

1. Rivers entered the lists in 1477 aboard a pageant hermitage while he himself
was dressed as a hermit knight. See *Triumph of Honour*, 123–5.

Readers of the *Arcadia* will recognize a remarkable precedent for Artesia's tournament in this Tudor chivalric drama.

Much of this new interest in the spectacular and dramatic possibilities of the tournament undoubtedly reflects the King's own wishes. Henry clearly wanted to stage a festival that would present his court as the equal in magnificence and status to any court in Europe. As with his disguisings and banquets, the tournaments had to be spectacular and fashionable. But much of the credit for this new interest in spectacle must also go to the men who planned and executed the four tournaments, primarily the Comptroller of the Household and the heralds rather than the knights themselves.

Henry assigned his Comptroller and Sergeant of the Armoury, Sir Richard Guildford, with the main responsibility for planning the tournaments.[1] One of his most trusted counsellors, Guildford had already arranged many of the court's most impressive jousts, including the one held in celebration of Prince Henry's creation as Duke of York. Guildford was more than just a provisioner of lances and builder of scaffolds. He took an active interest in the wedding tournaments from their initial planning, in the spring of 1500, to their final performance almost two years later. It was his show from beginning to end. He devised tents and provided equipment for the lists,[2] and he even presided over the performances of the knights:

> Sir Richard Gilford, Countroller of the Kinges Hous, and Sir Nicholas Vaus were ever for the most party in the feld every day of the justes right goodly beseen, bothe their horsis and ther rayement, with great and massy cheynes of golde abought ther nekkes, and by them the Kynges Grace did sende his myend and messages into the feld at his goodly pleasure. (4/543-9)

The King invested enormous sums in the pageantry and equipment for this tournament: 200 marks for the Duke of Buckingham, £50 for Lord Berners, somewhat lesser amounts for the rest.[3] To Guildford went the responsibility for seeing that it was well spent.

1. 'And asfor Justes Turneyes and suche other Cerymonyes they be remitted to þe said maste^r cometroller Sergeant of the kinges Armoury And asfor prouision of the Scaffoldes and all other thinges belonging to the said Justes maister cometroller and worley haue taken vpon theym the charge' (*M*, 10^v).
2. Cf. Public Record Office, MS E 101/415/3, 31 August 1501: 'Item for the frame of the tentt that Sir Charles and mast^r comptroller hath devised'.
3. Public Record Office, MS E 101/415/3, 9 April 1501, 11 April 1501, 23 April 1501, 21 May 1501, 30 June 1501.

The actual conduct of the tournament, however, was the responsibility of the heralds. They judged the worthiness of the knights to fight, enrolled them in the lists, measured the lances, scored the matches, and determined the winners. Above all, they drew up the tournament challenges, and in so doing they established the chivalric roles that the knights would play and specified whatever pageantry might be required to serve as the *mise en scène* for the tilting field.

In this case, the heralds drew up two challenges, and they were both proclaimed during Henry VII's meeting with Archduke Philip of Burgundy at Calais in May, 1500.[1] While the diplomats discussed matters of trade, the English knights discussed wedding festivals and points of chivalry with their Burgundian counterparts, who included the Grand Bastard of Burgundy, perhaps the most famous practitioner of the tilt then alive. Under these conditions, it is perhaps not surprising that both English challenges, written on behalf of the two groups of English knights in courtly French prose, should make provision for Trees of Chivalry, 'the most important of all tournament stage effects, and one especially popular a few decades earlier in the great Burgundian feats of arms'.[2] Indeed, the Burgundians responded to these English challenges with an answering challenge of their own.[3] Had the wedding of Arthur and Katharine occurred just three months after the Calais conference, as was then thought, many a Burgundian knight would have come to England to participate in a ritual of courtly playacting familiar to them but relatively new to the English.

The two challenges drawn up by the English heralds each provide for somewhat different versions of the Tree of Chivalry. In the first challenge, devised for the Earl of Suffolk, a single Tree was to be erected at Westminster near the tilting field. At the very top of the tree would be fixed the arms of Arthur and Katharine, 'for the honour and marriage of whom this feast will be held'. Just beneath, the arms of the challengers would hang. Finally, in a ceremony reminiscent of the *Pas de l'Arbre d'Or*, each 'answerer' would be required to deliver a shield of his own arms to a herald who would then hang them upon the tree beneath the challengers' shields (SC/144–64). The second version, devised for the Duke of Buckingham's challenge, proposed a

1. *Triumph of Honour*, 18–20.
2. Anglo, *Spectacle*, 100.
3. For the texts of the tournament cartels, see pp.lxxi–iv below. The answering challenge, proclaimed by the Burgundian knights, appears in British Library, MS Additional 46455, 9–10.

more ambitious version of this romantic, Burgundian device. Three Trees of Chivalry were to serve as a setting for the lists. The tallest, the 'one of most price', was designed as a cherry tree, one side painted red, the other white. A fortnight before the wedding, the challengers would hang their shields upon this tree—on the white side if they proposed to appear on the first day of the tournament or on the red if they meant to fight on the last day. At the same time a white 'pineapple' (*i.e.*, pine) tree would stand to the white side of the cherry tree while a red pear tree would flank its other side. A red and white fence would surround the entire arbour, broken only by a single gate from which would hang 'a bucyne or great horn'. By blowing the horn and hanging his shield upon one of these smaller trees, an answerer could accept the challenge, choose his day of combat, and offer his shield as a chivalric tribute to the honour of the wedding (BC/133–68).

We can almost certainly assign the idea for these chivalric stage settings to John Writhe, Garter King of Arms, who accompanied Henry to his Calais meeting with Archduke Philip of Burgundy. As the chief English herald, he would naturally take the lead in planning this, the most important tournament of the reign. Indeed, the Suffolk challenge explicitly charges Garter with the responsibility of circulating the articles of the tournament 'en ceste vostre tres honnourable court et en autres places ou il plaira a Vostre Grace' (SC/25–7). As it turns out, we have still more certain evidence of Writhe's participation. His personal copy of the English version of Buckingham's challenge, written either in his own hand or that of his son, appears in 'Ballard's Book' (College of Arms, MS M. 3, fols. 24ᵛ–26ᵛ), a manuscript Writhe had acquired from the widow of William Ballard, March King of Arms, about 1490.[1] What clinches Writhe's authorship of this challenge, however, is that he apparently modelled his prose style after one of Ballard's challenges, written for a royal wedding tournament in 1477 and recorded in the very same book. Ballard's preamble, for instance, cites the high and noble purposes of this tournament:

> And because the noble and laudable custume of this mat-
> remoniall and triumphault Royᵐᵉ in tyme passed hath be
> that at such high dayes of honneʳ excercise and fautes of the
> necessarie discipline of Armes were shewed and done to

---

1. According to a note on fol. 1. See Sir A. Wagner, *Heralds and Heraldry in the Middle Ages*, 2nd ed. (London, 1956), 108–9, for a discussion of this book.

experient and enable noblesse to the desiruyng of Cheuallerie
... (fol. 8ᵛ)

So Writhe's own wording closely follows Ballard:

> And forasmoche as the noble and laudable custome of this
> your triumphant reame have been in tyme passed, that at
> suche high festis and dayes of honour, excersice and faictes of
> the necessary discipline of armes have been shewed to
> thenabeling of Nobleness and Chivalrie ... (BC/11–15)

Indeed, Writhe even adapts a distinctive ceremony of choice from
Ballard's challenge. In both, the tournament articles are to be
posted in three places. At each of these places, the answerers
could subscribe their names beneath a heraldic symbol by way of
choosing the day they wished to fight.[1]

The actual stage setting, as described in the *Receyt*, evidently
struck something of a compromise between the two versions as
proposed in the challenges. Since each group of knights alternated
in the roles of challenger and answerer over the four days of the
tournament, some such compromise would have been necessary
in any case; Sir Richard Guildford could hardly be expected to
rebuild the stage setting each day. In addition, court politics may
have played an important part in modifying the design. The first
of the two challenges, after all, had originally been issued in the
name of the Earl of Suffolk, who subsequently defected from the
Tudor court and fled to Flanders.[2] In these unsettling circumstances, the Marquis of Dorset was conscripted to take over
Suffolk's role, and the Tree of Chivalry was modified to suggest
unity rather than conflict. 'Empainted with pleasant leaves,
flowers, and fruit', a single tree now stood enclosed by a fence.
The graphic counterpoising of shields hung from opposite
branches of a tree and the horn-blowing ceremony with its drama
of challenge and choice had been suppressed. Instead, all shields
now hung grouped together from the rails of the fence surrounding the arbour. In this undifferentiated grouping, they now
expressed unity of purpose rather than opposition and combat. In
a court embarrassed by the desertion of one of its most powerful
nobles, this final modification provided a welcome show of
chivalric solidarity for the Spanish guests.

On the tilting field as in the disguising hall, we find the English
court experimenting for the first time with fashions in spectacular
pageantry adopted from abroad. The Marquis of Dorset and his

---

1. For the 1477 ceremony, see College of Arms, MS M. 3, 9–10.
2. For Suffolk's flight, see Chrimes, 92–3.

knights, for example, arrived on pageant cars virtually identical to those that William Cornish had devised for the disguisings. The ship which carried Hope and Desire to the Castle of Love could not have been much different from the ones which later ferried Dorset's army onto the tournament field to attack the Duke of Buckingham's knights. The same team of heraldic beasts hauled pageant cars full of disguisers into Westminster Hall on one day, and then obediently pulled pageant cars laden with knights on to Westminster tilting field the next. Both entertainments were mounted aboard the first complete sets of Burgundian pageant cars that the English court had ever known. The disguising pageants, however, were patterned after the dream landscapes of the *Romance of the Rose*: rose arbours, castles of love, and other such allegorical palaces. The tournament pageants, by contrast, drew their inspiration from chivalric romances of knightly combat: dragons, hermit knights, maidens and unicorns, triumphal chariots, and wildmen. Just as the disguisings allegorized the marriage as an example of ideal love, so the tournaments defined that love as a theme of honour worthy of knightly combat.

TEXTUAL INTRODUCTION

THE MANUSCRIPT

College of Arms, MS 1st M. 13 (henceforth *M*), a Tudor herald's collection of texts relative to the English royal weddings of 1501–03, was made up in the late-sixteenth century by binding together a number of originally separate paper manuscripts. As we shall see, however, it has suffered some variation of contents when rebound in the eighteenth century. As a consequence, *M* today contains four constituent parts, three paper manuscripts dating from the turn of the sixteenth century and some blank quires of mid-eighteenth-century paper. They are:

1. A single quire of fourteen folio leaves measuring 292 by 209 mm and watermarked with a unicorn. It contains (on fols 1–11^r) a transcript of the Privy Council plans for the reception of Katharine of Aragon. The second of three extant versions of these minutes, the text dates from between October 1500 and March 1501.[1]

2. The *Receyt* occupies a second manuscript (hereafter *R*) of forty-nine folio leaves measuring approximately 300 by 216 mm, gathered into an initial quire of two leaves, followed by two quires of sixteen leaves and a final quire of sixteen leaves from which the ninth leaf has been cancelled, leaving a stub. It is watermarked with a gloved hand and star, similar to Briquet 11138 (dated 1500).

3. There then follow twelve leaves of mid-eighteenth-century paper, comprising three quarto quires watermarked with a fleur-de-lis above a shield (Strasbourg bend), the letters LVG (for Lucius van Gerrevink) below. These sheets are blank, except for a note scribbled on the verso of the final leaf and signed by 'E.L. Lancr' (i.e., Edmund Lodge, Lancaster Herald 1793–1822).[2]

---

1. *Triumph of Honour*, 173–4.
2. For Lodge's career, see W.H. Godfrey, Sir A. Wagner, and H.S. London, *The College of Arms* (London, 1963), 93. Lodge was responsible for publishing the text of *R* in the 1808 edition of the *Antiquarian Repertory* (see below, p. lv).

4. The final manuscript, a quire of four folio leaves followed by a quire of thirty-eight folio leaves measuring approximately 295 by 213 mm and watermarked with an ornamental letter P, comprises a narrative of Princess Margaret Tudor's journey from London to Edinburgh for her marriage to James IV of Scotland in the summer of 1503. Its author, John Young (then Somerset Herald[1]), accompanied the Princess on that occasion, and this manuscript, signed 'Somerset Le herault' at the end of the text on fol. 115[v], almost certainly represents his official journal of the event.

As its diverse composition suggests, M has experienced quite a protean history. Since all three of the original, constituent manuscripts show considerable wear on their first and last few folios, they probably existed as unbound pamphlets for some years before being bound into a single volume later in the sixteenth century. In their original condition, these separate pamphlets would probably have been covered with a fold of vellum and secured by stabbing rather than sewing—i.e. by stitching the quires together along the edges of their spine folds.[2] In fact, a reversed leaf in the R manuscript clearly shows the signs of this original stitching and cover. The text of the *Receyt* originally began on the verso of the first leaf, thus leaving a blank side facing outward to minimize possible damage to the text.[3] By the time the manuscript was bound together with its companions later in the century,[4] this leaf had become detached from its cognate. It was therefore reversed in binding so that the text might begin on the recto of fol. 27, even though the original blank side would now interrupt the text. As a consequence, the ten original stab holes, which mark the original spine-fold stitching, now appear about 14–18 mm from the present right-hand margin of fol. 27. By the same token, the absence of a title—or at least some description of the contents—on the blank, originally outward-facing side of fol. 27 points to the vellum fold that must once have covered R in its original form. Presumably, the title or

1. For Young's career, see *The College of Arms*, 107–8.
2. P.R. Robinson, 'The Booklet', *Codicologica*, iii (1980), 46–69. P. Gaskell, *A New Introduction to Bibliography* (Oxford, 1972), 234.
3. Since the four quires of the manuscript were only to be secured with stabbing rather than bound between boards, it was natural to expect that the first and last leaves would suffer greater damage than 'inside' leaves. As a consequence, these were left blank.
4. The presence of a folio numeral ('27') in the upper right-hand corner of the text side of the leaf shows that the leaf was reversed in the late-sixteenth century binding, not the mid-eighteenth century rebinding. The foliation was added between these two events (see below, p. xxxiv).

description was written on the cover instead of on the blank first folio, and was therefore lost when the binder discarded that cover.

Evidence of provenance suggests that the collector of the constituent manuscripts and original binder of *M* was a mid- to late-sixteenth century herald. The *R* manuscript certainly passed through the hands of Sir Christopher Barker, Garter Herald 1536–1550; between 1547 and 1550 he transcribed the *Receyt* into a personal collection of coronation ceremonials.[1] The rebus (MAR yorke) of Martin Marroffe, York Herald 1552–64, appears on fol. 1^r (the Privy Council orders), and the signature of William Colbarne, Marroffe's successor (1564–67), appears upon fol. 76^r (the first folio of Young's narrative). Other than John Young's signature at the end of his own report, there are no other personal marks of ownership on any of the manuscripts. However, Glynne Wickham has identified Colbarne's hand in the title added to the upper margin of fol. 1^r (now partly lost by damage to the paper)—a title which in any case could only have been written after 1553: 'Thordere of the [receaving] of Quene Kath[ren] dowager'.[2] This title has then been recopied just beneath Colbarne's script in the hand of Sir William Dugdale (Garter King of Arms, 1677–86). Together, these markings suggest that, whatever the origin of these various manuscripts, they had all become the property of a herald by the mid-sixteenth century who bound them into a single volume, and that the bound volume was owned successively by several individual heralds before being incorporated into the library of the College of Arms.

That Colbarne signed both the first and last manuscripts in the volume suggests that he may well have been the collector and binder in question. One of his successors as York Herald,

1. Barker's transcription of the *Receyt* appears in College of Arms, MS Vincent 25, fols 108^r–42^v; see below pp. l–li. I am indebted to R.C. Yorke, Archivist of the College of Arms, for the identification of Barker's hand. The MS can be dated between the coronation of Edward VI (1547), a description of which is included in the MS, and the death of Barker (2 January 1550).

2. For Wickham's identification of Colbarne's hand, see his MS 'Calendar of contents' appended to *M*. For Marroffe and Colbarne, see *The College of Arms*, 185–6. Sir Anthony Wagner, *Heralds of England* (London, 1967), 124 n. 1, thinks that William Wriothesley may have been the York herald who signed his official name on fol. 1^r, but he has apparently missed the MAR portion of the rebus. Katharine of Aragon's legal title, as a consequence of the Divorce, was '*Princess* Dowager': 'In whiche Parliament ... was enacted that quene Katheryn should from thence furth, be no more called quene, but princes Dowager, of prince Arthur' (Edward Hall, *Chronicle*, ed. H. Ellis (London, 1809), 795). As a member of the royal household and expert on protocol, a herald would be particularly sensitive to such a distinction. Only after Mary came to the throne could Katharine be referred to again as Queen Dowager.

however, is also a particularly likely candidate. Sir William
Dethick (York Herald 1570–87; Garter 1587–1606), a member of
the original Society of Antiquaries, was an avariciously determined collector of manuscripts, so much so that he was charged
with appropriating to his own personal library a number of books
properly belonging to his official library, and action was taken to
recover as many of them as possible. Whether or not *M* was
among the books recovered from Dethick by the College, the
press mark inscribed on fol. 1ʳ, '1st M. 13', tells us that it had
certainly passed into the library of the College of Arms sometime
in the seventeenth century, after the alphabetical system of press
marks evolved.[1] At that time, as a note on one of the eighteenth-
century fly-leaves tells us, the title 'written on the old Cover' was
'The Marr: of Queen Margaret da: to Hen: VII to the King of
Scots', a title that refers more accurately to Young's narrative
than to the *Receyt*.[2] We will return presently to the significance of
this title.

After the originally separate manuscripts were bound together,
the new volume was thoroughly foliated with Arabic numerals.
The Privy Council plans were numbered 1–14, the *Receyt* 27–75,
and Young's narrative 76–117. (The eighteenth-century leaves,
inserted between fols 75 and 76, are unnumbered.)[3] The pattern
thus shows that a manuscript of twelve leaves was removed, and
an equal number of blank leaves inserted, during the rebinding of
M in the eighteenth century. It is difficult to avoid the inference
that the blank leaves were meant, in some sense, as a replacement
for the lost quire.

To understand why these 'replacement' leaves are blank and
why they were bound in a different position than the quire they
replaced, we must attempt to identify the contents of the missing
manuscript. As it happens, we can do so with some certainty, for a
seventeenth-century heraldic manuscript, once the property of
John Anstis (Garter King of Arms 1727–54),[4] probably contains a

---

1. For Dethick's collecting activities and the foundation of the College library,
see Sir A. Wagner, *The Records and Collections of the College of Arms* (London,
1952), 12–14. *M* does not appear in the College's first library catalogue, dated
1618, but does appear in the 1690 catalogue. Presumably, the MS passed into
College ownership between these two dates, but it may simply have been absent
from the M press when the first catalogue was drawn up in 1618. I am indebted to
Mr R.C. Yorke, Archivist of the College of Arms, for this information.
2. This title has also been added, in pencil, to the inner margin of fol. 1ʳ.
3. This shows that the foliation was a result of the sixteenth-century binding,
not the eighteenth-century rebinding.
4. It was, in fact, a transcript of the Harvard manuscript, apparently obtained

transcript of at least half the lost leaves. Harvard, Houghton Library, MS English 1095 consists of two texts joined together as if they were a single narrative. The first, 'The Fyancells of Princess Margaret', recounts that princess's formal betrothal, by proxy, to James IV of Scotland in January 1502. It would fit comfortably in six of the missing leaves of M.[1] The second text, a copy of Young's narrative of Princess Margaret's subsequent journey to Scotland for her marriage to James in the summer of 1503, has clearly been transcribed directly from M, fols 76–117. The Harvard scribe has, in short, brought together two originally separate narratives to form a complete record of the pageantry and ceremonial of Princess Margaret's state wedding. That he found the 'Fyancells' as well as Young's narrative in M is suggested by M's original title, which, as we have seen, described the entire contents of the volume as a collection of papers relative to Princess Margaret's marriage. In its original form, at the very least, the Anglo-Scots marriage must have loomed much larger in M than the Anglo-Spanish marriage. Together, these circumstances argue strongly that the missing folios once contained the original version of the 'Fyancells of Princess Margaret', and that the seventeenth-century scribe of the Harvard manuscript copied both his texts from M.

If so, we need only assume that the 'Fyancells' manuscript was in poor condition in the eighteenth century to explain the presence of the 'replacement' folios.[2] Certainly M was in poor

from Anstis, that Hearne published in the 1770 edition of Leland's *Collectanea* (iv, 258–300).

1.   College of Arms, MS M. 1 *bis*, fols 84ᵛ–89, 90–95, also contains two duplicate copies of the *Fyancells*. Cf. L. Campbell, F. Steer, and R. Yorke, *A Catalogue of Manuscripts in the College of Arms Collections*, I (London, 1988), 91, 94. Both are early transcripts which once belonged to Clarenceux Hawley (d. 1557), and the first of these occupies paper of the same size and watermark as *R*. Each copy requires six folios.

2.   The two copies of the *Fyancells* in College of Arms MS 1 *bis*, fols 84ᵛ–95 (see preceding n.) seem to have formed a separate booklet of twelve leaves before being bound together with the rest of the contents of the MS. The original booklet belonged to Thomas Hawley (Clarenceux Herald, 1536–57), who signed his name on both the first and last leaves of the booklet (fols 84 and 95). Hawley accompanied Princess Margaret to Scotland for her marriage with James IV and served her there as groom porter of the Chamber (1503–07). He was thus associated closely with John Young, Somerset Herald, who also accompanied Margaret to Scotland, remained there in her service for two years, and wrote the narrative of Margaret's journey in M. These circumstances make it tempting to identify Hawley's twelve-leaf booklet as the missing twelve-leaf section in M, especially since his booklet uses, in part, the same paper as *R*. Hawley's booklet, however, seems to have been a part of MS 1 *bis* since the sixteenth century, when the present collection of MSS was bound together, perhaps by Robert Cooke

enough condition by that date to require rebinding. Once the
original volume was disbound by the rebinder, the separate
manuscripts could again be rearranged. At this point, it might
seem more logical to group the four constituent manuscripts by
placing the Privy Council Orders for Katharine of Aragon's
reception together with the *Receyt* and the 'Fyancells' together
with Young's narrative. But if the 'Fyancells' was too damaged to
be rebound, new paper could be inserted instead with the
intention of recopying the text on them at leisure. For whatever
reason, however, the recopying was never carried out and the
damaged leaves were discarded, leaving only the Harvard manuscript as a witness to the missing twelve leaves of *M*.[1]

Of the four original, constituent manuscripts, the status of the
Receyt is the most problematic. Young's narrative, because it has
all the characteristics of a draft report written in the hand of its
author, enjoys a great deal of textual authority. The 'Fyancells'
manuscript may also have been a similar draft report by Young.[2]
The Privy Council Orders, by contrast, is only one of many
copies of these ordinances that circulated among the various
departments of the household as a means of co-ordinating
preparations for the festival.[3] The *Receyt* falls between these two
extremes, claiming at times the authority of a fair copy, original
manuscript, betraying at other times all the signs of an indifferent
transcript of a copy somewhat distant from the author's original.

To begin with, the text has been transcribed by at least
three—perhaps four—separate hands, a circumstance suggestive
of multiple scribes creating a derivative text based upon a more
authoritative exemplar. The first hand (Scribe A) thus transcribed the main body of the text, from fol. 29^r to fol. 72^v. A
second (Scribe B1) then finished the job by transcribing the last
four folios of text (73^r–74^v). Next, a third hand (Scribe B2)—or
perhaps the second hand again, working less hurriedly[4]—copied

(Clarenceux Herald, 1567–93). Cf. *College of Arms*, 82–3, and Campbell, Steer,
and Yorke, *Catalogue of Manuscripts*, 91–2, 94.

1.   In the end, MS 1st M. 13 was rebound together with MS 2nd M. 16, another
volume apparently in need of rebinding at the same time. As a consequence, *M*
today occupies the first half of the combined volume.

2.   Hearne apparently describes both the *Fyancells* and the wedding narrative as
'written by John Younge', but this is merely an inference drawn from the fact that
both narratives are collected in the same manuscript.

3.   *Triumph of Honour*, 173–74.

4.   While the hands appear very similar, there are some apparent differences. In
particular, Scribe B1 customarily forms an *h* (usually in *the*) consisting of little
more than two loops, one above the other; Scribe B2, by contrast, generally avoids
turning the bowl of the *h* into a loop by bringing the pen upward and forward
from the descender to the next letter. The differences, however, might well be

the prologue (fols 27–28). Finally, a fourth hand (Scribe C) has inserted a number of words, lines, and even longer passages into the first scribe's work, either between lines or in the margins. The main scribe occasionally emends his own work as well, but the fourth scribe's work can be easily distinguished. He not only writes in a darker ink, but he often prefers an orthographical style different from that of the first scribe. He thus prefers 'espayne' to 'Hispayne' and generally writes 'off' rather than 'of' (cf. 1/51–6 and 1/94).

However easy his work may be to identify, the nature of Scribe C's contribution is particularly difficult to ascertain. Often, his work seems that of an editor correcting the work of a scribe against an authoritative copy-text. He thus corrects a number of scribal errors resulting from eyeskip (the dropped line at 4/418–9, for example) or transposition (the extended passage at 4/740–55, for example). At the same time, his work often takes on the characteristics of emendation, revision, or even original composition. He thus often adds to the margin passages of considerable importance that cannot so easily be identified as the results of scribal omission (as the passage at 4/948–53, which requires a considerable interruption in syntax to accommodate the insertion). Indeed, he is as likely to add superfluous and unnecessary qualifications (he tells us that Katharine's retinue was a goodly company 'off countess, baroness, and meny other honorable gentylwomen' at 1/55–6 and clarifies her status as Princess 'of Espayne' at 1/94) as he is to address important matters of substance. Such corrections as these resemble nothing so much as the revisions made by Victorian authors in their galley proofs.

In many respects, however, the physical composition of the manuscript points far more surely to some sort of authorial original than to a mere scribal copy. Book Five, for instance, (the account of Prince Arthur's funeral) was probably incorporated into the body of the text as something of an afterthought. Certainly the author of the *Receyt* seems to have brought his narrative to a close with his own description of Arthur's death at the end of Book Four. We can also establish on other grounds (below, pp. lvii–lxiv) that the book consists merely of an heraldic record of Prince Arthur's funeral which the author has incorporated into his own work by means of inserting chapter headings at appropriate places. In the *R* manuscript, however, we catch the author in the act of incorporating the heraldic record. The scribe

occasioned by the effects of haste in the portion of the text contributed by Scribe B1.

thus reflects the author's original intention by finishing the transcription of Book Four about three-quarters of the way down fol. 67^r and then leaving fol. 67^v blank. Moreover, the stub of a cancelled leaf between fols 67 and 68 shows that yet another leaf originally intervened between the end of Book Four and the beginning of Book Five. Since the scribe customarily leaves no blank space at all to separate one book from another,[1] the extraordinary separation he has allowed here shows that, in his mind at least, he was dealing with two quite separate texts. Furthermore, the text of the funeral report begins with a large, decorated initial letter—by far the most intricately drawn initial in the entire manuscript. Indeed, throughout the *Receyt* the initial letters of chapters and books have become increasingly perfunctory after a number of moderately elaborated initials at the beginning. The sudden appearance of such an intricately drawn initial, therefore, again suggests that the scribe thought he was beginning a new text altogether, not merely a new part of the same text he had been copying all along. If so, we may suspect that the cancelled leaf consisted of a title page to the new text, that it was removed in order to incorporate the funeral report into the body of the *Receyt*, and that the chapter heading ('the furst chaptre of the vth booke . . .') was a later addition inserted into the upper margin of fol. 68^r.[2] The awkwardness of these modifications underlines both the last-minute nature of this decision and the author's close involvement with the transcription of the manuscript. To make these modifications necessary, the author must have made his decision only after the transcription of Book Five had begun.

---

1.   On fol. 33^r, before he has fully settled on the copying conventions he will use, he concludes Book One after only six lines at the top of the page, writes 'ffinis p^{r}mi libri', and leaves the rest of the page blank. He avoids similar formal divisions at the ends of Books Two and Three, however, preferring on fols 45^r and 51^r to continue the next Book on the same page.

2.   The layout of fol. 68^r seems to imitate the features of the copy-text. The Wriothesley MS, which was apparently transcribed from the same copy-text, also begins part-way down the page and indents the first few lines of text to allow room for an ornamented initial (which in this case was never supplied). Instead of a chapter heading, however, the Wriothesley version places two sketches of Prince Arthur's arms in the top margin (for the relationships between the Wriothesley and *R* texts of the funeral account, see below, pp. lvii–lxiv). College of Arms, MS I.3, fols 14^v–17^v, which has been transcribed from the Wriothesley version, also attempts the same sort of format. Apparently, therefore, Scribe A was also attempting a similar imitation and only added the chapter title afterwards. Indeed, in order to work the title into the available space, he has had to combine a chapter title and book title in one, unlike his previous practice.

The prologue also seems to be the result of a late inspiration. Since it accurately outlines the *Receyt*'s division 'into v partes and small bokes' and specifically mentions 'the v [book] of the Princes lamentable deth and buriyng' (Pro./96–100), it could only have been composed after the author had made his decision to incorporate the funeral account into his narrative. Furthermore, it occupies its own exceptional quire of two leaves at the beginning of the manuscript, a circumstance that almost certainly establishes that the prologue was composed after the copying of the body of the text began. Otherwise, since the scribe seems to have been copying into a series of identical, sixteen-leaf quires, we would expect the prologue to occupy the beginning of one of these larger quires. Finally, that the prologue is copied in a hand different from that of the body of the text suggests that it must have been transcribed after Scribe A ceased his labours a mere four folios from the end of the text.

The picture that emerges is that of a scribal fair copy of the author's rough manuscript, prepared under continuing authorial supervision. Judging by his clear, professional court script, Scribe A was probably a professional. Even as he copied the text, however, decisions were being made about the narrative. Initially, the herald's funeral report was probably included in the manuscript as a companion piece to the main narrative; belatedly, this originally separate account was modified and incorporated as Book Five of the main narrative. After that was done, the author wrote a prologue and either set it aside to be copied when the main text had been completed or gave it to another scribe to prepare. In the midst of these manoeuvres, Scribe A was relieved by Scribe B1, an obviously non-professional copyist, virtually at the end of the task. This scribe completed the last four leaves of the funeral narrative, and then either he or a third scribe (B2) completed the job by copying the prologue on to two fresh leaves, which were then appended to the front of the manuscript.

Since the prologue was composed very late in this process, it would be tempting to identify the non-professional hand of Scribe B2, who contributed these leaves to the manuscript, as the hand of the author. More compelling evidence of the author's presence appears in the hand of Scribe C, who frequently corrects, emends, or even expands the text as copied by Scribe A. As we have seen, he not only carefully corrects scribal errors, but he inserts passages that seem more like authorial revision than mere correction. Still more suggestively, he makes no corrections or revisions whatsoever in Book Five, even though it can be shown that Scribes A and B1 committed a number of copying errors (below, pp. xli–ii). In short, Scribe C seems interested in correcting or emending only those portions of the text which were written by the author of the *Receyt*—he takes a more proprietary interest, so to speak, in the *Receyt* proper, but ignores the narrative of a herald which has been merely incorporated into his own text.

Unlike its companion manuscripts, *R* makes some pretence towards elegance. It is not merely an 'office' manuscript, a record compiled primarily as a precedent to be consulted when preparing similar festivals in the future. Rather, it is probably a fair copy of the author's rough draft, intended as a formal, literary memorial of the festival it describes. Such manuscripts—some of them elaborately illuminated—were widely known on the continent at the time, particularly in France and the Lowlands. The poets Pierre Gringore and André de la Vigne prepared a series of them at Paris (1504–17), one of them for Mary Tudor; Rémy Dupuys, the Duke of Burgundy's secretary and historian, produced a famous narrative account of the Archduke Charles's inauguration at Bruges (1515).[1] Playing the role of a Gringore or a Dupuys at the English court, the author has written a formal, commemorative narrative and had it professionally transcribed in a competent, but not lavish, fair copy.

In executing his commission, Scribe A performed his task with some unevenness. Especially toward the beginning of the manuscript, he frequently employs moderately decorated initials to mark the beginnings of chapter headings and paragraph divisions. He transcribes carefully, in his neat, well-shaped court script. He takes care to keep a wide, even margin, spaces his lines evenly, and carefully centres his chapter headings. His early folios are uncrowded, averaging about thirty lines per page. As he continues his task, however, the manuscript becomes progressively more crowded and less neat. The decorated initials become simpler and less elegant, and they appear more and more infrequently. Before long (fols 35 ff.) he crowds 40–45 lines on a page, the margins become narrower, and the decorated initials, when they appear at all, become little more than pen flourishes. Towards the end (fol. 60 ff.), his margins become increasingly untidy and his letters are less and less well-formed. Now writing in considerable haste, he once again fits fewer lines on a folio—about 33—but his script is

1.   C.R. Baskervill, *Pierre Gringore's Pageants for the Entry of Mary Tudor into Paris* (Chicago, 1934); H. Stein, 'Le Sacre d'Anne de Bretagne et son entrée à Paris en 1504', *Mémoire de la Société de l'Histoire de Paris*, xxix, 268–304; S. Anglo, ed., *La tryumphante Entrée de Charles Prince des Espagnes en Bruges 1515* (New York, 1973).

larger and sloppier. As the quality of his transcription deteriorates, he makes increasingly serious mistakes as when, for example, he transposes two longish passages at 4/740–55 which Scribe C has to rectify. He contributes his last decorated initial to the beginning of the funeral report on fol. 68^r, and then ceases to pay any more attention to such flourishes. At the very end, Scribe B1 copies out the last four leaves in a very broad and ill-formed script, managing to get only about 25 lines on each folio. The pattern of transcription, in short, suggests a task begun with care but finished with haste. The scribe started out with aspirations towards elegance, but found himself pressed to finish the job as quickly as possible.

On the whole, Scribe A produces only a moderately accurate transcription. On the one hand, he frequently falls victim to the usual scribal errors, principally word confusion (were/where, 5/232), transposition (5/152–5 and the chapter headings at 2/1 and 2/30), and eyeskip (5/104). This last category of error explains several important slips, particularly in the last half of the manuscript. Thus at 4/739 the scribe's eye skipped from the end of one sentence, 'the seid gates', over an intervening passage, to 'And when they were departyng homward' (4/740–8). As he continued to copy, however, he discovered his error. Since he could not rectify his mistake without spoiling the appearance of the page, he merely copied the omitted passage out of order, placing it at the end of the sentence which he was copying when he discovered his error. To correct this disorder, Scribe C had to insert the letters b, A, and c in the margin to indicate the correct order. While Scribe C has reduced the number of Scribe A's omissions, a fair number remain (e.g., the line of verse at 3/81 and the skipped word at 2/177). In particular, there are a number of serious omissions in Book Five where Scribe C has evidently lost interest in correcting the text. On the other hand, he is an accurate enough scribe to preserve, sometimes side by side, the differing lexical preferences of the various authors of his copy-text, as where a chapter heading, inserted into the funeral report by the author of the *Receyt*, promises a description of the 'ensencyng' of Prince Arthur's body, but Writhe's text itself describes how the prelates 'sensid' it. Here (as he frequently does elsewhere) the scribe has preserved one of the author's favourite stylistic devices, the addition of *ap-*, *en-*, and *em-* prefixes wherever possible to make his prose seem more Latinate and hence more portentous.

But if he succeeds in reproducing his copy-text's substantives with moderate accuracy, he seems to pay no particular attention to its accidentals. He is particularly cavalier in punctuating his text. Sometimes he supplies virgules, dots, or colons virtually at every clause; sometimes such marks appear seldom and randomly. In either case, the pointing rarely fills any grammatical or phrasal function. The same, often cavalier, attitude also appears in his treatment of abbreviations. Again and again he confuses singular, genitive singular, and plural nouns: e.g., *ordres/ordre* (5/100); *watchys/watche* (5/118); *coursers/courser* (5/175). Indeed, we can often catch him adjusting the accidentals of his copy-text to his own preferences. We have thus seen how he prefers *of* and *Hispayne* to Scribe C's *off* and *ispayne*. Similarly, Scribe C, at least in one instance, uses a thorn ('oþer', 4/418); Scribe A never does.[1] To the contrary, some evidence suggests that Scribe A found occasional thorns in his copy-text but transliterated them as *th*. He thus occasionally goes too far and mistakes a *y* for a thorn (e.g., 'fer in the contreth of the west', 1/29).

In sum, Scribe A produced a diligent and reasonably accurate transcript of his exemplar, one that preserves not only its substance but also a good deal of its spelling. His errors are distinguished almost entirely for their omissions and never for additions or deliberate improvements.

DATE

As the text itself makes clear, the author did not compile his account of the festival until several months after the funeral of Prince Arthur, the last event described in the narrative. Amidst his description of the wedding revels, the writer thus praises Henry VII for having 'contynued nobly and victorious unto this now the xviijth yere of his reigne' (4/820–1). Since Henry's eighteenth regnal year did not begin until 22 August 1502, the writer must have composed that passage, at least, no earlier than four months after the death of Prince Arthur (2 April 1502) and some nine months after the wedding revels which the passage describes. The elapse of so many months between events and

---

1. At this point, Scribe C is almost certainly restoring a passage inadvertently dropped when Scribe A's eye skipped from 'staves' at 4/418 to the same word at 4/419; as a consequence, the exceptional thorn here may represent something of a merely scribal error—Scribe C may simply have forgotton to transliterate a thorn found in his copy-text as *th* when he restored the forgotten passage. By its presence, however, it does at least establish another link between Scribe C and the author of the *Receyt*. It is at least possible that in the various corrections and emendations provided by Scribe C we catch the author superintending the final—and authoritative—version of his text.

historical description makes it unlikely that the author wrote his text in chronicle fashion, with new episodes being recorded virtually as they occurred. Rather, given its self-consciously literary divisions into Prologue, Books, and Chapters, the *Receyt* was more probably conceived and composed as a unit, after the writer had gathered together his notes and the various other materials which he incorporates into his text (for which, see below, pp. xliv–v, lvii–lxxi).

The death of Queen Elizabeth (11 February 1503) provides a probable terminal date for the composition of the *Receyt*. Since the writer apparently considers her to be still living at the time he is writing his account (he describes particular chambers in Richmond Palace as reserved for the Queen's use, for example; 4/851 ff.), the narrative must have been completed before her death. As a consequence, the date of composition of the *Receyt* may confidently be assigned to the first half of Henry VII's eighteenth regnal year, from late August 1502 to early February 1503, a period that includes the first anniversary of the festival it commemorates.

THE AUTHOR

Almost certainly a member of the King's household, the author consistently narrates his 'pusant and litle tretis' from the point of view of an attendant upon Henry VII. Consequently, his account is both unusually detailed in reporting events he has witnessed and vague in referring to those he has not. Although he devotes the entire first book of his narrative to the Princess's arrival at Plymouth and journey to London, for example, his account of these events is necessarily vague because he did not accompany one of the various parties that Henry sent out to meet and entertain the Princess on the various stages of her journey.[1] Only when the King himself abruptly decides to ride out and visit Princess Katharine at Dogmersfield does the narrative suddenly become detailed and circumstantial; at this point, he is reporting events he witnessed as a member, however humble, of the King's party. He thus records the colourful anecdote about the King's being denied an interview with the Princess on the grounds that she was asleep and that King Ferdinand had forbidden any such

1. The Privy Council Orders provided that only Richmond King of Arms, Somerset Herald, Rougedragon Pursuivant, and Montorgueil Pursuivant would ride to meet the Princess at Honiton, Devonshire, and attend her on her journey to London (British Library, MS Cotton Vespasian C. XIV, 95ᵛ).

meeting until after the wedding. Henry, the writer reports, observed that the Princess, having 'so far entrid into his empire and realme', was now subject to English law and threatened to visit her in her bedchamber if she would not receive him in a more suitable room (1/87–136).

Throughout the *Receyt*, indeed, the compiler characteristically reports his eyewitness experiences from a position very close to the King. He viewed Katharine's reception into London from a standing among the King's party at a merchant's house near the Standard in Cheapside (2/629–750), and he consequently does not note, as the civic chronicler did, that the Princess missed at least one of the speeches at an earlier pageant.[1] He gives us detailed, circumstantial descriptions not only of relatively public events, such as the wedding at St Paul's and three of the four tournaments, but also of more restricted events, such as the two wedding banquets, the ceremonial testing of the nuptial bed by the Earl of Oxford and its blessing by the assembled prelates, the King's offering at St Paul's two days after the wedding, all four of the court disguisings, and the King's 'consolation' of the Princess and her ladies after the departure of the Spaniards. He is particularly well-informed about royal decisions (e.g., the King's desire to send the Earl of Oxford with 'an especiall tokyn' to the Princess the day after the wedding, 3/327–33), and he pays particular attention to the 'addressyng and apparament' of the various chambers, halls, and palaces in which the events of the festival take place. In general, the author sees what the King sees and fails to see what the King does not.

To supplement his first-hand account of the festival, the author gained access to a number of court documents which he incorporates into his own narrative. Among these are the herald's report of Prince Arthur's funeral which, as we have seen, he divided into chapters to form Book Five of the *Receyt*. He also includes the verses spoken by the actors in the royal entry pageants; these probably derive from a copy submitted to the court for approval. His extremely detailed descriptions of the pageants themselves may have been the fruits of careful note-taking (since the pageants remained standing for some time after the festival, he had ample time to view them)[2] but the

---

1. A.H. Thomas and I.D. Thornley, eds., *The Great Chronicle of London* (London, 1938), 304–5.

2. S. Anglo, 'The London Pageants for the Reception of Katharine of Aragon', *Journal of the Warburg and Courtauld Institutes*, xxvi (1963), 54 n. 5, where payments are referred to in connection with the pageantry as late as 6 October 1502.

descriptions may also derive from the formal 'device' (written architectural specification) of the pageants which would also have been submitted to the court for its approval. Finally, he incorporates into Book Three of his narrative an anonymous poem on 'the joyful beholding' of the wedding ceremony, probably written by one of the King's many 'oratours'.[1] In all, perhaps a quarter of the *Receyt* consists of such incorporated materials.

All this eyewitness description (which must have involved notetaking) and deliberate collection of court documents fully justifies Glynne Wickham's conclusion that the *Receyt* constitutes a 'more or less official' history 'written by someone having access to information at source' and thus tends to confirm Edmund Lodge's conjecture that it 'was probably composed by the order of Henry VII himself'.[2] But who was this official, attendant historian?

Modern commentary has always identified the author as a herald because *R*, the unique manuscript from which all other versions of the main narrative descend, was bound into *M*, a volume of undoubted heraldic provenance, and because heralds often compiled similar narratives as a part of their official duties.[3] Although such a conjecture is not impossible, the weight of evidence suggests it to be extremely unlikely. To begin with, we have no real evidence of R's heraldic provenance before that manuscript was bound together with its three companion manuscripts to form *M* in the late-sixteenth century. *R* was certainly *collected* by a herald, but the evidence of provenance alone cannot show that it was *written* by a herald. For another thing, the narrative is most vague and unreliable in precisely those places where it should be most circumstantial and reliable were the writer in fact a herald. Court minutes tell us, for example, that immediately upon hearing of the Princess's arrival at Plymouth, the King's Council, as its first order of business, dispatched four heralds to meet, 'gief their attendaunce & serue the said princesse' as she rode from Devonshire to London.[4] The author's account, however, neither provides circumstantial detail of the Princess's journey (which presumably would have been easily obtainable

---

1. For the King's 'oratours', see W. Nelson, *John Skelton Laureate* (New York, 1939), 34–37.
2. Wickham, *Early English Stages*, i, 404; F. Grose and T. Astle, *The Antiquarian Repertory*, 4 vols (London, 1807–09), ii, 248.
3. See, for example, Wickham, *Early English Stages*, i, 404; Anglo, 'London Pageants', 54; Wagner, *Heralds of England*, 124 n. 1.
4. British Library, MS Cotton Vespasian C. XIV, fol. 95ᵛ.

from a brother herald), nor, still more tellingly, does it even mention the heralds' 'attendaunce' upon the Princess.

Along the same lines, the author's descriptions of the four tournaments are particularly misinformed and incomplete. Tournaments were indeed the herald's stock-in-trade, and these tournaments had been in the hands of the heralds since they had first been proclaimed at Calais in May, 1500.[1] Heralds presided over the entire ritual of the lists from the proclamation of the two challenges, to the enrolment of the knights who came to answer the challenges, to the devising of the trees of chivalry upon which the competitors hung their shields, to the umpiring and score-keeping of the various events, to the awarding of the prizes.[2] We should expect any English herald, as a consequence, to show professional interest in these events and to get at least the major facts right. The author, however, both gets his major facts wrong and shows a marked lack of interest in some of the major events of these, the most important tournaments of the reign. The extant score cheque for the joust thus shows that on the very first day of the competition, 'sir george herbert was hurt' and thereafter withdrew from the tournament. The compiler, however, not only overlooks this mishap, but has Sir George returning to the fray day after day.[3] Far from taking a keen interest in the jousts, the compiler does not even bother to describe the second day of the tournaments. Nor does he mention the participation of three Spanish knights, even though both the civic chronicler and the heralds' score cheque record their appearance.[4] Not does it occur to him to mention the winner of each day's event, as is usual in heraldic narratives and as even the civic chronicler unfailingly does.[5] On the whole, indeed, the civic chronicler makes a far more adequate narrator of tournaments than the author, at least from a herald's point of view.

What distinguishes the *Receyt* most sharply from true heraldic narratives, however, is its descriptions of the activities of heralds. Whatever else they may describe, true heraldic narratives always give generous attention to the ministrations of heralds. The three companion narratives originally bound with the *Receyt* in *M* pass this test easily; they describe the heralds' crying the King's

1. For the association of heralds with tournaments, see Wagner, *Heralds and Heraldry*, 25–6, 30, 46, 71–2. For the proclamations at Calais in 1500, see below, pp. lxxi–iv.

2. The two tournament cartels (Appendix) give a graphic picture of the duties and activities of the herald.

3. College of Arms, MS M. 3, fol. 25ᵛ.

4. *Great Chronicle*, 322; College of Arms, MS M. 3, fol. 25ᵛ.

5. *Great Chronicle*, 314–15.

largesse after the last course at the banquet table, escorting an English princess to Scotland, measuring lances and governing the ceremonial of the tilt, recording the jousters' scores, and gratefully listing the rewards they received for their services. They almost always identify one another by name. In this respect, Book Five of the *Receyt*, the interpolated funeral narrative, does indeed give a full account of the heralds' activities at almost every stage of the funeral ceremonies. Heralds escort the funeral procession, sometimes riding 'backward as was the maner' about the Prince's banner; they stand guard of honour about the casket; they accept cloth-of-gold palls from the noble mourners and lay them ceremoniously alongside the corpse; they begin the Dirge at the various funeral masses 'in a high voyce ... for Prince Arthur soule and all Cristen soulys, Pater Noster &c'; they receive mourning stoles and casket covers of black cloth for their 'fees'; and finally, Prince Arthur's own pursuivant, 'sore weping', casts his coat of arms into the grave atop the casket.[1]

By contrast, the author's own descriptions are characterized by their general lack of interest in the activities of heralds. In the first four books, he mentions the presence of heralds only twice, only then in passing, and only in such a way as to suggest that he himself is not a herald. In Book Two he thus describes the Princess' royal entry procession as it appeared 'to the Kinges sight' from his vantage point at the Standard in Cheapside (2/650–3). In recounting the participants in 'this solempne and ordinat entraunce', he mentions that 'the kinges of harodes and aroldes of armys in their cote armours of silver and golde of the Kynges armys of Englond ... made roome and weye and devyded the comon people right ordrely'. The heralds, in short, claim no more of his attention than the 'gentilmen belonging to therl of Northumberland' or the 'trumpettes, shalmewes, and sakbotes to a great nombre as cam with the Princes owte of Spayne' (2/653–76). Then later on, in Book Four, he closes his description of the first day of the tournaments with his only reference to the heralds who were, after all, presiding over this entertainment. Perhaps seeking to excuse the professional inadequacy of his own description, he tells the reader that the 'goodly feates [of arms] and therof the hooll discripcion appieryth weell pleynner and more opyn in the bokys of the haroldes of armys' (4/124–6).[2] In both cases, his remarks tend to disassociate him from the

---

1. 5/187–8, 317–21, 111–3, 253–4, 346–8.
2. Wagner, *Heralds of England*, 124 n. 1, cites this phrase as evidence of the author's status as a herald; in fact, it more likely suggests he was not one of 'the haroldes of armys' to whom he refers his readers.

profession of heraldry, in the first instance because he is apparently watching from the crowd while the heralds *en masse* march past him, and in the second because he seems to be contrasting his own enthusiastic but amateur description of the tournament to the professional recordkeeping of the heralds. Both the nature and number of these references, therefore, argue persuasively against heraldic authorship of the *Receyt*.

The indications which the author gives us of his own activities and interests at court suggest, in fact, rather a servant's than a herald's profession. Always deferential to nobility, he constantly remarks upon the 'addressyng and apparament' of the various palaces, halls, and chambers that he mentions. He sees the festival, in short, from the viewpoint of someone who must see to the comfort of his betters. Characteristically, he couples an admiring description of the great hall and chapel of Richmond Palace with special mention of the 'houses of office'—the pantry, buttery, cellary, kitchen, and scullery—which, by means of their economy, make possible the magnificence of the royal household (4/856–60).[1] Again, as we might expect from such a service-minded attendant, his accounts of the royal banquets, disguisings, and noble entertainments are much longer, more detailed, and professional than his descriptions of the jousts. He not only notices the great cupboards of gold and silver dishes which adorn the banqueting halls, but also appraises their value (cf. 4/970–5). In constant attendance upon the King and keenly interested in the functioning of the household, the author presents himself as one of Henry VII's small army of servants, perhaps a gentleman usher or groom.

An interesting, though inconclusive, case can be made for the authorship of one of Henry's grooms: Stephen Hawes. The poet was already well established as 'one of the gromes of the moost honorable chamber of our souerayne lorde kynge Henry the .vii.' by February 1503, when he received an allowance of black cloth for the funeral of Queen Elizabeth.[2] He might therefore have been present as early as October 1501 to witness the marriage festival, and he was certainly there in the very year in which the *Receyt* was composed (18 Henry VII).[3] Perhaps he was already known as a writer, for his first known work, *The Example of Virtue*,

---

1. For the importance of these offices in the royal household, see A.R. Myers, *The Household of Edward IV* (Manchester, 1959), 15, 174–97.

2. Public Record Office, L.C. 2/1, fol. 62ᵛ.

3. He was not listed among the court servants who received mourning at the funeral of Prince Edmund in 1500, however. He must therefore have entered the royal service after 19 June 1500 and before 11 February 1503.

appeared just a year after the *Receyt* was written (in 19 Henry VII according to the printer's introduction to that work).[1] In his *Scriptorum Illustrium maioris Brytanniae* (1557-9), moreover, Bale tells us that Hawes wrote both in prose and in poetry, and he lists among the poet's works something which he describes as *De coniugio principis*. Since Arthur was the only English prince who married in Hawes's lifetime, Hawes very probably wrote some work about the marriage of Prince Arthur.[2] Is *The Receyt of the Ladie Kateryne* to be identified with *De coniugio principis* as Hawes's first work written for the Tudor court?

Perhaps it is, but the stylistic evidence that would help us answer this question affirmatively is not very encouraging. To be sure, several passages in the *Receyt* resemble similar passages in one or another of Hawes's known works. Take the author's description of the roof of the great hall of Richmond Palace, for example:

> [the] rof is of tymber, not beamyd ne brasid but propir knottes, craftly corven, joyned and shett toguyders with mortes and pynned, hangyng pendaunt from the sede roff into the grownde and floure, aftir the moost new invencion and crafte, of the pure practif of gementri, cast owt with wyndowes glasid right lightsume and goodly.
>
> (4/799-805)

Compare:

> *The roof was wrought by merueylous gemetry*
> Colered with asure gold and gowlys
> *With knottes coruen full ryght craftely.*
>
> (*Example of Virtue*, ll. 248-50)

> With knottes sexangled gay and gloryous
> The rofe dyde hange ryght hygh and pleasauntly
> *By geometry made ryght well and craftely.*
>
> (*Pastime of Pleasure*, ll. 2560-2)

The author also aspires to the same elevated diction so characteristic of Hawes. Both, for example, have a particular fondness for French loan words: *pusant, enseasid, pastans, provents, curtilage,*

---

1. Stephen Hawes, *Minor Poems*, ed. F.W. Gluck and A.B. Morgan (London, 1974), 2.
2. It has been suggested that Bale might have arrived at this title by mistaking the frontispiece of *A joyfull medytacyon*, which shows the coronation of Henry VIII and Katharine of Aragon, for an illustration of their marriage (*Minor Poems*, xii n. 1). Bale, however, always translates titles directly from English to Latin; he rarely invents them. All the other titles assigned to Hawes can thus be identified as Latin translations of Hawes' own English titles.

cap-a-pe, and the like. Both also like to achieve dignity by adding the prefixes *ap-*, *em-*, and *en-* wherever possible: *apparament, appreparement, apperceyve, apparage, apparaunce, aproperyd; embrawded, empayntid; enduyed, ensence, enserche, encharge, enclyned, encompanyed, enfreight, enhaungid, enjoyned, ennouryd, enservyd*, and so forth. But on the whole, differences are as remarkable as similarities. Hawes's syntax never becomes quite so Latinate as does the author's (e.g., the clausal structures in such sentences as 2/88–9 and 4/1042–66). And while the author's dialect and grammatical habits generally follow those of Hawes as outlined in W.E. Mead's edition of the *Pastime of Pleasure*, there are some important differences. The author, for example, often uses *is* for *his* and *hit* for *it*, which Hawes does not do.[1] Conceivably, such differences might be explained by the differences inherent in Hawes's approaches to prose and poetic composition, or by differences in scribal and authorial choices, but we have no way of judging. As a result, the case for Hawes's authorship must remain a tantalizing but inconclusive one.

THE TRANSMISSION OF THE TEXT

1. The Main Narrative

For over a century after it was written, the *Receyt* lay virtually unnoticed. No historian cited it, no antiquary copied so much as a single passage into his own collections. In his *History of Henry VII*, Sir Francis Bacon spent several paragraphs describing in detail the pageantry and entertainments that took place at Prince Arthur's wedding, but he took all his information from one of the civic chronicles.[2] The text circulated only among heralds in the College of Arms. In the mid-sixteenth century, Sir Christopher Barker (Richmond Herald, 1522–36, Norroy 1536, Garter 1536–1550) transcribed the entire text, except for Book Five, into one of his own personal manuscripts (now College of Arms, MS Vincent 25, fols 108^r–142^v). Much interested in royal ceremonies, particularly coronations and royal entries, Sir Christopher transcribed the *Receyt* alongside other texts relative to the coronation

---

1. Stephen Hawes, *The Pastime of Pleasure*, ed. W.E. Mead (London, 1928), lxxxii–xcii.

2. Sir Francis Bacon, *The History of the Reign of King Henry the Seventh*, ed. R. Lockyer (London, 1971), 204–5. Bacon merely observes that 'there was a great deal of astronomy, the lady being resembled to Hesperus, and the Prince to Arcturus, and the old King Alphonsus ... was brought in to be the fortuneteller of the match'. This much he could have found out from the London chronicles.

ceremonial and pageantry for Henry VIII, Anne Boleyn, and Edward VI. Since the funeral account was irrelevant to the purposes of the volume he was transcribing, he not only omitted Book Five but also modified the wording of the Prologue to eliminate all references to that part of the text. He sometimes simplifies the author's syntax and inventively fills in lacunae. Although useless to an editor who wishes to establish the text of the *Receyt*, it is at least a careful, clear, and responsible transcript,[1] even if an uninfluential one, rarely consulted and never cited.[2]

Early in the next century, however, another herald produced a much more eccentric and much less accurate transcript which did circulate widely outside the College. *The book of certaine Triumphes* (British Library MS Harley 69) consists of a collection of materials relative to the ceremonial side of a herald's duties—tournaments, funerals, grants of arms, embassies, creations of Knights of the Bath, and the like. It is obviously the work of a herald who, about 1610, collected such passages out of manuscripts belonging to brother heralds as would be helpful to him in fulfilling the ceremonial duties of his office.[3] He could then turn to his collection to find examples of tournament challenges, noble funerals, grants of arms, and other heraldic functions useful in planning future ceremonies. He was not an antiquarian or historian *per se*, nor did he have Sir Christopher Barker's taste for collecting relatively complete documents. His excerpts from *R* appear at the end of his collection, at fols 28ᵛ–46ʳ.[4]

1. On the Vincent MSS in general, see Wagner, *Records and Collections*, 33–4, and Campbell, Steer, and Yorke, *Catalogue of Manuscripts*, 233–48. Barker introduces a number of scribal errors of the usual sort: 'lovyng bonde' becomes 'lovenge body' at Pro./83, for example, and he simplifies 'enserched' to 'serched' two lines later. Occasionally he adds a word or two ('Lady Kateryn *of Spayne*', Pro./82) or drops a phrase ('v partes [and small bokes]', Pro./96), but on the whole his is a remarkably accurate copy. He is not above filling in a lacuna, however (cf. 'with muche diligens', 4/1016), and he deliberately alters the Prologue at ll. 99–100 to omit a reference to Book Five, which he omits from his transcription.
2. Other portions of the MS, however, were noticed, particularly the portion relevant to Edward VI's coronation. See Leland, *Collectanea*, iv, 310–33, and J.G. Nichols, *Literary Remains of King Edward VI*, i (London, 1857), cclxxviii–ccciii.
3. The seventeenth-century bibliophile, Thomas Starkey, signed and dated the MS when he acquired it in 1617. Since the transcript includes portions from Book Five of the *Receyt*, it must have been transcribed from 1st M. 13, not from Sir Christopher Barker's version. The latest items added by the original herald-compiler concern the reign of Elizabeth I. Consequently, the MS must have been copied between 1603 and 1617.
4. Starkey added a few items on some blank folios at the end of the MS. The original compiler could have used those folios to extend his excerpts from *R* if he had been interested in doing so. In his transcription, the herald omits many words

This utilitarian bias explains why he copied only certain portions of *R* and arranged them in such an odd order. Primarily interested in strictly heraldic matters, he began his transcription with Books Four and Five of the *Receyt*, renumbering them 'Book One' and 'Book Two' in his version. Both of these excerpts speak directly of the ceremonial duties of a herald, whether as a devisor and judge of tournaments, an attendant upon the King at great state banquets, or an organizer of funerals. But in transcribing Book Four of *R*, he omitted Chapters VIII and IX because the *Receyt*'s account of the King's removal to Richmond and its admiring description of Henry's newly-rebuilt palace offered the herald no useful illustration of court ceremonial. He next, perhaps as an afterthought, turned to the beginning of *M* and copied out the Council's directives for the reception and marriage of the Princess Katharine (*M*, fols 1ʳ–11ʳ). Again, the herald's interest in this piece is utilitarian; it illustrates the practical steps necessary to the smooth performance of state ceremonials and details the contributions and interrelationships of the various branches of the royal household. He then completed his collection of excerpts from *M* by returning to *R* and copying out Book One, Chapters I–IV of the *Receyt*, skipping over the merely 'literary' Prologue. These four chapters describe the court's initial reception of the Princess Katharine, from her landing at Plymouth to her arrival at London. Since heralds regularly performed escort duties in such cases, this excerpt offered the herald-compiler another professionally useful example of successful court ceremonial. Further, it formed a useful companion piece to the Council directives that he had just copied; the one text illustrated the elaborate planning, the other the practical results of that planning. When he reached Chapter VI of his copy-text, 'thordre of the Citie of London for the receyte of the Princes' (1/206–7), he stopped; he made no effort to transcribe any portion of Books Two or Three. The *Receyt*'s accounts of the Princess's entry into London and of the wedding ceremony held no interest whatsoever for him; these ceremonies belonged to the provinces, respectively, of the city fathers and the bishops, not the heralds. In excerpting the 'useful' portions of the *Receyt* for his text, then, the herald transformed the writer's careful narrative structure into a rather awkward

---

and passages present in *R* but often follows the accidentals closely. His mistakes are often a matter of simple transposition (e.g., *have be seyn none/have none bene seene*, 1/121) or word confusion (e.g., *conteyning/contenuyng*, 4/580). There is no sign (such as the inclusion of a passage not present in *R*) that he derives any part of his text from any other source.

liii

anthology: Book Four (with omissions), Book Five, Council
directives, Book One (with omissions).

Since the text held no particular verbal authority for its
herald-scribe, he was understandably not very respectful of it.
Though greatly interested in the substance of the ceremonials
described, he was relatively indifferent about the language that
conveyed those descriptions. He often edited as he wrote,
sometimes condensing what he copied; he dropped or substituted
confusing words; he abbreviated titles and names; he 'corrected'
grammar. Moreover, he omitted those passages which he found
irrelevant, such as the *Receyt*'s description of the Spanish
rope-walker's performance (4/908–26). If he could not read a
word, he guessed; thus the *trone*-shaped pageant at 4/938 becomes
a *towre*-shaped one. As a copy wholly derivative from *R, The
booke of certaine Triumphes* (hereafter *H*) has no value whatsoever
in establishing the text of the *Receyt*; worse still, as a partial and
untrustworthy transcript, it badly misrepresents its text. One uses
the *H* version as a historical document at one's peril.

Nevertheless, *H* did have one undoubted advantage for
scholars: availability. In 1617 the manuscript came into the hands
of the bibliophile, Thomas Starkey, probably by way of one of the
several heralds in his acquaintance.[1] Upon Starkey's death in
1628, Sir Simonds D'Ewes pucrhased it from the estate, and from
D'Ewes it passed eventually into the great Harleian Collection
(1705) and thence to the library of the British Museum (1753).[2]
As a consequence, the text escaped the exclusive confines of the
College of Arms and became widely available in one or the other
of these great libraries.

For the next three centuries, scholars and antiquarians
frequently mined *H* for nuggets of value. Antiquarians primarily
culled it for illustrations of 'the elegancies, the luxuries, and the
general manners of a court almost as little known as those of
Egbert or Alfred',[3] while historians of the theatre plundered it for
illustrations of the early disguising and royal entry. As for the
antiquarians, seventeenth-century transcripts of *H* are represented by British Library MS Cotton Vespasian C. XI, fols

1. Starkey received manuscripts from William Sedgwick, an arms painter and
servant of Henry Lilly, Rouge Dragon Pursuivant (*College of Arms*, 222). He also
drew up his own pedigree, which found its way into the collections of another
pursuivant, William Radclyffe. C.E. Wright, *Fontes Harleiani* (London, 1972),
299–300; *DNB*. For Starkey's hand in other heraldic MSS see S. Anglo,
'Financial and Heraldic Records of the English Tournament', *Jour. Soc. Archivists*, ii (1960–64), 189–90, 192–3.
2. Wright, 131, 372.
3. *Antiquarian Repertory*, ii, 248.

112^v–126^v, and Bodleian MS Tanner 85, fols 60^r–107^v; an eighteenth-century transcript appears in the 1774 edition of Leland's *Collectanea* and nineteenth-century selections appear in Bentley's *Excerpta Historica* (1831). Historians of the stage, meanwhile, published extracts from *H* to document the early history of the masque. Collier, for example, quoted generous selections in his 1879 edition of *Annals of the Stage* while Alfred Goodwin (1844) and Paul Reyher (1909) included careful editions of the relevant chapters of Book Four in their studies of Tudor revels.[1] When such historians as Chambers and Withington compiled their influential histories of medieval drama and pageantry, it was to one or another of these versions that they turned for information.[2]

As one might expect, the accuracy of these many transcripts varies considerably. Unfortunately, the most unreliable of them all, the *Collectanea* version, became the one most often cited by historians of the stage. Printed from a condensed, stylistically 'improved' and often paraphrased transcript of *H* apparently supplied to the publisher by Joseph Edmondson,[3] it frequently manages to garble important details or omit them altogether. It not only repeats *H*'s error by describing the Richmond pageant as a *towre* rather than a *trone*, for example, but it substitutes *sea horses* for *woodosys* and *elks* for *ibexes*, while disguisers *issue from* rather than *alight from* their pageant cars (Book Four, Chapter Three). These unintentional errors aside, the Edmondson text is chiefly distinguished by deliberate omissions of 'unnecessary' verbiage and by efforts at stylistic condensation. All indications of chapter divisions are suppressed and the author's attempts at high style are routinely simplified, often mistaking the sense of the passage in the process. Thus an awkward attempt at high style:

> The morow clowdes were usually and after the curse naturall
> expellid; the clere beamys of the son full ofte tymes the
> myddell eires with their refleccions had striken. Then the

1. *Collectanea*, v, 352–81. S. Bentley, *Excerpta Historica* (London, 1831), 85–133. J.P. Collier, *The History of English Dramatic Poetry to the Time of Shakespeare, and Annals of the Stage to the Restoration* (London, 1879), i, 58ff. A.T. Goodwin, *Court Revels*, Shakespeare Society Papers, i (London, 1844), 47ff. Reyher, 351ff.
2. Chambers, *Mediaeval Stage*, i, 398–9; R. Withington, *English Pageantry*, i (Cambridge, Mass., 1918), 113–14.
3. 'Edmondson, who furnished those additions, was a coach-painter by trade, an antiquary by profession, and a herald by name. Little was to be reasonably expected from selections made by such a person' (Edmund Lodge, Lancaster Herald, in *Antiquarian Repertory*, ii, 248).

sides of their cursers with their spurres they began to tast
and extendid their passage unto the village of Esthampsted

(1/76–80)

becomes both simplified and garbled; the horsemen now strike
the sides of their coursers instead of the sunbeams striking the
'myddell eires':

> On the Morrowe the King's Grace, with all his Company,
> stroke the Sides of their Coursers with their Spurres, and
> began to extend their Passage towards the Village of
> Esthamsted.[1]

Indeed, so many liberties have been taken with the text that
scholars have found it difficult to tell which copy-text Edmondson had used for his contribution to the *Collectanea*.[2] Nevertheless, this paraphrased and stylistically improved transcript of a
transcript has often been the single source to which scholars have
turned for documentary evidence about the Tudor revels.

The inadequacies of the *Collectanea* version did produce one
good effect, however. Upset with Edmondson's transcript,
Edmund Lodge, Lancaster Herald, published a complete transcription of *R* in the 1808 version of *The Antiquarian Repertory*.[3]
In general a full and responsible text, it attempts something
approaching a diplomatic edition of *R*. While standardizing the
punctuation and capitalization according to nineteenth-century
usage, it attempts to retain *R*'s original spelling, and it preserves
abbreviation symbols. It even attempts to preserve the form as
well as the substance of *R* by keeping *R*'s paragraphing intact and
printing chapter headings in the style of the original. Like the *H*
scribe, however, Lodge had difficulties reading and transcribing
his copy-text. Even though it is the best transcription of all, it
suffers from many lapses. Words are misread or dropped; whole
lines are omitted; in one place, Latin is even mistranscribed as
garbled English.[4] Sometimes, in fact, Lodge's edition is so faulty
that important passages appear more accurately rendered in the

---

1. *Collectanea*, v, 353.
2. G. Wickham typically thinks that the *Collectanea* text was taken directly
from *R* (*Early English Stages*, i, 404).
3. *Antiquarian Repertory*, ii, 248–331. Lodge signs his contribution with his
initials only, but he has been identified in *College of Arms*, 93, and in *DNB*.
4. Cf. Wickham, i, 404; Lodge prints '"Of me ... trowe ye"' for 'O si me
inveniat' (*Antiquarian Repertory*, ii, *285).

Fig.1: The Textual Transmission of the Receyt

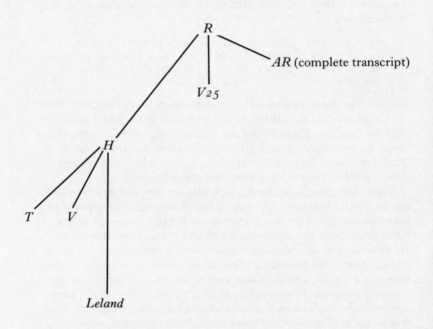

Sigla:

R—College of Arms, MS 1st M. 13, fols 27–75.

AR—Lodge transcript published in *Antiquarian Repertory*.

V25—College of Arms, MS Vincent 25, fols 108^r–142^v.

H—British Library, MS Harley 69, *The booke of certaine Triumphes*, fols 28^v–38^v, 44^r–46^r.

T—Bodley MS Tanner 85, fols 60^r–107^v.

V—British Library, MS Cotton Vespasian C. XI, fols 112^v–126^v.

Leland—Edmondson transcript published in Leland's *Collectanea*.

Edmondson version.[1] In the end, then, Lodge's version, though more complete than *H*, is about as unreliable.

The textual transmission of the *Receyt* is shown in fig.1. The editorial implications of this diagram are clear. Only *R*, a corrected, scribal copy of the author's rough draft, has any textual authority; all other texts are derivative.

2. *The Funeral Report*

Book Five of the *Receyt*, the funeral report, considerably complicates this neat pattern. This portion of the narrative has come down to us in two different textual traditions, one of them completely independent of the main body of the *Receyt*. A number of heraldic manuscripts—most of them funeral collections—include transcripts of the funeral report. These all derive from Sir Thomas Wriothesley's Register of Arms (British Library, MS 45131, fols 37–41) and are distinguished by their lack of chapter divisions. Both College of Arms MS I. 3 and British Library MS Egerton 2642 fall into this category, the former a full transcript of Wriothesley's text and the latter an edited and abridged one.[2] The more familiar textual tradition, which is distinguished by the presence of chapter divisions, derives from *R*. These include a sixteenth-century transcription in College of Arms, MS I. 11 as well as the seventeenth-century version in *H* discussed above.[3] Moreover, both *R* and the Wriothesley transcript (hereafter *A*) are reasonably accurate, independent witnesses to a now-lost, common original. Each supplies words, lines, even whole passages that have been omitted in the other, thereby allowing an editor to correct some cases of manifest error. At 5/151–2, for example, *R* leaves a large blank space where he has been unable to decipher in his copy-text the identity of the cleric who 'did the devyne service'; *A* fills in this lacuna with 'the

1. The Lodge text thus omits the information that the men and women performers coupled after dancing separately (cf. 4/337–40) at one disguising and omits as well the separate dancing of the men (cf. 4/630–2) on another occasion.

2. These versions of the funeral report have never been printed, although the text of I. 3 has been cited by F. Sandford, *A Genealogical History of the Kings of England*, ed. W. Stebbing (London, 1707), 475–6.

3. Although MS I. 11 has a very few readings which agree with *A* against *R*, these are the result of chance variation rather than evidence of a copy-text other than *R*. (I. 11 thus reads 'hym' with *A* at 5/34 rather than 'them' with *R*.) There is no doubt that I. 11 has been copied directly from *R*. Not only does it include chapter titles, which were introduced for the first time in *R*, but it occasionally transcribes some of these as if they were text rather than title. Similarly, it includes all of the passages not present in *A* but preserved in *R* and it omits all those passages present in *A* but omitted in *R*. Above all, it consistently agrees with *R*'s manifest errors.

bisshop of chestre'. In the same way, the *A* scribe skipped from
'hedes' at 5/169 to the same word at 5/172, thus inadvertently
omitting two and a half lines of text which *R* supplies. A number
of variants, however, cannot be identified as manifest error in
either version. Transpositions are especially frequent, but it is
impossible to say which is the original and which the transposed
version. Did the sergeants of arms go 'bifore hym to thofferyng of
that Mas Peny' (*R*, 5/285), or did they go 'to thofferyng of that
masse peny before hym' (*A*, fol. 40ʳ)?

Although the *A* and *R* versions have approximately equal
textual authority, the Wriothesley version reproduces more accurately the form of the original herald's report. As a study of the
contrasting verbal habits of the two writers shows, the chapter
headings in the *R* version clearly derive from the author of the
Receyt, not the herald. He inserted them into the herald's
originally undivided text to make its format appear consistent
with the rest of the *Receyt*. As a consequence, the characteristically elevated diction of the *Receyt*, with its fondness for *ap-* and *en-*
prefixes, continues to appear in these inserted chapter headings,
even though it often contrasts sharply with the simpler diction of
the herald's report. At 5/156, for example, the author's chapter
title promises a description 'of the *appreparyng* of the chare'. Two
lines later, however, the herald tells how 'the riche chare was
prepared' (5/158). Similarly, at 5/332 the chapter heading announ-
ces 'th*ensencyng* of the corse', but the text itself describes how the
'prelates cam and *sensid* the corse' (5/335–6).[1] Indeed, the
author's insertions, made more with an eye to their appearance
than to their sense, sometimes result in strikingly inappropriate
'chapter' divisions. The heading to Chapter VI, for example,
promises a report on the provision of torches and torch bearers for
the funeral masses at Ludlow. In fact, it describes the funeral
cortège's departure from Ludlow (accompanied by torches and
torch bearers) together with its arduous journey to Bewdley. The
next heading (VII) then promises to detail the 'noble rewards'
given to every church where the body remained overnight on its
journey to Worcester; instead, the 'chapter' mentions these only
in a very brief and general reference before describing at length
the cortège's ceremonial reception at Worcester.

1. Different forms of names and titles also sharply distinguish the two writers.
The author's 'abbot of Burie' (1/164) becomes the herald's 'abbot of Borey'
(5/149), for example, and where the author only knows Don Pedro de Ayala by
title as 'the protonotory of Hispayne', the herald knows him by name and a
different title: 'thambassatour of Hispayne, called Don Peter de Yeaule' (5/138–9;
he was, in fact, both papal protonotory and Spanish ambassador to Scotland).

In its original format, the funeral report represents an entirely distinct narrative tradition from the *Receyt*. Instead of a self-consciously literary narrative—a 'pusant and litle tretis' some-times redolent of Malory—the herald's report merely seeks to record pomp and elicit pathos. It serves as both a ceremonial record and as testimony of communal grief. The genre was a relatively new one as the heralds were relatively new at organizing funerals. The first extant examples date from the 1460s.[1] The most influential of these reports, one written to commemorate Edward IV's funeral, established both a ceremonial precedent for the conduct of subsequent royal funerals and a literary precedent for the composition of funeral reports.[2] As a consequence, not only does the ceremonial of Prince Arthur's funeral closely parallel that of Edward IV's obsequies, but the herald's report also closely models its descriptions after the Edward IV narrative. The indebtedness, however, is not so much one of phraseology as topicality. In short, the herald seems to have used the earlier narrative as a topical outline for his own composition. He thus describes the same items, often in similar language, in about the same order, whenever parallels in ceremonies permit. In describ-ing the removal of Prince Arthur's body from Ludlow Castle to the parish church, for instance, he follows his model's description of the removal of Edward IV's body from Westminster to Windsor. Like his predecessor, he begins by enumerating the names of the casket bearers, then describes the canopy and names its bearers, then details the four funeral banners and their bearers, then describes the personal ensign and its bearer, then concludes by naming the nobles who followed the procession in their mourning habits.[3] The genre, indeed, lends itself more to simpler syntactical constructions than to the long, Latinate sentences preferred by the author of the *Receyt*. Such narratives are often

---

1. Wagner, *Heralds of England*, 106–8.
2. The Edward IV narrative almost always appears in the funeral collections of sixteenth-century heralds, among them: College of Arms, MSS I. 3 (fols 7ᵛ, 8ᵛ–10), I. 7 (fols 7–10), and I. 14 (fol. 186ff.); British Library, MSS Additional 45131 (fol. 23ff.), and Stowe 668 (fol. 89ff.). It has been printed in *Archaeologia*, i (1770), 348–55 ('from a MS. of the late Mr. Anstis') and in *Letters and Papers Illustrative of the Reigns of Richard III. and Henry VII.*, ed. J. Gairdner, Rolls Series, i (London, 1861), 3–10 (from College of Arms, MS I. 7). In several of these manuscripts, a copy of 'the Ordenaunces which shalbe done in the observaunce at the deth and buryall of a annoynted king' immediately prefaces the funeral report itself, and the descriptions of the ceremonial in the report show that the 'ordinances' were carefully followed. This suggests that the 'ordinances' may first have been codified for Edward IV's funeral, which as a consequence became the single most important precedent for later funerals.
3. *Letters and Papers*, 5–6.

little more than expanded lists, successions of torches, flags, yards
of cloth, funeral cars, marchers in processions, mourning garments, and the offerings of Mass pennies.

But if the herald consciously imitates this prosaic model, he
also deserts it from time to time. On several occasions, he adopts a
first person narration quite distinct from the anonymous detailing
of ceremonies and enumerating of minutiae prescribed in his
Yorkist precedent. On these occasions, his prose becomes vivid,
emotionally affecting, and vigorous. He demonstrates something
of a flair for the dramatic. If he had merely followed his model, he
would have begun his report with an account of the preparation of
Prince Arthur's body and its lying in state. Instead, he postpones
this obligatory reportage until he has first narrated the beginning
of the story as he himself had experienced it. He thus sets his
scene at Greenwich just as the King's confessor, arriving to break
the terrible news to Henry, prepares his royal master to hear the
worst with a quotation from Job. The herald, who was apparently
a witness to this event, then tells how the King called for the
Queen so that the two of them might 'take the peynfull sorowes
toguyders', and he then vividly dramatizes their mutual attempts
to console one another 'as I harde sey'. Abruptly, he then recalls
himself to his official task and sets about the business of
describing the funeral preparations, much of it information
necessarily gathered at second hand after he had arrived in
Ludlow. But as he warms to his task, he frequently abandons the
official style for vivid, first person narration whenever his
experiences have been particularly affecting. He confides, for
example, his frustrations with the task of moving the heavy
funeral cart along almost impassably muddy roads on the 'foulist,
caulde, wyndy, and rayny day and the werst wey that I have
seen—ye, and in some place fayne to take oxen to drawe the chare,
so ill was the wey' (5/190–2). And he is particularly moved,
towards the end of his report, by the 'pitious sight' of the Prince's
household officers, all weeping uncontrollably, breaking their
staves of office over their heads and casting them into the grave
(5/346–54). At such times as these, the pedestrian report achieves
some considerable success in literary narrative.

These personal intrusions into an otherwise anonymous report
allow a reasonable identification of the author from among the
five heralds who officiated at Prince Arthur's funeral: Garter
King of Arms (John Writhe), Somerset Herald (John Young),
Bluemantle Pursuivant (Laurence Alford?), Rouge Dragon Pursuivant (name unknown), and Wallingford Pursuivant (Thomas
Writhe, later Sir Thomas Wriothesley, eldest son and successor as

Garter to John Writhe).[1] Of these, the two pursuivants are the most unlikely candidates; clearly the junior partners on this mission, neither is known to have written anything at all. Although a senior herald and author of similar heraldic narratives, John Young can be eliminated on stylistic grounds as even a cursory glance at his other narratives (above, pp. xxxii, xxxv–vi) will allow. This narrows the field to John Writhe and his son, Thomas.

Sir Thomas Wriothesley's position as Wallingford Pursuivant to Prince Arthur would seem to press his claim as the apparent author of the funeral narrative; the text itself, however, decisively rules out this possibility. For one thing, the herald-author narrates his report, as we have seen, from the point of view of someone who was at Greenwich when news of Arthur's death reached the King. Indeed, the author reports Arthur's death in only the most general terms and has nothing very concrete to say about funeral preparations before the moment when the royal party, dispatched from London, reached Ludlow. Unlike the other four heralds whom the court sent off from London, however, Wriothesley had been part of the Prince's household in Ludlow. Almost certainly, he was there when the Prince died. Whoever took the news of Arthur's death to London, he did not; protocol demanded that he remain continuously in attendance upon his master's body until, at the burial, he cast his herald's tabard into his master's grave to symbolize his new status as a masterless man (cf. 5/346–54 and n.). Similarly, at another telling point in the narrative, the herald-author leaves the funeral procession at Bewdley and rides to Worcester with Sir Richard Croft and Sir William Uvedale to make further arrangements there. Again, Wriothesley could not have done that; his place remained beside the casket of his dead master. Finally, the obvious corruption of the *A* text argues strongly against Wriothesley's authorship. It is difficult to imagine that Wriothesley, who had the funeral report professionally transcribed into his own official Register, would accept such an inaccurate version of his own work in a personal manuscript obviously meant as an authoritative fair copy.

1. Public Record Office, MS L.C. 2/1, fols 15ᵛ, 28ᵛ, lists the four heralds who received eight yards of cloth for mourning garments as they were sent off to Prince Arthur's funeral. On fol. 17ʳ, an expense is recorded for painting 'v coates of Armes for v harauldes to attende vppon the chare'. The fifth herald, Prince Arthur's personal pursuivant, Wallingford, would have been with Arthur in Ludlow and did not receive cloth with the other four in London. He is also identified at 5/346–54 in the *Receyt*. For biographical information on these five heralds, see *College of Arms*.

This leaves Sir Thomas's father, John Writhe, as the most probable author. Logically, the responsibility of drawing up a report would fall to him in any case as the most senior herald on the mission.[1] Moreover, Writhe's compositional habits closely parallel those of the author of the funeral report in their somewhat exaggerated respect for literary and heraldic precedent. In drawing up Buckingham's tournament cartel, for example, he imitates the style and wording of a Yorkist challenge in much the same way that the herald-author takes a Yorkist funeral report for his model (see above, pp. xxvii–viii). Further, the very evidence that eliminates Sir Thomas Wriothesley from consideration tends to support the claims for Writhe. Not only was Writhe in London when news of Arthur's death reached the court,[2] but as the virtual heraldic symbol of royal authority, Garter would have been the most likely herald to accompany Croft and Uvedale to Worcester. Similarly, Writhe's authorship better explains the textual corruption of the *A* manuscript than does Wriothesley's. Sir Thomas inherited his father's manuscripts in 1504 and often incorporated copies of these into his own heraldic collections.[3] In compiling the *A* manuscript, Sir Thomas's scribe would be unlikely to single out the funeral report as having any special significance apart from the other 'old' texts he was copying from Writhe's books into the new Register. Having copied it professionally, albiet inaccurately, into the imposing new volume, he may even have discarded Writhe's original.

In transcribing this lost (and possibly discarded) original, Wriothesley's scribe was considerably less accurate than the *R* scribe. For every word of phrase which *R* drops, *A* drops two. Never does *R* drop whole lines; *A* does on several occasions (in addition to 5/169–72, see 5/58–60 and 5/189–93). Nevertheless, as the Register of Garter King of Arms, Wriothesley's manuscript enjoyed a prestige that the original report lacked. Thus when Wriothesley was called to give testimony in the divorce trial of Katharine of Aragon, he read into the record a passage from this

1. The claims of Garter to be sovereign in the Office of Arms had not yet been accepted. In some respects, indeed, Roger Machado, Richmond King of Arms, enjoyed equal, if not greater, status to Garter. Garter, however, was clearly the most senior herald in attendance at the funeral. For the controversy, which came to a head in 1530, see Wagner, *Heralds and Heraldry*, 62–4, 87–99.
2. The account book entries clearly imply this; Garter and his three fellow-heralds were given mourning-cloth, presumably in London, before setting out for Wales. Wallingford (Wriothesley) was not then given mourning-cloth because he was already in Wales. See p. lxi n. 1.
3. Wagner, *Records and Collections*, 9–11. Sir A. Wagner, *A Catalogue of English Mediaeval Rolls of Arms*, Harleian Society (Oxford, 1950), 111–16, 120–4.

Fig.2 : Manuscripts of the Funeral Report

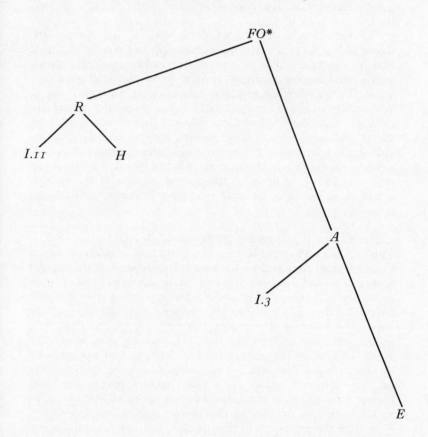

Sigla :

FO*—Writhe's? original funeral report, no longer extant.
R—College of Arms, MS 1st M. 13, fols 68^r–74^v.
H—British Library, MS Harley 69, fols 35^v–38^v.
A—British Library, MS Additional 45131, fols 37–41.
I.3—College of Arms, MS I. 3, fols 14^v–17^v.
I.11—College of Arms, MS I. 11, fols 10^r–14^r.
E—British Library, MS Egerton 2642, fols 174^v–176.

very transcript rather than from the original report to establish certain facts about the death of Prince Arthur.[1] In short, the prestige of the Garter Register outweighed textual or even historical accuracy. As a consequence, all accounts of the funeral report, except those few dependent upon *R*, derive entirely from *A*.

The textual relationships of these various manuscripts are shown in Fig. 2. Two independent transcripts of Writhe's original were made; the author of the *Receyt* incorporated one (with interpolated chapter headings) into the *R* manuscript about a year before Writhe's death. Some time between 1525 and 1532,[2] one of Wriothesley's scribes incorporated another transcription (preserving this time the original form without chapter headings) into the *A* manuscript. As a consequence, both *A* and *R* represent independent witnesses to the original funeral report. Since *R* remains the more reliable version, it naturally must serve as the copy-text for any edition of the funeral portion of the *Receyt*. However, *A* can often be used to correct *R* in cases of manifest error.

3. The Royal Entry Pageants: Speeches and Descriptions

The author's account of Katharine's entry into London occasions similar textual complexities to those encountered with the funeral report. The majority of Book Two is compiled rather than composed; it consists of pageant descriptions and speeches that have been interpolated into the author's own narrative. Only those few chapters that report the progress of the Princess's procession from St George's field (I), past the King's vantage point (IX), to its destination (end of X) represent the author's own reportage. The rest derives from a copy of the speeches performed by the actors upon their pageant stages and from formal descriptions of the various pageants themselves which, as we shall see, were probably drawn up by the show's designer.

At least three versions of the pageant speeches exist, including the transcript incorporated into the *Receyt*. As Busch, Thomas, Thornley, and others have shown, the versions preserved in the two extant civic chronicles, British Library Cotton Vitellius A.

1. Cambridge University Library, MS Dd. 13. 26, fols 57ᵛ–58ʳ.
2. C.E. Wright, *English Heraldic Manuscripts in the British Museum* (London, 1973), 4, dates Additional MS 45132, a companion manuscript, 'between 1525 and 1534'. The narrative of Arthur's funeral, however, must have been entered into Wriothesley's Register by 1532, when Wriothesley cited the volume as part of the royal divorce proceedings. The A manuscript has been expertly described in British Museum, *Catalogue of Additions to the Manuscripts 1936–1945* (London, 1970), pp. 5–8.

XVI (hereafter *C*) and Guildhall MS 3313 (hereafter *G*), were
transcribed independently from a common source, perhaps the
lost 'Main City Chronicle'.[1] Both therefore derive ultimately
from a copy of the verses in the City's possession, perhaps an
actor's version or a copy presented to the London Common
Council for its approval.[2] Whatever the exact source of the civic
copy, it was distinguished by two features: it prefaced each speech
with a Latin distich, and it placed Prelacy's speech in the wrong
pageant. The Latin distichs, which gave the general tenor of each
English speech, were probably painted on the pageants for the
benefit of those Spaniards—like the Princess Katharine herself—
who could not understand English.[3] The misplacement of
Prelacy's speech suggests that the verses came to the scribe of the
Main City Chronicle in the form of speeches written on separate
pieces of paper rather than in a roll or book. Such a format would
encourage the misordering and misassigning of individual speeches. Both of these features again point to the civic provenance of
this version. Not only do speeches copied upon separate sheets of
paper suggest a text derived from actors' parts, but the preservation of the Latin distichs reflects the city's practical provision
for communicating the sense of the show to their non-
English-speaking guests.

The version incorporated into the *Receyt*, by contrast, probably represents a copy circulated at court. The court was as keenly
interested in these pageants as the city. A household ordinance
dating from the mid 1490s, for example, already calls for the
construction of pageants representing 'heavenly places' should it
transpire that a foreign princess might be received into London
on the occasion of her marriage to an English prince.[4] Indeed, one
civic chronicle apparently records civic displeasure at court
interference in the preparation of these very pageants.[5] Under
these circumstances, it would be safe to expect that a copy of the
pageant speeches was presented to the court commissioners,

---

1. Busch, 405–15; C.L. Kingsford, *English Historical Literature in the Fifteenth
Century* (Oxford, 1913), 99–101; *Great Chronicle*, lxix–lxxvi.
2. The Council did, in fact, oversee the construction of pageants and the
writing of verse for civic triumphs with some care. They asked for a copy of
William Lily's verses in 1522 'to thentent that they may be entered for a president
herafter' (Corporation of London, *Repertories*, VI, fol. 4), and they dispatched a
committee to see whether another pageant was suitable for the civic triumph of
Philip of Spain in 1554 (*Repertories*, XIII (1), fol. 185ᵛ).
3. For an earlier example of such verses being painted upon a London pageant,
see Wickham, *Early English Stages*, 329.
4. *Antiquarian Repertory*, i, 303.
5. *Great Chronicle*, 310; *Triumph of Honour*, 99 n. 8.

headed by Lord Abergavenny and Sir Reginald Bray,[1] and reached the author of the *Receyt* in this way. To judge from the extant transcript in *R*, the court copy lacked the Latin distichs. There is little reason to suppose that the author of the *Receyt*, who frequently records Latin tags and who himself aspires to a Latinate syntax, would have consciously suppressed the distichs.

The substantive variants in the texts also divide the three manuscripts into two traditions of textual transmission and confirm the order suggested by the foregoing circumstances:

1. *R* (2/67)   I remember well, Lady, in your first entre
   G   I rembyr well, In yowyr ffyrst entre
   C   I remember wele In your first Entre

2. *R* (2/197)   And that to the comonweall I have a singler Ihe,
   G   And that I, to the comon weal, have a synguler Ie
   C   And that to the comon wele I haue a synguler Joy

3. *R* (2/374)   Doughter, the sonne, signifiour of kinges,
   G   Dowgthyr the same, syngnyfyour of kyngys
   C   Doughter, the same signifiour of kynges

4. *R* (2/403)   The tyme is com, right glad am I
   G   The tyme is comyn, whereof rygth glad am I
   C   The tyme is come, wherof right glad am I

5. *R* (2/454)   In astronomy houghe that euery thyng
   G   In astronomy, how that In every thyng
   C   In Astronomy, how that in euery thyng

In all but example 2, *C* agrees with *G* against *R*. In this case, however, the agreement of a court and city manuscript against another city manuscript probably represents *G*'s individual error —a transposition in word order—while both *R* and *C* have independently preserved the correct reading. None of these copies is an absolutely reliable version. On the one hand, *R* certainly preserves the correct reading, 'sonne', in example 3, while the civic manuscripts copy the erroneous reading, 'same', from the Main City Chronicle. On the other hand, *G* and *C* preserve the correct reading, 'in euery thyng', in example 5, while the court manuscript, *R*, erroneously reads 'euery thyng'. The other two examples must be decided upon metrical rather than textual grounds, if at all. Probably the court tradition preserves the correct reading in example 1 (*R*, 'Lady') while the civic tradition

---

1. For the Privy Council Order which established Lord Abergavenny's commission to oversee the civic reception, see M, fol. 5[v].

is more accurate in example 4 (*G*, *C*, 'whereof'). In both cases, the lines are one measure too short without the extra word.

In conjunction with these verses, the pageant descriptions form an especially puzzling feature of the author's narrative. In their detail and careful specification of the structure of the individual pageants, they are unprecedented among descriptions of royal entry pageantry not only in England, but in all of Western Europe. Rather than reporting what the pageants looked like to the observer, these descriptions tell how they were made. They often give measurements, specify materials, and fully detail the decorative scheme of each pageant. The third pageant, for example, begins by specifying that it was four-square in shape, the bottom three feet painted to look like a freestone foundation, the rest painted to look like a brick wall. Two portcullised gates breached this mock wall, and these were framed by three pillars (the two outside ones painted to look like green marble, the middle one like red marble). All this was topped by a mantle a foot-and-a-half wide, which supported a still more detailed superstructure. Thus only after all this detailed description of the lower parts of the pageant does the writer get to the pageant stage itself, which was located in the superstructure. There follows an equally detailed description of the room in which three of the four actors appear: it held a bench decorated with green and white chequers and its walls were decorated with the same design overlaid with heraldic emblems. On the ceiling above hung a blue 'volvell' with the signs of the moon displayed upon its circumference and four angels painted upon it. Curiously, after all of this very particular description of the architecture and decoration scheme of the pageant, the actors are not described at all: 'upon this rehersid sete there sate such persones as their speches shall declare'.

By contrast, the civic chronicler describes the very same pageant in the more conventional manner. In a very few lines, he tells us what the pageant represented rather than how it was built, and he centres his description about the actors:

> a pagend ... wheryn was contryvid the zodyak with the xij sygnys In a volvell, and theryn was shewid the encreace & wane of the mone wyth many othir conclucions of astronony, Ovyr the which volvell or zodyak sat In a stage or pynnakyll tharchangell Raphaell, and undyr the said volvell satt iij personagis Representyng kyng Alphons fforenamyd by vertu, Job & Boecius, The which were Reputid ffor iij the most cunnyng as Alphons astronomer Job dyvyne & Boecius phylyzofyr by theyr dayes, And soo soon as she was

> approchid nere to this pagend Raphaell with his goldyn &
> glyteryng wyngis & ffedyrs of many & sundry colours, began
> this prepocicion.[1]

Here the chronicler mentions only those details of pageant
structure and costuming which are important for understanding
the performance. Gone is the overwhelming enumeration of
architectural detail; he merely locates four characters—three
'cunning' men and an angel—in relationship to the pageant's most
important symbolic feature, the volvell.

Elsewhere in the *Receyt*, the author himself describes other
pageantry in exactly the same way that the civic chronicler
describes this pageant. The castle, ship, and mountain pageants
that provide the setting for one of the most spectacular of the
disguisings, for example, only earn two or three lines of description each, none of it characterized by the wealth of constructional
detail devoted to each of the civic pageants:

> the secunde pagent was a shippe ... sett uppon whelys
> without any leders in sight, in right goodly apparell, havyng
> her mastys, toppys, saylys, her taclyng, and all other
> appurtenans necessary unto a semely vessell, as though it
> hade been saylyng in the see.

> (4/179–83)

Had the author described this pageant in the manner of the royal
entry stages, he would have carefully detailed the 'right goodly
apparell' and the 'other appurtenans'. But like the civic chronicler, he is not interested in the construction of the pageant or the
details of its decoration. Indeed, wherever else he describes such
pageantry, the author always describes it in this briefer, less
technical form, more as a record of the impression the pageant
makes upon a viewer than as a record of the design and decoration
of the pageant itself. On the whole, therefore, the account of the
civic pageants stands apart from the author's usual mode of
description and suggests that he is once again incorporating into
his narrative a text composed by someone else for some other
purpose.

One probable source for such detailed and constructional
descriptions of the royal entry pageantry could have been found in
the pageant designer's 'device' (written architectural specification). As Geoffrey Webb points out, 'the part played by
drawings, whether plans or elevational designs, in the architecture
of the Middle Ages was, by comparison with modern practice,

---

1. *Great Chronicle*, 301.

small'. Instead, architects drew up written descriptions—known
as 'devices'—of their projects. Drawings ('plats') were, of course,
used, but usually they were 'only diagrammatic illustrations of a
verbal text. And generally speaking, when a building existed on
paper, it existed in words and not in line.' For the medieval
designer, verbal 'devices' serve as the 'legal documentts on which
the builder makes his bargain, and by which he is bound'.[1] For
historians of the stage, perhaps the most familiar such device
appears in the contract for the Fortune Theatre:

> The frame of the saide howse to be sett square and to
> conteine ffowerscore foote of lawfull assize everye waie
> square withoutt and fiftie fiue foote of liek assize square
> everye waie within, with a good suer and stronge foundacion
> of pyles, brick, lyme and sand bothe without & within, to be
> wroughte one foote of assize at the leiste aboue the grounde
> . . .[2]

Certainly the pageant descriptions of the *Receyt* read like architectural devices. Compare the opening of the third pageant, for
example, with the language of the Fortune contract:

> And from this pagent of the Castell of Portcullys, they
> extendid their jorney and passage to the thirde pagent in the
> myddes of Cornell enjoynyd to the condute, there beyng iiij
> square, empayntid three foote from the grounde of colour
> like frestone, havyng in his forefrunte iij great pylours . . .
>
> (2/273–7)

Here only a slight revision, mostly in the tenses of the verbs,
transforms this description into the sort of legal 'device' familiar
to the medieval architect:

> The thirde pagent in the myddes of Cornell *to be joyned* to
> the conducte . . . *to have* in his forefrunte iij great pylours . . .

Certainly, if the author has not modified a 'device' in order to
incorporate it into his narrative, he has achieved a striking
approximation of one all on his own.

Quite possibly, then, the author's copy-text for Book Two of
his narrative consisted of the pageant designer's 'device' with
verses attached. The author merely modified the device to seem
like a description and added a few narrative directions: from this

---

1. 'The Office of Devisor', in *F. Saxl 1890–1948*, ed. D.J. Gordon (London,
1949), 297–8. As Webb points out, not all such devices were strictly architectural.
A number consisted of verbal directions to painters, sculptors, or other artisans for
a scheme of decoration, a manuscript illumination, or a tomb sculpture (300–5).
2. Chambers, *Elizabethan Stage*, ii, 436.

Fig.3: The Textual Transmission of the Pageant Verses

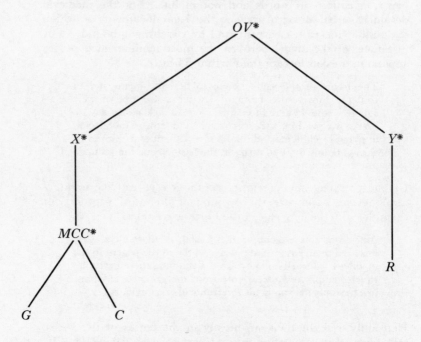

Sigla:

OV*—Original copy of pageant verses.

X*—Actors' copy of verses, with Latin distichs attached.

Y*—Court copy of verses, without Latin distichs.

MCC*—Main City Chronicle.

G—Guildhall MS 3313 (*The Great Chronicle of London*), fols 276^r–285^v.

C—British Library, MS Cotton Vitellius A. XVI, fols 183^r–195^r.

R—College of Arms, MS 1st M. 13, fols 27–74.

pageant they went on to the next one; then Raphael said the following speech. Some such document would probably have come to the attention of the joint civic–court commission headed by Lord Abergavenny which was charged with overseeing the city's reception of the Princess. From Lord Abergavenny, it would have circulated to the court and come to the attention of the author.

The textual relationships of these various manuscripts can thus be summarized as in Fig. 3. Two transcripts of the original verses were made. One, an actor's copy, was in turn transcribed into the lost Main City Chronicle, and the extant civic chronicles, *G* and *C*, took their texts from the Main City Chronicle. The other copy, a fair copy of the verses probably combined with a 'device' of the pageantry, circulated at court, where it was copied into the *Receyt*. As a consequence, all three extant manuscripts are substantive versions, but all descend from the same common original through various intermediaries. Through *G* and *C* we can recover many of the readings of *MCC**, and we can compare these readings with *R* to correct obvious cases of manifest error, or at least to define our editorial alternatives.

TEXTS OF THE TOURNAMENT CHALLENGES

A. The Buckingham Challenge

Two copies of this challenge—one in French, one in English— represent the version first proclaimed at Calais in May, 1500. Both announce that the wedding will occur shortly after the Calais conference, 'before thende and laste daie of the moneth of Septembre nowe next ensuing or nere thervpon' (BC/5–6 text note). The English version, a late-sixteenth century transcription of the original English challenge, appears in the New or Great Cartulary containing transcripts and abstracts of Stafford muniments among the Bagot papers in the Staffordshire County Record Office (MS D.1721/1/1, fols 425–7). The challenge thus forms part of the collections of the Stafford family archives compiled by Duke Edward's grandson, Edward, Lord Stafford, in the 1590s.[1] This provenance gives us good reason to suspect that the original document (which was apparently discarded after being transcribed into the folio collection) was an especially authoritative one, perhaps the original letter of challenge as prepared for the Duke of Buckingham by Garter Writhe.[2] The

1. C. Rawcliffe, 'A Tudor Nobleman as Archivist: The Papers of Edward, Third Duke of Buckingham', *Journal of the Society of Archivists*, v (1974–77), 297.
2. For the most part, only copies of the original letters of challenge survive.

French version (British Library MS Additional 46455, fols 6ʳ–8ᵛ), a translation of the English text, stands almost as close to the original source. It appears among the papers of Jean Blicquy de Houppelines, who was French Secretary to the King's Council at Calais during the Anglo-Burgundian conference of 1500. It is in Houppelines's own hand, apparently a somewhat hasty transcription, made for his own use, of the version proclaimed to the Burgundian knights.

A third, and perhaps most authoritative, text records the challenge as revised to suit the altered circumstances of the wedding tournament when actually performed in November, 1501. It alters the dates of the tournament and the numbers of challengers accompanying the Duke, but otherwise it contributes but few intentional variants to the text. Since it gives the correct date of the wedding (14 November 1501), this version must have been compiled shortly after 2 October, when word finally reached London of Katharine's unexpected arrival in Plymouth; only then could a firm date for the wedding be fixed. This version of the challenge gains special authority from the circumstances of its preservation. Copied onto some blank folios of 'Ballard's Book' (College of Arms, MS M. 3, fols 24ᵛ–26ᵛ) either by John Writhe or by his son, Thomas Wriothesley (above, pp. xxvii–viii), it is accompanied by the score cheque for the entire tournament. This version thus stands as the more-or-less official version of the challenge, the one which actually governed the performance of the tournament. As such, it naturally serves as the copy-text for this edition.[1]

B. *The Suffolk Challenge*

Only two copies of this challenge exist, both French and both found among the diplomatic correspondence of the Calais conference. Perhaps the better of the two texts—the one used here as copy-text—is found among the correspondence of Don Pedro de Ayala, Spanish Ambassador to England. Don Pedro accompanied Henry to Calais[2] and reported minutely on the substance of the Anglo-Burgundian negotiations to Ferdinand and Isabella. In his

Anglo thus reports that 'to my knowledge only one original challenge, that is the actual document circulated amongst the knights, signed both by Challengers and Answerers, and proclaimed aloud by the heralds, has survived' ('Financial and Heraldic Records', p. 187).

1.   College of Arms, MS M. 3 has been fully described in The College of Arms, *Heralds' Commemorative Exhibition 1484–1934, Held at the College of Arms* (London, 1936), 57–9, and in Wagner, *English Mediaeval Rolls of Arms*, 111–16.

2.   For the roster of those attending the Calais conference, see British Library, MS 1757, 361, printed, with errors, in Gairdner, *Letters and Papers*, ii, 89–94.

report, he also mentioned the preparations for the royal wedding, which were being gossiped about at Calais.[1] As an example of the latter, he encloses in his dispatch a copy of the Suffolk challenge (Archives of Simancas, MS P.R. 54–14, fols 5–8). The product of a professional scribe rather than his own hand, this copy may well have been one especially prepared to circulate among the Burgundian knights—a 'published' version, in effect. It is a fair copy in a clear hand, written with some pretence to elegance of script. Another, independent version of the same text occurs alongside the French copy of the Buckingham cartel among the papers of Jean Blicquy de Houppelines (British Library, MS. Additional 46455, fols 4^r–6^r). Instead of the careful, professional script characteristic of the Ayala version, this one, written in Houppelines's own competent but hasty script, constitutes a private record of the text rather than a 'public' fair copy, but it does provide a number of variants useful in establishing the text.

Since both copies of this cartel were prepared for the eyes of Burgundian knights at the Calais conference, it is difficult to say whether an English version ever existed. Conceivably, the original letter of challenge might have been drawn up in French by Guisnes Pursuivant, a herald associated with Suffolk.[2] At least two bits of evidence, however, point to an original English version. First of all, the text of the challenge explicitly mentions Garter as the herald in charge of supervising the circulation of the articles throughout the Court and such other places as the King might choose (SC/24–7). Secondly, articles xiij–xxj of the challenge are in fact literal translations of the ordinances devised in English by John Tiptoft, Earl of Worcester, to govern Jousts Royal (cf. SC/125 ff. n.). This much of the text, at least, is a translation from the English. Together, these circumstances again point to an original English challenge drawn up by Writhe and translated into French as was the Buckingham challenge. Presumably, this text was also modified, like the Buckingham text, to accommodate changes made necessary by the postponement of the wedding and by the defection of Suffolk, who was replaced as Chief Challenger by the Marquis of Dorset (the Marquis appears as 'Lord Harrington' in this version[3]). If so, the emended version

1. Ayala's letter is Archives of Simancas, MS P.R. 54–14.
2. Guisnes Pursuivant, probably a relative of Sir Robert Curson, was executed for aiding Sir Edmund de la Pole. See *College of Arms*, 260–1.
3. Thomas Grey I, 1st Marquis of Dorset, died just before the royal wedding on 20 September 1501. His son, Thomas Grey II, immediately succeeded to the title and fought the wedding tournament as Marquis of Dorset. Before then, he was known as Lord Harrington. His tournament pageant, a hermitage escorted by

has not survived. The events described in the *Receyt*, however, generally follow the events as proclaimed in the challenge.

THE TEXT OF THIS EDITION

The aim of this edition is to establish the text of *The Receyt of the Ladie Kateryne*, insofar as possible, by correcting *R* against the other three substantive texts: *A* (Book Five) and *G* and *C* (Book Two). All departures from copy-text, as well as all substantive variants from these texts, are duly noted in the textual apparatus. A few readings from *V25* also appear in the textual apparatus at textual cruxes and where ink blots or damage to the MS have obscured the text.

In printing *R*, capitalization and punctuation have been modernized. The letters *i, j, u,* and *v* have likewise been modernized, but otherwise the spelling of the original has been preserved. All abbreviations have been silently expanded in conformity with the scribes' normal spellings. The transcription of the manuscript is often made difficult by Scribe A's practice of using very similar symbols both as expansion signs and pen flourishes. He will often place an expansion sign at the end of a word where, presumably, no expansion is intended, as in *vpp, even, sonne, iron.* By the same token, he will often use an upward flourish in a word ending with an *m* or an *n* to indicate an expansion, as in *dispocon = dispocicion*; *itm = item*; and *com = come.* Just as often, he will use the same symbol merely as an elegant pen flourish, as in *man, theron, morn.* On the whole, this edition errs on the side of liberality in transcribing these often ambiguous symbols; where an expansion seems possible, one will be supplied (e.g., *comyn = commyn; sen = seen*). Ampersands are spelled throughout as *and*, except in the form *&c*, where the symbol is retained. *Xpen* is expanded as *Christen.* Roman numerals appear throughout in their original form. *ff* is rendered as *F* only in those cases (i.e., the beginnings of lines of verse or the first letters of a sentence) where a capital is clearly necessary. Word division has been generally modernized, except in cases of deliberate elision, particularly in those cases where the author seems to be imitating French habits of dropping a vowel between a definite article and a noun (*thestates*) or adjective (*tholde*). ˋAngled ticksˊ enclose interlineations and marginal additions.

a hermit and thirty beadsmen dressed in black, may refer to the recent loss of his father.

[Square brackets] identify editorial intrusions. ⟨Angled brackets⟩ indicate the loss of words or letters through ink blots or paper damage. The paragraphing of *R* has been preserved.

[PROLOGUE]

fol.27ʳHere begynneth the note and tretise of the moost goodly
behavor in receyt of the Ladie Kateryne, daughter unto
Phardinand, the Kyng of Espayn, yoven in mariage gainct to
Prince Arthure, son and heir unto our noble Sofreynge of
Englond, King Henry the vijth, in the xvij yere of his reign.   5

Microcosmus, the lesser world, by his diffinicion properlie
resemblant is unto mankiend thrugh certayn disposicions in
theym by great studie of the lerned persones sought by their
long labour and diligent investigacion, emonges the which
nombre of disposicions I specially note, and to my purpose do   10
bring and alledge, the singuler veynes of blode in mannys
bodie, being direct from the hed and also from the herte to
every parte of the corps of mankiend inward, not suffring the
said parties for fervent drynes to be perisshed ne utterly
overcom. Such veynes by symlitude in the erthe we fiend hym   15
wonderfully `and´ in dyvers parties compassing to thencrease of
frutes, erbis, and all thinges that burgenyth and hath the
plesurefull gifte and suffrans of lyve in this world. The great
huge and moost morvelous veyn of all moisture is the occean
see, that for her excellent plenty of waters maketh all othre sees   20
and ryvers owte of hyr to have curse and issue. So lardge and
so depe she is and so farre above all othre, that under the spere
of the mone of `all´ moisturesse [she] may be named the hed
and the mother. With her watrie wynges she spredith the
ground holy in compas, except that the will of Almyghtie God,   25
for then⟨ch⟩esion that generacions shold multiply, thre partes
stable ar left withowt mobilite and waves of his said stremys.
The names of thoes partes, the stories of old and auncient
writers, the which have commend to their memorie the great
journes of dyvers persones in therth, callid theym Asia, Affrica,   30
and Europa. The High Prince of Heven hym self hathe /
fol.28ʳvarnesshid thies forsaid costes and places of therth with

1   tretise] *the letters* tise, *though obscured by an inkblot, are readable* R.
26   then⟨ch⟩esion] *an inkblot has obliterated the* ch *and part of the* n *in this
word* R.
32   f.28ʳ] *f.27ᵛ is blank; f.27 has been reversed in binding, so that the text, which
originally began on the verso page, now begins on the recto page, leaving the blank
side to interrupt the text.*

wonderfull aboundance of rotes, erbis, trees, frutes, grayne,
fowle, and bestes to thonly sustentacion and comfort of his
ellect and dere creature, man. In the low fote of Europa and   35
vale from the son stondith and is set our owne moost cristen
regiowne of Englond, fulfilled and occupied with moost goodly
people, devowt ever and right full of vertue. Saynt Austyne
named thies people for their faire countnans 'Englesh'—
'aungels' by his furst nominacion. He was the furst doctour   40
that in this region prechid the lawes of God. And where we
were blynde with therrore of old sectes and gentilite, he us
revoked by tholy baptym and feithe of Cristendom. Now [we]
stedfastly observed the preceptes of God, the which be chefly
to honour and love our maker above all thing; secondly our   45
neiburs and our evencristen as ourselfes. We shold desire and
appetite as well to enyoie the felicite and helth of their bodies
as after the seperacion of their lyves to be everlastingly in the
fruicion of blissednes. Many noble princes in the world have
ben perceyved and knowen bifore this often tymes the love and   50
unyte of the commons, and their neiburs `to´ have litell
pondred and regardid, thinking the great praise and mag-
nificens of theym to be in effusion of blode, stryve, and
batelles especially consisting, contrary and ageynst the sawes and
verdutes of the proved wisedom affermyng peax above all   55
thinges moost profitable and necessarie. Thexemplar therof by
Rome, that noble cite and maistres of all Christen faithe, is
apparantly pictured unto thunderstonding and knowledg of
every man, that thrugh lernyng, wisdom, vertue, their stable
faieth, and pesyblenes of Sayntes Petre and Pawle hath pur-   60
chased more dignite and rewle emonges the people then ever
the great manhode of the ij brothren Remus and Romulus,
of whom the oon slue thoder, by their such slaughter kowd to the
fol.28ᵛsaide / empire subdue or employ. How long had Alexander the
clere possession of the realmes and straung countreis of the   65
worlde, that with his great labour, payne, and losse of his
people he conquerid and subdued to `his´ dominion? A small
while, whiles he lyved, and straight aftir his disceasse every
prince had his londes and kyngdoms forthwith in peax. Criste
fought not with the Jues into this worlde when he cam to   70
redeme and to heven restore the sowle of man, yet we trust that
they with hym shall persever in blis perdurable withowt payn

51   and their neiburs] to *cancelled between* and *and* their R.
59   wisdom] visdom R.   67   dominion] don R.

forever. The moost noble and prudent kynges in the world, as well our excellent Suffrayng and Prince of Englond, Kyng Henry the vijth, as the worthy and famous Prince, Fardinand, by provysion of God, King of Espayn, in likewise have allowid the sentence of unite and peax to be moost expedient. To thaccomplishment wherof, and contynuall in their heires the stedfast observyng, they have propond everych to other ther worthy and goodly issue, that is to sey, the King of Englandes son furst begoten, Prince Arthure, and the Kyng of Espayn, the Ladie Kateryn his daughter and princesse, to be cowplid in the lovyng bonde and sacrament of wedlok, the which after by meny and dyvers enbasshions right well and prudently examined and enserchid with moost great leisure and good consideracion, was utterly affirmed and diffined, wherupon the moost excellent Prince Phardinand, the rehercid King of Espayn, hath honorably and after truth and justyce, with a right goodly company in shippis by water, delyvered and sent his daughter and princesse, the Lady Kateryn, of whois arryving, receite, mariage, with the circumstans, this pusant and litle tretes folowing is drawen and compiled, conteyning truly and withowt fables the very gest and fourme of the mater, nothing being in his dedes abbreviat, neither by eny superflu-ous addicions fayn thinges representing. This said tretise is devyded into v partes and small bokes—the furst of her departing and arryving; the second of her receite into the noble Cite of London; the iij of her mariage and feast roiall; the iiij of the justes, banquettes, and disguysing; the v of the Princes lamentable deth and buriyng—with their singuler titles and chaptiers as afterward severally in the book it is appiering.

75
80
85
90
95
100

83   lovyng] louung *R*.

[BOOK I]

The furste chapiter: how the Princesse departid from her fathre and mothre, beyng in Hispayne, and what wiendes and jeopardies she suffred in her passage.

Whan that after the prefixed promyses `bitwene´ the noble   5
kinges of the roiall realmes of Englond and of Hispayne, the
doughter and princesse of the said King of Hispayne, for
thentente of matrymonie legallie to be fynesshid and concludid,
[went] to her prepaired navye of shippes with the right
sufficiaunt gardie and companye of noblis of that contreth to   10
her assistentes lymyted and assigned theymself shold brefly
order and condute. Thympacient wiendes of that coostis shold
seme to have ben greatly aggreved and not peasably to suffer
the bifore-desired passage of the said Princesse to the coostes of
Englond, fatally ordynate and predestynate, the gieftes and also   15
the dowrie of soo goodlie a ladie and princesse. Wherupon they
cruelly with right great hudgenes of storm and tempest
oppresed with their oultragious blastes the clothis of the said
shippes, enhaunced their mastes owte of their sokettes, distrobled their takling and all their hoole remyge. The perilous   20
seas with waves soo fearfully wrought and arrerid that unto the
rulers and craftie maryners was, moost to thenfreight persones
to be savegardid, expediently thought to som of their owne
lately forsaken havens they shold retourne their course. Where
within short seasons it contentid Almyghtie God that more   25
plesant wiendes shold goodlie rule the journeis of the cleer
eires above, thrugh whoes help and aide unto thenglisshe
parties they were right shortly conveied, and fortunatly they
arryved at Plymmouthe, fer in the contreth of the west.

---

5 promyses bitwene] of *cancelled after* promyses *R.*

The second chapter: of her arryvinge in Englond   30
and of the meting of the Kinges Grace and dyvers
othre estates of the londe.

fol.29ᵛ/ Than as sone as this glad entres of the ladie was knowen and
apperceyved to thestates and gentiles, borderers of the said
contreth `off the west´, with all goodlie maner and haste [they]   35
sped theymself with right honorable gieftes to repaire to that
noble princesse. And there they goodly with all requyred
poyntes and features of curtesie saluted and welcomed her, so
escapid graciously her perilous jeopardies, with their pleasures,
presentes, and their attendancis, as well in the said furste   40
arryving as in contynuall servyce, waiting, and guyding `to´ the
`sayd´ Princesse into the further entrans of the realme of
Englond toward the honorate and aunciant Citie of London,
where at that tyme the Kinges Noble Grace was lodged and
abiding.   45

And furste the Lorde Broke, Stuard of the Kinges Howse,
was by thassignement of the Kinges Grace directid and sent to
thentent to purvey and provyde for the Princesse and her
retynue in their journey and passage, as well for their viand,
horses, and cariage as every other necessite, and right conveny-   50
ently `so´ he did. `After that, therl off Surrey with divers other
lordes temperall off the lond ensuyd unto the metyng and
attendaunce off thys whorthy Estate and Princesse.´

And after them the Duches of Norffolke, by a like assent and
will of the King, with a goodly companye with her `off   55
countess, baroness, and meny other honorable gentylwomen´,
repaired unto this noble Princesse, and there `at her´ suche
metyng had, she kept forth on her contynuall company and
waiting.

Notwithstanding, His Highnes and Grace was not soo   60
intentifly satisfied with the chere, servyce, and diligente atten-
dans of his said subjectes gentils, but bountuously let hymself
with a semely company of his estates—dukes, erlis, and barons
with othre dyvers of knyghtes, esquyeris, and gentilmen—to
be the iiij day of Novembre removed from his maner of Riche-   65
mount towardes the meting of this goodly ladie, whois spedefull journey was annoied and suffred impedyment, and of
fol.30ʳhis / encrese was sore abreviat by thenchesion that he and his
present lege servantes, the day right fer spent, so late were

horsid at their said remove, the silens of thevenyng full hastily   70
did theym approche, that they were compellid by convenyens
at Chartsey, not veray fer from the said Manour of Richemount, to purvey and harbage for their reposing that nyght.

The third chapiter: of the meting that the Prince
gave the King at Esthampsted.   75

The morow clowdes were usually and after the curse naturall
expellid; the clere beamys of the son full ofte tymes the
myddell eires with their refleccions had striken. Then the sides
of their cursers with their spurres they began to tast and
extendid their passage unto the village of Esthampsted. There   80
myght the true and lovyng Englisshe people pleasauntly
perceyve the pure and proper Prince Arthure, the heire of their
lefull londes and successour by grace grantid of God, full
solemply to salute his sage fathre bifore their owne presens, the
which was great gladnes to all trusty hertes that of everych   85
realme by wise sawes ar named for the treasure.

Loo thus with his sonne the moost noble Henry of Richemount, of Englond the vijth king of that name, full pleasantly
passid over the season of that nyght, and in the next morow to
the playnes he departid, where met with hym the Prothonotary   90
of Hispayne, and ensured hym that they had receyved bie
streite injunction and commaundement of their Soveraigne
Lord of their lond that they shold in noo maner of wise
permytt ne suffer their ladie and Princesse `of Espayne´, whom
they had to guyde and in gouvernans, to have eny meting, ne   95
fol.30ᵛuse eny maner of / communycacion neither company, unto
thincepcion of the very daie of the solempnisacion of the
mariage. Wherupon after certayn musing of this myend of the
Kinge of Hispayne, immediatly there in the feldes `the Kynges
Grace off owr realme off Englond´ let all theym that were of his   100
moost honorable Councell to be in that mattier advertised how
they thought moost to reason aggreable, either tenclyne to this
declarid purpose, or as he entendid to that lady he shold
maynteyn his passage.

And sone after the prudent enserche of every persones both   105
spiritual and temperalles aunswere, it was holy by their sentens
concludid that forasmoch as due agrementes in a maner

99   the Kynges] the *modified from* he *by hand C to prepare for interlineation*
R.

accomplisshed, sithe they were so far entrid into his empire and
realme, they shold seme to be in partie dischardgid annempste
their Soveraigne, and of all gouvernay of their said Princes   110
avoided and excludid, and the pleasure and commaundment of
her to lie in the power in grace and disposicion of oure noble
Kyng of Englond.

The iiijth chaptre: of the demeanure of the King
and of the Princesse in their furst metynge.   115

Thus His Highnes avaunced hymself, levyng the Pryns behynde
upon the playne, and in the tyme of ij or iij of the clok at after
none, His Grace entred into the towne of Dogmersfeld, where
the Pryncesse was ij or iij owres bifore his said comyng right
well accompanyed and right richely beseyn, so as hertofore   120
have be seyn none like her, havyng with her an Archbusshop, a
Busshop, and an Erl, with meny other noblis of Hispayne, and
meny ladies and gentilwomen of the same contreth to the
fol.31ʳnombre of thre score, and ladies and gentilwomen of / this
region right nygh as meny.   125
    And as sone as the Princesse servantes were asserteyned of
the commyng of the Kyng, `as tharchebusshoppe, the Bussh-
oppe, therl, with other off her retynue and councell´ they
shewid hym that the Princesse was in her rest, whom he
aunswerd in such fourme, that if she were in her bed, he wold   130
se and commone with her, for that was the myend and thentent
of his commyng. And thus convenyent leisure to her respited,
she gave hym an honorable metyng in her third chambre,
where were perused the mooste goodly wordes and uttred of
the langueges of bothe parties to as great joye and gladnes as in   135
eny persones myght ever covenably have ben had.
    After the which welcomes and communycacion endid, the
Kinges Grace deposid his riding garmentes and chaunged
hym, and by half season of oon owre the Prince was also
knowen to be present, and ensueyng the Kinges Highnes and   140
the Lord Prynce made their second resort toguydre to the
chambre of the Pryncesse, and there thrugh thenterpretacion of
busshoppis the spechis of bothe contrethis be the meane of
Laten were understonden. And whereas tofore they were by
deputies contractid, they here now were in their either othre   145
presens spousally ensured. The which semly ensurans, so as it
is promysed, honorably endid, the King sped hym to his
souper. And after that he had souped full curteisly, with the

Lord Prince visited the Ladie in her owne chambre. And then
she and her ladies let call their mynstrelles, and with right   150
goodly behavour and maner they solacid theymself with the
disportes of daunsyng, and afterward the Lorde Prince in like
demeanure with the Lady Guldford daunced right plesant and
honorably.

The vth chaptre: howe the Princesse departid from   155
Dogmersfeld to Londonward, and how the King
removed another wey to the same cite.

fol.31ᵛ/ Upon the morow, the vijth day of the rehersid moneth of
Novembre, the Princesse on her bihalve toke her journey to
Chartsey and ther lodged all that nyght, and from thens   160
towardes Lamehith. And or ever she cam fully to the said
town, `beyond a´ village callid Kyngeston upon Thamyse, the
Duke of Bokingham on horsbak full richely beseyn, therle of
Kent, the Lord Henry the dukes brothre, and thabbot of Burie
(the which after the Duc had saluted Her Grace, declared goodly   165
in Laten a certayn proposicion of her welcomyng into the realme),
with a great company of the `Dukes´ gentilmen and yomen in
his lyverey of blak and red to the nombre of iij or iiij hundreth
persones, met this noble ladie, `and at that vyllage they lodgyd
all that nyght,´ and so accompanyed with her as a guyde, `in the   170
morne´ right honorably condutid her to her said lodging at
Lamehith, where she contynued unto such season as her
entring into the Citie of London myght moost convenyently in
every maner bihalve be prepared, as well on her partie of the
retynue of Hispayn, as in the to her assistentes of the realme of   175
Englond by our Sovereign assigned, partly to thencres and mag-
nyfiyng of her honour and estate, secundly to the mayntten-
ans of olde and famous appetitis that thenglisshe people have
ever used in the welcomynge of their acceptable and wel-
biloved straungers.   180
    The Kinges Highnes also in his partie removed from the said
Princes another wey towardes the Cite of London, and the
furst nyght he lodgid at Esthamsted, whereas His Grace had
ben bifore in his furste commyng to the Lady Princesse. And
upon the morowe, the viijth daie of the rehersid moneth of   185

150   mynstrelles] mynstelles R.
162   beyond a] added by hand C over erasure at beginning of line R.
171   said lodging] said cancelled between these words R.

Novembre, he nyghtid at his castell of Wyndsore. The ixth
daie of the same moneth in his maner of Richemount hymself
he reposid, where the Quenys Grace met with hym, whom he
asserteyned and made prevy of thactes and demeanure /
fol.32^rbitwene hymself, the Prince, and the Princesse, and how he   190
likyd hir person and behavour. And the xth day ensueng, he
rode till he came to Paris Gardeyn uppon the further side of
the ryver from London, and there he toke his barge and was
sett upp at his lodgyng callid Baynardes Castell within the
same cytie, set uppon the Tamys side, right pleasauntly   195
sheweng toward the water—withinforth ful weell garnysshid
and araide, full strongly with wallys encompased without—
where to his noble and prudent audiens al maner of matters
hade ther recourse that to his owne person were apperteynyng
for his owne honour and right to all his hooll realme for   200
comfort and justice, and also for the goodly endutyng of this
noble lady and Princes of Hispayne. And at his there settyng
upp and landyng, the Quenes Grace by watir in hir barge with
her goodly company of ladyes was there presently landid and
entride in.   205

The vjth chaptre: of thordre of the Citie of London
for the receyte of the Princes.

In the meane season, the stedfast, sure, and secret chambre of
Englond, the opulent rehersid Cytie of London, was than full
excellently accompanyed with the moost great multitude of   210
people—what for the citesens inhabitauntes of the same, what
for the estates of every contreth, shire, and party with ther
servantes unto them awaytyng, what for other of honest
comons of every town, holde, and border of the realme of
Englond—that eneth ther might be lodging, ostrie, or roume for   215
the seid great resorte fownde or begotyn within the wallis
neithir suberbys of all the seid citie. Every lord both spirituall
and temporall was kepyng their opyn housseholdes with right
great ryaltie of fare and vitall, ich gentill his lyvereys, bagges,
and conysances opynly worne, that every man might   220
apparently perceyve and know every gentilman his servant, the
oon of them from the other in that tyme.

---

215 ther might be lodging] ther might be lodgiding *R*; *the scribe has
attempted to correct* the might be lodgid *to* ther might be lodging *by adding* -r
to the and -ing *to* lodgid.

First oure honourable and Leage Lord, oure Suffreyn the
Kynge, hade to his noble and propir parson the moost `and´
great diligent waytinges and attendaunces. He was also daily   225
encompanyed with his valiant and sage lordes, the hede and
principall officers of his ryall realme.

Of the spiritualte there was tharchebusshopp of Cantibury,
Metropoliton and Primat of the realme; thearchebusshop of
fol.32ᵛYork; / the Bushopp of Wynchestre, the Lord of the Privyseall;   230
the Bushop of Salisbury; the Bushop of Excetour; the Bushop
of Rouchestre; the Deane of his Chapell, with the solempne
and excellent company of his chapleyns, queremen, queresters
to his devoute Chapell belongyng; his Secretory; and all other
officers spirituall with many moo of bushoppis, abbottes, and   235
priours and doctours of the chirch, knightes and esquyers for
his body, lougher officers of his seid houssoulde, that to
nombre of his great retynue might not easely ne convenyently
be rekenyd. Over this His Highnes had Yomen of his Garde in
clothing of large jakettes of damaske, whight and grene goodly   240
enbrowdred bothe on ther brestys bifore and also on their
bakkys behynde, with rownde garlandes of vyne braunchs
besett before richely with spancles of silver and gilte, and in the
myddell a rede rose beten with goldesmethis werk, the which
were of the chosen persones of the hole contreth proved   245
archeers strong, valiant, and bold men with bright hawbertes in
their handes to the nombre of thre hundreth, evermore stondyng by the weies and passage upon a rowe in bothe the siddes
where the Kinges Highnes shuld from chambre to chambre or
from oon place to anothir place at his goodly pleasure be   250
remeovid.

The Mayour, Aldremen, Sherevys, with othir of the conservatours, councellours, and ayders of the Cytie of London, so
ordurly with good polesye hade provydid the seid cytie that the
felawshippis of every crafte shulde—all thinges leied aparte in   255
ther severall lyverys and hodys of their manour—be present at
the comyng of this moost excellent Princes. And for the seid
great nombre of craftes were barrys made on every sid of the
weys fro the myddys of Gracechurchs Strete unto the entryng
of the chirch yard of Powlis that they might from the comers   260
and comon people have ther space and ease and also be seen.
The mydweyes were also gravelld and sondid so that the
horsis, mulis, and cursers of the wayters and condutes of this

254   provydid] *the suffix, -id, added in lighter ink and squeezed into the space
between words.*

noble lady might without jobardie or hurte be goodly avauncyd
and shewe their pleasaunt currages. They hadde also ordeyned   265
vj stacions and places of pausing where were wrought and
arreysid vj costly, pleasaunt, and goodly pagayntes with cer-
fol.33ʳ teyn personys in everych of / theim to have and use their
spechis and salutes unto this great estate and gentilwoman as
she sholde passe by, `the´ which shall heraftir be more pleynly   270
opyned and declared. All thes nobles in generall before
rehersid with their attendours abydyng and entendyng thentres
of this moost worthy Princes.

Finis primi libri

[Book 2]

fol.33ᵛ   The `first´ chaptre of the secunde booke: of
thorderyng of their raies in Seint Georges Feld.

Now it is that we be comyn into the moost joyefull and lengest
desired and acceptable season, the fryday the xij day of the
moneth of Novembre, uppon whom this great Princes of   5
Hispayne, aftir that she had dyned at her lodgyng of Lambeth
at oure Soverayn his will, pleasure, and myend of Englond, she
shulde make her entres, assemblyng ffirst her owne retynue of
the contreth of Spayne, and than procedid forth into Seint
Georges Feld, where were redy present uppon horsbak a right   10
semely company by the Kinges Grace assigned for the ryall and
solempne inducyng of this noble estate, adjoynyng nygh to her
seid lodging.

Furst there was for the spiritualte of Englond: tharchebushop of York, with othir bushoppes; the Deane of York,   15
with othir prelates of the chirch. For the temperalte: the Duke
of York, the Duke of Bokyngham, therl of Northumberlond,
therl of Surrey, therl of Essex, therle of Kent, the Lord Henry
of Bokyngham, the Lord Burgeveny, the Lord Straunge,
the Lord Barners, the Lord Suche, the Lord Willughby, and   20
other lordes right weell horsid and richely beseen, with many
knightes and esquyers to a great nombre in lyke wise horsid
and beseen.

The secunde chaptre: what solempnyte was usid in
hir receyte in`to´ the Cytie of London.   25

Thus they made owt their raies and sett furth ordurly, every
person in his rumme convenient, and passid thorough
Southwerk till they cam to the enteraunce of the great bridge of
London, wheruppon was the furst pagent in maner and fourme
folowyng: that is to sey, there was on the myddes of the bridge   30
erecte a tabernacle of two flouers, assemblaunt unto tweyne

1–2 of thorderyng ... Seint Georges Feld] *R incorrectly places this chapter*
title at the head of the second chapter, and transposes the title of chapter two here.
14 Englond] Egglond *R.*
24–5 what solempnyte ... London] *R mistakenly transposes this chapter*
heading to chapter one.

rodeloftes, in whoes lougher floure and particion there was a
sete. And within the sete a faire yonge lady with a wheel in hir
hand in liknes of Seint Kateryne, with right many virgyns in
every side of her. And in the ijde and higher floure and story, 35
fol.34ʳ there was anothir lady / in liknes of Seint Ursula with her great
multitude of virgyns right goodly dressid and arayed. Above
the bothe flours there was the pictour of the Trinyte, and upon
iche side of thise iij storyes, oon small tabernacle square with
propir vanys, and in every square of the small tabernacle, the 40
Garter invyrond with his poysye in Frenche: *Onye soit que male
pens.* And in the myddis of the Garter the rede rose regall, and
so in the numbre of bothe siddes were six smale tabernacles,
uppon whoes toppes were six angelles ensensynd the Trynyte,
Seint Ursula, and Seint Kateryn. The wallis of the saide flours 45
or loftes were peyntid with hangyng courteyns of cloth of
tissue, blue and rede. And a party space bifore this pagent were
ij great postes set, enpayntid with `the´ thre estriche fethers,
rosis red, and portcullys, and on every of them a red lyon
rampand, holdyng a vane enpayntyd with the armys of Eng- 50
lond, and all the hoole werke corvyn of tymbre gilte and
peyntid with golde, byse, and asur.

The thirde chaptre: of the speches that were utteryd
in the furst pagent.

Thise were the speches that the saintes in the pagent had unto 55
the Lady Princes. And first Seint Kateryn enteryd in her
proposicion:

[Ne grave sit patrias, Katharina relinquere sedes
Plus tibi splendoris, Regna aliena dabunt.]

I, Kateryn, of the Courte Celestiall, 60
Where as is joye and pardurable blisse,
From whens all grace and compforte doeth and shall
Alwey procede, for veray love, iwisse,
Am com to you, faire lady, sithe that this

58–9 Ne grave … dabunt] *om. R.* 58 Katharina] katerina *C.*
64 Am] *the letter* m, *in lighter ink, squeezed into the space between* A *and* com,
R.

Into this cytie is your first resorte,   65
To welcom you, ayde, assiste, and compforte.

I remembre well, Lady, in your first entre
Into this world, the trust and affeccion
That ye and your frendes bare towardes me,
In your baptisme to be shelde and protection,   70
Not of adventure, but of fre Eleccion
Ye toke this name, Kateryn, for very trust and love,
Which name is regestrid in the High Court above.

fol.34ᵛ   And as I holpe you to Crist your first make,
So have I purveyed a secunde spouse trewe,   75
But ye for him the first shal not forsake;
Love your firste spouse chef, and aftir that your newe,
And thise rewardes therof shall ensue;
With the secunde honour temporall,
And with the first glory perpetuall.   80

Holde on your wey and ye shall sone espye
A goodly castell, wherof the capytayne
Is wise and famous, callid Pollicie,
Without whoes helpe all they that thinke to reyne
Or longe to prospere labour all in vayne.   85
Pollice to honour will you convey;
Hast you therfor; God spede you in your weye.

This proposicion of Seint Katiryn so goodly by declaracion
endid, Seint Ursula spekyth in her maner thus:

[Sis ffelix Katherina meis, ffaustum que Britannis   90
Sidus nam tute, hiis Hysperus alter eris.]

Madam Kateryn, because that I and ye
Be come of noble blod of this land
Of Lancastre, which is not oonly of amyte
The cause, but also a ferme band   95
Betwene you and this realme to stonde;

67   Lady] *om. GC.*   69   towardes] toward *C.*   72   trust] trist *C.*
74   holpe] halp *GC.*   79   honour] an honour *GC.*   81   ye] you *C.*
86   will you convey] will you streite convey *GC.*
87   in your weye] on your waye *GC.*
90–1   Sis ffelix ... eris] *om. R.*   93   come] cummyn *GC.*

Nature shall meove us to love alwey
As two comon owt of oon cuntrye.

Trouthe it is that owt of myn lynage came
Arthure the wise, noble, and vaillaunt kyng,   100
That in this region was furst of his name,
And for his strength, honour, and all thyng
Mete for his estate, he was resemblyng
Arthure, the noble signe in heven,
Beautee of the northe, with bright sterres sevene.   105

Unto this kinge, stronge, famous, and prudent,
Nere kynne am I, and named am Ursula,
By which name I also represent
Anothir ymage callid Minor Ursa,
That otherwise is callid Cynosura,   110
Set fast by Arthure, with other sterres bright,
Gevyng great compforte to travellours by nyght.

fol.35ʳ   As Arthure, your spouse, than the secunde nowe
Succedith the furst Arthure in dignite,
So in lyke wise, Madame Kateryn, yow   115
As secunde Ursula shall succede me;
Wherfor goo now to Pollici, for he
Shortely to Honour shall se you conveyed,
So as my suster Kateryn hath to you seied.

This doon the Lady Princes and her goodly company procede   120
forth   unto   the   secunde   pagent   called   the   Castell   with
Portculleis.

The iiijth captre: of the descripcion and speches of
the secunde pagent.

Which was edified in the strete callid Grasechurch Strete in the   125
place where as the said strete was mooste of brede, and was
bildid in fourme as ye shall perceyve. That is to sey, ffurst
there was in the myddis of the strete where as the watir
runneth in the chanell a foundacione off stone of iij or iiij foote
in highte, havyng the seid curse and voydans that the watir   130

99   myn] my *GC.*   106   this kinge] the kyng *GC.*
117   Wherfor] whefor *R.*   117   Pollici] *a final* e *has been erased R.*
119   hath to you seied] hath seyd *GC.*

might usually be curraunt as he did, upon the which foun-
dacion the castell was erecte. And within a manys highte from the
stone werk were batilmentes of tymber, covered and leyed over
with canvas enpeyntid like frestone and whight lyme, so
that the semys of the stones were perceyved like as mortur or   135
sement had ben betwene. And in every batilment and voyde of
batilment in ordour and curse were sett certeyn bagges: furst a
red rose and a whight in his myddes, with a crowne upon the
hight of golde; the secunde was thre garters of blew with this
poysie in Frenche written, *Hony soit que male pens*, inviround   140
and in his myddes `and´ on his height a crown of gold; the
thurd was a flowrd luce of gold; the iiijte was the portcullys of
gold and ij cheynes hangyng on iche sid, and on the height of
the portcullys a crowne of gold. And sum part also were
clowdes with beamys of golde, the grounde as it were thayre   145
blew; in othir places whight hertes, in summe other pekokkes
displayed. And above this first batilment, of manys hight from
the grounde, there was a greate gate with foldyng leves full of
great barris of iron with many naylys affixed, and over the gate
a lardge portcullys, and in every joynte of the portcullys a red   150
fol.35ᵛrose. / Over this grete gate as it were on the stone werk, a
shelde quartered with blewe and red with the Kinges armys of
Englond, that is to sey in every quarter of blew iij floure de luce
of gold and in every quarter of red iij lyons of golde, which
sheld was uppehold and susteyned with `ij´ goodly bestes, the   155
oon of them on the right sid, a red dragon dredfull, the othir of
the lyfte sid, a whight grehound, and a yard from the sheld on
every sid a great rede rose of half a yard brede. And above this
gate was batilmentes and bagges as it is declared before in the
historye. Bynethe in the openyng stode an armyd knight cape-   160
a-pe, as a capeten or a venturous knight, callid Pollici. And
from this gate and bildyng stretchid forth on ich side of the
strete into menys wyndowes and stallis ij other portcullys
embatilmentid, and on ich of them the sheld bifore rehersid
with bagges of rosis red, dragons dredfull, displayed pecokkes,   165
clowdes with beamys above of gold, and fanys uppon everych
of the seid batilmentes right goodly gilded. And on every
corner and egge of this myddell story and great towre extendid
a turret right pleasauntly dekkyd with rosys, grehoundes,
portcullys, and Seint George crossis of whight and rede, and   170
every turret vij square in his toppe, and on every square a

139   of blew] of *is written over a cancelled* was *R.*
147   of manys hight] of *is written over an* A *R.*   167   every] euʳ *R.*

pynnacle and a fane. Yet above all this great story there was
anothir large dore wherin stode a knight with an hedepece
callid Noblenes, and on his right hand a bushop who was
named Vertue. This towre was sumwhat lesser then the   175
lougher, ledid above and goodly payntid, and was iiij square
and had iiij [. . .] goyng upp on `his´ iiijor parties like ragge and
flynt stone, with holow crossis, wyndows, and gunholys, and
on the toppys great fanys with the kinges armys, and on the
highest of all the hole pageant a rede dredfull dragon holdyng a   180
staf of iron, and on the staf a great crown of gold. The hors
weyes and passages was undre the wynges of this seid pagent.

   Now Pollici entreth his proposicion, seieing thus:

            [Est sana virtuti, arx hec, nec non nobilitati
            Sed sine me nullus, huc patet introitus.]   185

       Who openyd these gatis? What, opened they alone?
       What meanyth this? O now I se weell why:
       The bright sterre of Spayne, Hesperus, on them shone,
       Whoes goodly beames hath persid mightily
       Thorugh this castell to bring this good lady,   190
       Whoes prosperous comyng shall right joyefull be,
       Bothe unto Nobles, Vertu, and unto me.

fol.36ʳ   Welcom you be, right excellent Princes,
       And more welcom for that I, Pollici,
       Se in you tokenes of vertue and nobles,   195
       Two thynges to the comonweall necessary,
       And that to the comonweall I have `a´ singler ihe,
       Therfor I me enforce alweay to thencreas
       Of thise two thynges, vertu and noblesse.

       Than forasmoch as I perceyve and se   200
       You disposed to noblesse and vertue,
       Ye seme right apte to have auctoryte

177   iiij goyng] *the scribe has probably omitted a word here.*
184–5   Est sana . . . introitus] *om. R.*
186   Who openyd] Whoo openyth *GC.*   193   you] ye *GC.*
195   Se in you] Se & in you *C.*   196   necessary] rygth necessary *GC.*
197   And that to the comonweall I have a singler ihe] And that I, to the
comon weal, have a synguler Ie *G*, And that to the comon wele / I haue a
synguler Ioy *C.*
198–9   Therfor . . . noblesse] *C reverses the order of these lines, but has placed*
the letters A and B beside the lines to indicate their correct order.

Within thys realme. Wherfor as it is due,
I counsaill you to labour and pursue
To them two, now beyng in this towre,   205
And there shal be while I am governoure.

Than be profounde eloquens, Noblesse his proposicion full
goodly purposith, seyeng in this wise:

[Si virtus absit census genus atque potestas
Nil preter nomen, Nobilitatis habent.]   210

Madame, sith ye have entred the gate of Pollici,
And the presens approchid of me, Noblesse,
To vertue streight ye shal be ladde therby,
For this is trouthe, no maner man doubtles
Can me and Vertue suerly atteigne, onlesse   215
That he of Pollici entre first the gate,
For we in noo wise may be seperate.

Wherfor, Madame, me thinke it very good
With me, Noblesse, to have acqueyntaunce
Because ye be come of noble blode,   220
And therfor now myself I shall avaunce,
As I am bounde, with all my puissaunce,
You to convey to vertu in generall,
Dystingued in theoryke and cardinall.

Vertue apperteyneth to every estate,   225
As well to noble as folke of low degre,
But yet the noble, aftir anothir rate,
Be applied of their right propertie
To be vertuous and to have regalee,
Guydyng the people, by strenght for defens   230
Of them and thers, by singler prudence.

209-10   Si virtus ... habent] *om. R.*   210   habent] habens *GC.*
211   sith] sythen *G.*   211   gate] Gatys *GC.*   213   ladde] led *C.*
218   me thinke it very good] me thynkyth verray good *GC.*
220   of noble blode] of soo noble blood *G.*
224   theoryke] *R originally wrote* the Oryke *but corrected himself by enlarging
the* e *and* O *to fill the space between words.*
225   to every estate] unto every astate *GC.*
228   applied] apployed *C.*   230   Guydyng] Guyvyng *C.*

fol.36ᵛ   Preas forth to Vertue. She is debonayre,
    Treatable, and meke, takyng noo disdayne
    Of noo creature that to hir will repaire.
    Ye shall hir purchas, and that with litill payne,   235
    But without her and me, all labour is in vayne.
    To come to Honour, therfor, I shall provide
    That Vertue to Honour shal be your guyde.

Thus Vertue in his proposicion doeth conclude, and aftir
Noblesse spekyng, seyeng in this wise: 240

    [Si tibi virtutem, licet absint cetera solam
    Conciliabis eris, Nobilitata nimis.]

    Trouthe it is that Noblesse, Lady Kateryn,
    Without me, Vertue, wol not acheved be:
    Who that oon will have, that other must he wynne,   245
    But all the craft is to fall in with me.
    I am so straunge that many fro me fle,
    For I, Vertue, myself all wey addresse
    To thinges of great difficultie and hardnesse.

    But notwithstondyng, Madame, yet shall ye   250
    Wynne me `with´ moore ease than othir shall,
    For men in you may weell perceyve and see
    A very dispocicion naturall
    Apte to receyve everych Vertue Cardinall,
    And therfor with lesse labour and peyne   255
    To myn acqueyntaunce ye shall weell atteigne.

    Moreover, the excellent dispocicion
    Of your dere spouse, the noble Prince Arthure,
    So toward is, so goodly of condicion,
    That your dispocicions clene and pure   260
    Joyned toguydre, ye must nedis be sure
    Of myn acqueyntaunce, and therby espyre
    To Noblesse, here, whoes favour ye desire.

---

234   Of noo creature] Of any creature G.
241–2   Si tibi ... nimis] om. R.   245   Who that] Whoo than G.
245   must he wynne] must wyn GC.   250   yet shall ye] it shall ye C.
251   Wynne me] wᵗ cancelled after wynne R.
251   than] corrected from then R.   254   everych] ecch G; euery C.

Of these matiers to you shall pronunce,
Or it be longe, not oonly an Angell,   265
But also your kynnesman, King Alfons,
Which of austronomy was the very welle,
And of your fate the dispocicion can telle.
Hym shall ye mete with other moo electe,
That toward your seid spouse shall you directe.   270

fol.37ʳ   The vth chaptre: of the iijde pagent and speches
           utteryd of the persones there beyng in hyt.

And from this pagent of the Castell of Portcullys, they extendid
their jorney and passage to the thirde pagent in the myddes of
Cornell enjoynyd to the condute, there beyng iiij square,   275
empayntid three foote from the grounde of colour like frestone,
havyng in his forefrunte iij great pylours: ij grene marbill, on
every sid j, and in the myddis oon pelour of red marbill
empayntid; and all the voyde space betwene the pilours of werk
like brikk wallis, havyng two portcullys in the seid forefronte of   280
yelowe, and on every side of the portcully a crosse voydid with
gunholys in every poynt of the cros. Above this brikke walle
there was a mantill cumpassyng the hole pagent, vyrond of a
fote and an half brode with ij rollys, oon beneth of whight and
grene, another above of blak and yelowe, and in the space   285
betwene the ij roullys many dyvers bagges: first a rede rose and
a whight in his myddis crownyd with gold, portcullys crownyd
with golde, a whight grehound, and a red dragon dredfull. And
thus they were sett orderly, iche aftir othir in all the hooll
compasse and circute. Uppon the toppe of the oon grene pelour   290
of marbill, uppon the right hand, a rede dragon dredfull
holdyng a shelde with the kinges armys quartered with blew
and rede, and in the blue iij floures de luces of golde, and in the
rede quarters iij lyons of gold. And on the topp of the pelour of
grene marbill, on the lefte hand a rede lyon rampaunt holdyng   295
also a sheld of like armys to the othir rehersid. Above this and
within this pagent there was a sete like unto a beanche,
enhauncid in the myddill sumwhat higher than the siddes, the
which beanch was of grene chekirs very thykke with frenge of
rede, and in every cros of chekyr a rede rose and a whight in his   300

265   be longe] belonge R.   270   shall you directe] shall direct GC.
271   pagent] written over an erasure R.
278   pelour] plelour R.   286   betwene] betwe R.

myddill. Abought this sete as uppon the wallys were chekyrs of
whight and grene besett full of rede rosys crowned with golde
floures de luce, rede dragons, whight grehoundes, portcullis
crownyd also with golde, and upon his edgis and siddis ij smale
postes with chekirs of rede besett full of whight estriche fethers   305
and floure de luces of golde. Upon this rehersid sete there sate
such persones as their speches shall declare. And above the
hedys of these sitters was a blew spere of the mone especiall
fol.37ᵛwith / othir planettes and sterrys in their curse and ordre. And   310
in the circumferens of this spere were the signes of the mone,
and with `owt´ the circul of the spere were iiij angels in the
iiijor costes and partys of the worlde, that is to say: orientall,
austerall, occidentall, and boriall. Above this blewe spere there
was a sete and an angell therin, the which was callid Raphaell,
the angell of mariage, and on every side of the angell, this   315
shilde of the Kinges armys upholde with a rede dragon and
grehounde. And over this sete were pynnacles with fanys of
goolde full goodly wrought, and all the hooll pagent chekiryd
with whight and grene as well without as within, set with
bagges and conizansis as it was shewed. And this Pagent of the   320
Mone was appropriat to the Princes, sheweng her fatall
disposycion and destyny.

Now foloweth the proposicion of thangell of mariage callid
Raphaell, seyeng in his proposicion thus:

[Corpora spiritibus reddit Deus, ymaque summis   325
Nil fiat ut noster absque ministerio.]

Though philosophers of God knowladge did opteigne
By the meane of creatures, yet be ye sure
This knowladge was never hade sufficient and pleyne
But by the techyng of angell, more perfight and pure   330
Than the instruccion of any bodely creature.
They be Goddes massengers that oonly can
Declare such hevenly mysteres to man.

Who taught the prophetes and the patriarkes
The unyte of God and trynyte of persone?   335

302   rede rosys crowned] Rede Rosys whight ande grene Crowned *R*.
304   upon his edgis] his *cancelled between* his *and* edgis *R*.
325–6   Corpora ... ministerio] *om. R*.
330   by the techyng] by techyng *G*.
334   and the patriarkes] and patryarkis *GC*.

Who enfourmed theim in the marvelous werkes
Of Cristis incarnacion, but angell alone?
Angell taught the providence that God in his trone
Hath over all creatures, as well lowe as highe,
Which provydence dyvers philosophers denye.   340

Madame, we be mynesters of Goddes providence,
Whom Almighti God to his people doeth sende
To geve them instruccion, ayde, and assistence.
Also God doeth ich man at his birth commennde
To his propre angell to socour and defende,   345
Eke cities and realmes to archaungelis that move
These orbes and speeres in the regions above.

fol. 38^r   Moreover I, Raphaell, on of the seven
Alwey stondyng in Goddis highe presens,
Have especiall charge to me gevyn   350
Over mariages, by Goddis provydens
To be made for love with vertu and reverence,
For procreacion of childern, aftir Goddis precepte,
Not for sensuall lust and appetite to be kepte.

Wherfor, ageynst your mariage I com hether   355
To sett you coupled to your noble make,
In like maner as I brought toguyder
Thoby and Sara, only for vertues sake.
Wherfor, Madam, your wey nowe maye ye take,
And ye shall shortely of your spouse Arthure   360
See a more perfight and expresse figure.

Now by great eloquens and famous speche Gabriell his
proposicion hath opynly pronunced, Alfons by ordre to this
nobill lady expressith his myend, seieng thus:

[Longa resarcito, Arthuri post tempora Regno   365
Huc te venturum, sidera prodiderant.]

338   taught] thorwth GC.
339   lowe as highe] & cancelled and as interlineated between lowe and hye C.
346   cities] citie R; Cytees GC.
346   to archaungelis] tharchangels GC.
347   speeres in] sperys `rule´ In G.   350   especiall] a speciall GC.
353   childern] chyldyr GC.   355   ageynst] agayn GC.   356   sett] see GC.
363   pronunced] -ed written over -iat R.
365-6   Longa ... prodiderant] om. R .

Doughtir Kateryn, I, Alfons, remembre
Certayn constellacions passid many a day
Sheweng a goodly princes, yonge and tendre,
Of myn issue, shuld frome her owne contray   370
Towardes northwest take a great jorney,
And to a noble prince shulde there maryed be,
Aspiring to honour and dignyte.

Doughter, the sonne, signifiour of kinges,
Entryng the Sagittary and his triplicite,   375
To whoes conjunction approximate is
Hesperus and Arthure, the signifiour as we se,
For the more parte, in the same house to be.
Loo, Lady Kateryne, these tokenes signifie
What dignyte ye shall opteygne, where, and why.   380

Ye shall achewe the dignite of a quene
By meane of mariage in this noble land,
The land of Sagittary, as is evidenly seen
By theffecte therof, and it doeth subgiet stond
Undre the firy circumferens and bande.   385
Weell may ye joye, whom the hevens assure
So prosperous filicite longe to endure.

fol.38ᵛ   And `for´ more concordauns, ye shall undrestond
Ye, Lady, bere the bagge of Sagittary,
Somtyme the auncient armys of this lond   390
As appiereth by blason of auctoryte,
And by the same signe opteigned victory
Of enemys, there numbre beyng great,
And no marvall, that signe is so mete.

Hit is the signe that Noble Prince Arthure   395
Was borne undre, your spouse fortunate,
In triplicite of the Lyon sure.
His house domified and so procreate,
It is the signifier of greate estate,
And is of Jopiter the house, fortune of Heven,   400
In which aspectes and signes ye be com even.

Therfor I se weell, by experience,
The tyme is com, whereof right glad am I,

371   Towardes] Toward GC.   374   sonne] same GC.
389   of Sagittary] of the Sagittare G.   395   the signe] that sygn GC.
400   fortune] fourmyd GC.   401   which] whoos G.
401   signes] signe C.   401   ye be com] ye comyn GC.
403   com] comyn G.   403   whereof] GC, om. R.

And eke the hevens, by Goddis high providens,
Doeth the same thyng assure and ratifie,   405
As your self may se here evidently,
Beholdyng Arthure in his hevenly spere,
Signifiour of your noble spouse so dere,

To whoes seid signifiour, the bodies celestiall
Stand very benyvolent and frendly directe,   410
And eke your owne sterre, Hesperus especiall,
Hath of everych planete right prosperous aspecte,
Which signyfieth very fortunate effecte
To folow upon your noble mariage
To Prince Arthures worthy personage.   415

This speche here foloweng is the argument of Jobbe, the holy
prophet:

[Contemplare Deum, pocius quam sidera nam ille
Presidet omnibus hiis, munifice que regit.]

Hit is to vertue full good and necessary,   420
The astronomy of the philosophers,
But notwithstondyng, Madame, yet shall I
Shew you anothir astronomy that is
More necessary to be knowen, and it is this:
To knowe Himself that creatyd and wrought   425
Heven, erth, and all creatures of nought.

fol.39^r Alfons hath shewed you the hevenly bodies
For your compfort, and of your spouse a figure.
But now, Madam, loke up above all this
And ye shall fiend a more speciall pleasure   430
To knowe and beholde the great Lord of Nature,
Almighti God, that creatyd and wrought
Arthure, Hesperus, and all the heven of nought.

It is the Sonne of Justice, therthe illumyneng;
This is the very Hesperus that shone so bright   435

406   As] GC, And R.   412   everych] euery C.
412   aspecte] aspette R.   418-9   Contemplare ... regit] om R.
418   Contemplare] G, Contemplar C.   425   knowe] knew C.
427   shewed you] shewyd to yow G.   432   creatyd] creat C.
433   all the heven] all thyng GC.   435   This] That GC.

In the west, to oure compforte, by his dethe fallyng;
This is the Lyon of Juda, that venquysshid in fight,
Rysyng from deth to lyf by his owne myght;
This is Arthure, illumyneng iche cost
With vij bright sterrys, vij yeftes of the Holy Gost,   440

Which hath not knet Arthure and Esperus oonly
Togither, as Alfons your kynnesman hath seid,
But also by Goddis provydence almighti
His predestinacion and grace therto leyed
To be joyned in maryage, with His helpe and ayde,   445
For concordauns of the Cardinall Vertue
Of Atemperance betwene your spouse and you.

Boetius also maketh reasons foloweng unto the rehersid mattir
and entent:

[Pulcrum est nosce Deum, solem lunam que sed hec quid   450
Si tute ignores, utilitatis habent.]

Madame, as the noble Alfons king
Hath evydently shewed, by good argument
In astronomy, houghe that in everythyng
The hevenly bodies, right benyvolent,   455
Stand in aspectes full equyvolent,
Everych fortunate in his region,
Disposid to your mariage and unyon,

Right so Job, exsperte in divinite,
For convenyences founde in your personage,   460
Hath shewed and proved by auctoryte
That ye and your spouse ought in mariage
Be joyned as two of ryall parage,
To Goddes pleasure and effectes naturall,
Ffurst causid in the bodies spereycall.   465

fol.39ᵛ   Of the furst cause than procedeth the secunde,
Lynked and knyt by a goldeyn cheyne,
Theffectes, I meane, that you shall make habunde,

439   Arthure] Arthurus G.   439   illumyneng] enlumynyng GC.
447   betwene] atwene GC.   450–1   Pulcrum ... habent] om. R.
454   in everythyng] GC, euery thyng R.
465   spereycall] spyrytuall GC.
466   than] that C.   468   habunde] habound GC.

In honour and dignite forever to reigne.
Wherfor of reason, we thre accorde certayne,   470
Astronomer, philosopher, and devyne,
You to be joyned, and so we all determyne.

The vjth chaptre: of the iiijte pagent and speches
uttiryd there, of the persons beyng there`in´, and of
all other behavys.   475

And from this pagent of the mone in Cornell they procedid in
their seid former ordre and raise unto the iiij pagent, which was
in Chepesid betwene the Great Conducte and the Standard,
the which was corneryd with iiij great postes, two bifore and ij
behynde; upon the ij former postes a red dragon upon oon of   480
them and on the tothir a whight hert with a crowne of gold
abowte his neke and a chene of golden lynkys comyng from the
crown; the other ij bestes on the othir postes, the oon of theim a
rede lyon rampand, the othir a whight grehound. And in the
face of this pagent there was a whele wondurffully wrought   485
with clowdis abought the compasse owtward; and undre thys
whele was there a skochon of whight with Seint Georges crosse
and a red swerd, and in the ij lower corners ij astronomers, oon
with a tyrangill and the othir with a quadrat, havyng their
speculacion to the bodies above. Upon the uppar part above   490
directe was the Father of Heven, and on the ij corners besid
him ij anglis with trumpettes and armys uppon theim bothe,
the oon of theim havyng a scripture written: *laudate dominum
de celis*, the othir his scriptour aunsweryng: *laudate eum in
excellis*. Over the Father there was many angels havyng scrip-   495
tours of *te deum* and *tibi omnes* &c. Within the medill of this
great whele there was a chare, and within the chare a prince stondyng full richely beseene. Benethe his chare there was iiijor
great sterres like iiij wheles runyng very swyftly, and betwene
the ij former sterres, the centour of erthe. In the brede of this 500
whele, there were many dyvers figures—sume of berys, sume
lyons, sum hors, sume wormys, sume fisshis, sume marmaydes,
sume bullis, sume virgyns, sume nakyd men, sume ramys—
stikkyd full of sterrys as they be apropered and namyd in bokys
of astronomy, havyng lynys—sum red, sume whight—deducte   505

471   and devyne] & hooly dyvyne *GC*.
472   determyne] termyne *GC*.   501   there were] the were *R*.

fol.40ʳ from iche sterre, planet and / signe, and aftir the aspectes that
naturally iche of theim hath unto othir. In the brede of this
whele were iij armyd knightes, the which, as they wolde
ascendid, tornyd this whele very swyftly all the season of the
comyng of this Princes. The highte of this pagent was goodly   510
wrought with penacles and lanternys holow with wyndowes,
many and craftyly wrought and empoyntid, and gilte full
costeously, bothe within and without, and this was named
the spere of the sunne, apropriat to the Prince of Englond,
sheweng `and´ declaryng his fatall dispocicion and desteny.   515
    These foloweng be the speches of the iiijte pagent:

                [Volvitur Arthuri triga aurea cardine semper
                Inmoto, nec Aquis mergitur Hesperiis.]

                Welcome, faire ladie, fairer than Esperus,
                Welcom, noble princes, into Brytayn,   520
                The land of Arthure, your spouse most bounteous,
                Whoes expresse ymage and fygure certayne
                Ye may behold, all armyd not in vayne
                With corporall armour oonly, but in like wise
                With the sperituall Armour of Justice.   525

                Which Armour of Justice, as the prophete seith,
                Is of everych realme the peasible conservature.
                Wherfor as ye se here this chare on hight
                Stondith in his compas alwey ferme and sure,
                Lykewise the realme of your worthy spouse, Arthure,   530
                Shynyng in Vertu, shall stond perpetually
                Within the compas of his noble progeny.

                Wherfor, Madame, greatly rejoyse ye may,
                For whoes mariage, of a speciall favour,
                It pleasid hath Almighti God to purvey   535
                A prince of all princes the very floure,
                With whome ye shall aspyre to great honour.
                Go ye forth to the joyefull semblaunce now
                Of the mariage betwene your spouse and you.

515 dispocicion] dispocon R.
517–8 Volvitur ... Hesperiis] om. R.
518 Hesperiis] hesperius C, hisperius G.
524 oonly] om G.   527 everych] every GC.   530 worthy] GC, om. R.
532 Within] Wyth GC.   532 his] GC, this R.

The vijth chaptre: of the vte pagent and speches   540
usid therin.

fol.40ᵛ/ And from this Pagent of the Sunne at the Great Conducte,
they procedid in their former ordre and raise unto the vth
pagent at the Standard in Chepe. And in his forefrunt of man
highte he hade a great and a large rede rose with a grehounde   545
on his oon side whight, and on the other sid a rede dragon, and
at his iiijor uttirmest corners iiijor great postes. And upon these
postes were iiijor sage personys aftir the auncyent fachion
arayed, sum with marvelous hoodes, and sum with hattes, and
their robys sett full of perlys, and were semblaunt unto the   550
prophettes. And upon and above the forefront and behynde the
pagent were great lyons and dragons and grehoundes of leed
poyntid. And above all this there was a trone compassid
abought with many candilstikkys of golde, and wex tapers with
goodly bolles and floures sett in theim, and these tapers were   555
brennyng. And within this trone, there was the Godhod sittyng
full gloryously, and abought Him in circute ennumerable of
angels singing full armoneously as it had been in a chirche with
a swete and a solempne noyse. And in the hight of this hooll
pagent were many goodly penacles, wyndowes, and fanys right   560
goodly besett. And in every unche space of this werk were
perlys of sylver counterfetid right great and right coryously
wrought. And this was callid the Temple of God, exortyng and
meovyng this goodly Princes to the love of God and of Holy
Chirch.

The viij chaptre: of the vth pagent and of such   565
speches as the presentes there uttered unto the
noble Princes.

[Hunc veneram locum sexteno lumine septum
Dignum que Athuri totidem astra micant.]

I am begynnyng and ende, that made iche creature   570
Myself and for myself, but man especially,
Both male and female, made aftir myn owne figure,
Whom I joyned together in matrimony,

568–9 Hunc ... micant] *om. R.*   571 especially] specially *C.*

And that in Paradise, declaryng opynly
That man shall weddyng in my Chirch solempnyse,   575
Figured and signified by the erthly Paradise.

In this, my Chirche, I am alwey resident,
As my cheef tabernacle and moost choson place,
Amonge thise golden candilstikkes, which represent,
My Catholyk Chirch, shynyng bifore my face   580
With lighte of feithe, wisdame, doctryne, and grace,
And marvellously eke enflamed toward me
With the inextinguible fire of Charyte.

fol.41ʳ   Wherfor, my wilbeloved doughter Kateryne,
Sith I have made you to myn owne semblaunce   585
In my Chirch to be maried, and your noble children
To reigne in this lande as in their enherytaunce,
See that ye have me in speciall remembraunce.
Love me and my Chirch, your speritull moder,
For ye despising that one despise that other.   590

Loke ye walke in my preceptes and obey them weell,
And here I geve you that same blissing that I
Gave my wil beloved children of Isarell:
'Blissid be the frute of your bely,
Your sustenuce and frutes shall encrease and multiplye,   595
Your rebellious enemyes I shall put in your hande,
Encreasyng in honour bothe you and your lande'.

This speche foloweng is of the Prelate of the Chirche:

[Septimus extremis te sponsam Henricus ab oris,
Arthurum ut nubas, virgo decora, vocat.]   600

Thoughe man, for his offence and greate demerite,
Felle from his honour, by right and justice,

575   man] men GC.   580   bifore] affore GC.
583   inextinguible] extyngwible GC.   585   myn] my C.
591   Loke ye walke in my preceptes] Look that ye walk, In my preceptis G,
Loke that you walk my preceptes C.
592   that same] the `same´ G.   593   children] childyr GC.
595   sustenuce] substance GC.   595   frutes shall] ffrutys, I shall GC.
596   rebellious] GC, Rebellours R.
599–600   Septimus . . . vocat] om. R.   599   extremis] extremus GC.

To infinite sorowe, God of His goodnes yet
The remedy for man did himself devise,
And in conclucion, the moost convenient wise   605
For manys Redempcion was thought to be than
The maryage of God to the nature of man.

This mariage was so secret a mystery
That oure Blissid Savyour, Crist Jhesus,
Compared it to a maryage erthely,   610
To make it appiere more open and pleyn to us
By a parabill or symylitude, seyeng thus:
The Kyng of Heven is like an erthely kyng
That to his sonne prepareth a weddyng.

And right so as oure soveraign lord, the Kyng,   615
May be resemblid to the Kyng Celestiall
As well as any prince erthely now lyvyng,
Sittyng amonge the vij candilstikkes roiall,
As he whom hit hath pleasid God to accept and calle,
Of all honour and dignite unto height,   620
Moost Cristen kyng and moost stedfast in the feithe.

fol.41ᵛ   This noble Kyng doeth a mariage ordeigne
Betwene his furst begoten sonne, Prince Arthure,
And you, Dame Kateryne, the Kinges doughter of Spayne,
Whom Pollici, Noblesse, and Vertue doeth assure   625
To bothe realmes honour, proufite, and pleasure.
Wherfor, Madame, to Honour ye shall procede,
Beyng of the vertues the guerdon and the mede.

The ixth chaptre: of the vj pagent and of such
speches as were uttered in the same.   630

And unto this rehersid pagent at the Standard erectid, the
Kinges Highnes hade conveyed himself sumwhat prevy and
secretly and stode in a marchauntes chambre, and with him the
Lord Prince, therl of Oxinford, therl of Darby, therl of
Shrewesbury, my Lord Chamberleyn, with many othir estates.   635
And not very ferre thens in anothir chambre stode the Quenes

610   it] yit C.   611   appiere] to appere GC.
614   prepareth] preparid G.   620   unto height] unto the heyth GC.
628   the vertues] those vertuys GC.

Good Grace, my Lady the Kynges Moder, my Lady Margarete,
my Lady her sustir, with many othir ladies of the londe,
not in very opyn sight, like as the Kinges Grace did in his
maner and party, there they bothe beholdyng the persones,   640
their raise, ordre, and behavynges of the hole company, bothe
of Englond and of Spayne, as well of their apparell and their
horsis as of their discreate and goodly ordre, poyntes in
features of their demeanour. Above in wyndowes, ledis, gut-
tours, and batilmentes stode many of the Yemen of the Garde,   645
and also benethe in the strete the servantes of my Lord Prince,
my Lord of Oxinford, my Lord of Darby, my Lord of
Shrewesbury, my Lord Chamberleyn, with othir dyvers to a
great and a howge nombre on bothe the siddes of the strete.
And eftsone the beganne to approche to the Kinges sight in the   650
moost goodly wise that ever was seen in Englond or in any
othir realme that of qweke and recent memory may be knowen
or undirstond. And first in this solempne and ordinat entraunce cam rydyng the Mayre on horsbake in cremsyn saten
with a riche colour of golde abought his neke, and bifore him the   655
Sworde Berer aftir the guyse of the Citie, and aftir him the Recorder in blake velvet, the ij Shrevys and the xxiiijti Aldremen
in skarlet and their servantes right weell horsid and beseen.
Aftir that they hade made their salutes unto the Princes upon
the Bridge in the entrynge of the Citie and made a goode space   660
in the stretes, rum and passage for the Princes and hir greate
multitude and retynue, aftir them cam the kinges of harodes
and aroldes of armys in their cote armours of silver and golde
fol.42ʳof the / Kynges armys of Englond, and also made roome and
weye and devyded the comon people right ordrely. Enseyng   665
appered fresshely apareld vj goodly galauntes of therl of Essex
in yelow cercenet with many estrich fethers upon right pleasaunt cursours of corage, trapped and besett full of silver bellis,
avaunsyng their horsis aftir the moost coriouse maner. And
aftir them rode the gentilmen belonging to therl of North-   670
umberland, and than the gentilmen belongyng to the Duke of
Bokyngham, and aftir theim the squyers and knightes appoyntid by the Kyng, and aftir the seid lordes, therlys of Northumberland and Kent, and aftir theim the Duke of Bokyngham,
and aftir them such trumpettes, shalmewes, and sakbotes to a   675
great nombre as cam with the Princes owte of Spayne, and aftir
theim straungers of Spayne, as well thestates as gentilmen,
every of them rydyng upon the right hand of an Englishman as
they were in degre and honour except therl, tharchebushop,
and the Bushop that cam with this Lady, who rode all three   680

toguyders. And aftir theim rode the Princes upon a great mule
richely trapped aftir the manour of Spayne, the Duke of Yorke
on her right hande and the Legate of Rome on her left hande.
She was in riche apparell on her body aftir the manour of her
contre, and upon her hed a litill hatte fashounyd like a   685
cardinalles hatte of a praty brede with a lase of golde at this hatt
to steye hit, her heere hanging down abowt her shulders, which
is faire aburne, and in maner of a coyfe betwene her hede and
her hatt of a carnacion colour, and that was fastenyd from the
myddis of her hed upwardes so as men might weell se all her   690
heere from the myddill parte of her hed downward. And as
well her owne foteman weell apparellid as the Kinges fotemen,
to a great nombre richely apparellid, were abowte her, and aftir
her rode viij ladies, iiij of Englond and iiij of Spayne,
apparellid in clothe of golde. The furst lady of Spayne rode   695
upon a mule trappyd. Her sadill was like a fouldyng stole with
iiij stavis, to behynde and ij bifore, eithir of theim crossyng
other, richely enclosid, and she sittyng upon the wronge side of
the mule, her bake to the contrary sid aftir the rydyng of gentilwomen in Englond, and a lady of Englond apparellid in clothe   700
of golde rydyng by her to kepe her company in maner of a leder
of her hors, but the lady of Spayne rode upon the right hande
of the Englisshe lady, so as whan they bothe were toguydres,
the bake of the oon lady was to the bake of the other, her heer
hanging down abowte her neke, and a good large hatt uppon   705
her hed proporchyoned aftir the fachion of a cardenalles hatte
as the Princes hade. And aftir them rode the secunde lady of
fol.42ᵛthe seid / foure ladies of Spayne all in blake, callid Lady
Mastres, with kerchiers upon her hed, a blak thinge of clothe
over her kerchiers like unto the fachion of a religious woman   710
aftir the maner of Spayne, her sadill, aftir the maner of the
other ladies sadylles of Spayne, coverd with blak and sate upon
the wronge side of the mule as other ladies of Spayne did. And
the Englisshe lady rode by her in clothe of golde as thother two
rode bifore. And aftir theim rode the thurde lady of the seid viij   715
ladies of Spayne aftir the same fourme and apparell as the furst
lady of the seid viij ladies, rode with an Englysshe lady in
clothe of goolde bake to bak as the othir rode. And so aftir the
same fourme and undre such apparell rode all the remenante
Englissh ladies bak to bak, and aftir theim cam an hors-lytter   720
richely beseen, and aftir the hors-litter iij yonge Englissh
ladies, maydynes of honour, in like sadilles, sittyng upon the

712   coverd] couᵉrerd R.

wrong side of their palfreis, every of them aftir othir as though
they had ben folowers. Ther apparell was cloth of gold, and
every of their palfreis were ledd by a foteman. And aftir them   725
cam a spare palfrey with a sydde sadill and a pilyon of estate
aftir thenglissh maner, richely apparellid, which palfrey was
led by the Mastir of the Quenes Hors, the seid Mastir beyng on
horsbak richely beseen. And aftir them cam iiijor spare hors,
every of them aftir othir, led by a foteman rychely apperellyd,   730
and every of thoes iiijor hors havyng such highe quyshons upon
their bakkys as the mule hade of the Princes. And aftir thoes
iiijor spare hors came other ij spare hors, either of them aftir
other, richely apoyntid. And upon either of the seid ij hors
bakkes a sadill with stavys such as the other ladies of Spayne   735
rode inn, and a styrop gilte for a lady hangyng upon the wronge
sid of the hors, which stiroppis were very greate and of a
marvelous fashion. And aftir thoes ij spare hors cam v charys
richely beseen, in every of the which charys were Englissh
ladies. And aftir every of thoes v chares folowed vj ladies and   740
gentilwomen fresshly beseen and rydyng on palfreis. And aftir
thoes v charys came ij other charys not so richely beseen, in
which ij charys were Spanyssh women apparellyd aftir the
Spanysshe fachion. Ther apparell was busteous and marvelous,
and they were not the fairest women of the company. And aftir   745
thoes charys cam the yomen belonging to the Duke of
Bokyngham all in a lyvery on horsbak and aftir that the yemen
belongyng to therll of Northumberland all in a lyvery on
fol.43ʳhorsbak, / and aftir them othir lordes and gentilmen is
servantes that rode bifore the Princes.   750

The xth capture: of the vj pagent speche ande
demeanour there.

And from this pagent at the Standard in Chepe they procedid
in their seid former ordre and raise unto the vj pagent, the
which was in the furthest ende of Chepe and next unto the litill   755
conducte, the which was the last, and in the enteraunce of the
Chircheyard of Poulis, and was goodly poyntid and gilte, with
many pelers in the myddis, and betewene every rybbe of the
pelours, pictours of lyons, dragons, and grehoundes, and on
everych sid of the pagent a great peier of steires goyng up. And   760
upon the floure at the hede of the steires stode the vij vertues,

755   Chepe] shepe R.

the iij Theologik and iiij Cardinalles, that is to seye, Feith,
Hope, and Charite, Justice, Temperauns, Prudens, and For-
titude or Strength, and abought theim many vyrgyns in whight
garmentes of poudrid armyns, and above theim was there iij   765
seetes, and in the myddis satt oon full pleasauntly beseen in
purpill velvett, and he was callid Honour. And in the two other
setes upon the right hande and on the left hande was there ij
cusshons, with iche of theim a ceptour and a cronell of gold in
tokyn that they were recerved and kept for the Prince and the   770
Princes, and above their hedes tabernaclis, pynaclis, armys,
and bagges full pleasaunt, riche, and goode, bothe within and
without.

          Thus and in this manour and fourme spoke the
          noble person, Honour, unto the Princes.   775

          [Omnium felix Arthurum nacta maritum,
          Non deerit capiti digna corona tuo.]

          I am Honour, whom folk of every degre
          Pursue to have, but many of ther purpos mysse,
          For I without vertue can not acheved be.   780
          Honour, ye wott well, the rewarde of vertue is,
          And thoughe that vertuelesse many a man or this
          Hath semyd honourable, yet was he not so;
          Such honour is countirfaite and is lightly goo.

fol.43ᵛ   Tholde Romayns, though they blynde were   785
          In the errour of old gentilite,
          Yet of me they dremyd in a manere,
          Thinkyng the wey to me shuld Vertue be,
          For which two templis of Vertue and me
          They joyned toguyder whan they made them new,   790
          In tokyn that Honour is annexed to Vertu.

137   two] *written over an erasure R.*
770   recerved] *altered from* receyved *R.*
776–7 Omnium ... tuo] *om. R.*
780   vertue] wertue *R.*
783   he] *GC,* ye *R.*   784   goo] agoo *GC.*
788   shuld Vertue be] vertw shuld be *G.*
791   In tokyn] *in R, these words are separated by an erasure.*

Also your self see weell that in the wey
And in iche stappe toward us ascendyng
There dwellith a vertue, so that no man may
Asspire to us for any maner of thinge   795
But sithe they be ever more dwellyng
In the wey. All folkes of necessitie
Must come by thise vertues or thei com at me.

Wherfor, noble Princes, if that ye persever
With your excellent spouse, than shall ye   800
Reigne here with us in prosperite for ever.
Also these crownes and seetes on ich side of me
All voyde and unoccupied yet, as ye see,
Ar kept as reward for Noblesse and Vertue,
That oon for your noble spouse, that other for you.   805

Whan that the Princes had passid by the pagentes in ray
ordyned and sett in the stretes of London, and with grate
pleasure harde and beholden the goodly sightes in theim
severally, at this last pagent beforeseid, the which was in the
entraunce of the Chirche Yard of Poulys adjoyned and anexed   810
to the Litill Conducte, the Mayre of the Cytie, the ij Shrevys,
the Recordar, and the xxiiijti Aldremen with other of the
Citie—they aboode her honourable comyng and with moch
treasoure and great plentie of plate of silver and gilt, as basones
and pottes fulfillid with coyne to a great summe—salutid,   815
presentid, and also gave unto her the seid gieftes, and with
agoodly countenances and demeanour. And in like wise, her
goodnes full amyable, aftir moost lernyd maner, she receyvid
with great thankes the plate goold and specially their good
myendes. And thus she and her nobles procedid till they cam to   820
the dore of Seint Powlis, where she was solempnely with
honour receyved of tharchebushop of Cantirbury, the Busshop
of Derham, and the quere of Poulis with many prelates of the
Chirch of Englond in procession, and so leed and condute to
the `auter and from thense to the´ shryne of Seint Erkenwald,   825
fol.44ʳat the which shryne she made her devout / offeryng. And
incontynente the estates waytyng to hir in this rehersid jorney

794   so that] so there C.   798   vertues] om. GC.
798   at] to GC.   802   on] In G.
803   unoccupied] uncumpanyed GC.
805   spouse, that] spowse, and that GC.
808   harde] hade R.
824   condute] -te added by hand C over erasure R.

brought her to the Busshoppis Paleis of London without the
west doore of the Chirche of Powlis. And this doon the gentils
departid every man to his owne lodgyng, ffurst the Busshopp of   830
Cantirbury to the Blakeffreres, the Duke of York and the
Bushop of Derham to the Paleis of Derham, the Duke of
Bokyngham, therl of Northumberlond, with all the residue of
estates to their places, lodginges, and innys. Thus this joyefull
and honourable day was fortunatly brought to his ende. And   835
the Princes there in her lodging passid over full conveniently
all the hoole nyght.

No marvell though that matter to theffectes of felicite to be
fynnally deducid and conveied, the which mediat grace
and leafull purpose meovith—ffirst to ther incepcions and   840
begynnyng (thexperyence wherof might be evident and aproperyd in this present day to deme and juge Almighti God
in this mariage content and pleasid), heraftir with great influens
of strength and vertu to assiste the parties in their weyes and
intentes—that notwithstandyng the wonderfull preyse of the   845
people, the cruelnes of their cursours and sterne horsis, the
jeopardies, standynges in highe places, wyndowes, and housys
of the stretes within the Cytie of London, yet there was that
daye no myschaunces of oppressyng man, woman, ne childe,
neithir stroke with hors ne infortunat fall, praysid and lovyd be   850
Almyghti God.

The Satirday `now´ is entryd aftir the succession and curse of
tyme in whom the estates and embasadours of Hispayne—
guyders, save-conduters of this noble Princes—thought it
expedient to intrete before the Kingez wurthy presens—their   855
messages, embasshions, and singler titles of their Lord
Soverayne of their realme his commaundement—of and uppon
the frendly and lovyng aggreamentes of mariage in this noble
issue betwene them oftyn encompassid and concludid. Wherto
the Kinges Highnes agreable lett purvey and ordigne him to   860
the receyvynges of their seid declaracions, and for that behalve
and cause made addresse and array oon of his great chambers
within his lodging of Baynardes Castell, hangid with riche
cloth of arras, and in the hed and uppar parte of this large
chambre a sete regall covered over with a cloth of estate   865
precious and riche costly, where undre is magestie was settyng
upon cusshons of cloth of golde (as in tribunall the aunncient
and honourable kynges in antiquyte have in their matters of
charge be accustumed to occupie their verdutes and sentens `of´

832   to the Paleis of Derham] *written over an erasure R.*

grante), is dere and wilbeloved sons, the Lord Prince on the   870
fol.44ᵛright hand / and the Duke of York on his left hand. To which
thus in such rialtie settyng these seid straungers were suffryd
and promysyd to enjoye and have their lyberall accesse, and
unto his grace they made and expressid in right goodly maner
the everych poynt and circumstaunce of `their´ commyssion,   875
the which conscideryd not oonly the besy and deligent attendaunces and company of her persone by the seid straungers, and also dyvers cuntreis and costes that they shuld by ther
ventures of wyndes and tempest avertyd and dreven, but also
for the suertie, and to this virgyn and Princes so pure and   880
without distres of any malicious person to such corupcion of
her disposid or ennormly enforsid. And in thies singler articles
of her conveyaunce, by right great pollicy—as of the assurenes
of hir virginite, with thool myend and massage of the Kyng
[of] Hispayne—they publisshid full wise and perfightly byfore   885
the Kinges Highnes, (there beyng abought him present right
many lordes bothe spirituall and temperall and thoes that to his
noble councell were assigned and aperteyned), they upon this
desireng to be now dischargid and exonerat of this great and
dredfull custodie, and as true, juste, and liege servantes to be   890
notid and regarded to their Prince. To the which desire,
request, and leafull peticion the Kynges Grace moost prudently enclyned aftir due and reverent thankys, with wordis of
grate kyndnes and favour unto theim by his owne person
utteryd with moch discression. He them dischargid therof,   895
with all the othir of the singler promisses. Thanswere and
satisfyeng was by the Busshop of Rochestre, to that entent
assigned, full clerkly in Laten shewed and propounde.

The same day also the Princes, forasmoch as she had not
seene the Quenes Grace no season syn her arryvyng first in to   900
the costes of Englond, as due reason did requyre, causid
honourably her company to be warnyd for the convenient and
goodly visiting and sight of the Quene, then toguyders with the
Kyng her husbond in the seid lodgyng of Baynardes Castell.
Upon this there was a `right´ great assembly both of gentilmen   905
of this cuntreth and also of Hispayne, in apparelles of silk and
gold full richely beseen. And so on their horsbak they repaired

876   oonly the] *these two words separated by an erasure R.*
882   singler] *this word is a later addition, perhaps inserted by the corrector,*
written in a space at the end of a line.
887   lordes] lord *R.*   891   regarded] regard *R.*
897   by the Busshop] by thoo the busshop *R.*

to the seid place, and in that rydyng was the Mastir of the
Quenes Hors ledyng an hors-lyttir aftir all the ladies and
company of gentilwomene, the seid hors-lytter beyng covered   910
fol.45ʳand aparellid right / costely bothe within and without. In the
aftirnoon, abought thoure of thre or iiijor of clok, she was
solempnely with moost honoure and behavour receyved and
acceptid to the Quenes Grace, and with pleasure and goodly
commynycacion, dauncyng, and disportes thei passed the   915
season full conveniently. And in the same evenyng late, with
torchis light to a great nombre, she was conveyed and brought
honourable to her lodging at the Bushoppis Paleis of London.
And thus with honour and merthe this Satirday was exspired
and doon.   920

915   thei passed] *written over* to passe *R.*

[BOOK 3]

The thirde boke: of `the´ mariage and fest riall and othir circumstauns there aboughtes.

The furst chapeture: of thordryng of the Chirch of Powlis.

The Cathedrall Chirch of Seint Poulys within the Citie of 5
London was ennouryd in all behalvys bothe autier and quere, and also the body of the chirche with the moost excellent ornementes apperteynyng unto the worship of God and honour of this joyefull maryage and unyon of the moost reverent Prince and Princes: ffurst thauter with their plates, jowelx, and 10
relikkes of wondrefull riches and precyousnes, with copys and vestmentes in their suetes honourably to the mynystres abe-hovabill of full great valoure, the quere also enhaungyd with clothis of aras. And from the quere doore, the which is of xij or xiij g⟨res⟩es enhight from the pament, extendid a weye and pas- 15
sage callid a levy, like unto a brydge of tymbre byllyd and `a´rays-id upon great and many postes, railid upon bothe the siddes, with red say nailyd and covered upon the seid reylys all the lengeth of the body of the chirche unto the nyghyngys and approx-imacion of the west doore, the which is of vj or vijth hundreth 20
foote of lengeth. And nere unto the lougher ende of thys levy there was enhaunsid a certayne porcion of v or vj greses like a stage rownde encompasse, covered with red say takyd fast with
fol.45ᵛgilte nailys, uppon the / which the Prince, Princes, and mynysters of the Sacrement of Matrimony might conveniently 25
stond. And in objecte annempst this place where as the courte and constory is usyd to be kept, above in the vaute, there was a closet made propirly with lates wyndowes enclosid, within which closett the Kinges Grace and the Quenes might stond secreatly to se and apperceyve the fourme and manour of the 30
mynystracion. The wallys also of the body of the chirch, contynuyng the lengeth of the levy of a great hight and brede, were hangyd with costely and riche clothis of Arras, whoes

---

2 aboughtes] -es *added in different ink R.*
10 jowelx] and *cancelled before* jowelx *R.*

werkes and texturys representid the noble and valiaunt actes,
storis, and gestes that for the moost partie poetes and oratours 35
writt and remembre in their commentes, bokes, and scripture,
as well `in´ the besegyng of noble cities as othir batalles [and]
turneis, their horsis and persons aftir the moost goodly picture,
shapp, and fachyon, with thendeovour and practif of the maker
`his reason´ and imaginacion. 40

　　Here ensueth certayn mattirs of the joyeful beholdyng of the
Prince and Princes to entir into Powlys:

The prophetez sage we rede in storys and comment,
Patriarchis and they `that´ to the temples were
Deserviant and longyng, thought their lyves spent 45
Right well, and their prayours with wepyng of many a tere,
So that they might abyde without drede or fere
The commyng and the birthe of that noble childe
That with our aunncient enemy shuld hold and kepe the feld,

And in that bataill mekely though that he were slayn, 50
And unto thende mortall if he shuld be brought,
The thirde day by his owne powre he shuld aryse ageyn,
Secundly redemyng that first he made of nought.
Who that the true scripture hade enserchid and sought
Shuld the holy Symeon esspecially fyend 55
Amonge is hole peticions desire non othir thyng

fol.46ʳ | Save oonly that sight or ever that he died,
Oftyn in is orysons seyeng to Almighti God:
O si me inveniat, trowe ye I shall abyde
To se thalmon and frute that spryneth of Aron is rode; 60
The granys of this tre were sowyn all abrode,
Is rote perisshid the egge and depe places of peyne,
The bowes beyng in therthe, the toppe in Hevyn ageyn.

This vertuouse man at the last did fynally asspire
Unto his request, and grauntid it was to hym 65
By thalmighti God theffecte of his desire:
Is age still contynued, hough be it is eyn were dyme,
For his clene lief and purenes without synne.
The sonne of Hevyn and Maris, as ye be advysid,
Was present to the Temple to be circumsisid. 70

With mooche joy and gladdnes he resounde this noble songe,
Enbrasing this babe betwix his armys two,
Seyeng: here is nowe commyng us amonge

The light of the Gentils and glory of Isarel also;
Now, Lord, dimitt thy servant in peas and lett me goo.   75
I thanke thyn especiall grace of suffraunce that I might
Persever in my yeeres to se this joyefull sight.

The furst daie of Januare, the leder of the yeer,
Jhesus to be circumcisid was takyn from his moder;
The xiiij day of Novembre, allege him for his pere,   80
[...]
Of pleasure, joye, and gladnes above many othir,
The Sonday, the xvij yeer of vijth Henry the Kinge,
Uppon the which Sonday shulde be the goodly weddyng

And everlastyng unyon of Englond and of Ispayne,   85
The most noble regions undre the Hevyn is cope,
Now tournyd and made but oon realme that byfore was tweyne.
Blissid be the begynners that of the matier spoke,
For this bond and unyon, I trust, shall never be broke.
In Poulis many Simeons thought they hade well taryed   90
To see thus Spayne and Englond toguyders to be maried.

The ijde chaptre: of the company and bryngyng into
the chirch of bothe the Prince and Princes.

Thordre due was not pretermisid that first the Temple of God
fol.46ᵛ/ that tyme shuld have his duetie and serymonyes of annoure-   95
ment, neithir aftir `that´ thoffice ne the service of thonour
temperall, wherupon in this chirch thus, as it is premisid,
apprepared in is solempnites, was a great and a right pleasaunt puysauns of people to thentent of reverent awaytyng and
diligent attendauns (hough be hit commonly it is seen great   100
resorte often to be made for wonderyng and pleasure in their
owne sightes, and in volgar speche callid gasynges of the rudes
and unlernyd persons). Besides whom there were of the nobles
of the realme electe, chosyn, and assigned by the Kinges Grace
for thonoureabyll and goodly company and attendauns to the   105

---

80   xiiij] xviij R.
80–2   pere, ... othir] *the scribe has evidently dropped a line, although it is
uncertain whether he dropped the fourth or fifth line of this rime-royal stanza.
Here I assume that a line parallel with the second line, perhaps beginning 'Arthur
to be maried', has been dropped, thus duplicating the parallelism of the first and
third lines.*

reverent persons of the Prince and Princes, as the noble yerle of
Oxinford, Great Chamberleyn of Englond, and therl of Shrewisbury, with many dyvers of thers and othir with them
encompaned. The which, furst upon the seid Sonday in the
morow abought thoures of ix and x of the clok set the Lord   110
Prince from his lodging, at that tyme callid the Kinges
Wardrope, and with right semly attendauns and worship
brought him to the southe doore of Poulys, were he alytid
and—is devocion there and obediens humbly hade to Almighti
God and is holys—went thorugh the chirche before rehersid   115
unto a privy and a secret chambre within the Paleis of the
Busshoppis of London, where he chaungid his vesture and
induyd himself the ryall and comfortable apparell of weddyng
and spousage, and thein immediatly in his priour fourme and
with is rehersid company was conductid ageyn to the seid   120
Chirch of Poulys. By the which season the often remembrid
Princes—encompaned with estates of Englond and of Hispayne, bothe lordes, knightes, and gentilmen, ladies, and othir
gentilwomen to a great and a goodly nombre, herself ledde by
the two honourabill persons of estate, the Duke of York and   125
therl that cam with her owte of Hispayne, the Lady Cecill
beryng her trayne—made so furth hir ordinat progression owte
of the paleis her lodging toward the entres of the Chirche of
Poulys in at the west doore, tyll she cam to the gres where she
shulde be maryed. At the which place the Bushop of Can-   130
tirbury, with the nombre of xviij mooe bushoppes and
honourabill abbottes mighteryd full solempnely, gave her
meatyng with procession moost devoute and worshipfull.
Where stode also present and redy the discrete and weell-
lernyd the Kinges Councell, and there made oppyn and   135
knowen by proposycions of all the aggreamentes and accorde
betwene the Kinges of bothe the realmes: firrst for the gieft and
porcion that her father shuld devyde with her to her maryage;
secundly were partid unto her certayn writinges and opynly
declared ensealid, as well be the Kinges Grace as the Lord   140
Prince; the seid lettirs patent thus contryved and ensealid
fol.47ʳ implied and conteyned her suertie and endowment. / A right
goodly multitude of estatis—the lordes and gentilmen in their
araye and ordre, by ij and ij, arme in arme, in apparell of silkes
and many in goold with riche and massie cheynes and colours   145

107–8   Shrewisbury] Shrevisbury R.
121–2   remembrid Princes] the *erased between* remembrid *and* Princes R.
126   therl] therk R.   128   paleis] plaleis R.
140–1   Lord Prince; the] of *erased between* Prince *and* the R.

of goold aftir dyvers and goodly werkes and fachion—precedid
this beautyfull Princes; and her ladies and gentilwomen in like
cours and beseeng, folowed also by ij and ij as the men did in
their former ordre and guyse. All the hooll company, lordes,
ladies, gentilmen, and women, thus conveyed her to this, the   150
very stacion before rehersid, assigneid for thexecucion of the
Sacrement of Matrimony. The garmentes of the Lord Prince
and Princes bothe were of whight saten, but for the straunge
dyversitie of rayement of the countreth of Hispayne to be
discryvyn: she were that tyme and daye of her maryage uppon   155
her hed a coyf of whight silk with a bordre of goold, perle, and
precious ston, beyng of an unche and an half of brede, the
which covered the great parte of hir visage and also a large
quantite of her body toward her wast and myddill; her gown
very large, bothe the slevys and also the body with many   160
plightes, moch litche unto menys clothyng; and aftir the same
fourme the remenant of the ladies of Hispayne were arayed;
and beneth her wastes certayn rownde hopys beryng owte ther
gownes from ther bodies aftir their countray maner. The
Kynges Highnes and the Quenes, bycause they wold make non   165
opyn shew nor apperaunce that day, whereas they uppon the
nyght before had comyn secreatly to the place of the Lord
Burgevenyes nere unto the seid Chirch of Poulis adjoynyng, so
in like wyse prively they had conveyed themselfes to the
rehersid closett above the consistory aright annempst the place   170
where the solempnyte of mariage shuld be executid, where they
beheld the Archebushop of Cauntirbury, encompanyed with
bushoppis and abbottes as it was lately expressid aftir the
fourme of Cristen religion and lawe, couple and conjoyne their
noble persons toguyder as the custom and sacrement in this   175
behalve doeth requyre and aske. This honourable and highe
solempnyte perduryd there by the space of [ ] houre and
more, aftir the which peracte and doon, the remembrid rayes
fol.47ᵛand ordre of tharchebushoppis, bushoppis, / and abbottes,
lordes, knightis, and gentilmen precedid the goodly Prince and   180
Princes, the ladies and gentilwomen foloweng in like course
and maner. The mynstrelles also—bothe trumpettes,
shalmewes, and sakbottes—strake upp and made such melodies
and myrthe as they coude, the which was confortable and

146   precedid] *corrected from* procedid *R.*
148   beseeng] -g *added by corrector R.*   169   wyse] Royse *R.*
171–8   *a pointing hand is drawn in the left margin opposite this passage R.*
177   space of [ ] houre] thre *has been erased leaving a blank R.*

joyefull to here. The Prince and Princes, hand in hand, he   185
beyng on hir right side, went thus moost solempne and goodly
toward the highe autier upon the levy before rehersid, and or
ever they entryd in to the quere dore, they curtesly bothe
turnyd them to the southe and to the northe parties for
thentent that the present multitude of people might see and   190
behold their persones, the which people were so breme and
many, that in the rodeloftes, vautes, wyndowes, and on the
pavmentes were to conscidere and behold nothing but visages.
Of this multitude were dyvers showghtes and noysys made,
sum cryeng 'King Henry', sum in like wise cryeng 'Prince   195
Arthure'.

The thurde chaptre: of the ascendyng to the autier and
of the masse and their retournyng to the Paleis to their
dener.

From thens `thei´ ascendid to the aultier unto the moost   200
solempne, devout, and glorious Masse of the Trinyte, celebrate
and mynystrid by tharchebushop of Cantirbury, there doyng
the obsequens the rehersid honourable company of bushoppys,
abbottes, and othir prelates of the Chirche with songe and
orgons moost pleasure and excellently. And whan this Masse   205
solempne with his moost due observans was endid, in the tyme
of the benediccions of the bredes, wynnys, and spices and othir
thinges of comfort, and to the refresshyng of the presentes
aftir the curtesy of Englond shuld be distributid, the Duke of
York with therl of Hispayne, aftir the seid refresshyng, the   210
moost excellent Princes—fully sacrid aftir the preceptes of the
fol.48ʳ Chirche—leed / and conveyed with the rehersid goodly multitude of nobles and estates towardes the Paleis of the Bushoppis
of London, the place riall of this great and noble fest of the
mariage. And when they cam without the west dore of Poulys,   215
there was the vij pagent runnyng with wynne all the tyme of
the mariage and Masse, and was a goodly mountayne or
mounte, bullid and made in fourme and maner foloweng: that
is to sey, the seid mountayne was grene, and many herbis and
trees with many rochis and ragges of stone, geat, ambir, and   220
currall, with othir marvelles ores of metalles groweng and
apperyng owt of the siddes of the `seid´ mountayne. And uppon
the hight of this mountayne grew three great trees, wherof oon
uppon the right hand was grene beryng floures of goold, and
summe were red rosys, and in the toppe of oon of the rosys   225

stode, as it hade been groweng, a whight grehounde. And
ageynst the body of the tre stode the King of Fraunce, pictured
in clene armour, beyng in the myddes of a whight hert, within
the body of the seid hert upp to the knees, with a rounde ball of
silver in his hand. The secunde tre was also grene with many   230
rede rosys, and owt of the toppe of this tre of oon of the rosys
sprange a rede dragon dredfull. And annempst the myddill and
body of this tre stode the King of Englond harnessid complet
with a sword in his hand, beyng in the myddes of a shipp, and
appiered above the seid ship by the myddill. The thirde tre was   235
also grene, and is frute was also appulles or oranges, and owt of
oon of thoes oranges spronge a red lyon. And annempst the
myddill of this tre stode the Kyng of Spayne in complet
harnes, in the myddes of a castell, with a ball of silver in his
hand. And everych of thise kynges hade their skochons and   240
armys above their hedes. And in the myddes and depnes of this
pagent the conducte was runyng with wynne all the tyme of the
mariage, and without a pale compassid all the hooll pagent, and
therin a gate for people to entryn at to fetch and drynke the
seid wynne that thus so ubertly rann owt of this conducte.   245

The iiijte chaptre: of the addressyng and apparament
of the chambers and halle where as the fest riall was
kepte.

fol.48ᵛ/ By this pagent they passid unto the very entyraunnce of the
Paleis where was a great chambre moost pleasaunt and astately   250
addressid with hangynges of rialtie and every annowrement
that might belonge to so noble estate, in whoes ever parte there
was a stondyng cuppbord with plate of clene gold very precious
and riche and also of right great plentie. There was also two
burdes of honour, oon of theim for the Princes, and anothir for   255
persones of great reputacion. At the first and higher burde that
was of honour sate the goodly and noble Princes in her estate
and the Bushop of her countreth. And at the lougher partie of
the seid burde and meas were sett the Duches of Norfolk, therl
of Hispayne, and the Cownties, and were servyd that day with   260
lordes and noble knightes, and non othir shuld be permyttyd
ne suffred to bere disches, cuppis, ne othir curse of service.

250   astately] astely *R.*
252   noble estate] *one or more illegible words interlineated between* noble *and*
estate *in R.*

Their vitaill was not to be singlerly named, for the moost
delecates, deynties, and curyous metes that might be purveyed
or goten within the hooll realme of Englond—the which ever   265
therof hath opteyned the praise and commendacion emonge all
other cuntries or nacions in the world, blissid by thauctor,
Almighti God—bothe flesshe, veneson wild and tame, fisshe,
and the remenant of every maner of viand, wynys of all maner
kiend, spices, pleasures, and subtilties of the cunnyng appre-   270
paryng of the cookes, were not that day to seke nor myssyd.
At the secunde table in this chambre by the siddes of the wallys
were sett enspeciall company of ladies, the chief and principall
of the lond, every of theim assigneid to the chere and solas and
to bere the goodly and convenient company to the ladies   275
straungers of Hispayne. In the halle also ryall there was erecte
another highe and a large stondyng cupbord of plate silver—
moch therof gilte—with dyvers tables and burdes apprepared
and covered, in whom were the residue of the gentils and
persons of honour as well of Englond as of Hispayne, moost   280
fol.49ʳ ordrely sett and served with knightes, squyers, and / gentilwomen, with vitalles, delecates, and wynys bifore rehersid,
habundaunt and bountiously. And this solempne dener and
great fest contynued `unto´ thourys of iiijor or fyve of the clok
at the aftirnon, by the which season therl of Oxinford, Great   285
Chamberleyn of Englond, was direct and sent from the Kynges
Noble Highnes unto the Duches of Norfolk, the Countes of
Cabra, the Lady Mastres to the Prince and Lady Mastres to the
Princes, for thentent to have the oversight and apparament of
the chambre and bedde that the Prince and Princes, aftir the   290
condicion of wedlok, shuld take in their reaste and ease. The
which Duches, Countes, and Lady Mastres to the Prince and
Princes, aftir the convenient and leysure of two or iij hourys,
sertefyed the seid Erl of Oxinford of thexpedicion and requyred addressyng of the bothe chambre and bedde of estate, who   295
than incontynent repaired to the seid chambre himself, and
there, furste uppon the side that the Prince shuld lighe and
eftsones on the side that the Princes also shulde reste, toke the
say with right honourabill maner and behavyng. And ensueng
the Lord Prince, and His Grace, and nobles aftir the goodly   300
disportes, dauncynges with pleasure, myrthe, and solas before
usyd, departid to his seid arrayed chambre and bedde, wheryn
the Princes bifore his comyng was reverently leied and reposid.

273   enspeciall] -y *erased at end of word R.*
299–300   ensueng the Lord Prince] ensueng lymytt the Lord Prince *R.*

Than aftir the congruent usages and custom in mariages of
persones of noble blod, their seid bedde and lodgyng was   305
blissid with theffucion of certayn orisons therunto limyt and
appropriat by the bushoppis and prelates there present; than
furst refresshid curtesly with wyn and spices, were, as it was
convenient, required and monisshid to their singler departure.
And thus thise worthy persones concludid and consummat   310
theffecte `and complement of the sacrement of matrimony. The
day thus with joye, mirthe, and gladnes deduced to his ende.´

> The v chaptre: hough the straungers were desired to
> repast with my Lady the Kynges Moder and
> othir nobles of Englond.   315

The Monday immediatly ensueng aftir this great, goodly
solempneties, every person was allevyat and dischargid from
the burdeyn of their attendauns, ne were callid uppon to non
acte of chargeable buysynes aboute the service of the Prince or
Princes, but at their libertie and pleasure might use themself   320
unto their ease and commodities. And within the Paleis of the
fol.49ᵛfest riall every thing was undir silence, for the Princes / that
day, aftir due and moost honourable maner, kept and observed
her secret chambre sole with her ladies and gentilwomen, to
whoes presens non accesse utterly was suffryd to be had,   325
neithir by straunger of Englond ne of Hispayne, savyng oonly
the Great Chamberleyn of Englond, therl of Oxinford, was
directe and sent from the Kinges Grace unto her with an
especiall tokyn, and goodly salutid her with wordes of mooste
favour and reverens, seyeng that his Highnes wolde here above   330
all thinges to be of good compfort, and that he thought longe
unto the tyme that he might see her to his great joye and
gladnes. This present day the chief and principall estates of
Hispayne—tharchebushop, therl, and the Bushop, with the
residue of Hispayne—of honour were desired to repast and   335
dener to the reverent and moost wourshipfull my Lady the
Kyngez Modre at her lodgyng within the Cyte of London
callid the Couldeherber, for whom that place was right ryall

306   limyt] *this word is very smudged R.*   307   appropriat] appʳat *R.*
311–2   and complement ... his ende] *written partly over an erasure and
squeezed into the one-line space at the end of the chapter R.*
318   burdeyn of] *written over an erasure R.*
324–5   to whoes] towhas *R.*

and plesauntly beseen and addressid, enhaunged with riche
clothes of Arras, and in the halle a goodly cuppbord made and   340
erecte with great plentith of plate, bothe silver and gilte. And
they were sett at the [high]ther burde, encompanyed and
couplid every of theim, as well the men as the women, with hys
companyon of Englond to make them chier and solas. They
were also enservyd aftir the right goodly maner bothe of their   345
vitalles, deynties, and delecates, and with dyvers wynes abundaunt and plentuously. And in like wise and fourme, therl of
Darby had theim ageyn with him at his lodgyng at their soper
with right worshipfull chier and parleyaunce as my Lady the
Kynges Modre did unto theim at their dener. And in the   350
aftirnon towardes the nyght, the Kynges Grace lete warne and
monysshe in generall all the nobles of the realme and estates
that were within the Cytie of London to be redy in the
mornyng at ix of the clok to geve their attendauns and wayting
uppon his Highnes to the Chirch of Seint Poule for his   355
honourable and devout offeryng, there for thentent of love and
praysing to Almighti God that so prosperously his goodness
had suffrid every thinge of this noble and excellent acte to be
brought to his moost and laudable conclucion.

The vj chaptre: of the offeryng of the Kinges Grace   360
with all his nobles at the Chirche of Powlys.

Upon the Tuesday foloweng, the multitude of nobles, aftir
their commaundement and charge geven unto them in the
fol.50ᵉ evynnyng, assemblid them toguyder, and at thoure prefixed /
hade made their repairellys and were redye at the Kinges   365
lodging callid Baynardes Castell, every of them in riche,
pleasaunt, and coostly appairell upon their horsbak, bothe of
the spirituall and temperall, tareyng the Kinges comyng forthe,
where anon his Highnes and the Lord Prince made forth ther
passage in this semble and in moost goodly wise unto the   370
Chirch of Poulys. Where his Grace, aftir that he had hard
masse and devoutly offeryd at the blissid and holy rode of the
north doore, than the moost excellent and wurshipfull

341   plate] place R.
342   the highther burde] the [erasure] ther burde R.
349-50   my Lady the Kynges Modre] the Ladies the kynges modre R.
353   London to be redy] the phrase vpon their allegiauns has been
cancelled between London and to be redy R.

multitude of gentils made their arais and ordre and before the
Kinges Mageste and Highnes: ffurst the gentilmen of the   375
realme, esquyers; and aftir them the knightes, lordes, barons,
and othir many noble estates; and aftir them the Bushop of
Hispayne and tharchebushop of York; and aftir therl of
Shrewisbury and therl of Hispayne uppon his right hand.
Whom also folowed tharchebushop of Cantirbury, tharche-   380
bushop of Hispayne upon his right hand. In this ordre toward
the Kinge, the lordes officers of the lond: and mediatly before
His Grace the Duke of York, Cunstable of England, upon the
right hand, therl of Darby, Marshall, of the left hand; therl of
Oxinford, Great Chamberleyn of Englond, upon the right   385
hand, sumwhat nere to the Kinges person. And aftir the
Kinges Grace folowed the Lord Prince, the Duke of
Bokyngham, therl of Northumberlond, therl of Essex, and
therl of Kent with many othir in this company of barons, erls,
marques; and aftir them all the Yomen of his Garde right weell   390
beseen as they have been discrivyd tofore. And in this season,
the Princes was secretly conveyed unto the closett where as the
Kinges Grace stode in the `tyme of´ mariage upon the Sonday,
to see and perceyve this goodly pusauns and nombre of gentils,
where were accountid and rekenyd the mountenans of fyve   395
hundred, three score, and three, with chenes and colours of
golde worne of the gentils and nobles of this rehersid companye. And in the meane season, while they passid by thorowh
the Chirch of Poulis unto the paleis gate, the Princes had
returned ageyn to her lodgyng. And in the doore of her secunde   400
chambre she honourable mett the Kinge her faders Highnes,
fol.50ᵛand there betwene them were proferyd and / utteryd right
pleasaunt and favorabill wordes, salutes, and commynycacions,
aftir the which the King departyd, and was with this goodly
attendauns and company brought to his lodging of Baynardes   405
Castell. The Princes was ordred to hir dyner, and this day,
where as she ever tofore was servyd aftir the guyse and maner
of Hispayne, now unto hir was usid the accostomed service of
the Realme of Englond with moch curyousnes, apparement,
and behalve. And aftir that Her Grace had thus with hir   410
retynue repastid and dynde, she with her attendours repaired
unto the Kyng and to the Quene at Baynardes Castell where

380   Whom] added in darker ink R.
395   and rekenyd] the cancelled between and and Rekenyd R.
409   apparement] appʳarement R.
411   repastid] Repast with expansion sign usually meaning -er R.

the hooll rehersid company of estates that waytid uppon his
Highnes in the fornoon were present, and over them the
Mayour, Aldremen, and Craftys of the Cytie of London, and   415
than the Kynge, the Quene, my Lord Prince, my Lady Princes,
with all the lordes spirituall and temperall, with othir of the
nobles of the londe—the seid Mayour and Craftes severally
havyng their barges in right goodly manour, fornysshid and
accompanyed every of them with their owne servantes—   420
brought the Kinges Grace to Westmestir to the nombre of xl
barges and moo, right weell dekkyd and arayed, so as hertofore
have not ben seen so many barges so well accompanyed uppon
the Thamys at onys in assembly with mynystrelles of trumpettes, claryons, shalmews, and sakbotes that wondre hit was   425
and joye to here that goodly and pleasaunt noyse. And that
nyght such as were appoyntid to be Knightes of the Bathe
repaired to their baynes to the nombre of lviij, and there that
nyght the Kyng himself gave unto fyve of them ther charges
aftir thordre and lawe of the Bathe, and commaundid therl of   430
Oxinford, Gret Chamberleyn of Englond, undir and by the
vertue of his auctoryte, aftir the same fourme to encharge the
remnaunt, and in this maner the daye and also the great part of
the nyght was occupyed and expendid right laudably.

The vij chaptre: of the dubbyng and ordre of the   435
Knightes of the Bathe.

fol.51ʳ/ The morow of the Wedenysday next folowyng the Knightes
of the Bathe that had entrid into the begynnyng and certen
requisites apperteynyng aftir the Lawe of Armys unto thordre
and degre of the Bathe were warnyd and assignid unto their   440
attendaunce uppon the Kinges Grace to have and enjoye the
perficte accomplisshement of all the necessary poynties and
dueties to that solempne and highe knighthod apperteynyng.
And so they were redy and gave their diligens and wayting with
ther horsys, swordes, with their sporys uppon their helys, and   445
that shuld be for them nedfull, and there were by the Kinges
hond—in his Great Chambre at his Carpet and `under is ryche
clothe of estate´—dubyd and girtid with their swordes. They
shuld a redyn also that tyme in their rialtie, but of that they

447–8   under ... estate] *worked into left margin at end of one line and over an
erasure at beginning of next line; hand C, R.*

were pardoned bycause the wedir was not clere ne convenient   450
bycause of moch wete. There was also at that season addid by
the Kinges will and pleasure xviij moo knightes that had not
been in the baynes, and were dubyd knightes with the rehersid
nombre of lviij. So in all there were thre score and xvjten,
wherof so great a nombre and multitude have not been seen   455
heretofore in Englond at oon season made. The aftirnoon and
remnant of this day was with moch pleasure, myrth, and rialtie
occupied and consumyd.

[BOOK 4]

The iiijth boke: of the justes and bankkettes and
disguysynges.

The furst chaptre: of the arraies of the tentes and
feild of justes and turneamentes.

Uppon the Thursday the great and large voyde space bifore   5
Westmenstir Halle and the Paleis was graveld, sondid, and
goodly ordred for thease of the horsys and a tilte sett and
arreysid all the holl lengeth from the watir gate upp welnyghe
to thenterauns of the gate that openyth into the Kinges Strete
toward the sentwary. And att the uppar ende of the tilte by the   10
watir gate on the north parte a certen space beside from the
seid tilte there was a goodly tre enpayntid with pleasaunt levys,
floures, and frute, and sett upp encompassid and closid with
pale rownde abought, undre the which tre uppon railys were
hangyd the skochons and shildes with tharmys of the lordes   15
and knightes chalengers and they that entendid to take uppon
theim the nobill and valiant actes, justis, and turneamentes
fol.51ᵛriall. And on the southesid of this place, / ordred and addressid
for this runynges, there was a stage stronge and substauncially
byllid, with his particion in the myddis, whoes part upon the   20
right hand was apparellid and garnysshid for the Kinges Grace
and his lordes full pleasauntly with hangynges and cusshons of
golde, and the lougher parte upon the left hond in like maner
addressid and purveyed for the Quenes Grace and all her
goodly company of ladies. And annempst this particion there   25
were greces and steyers downe to the place of turney for
messangers and thoes by whom hit pleasid the Kinges Highnes
to have his myend and erand doon. Into this tent was enterans
that the Kyng, the Quene, the Prince, and my Lady Princes—
with all the othir nobles and estates—might thorugh West-   30
menster Halle by the Chekyr Chambir, without any more shewe
`or´ apparens, com in to this seid stondyng and stage. In the
northsid, annempst the stage of the Kinges, there was anothir
stage covered with red say for the Mayour of London, the

28   myend and erand] and *cancelled between* myend *and* and *R.*
32   com in to this] cam in to this *R.*

Shrevys, Aldremen, and worshipfull of the Craftes. And in all 35
the circuyte of this feld of werre, by and uppon the wallys,
were duble stages, very thyk and many, wilbyldid and plankyd,
for the honest and comon people, the which by the greate price
and coste of the seid comon people were hiryd. The feld nygh
unto the tylte was barred to thexcheweng of the rudes and their 40
discurse and wandryng amonge the sperys, horsys, and cur-
siours, as well for thease and regarde of ther hurte and
jeopardies as the distroublyng and impedyment of the present
goodly enacters of the noble feates of armys and werre. Then as
sone as dyner was doon in the courte, the Quenes Grace, my 45
Lady the Kinges Modir, the Princes, the Lady Margaret, and
her suster—wil-beloved doughtirs unto the Kyng [and] the
Quene—with many othir ladies and gentilwomen of honour to
the nombre of two or three hundreth, entred into this goodly
and weell-prepared stage. And aftir that immediatly the Kinges 50
Highnes himself, the Lord Prince, the Duke of York—his
noble heiers and issue—therl of Oxinford, Great Chamberleyn
of Englond, therl of Darby, Constable of the seid Realme, therl
of Northumberlond, therl of Shrewesbury, therl of Surrey, the
lordes straungers of Hispayne, with the moost excellent com- 55
pany of the lond—knightes, squyers, gentilmen, and Yomen
of his Garde to his noble estate and grace awaytyng—repaired
and cam to his forsaid stage, the Mayour and also his company to
their place rehersid. The stagis, wallys, batilmentes, and
wyndowes were furnysshid and fulfillid with wondrefull multi- 60
tude and puysauns of people, that unto sight and perceyvyng
was no thinge to the yee but oonly visages and faces without
apperans of their bodies.

fol.52^r   / The second chaptre: of thentiryng into the feld of
noble dedes of werrys doon and shewed by the 65
chalengeours and defendours.

Now ye shal be advertisid and also ye shall here of the moost
worthy, laudable, joyefull, and pleasaunt enteryng of the feld of
were and armys made and shewed by the goodly and valiaunt
Duke, Merquyes, erls, lordes, and noble knigtes of the 70
worshipfull and aunncient blod of Englond. First, the trumpettes blew to the feld a great season, rydyng abought the

41   sperys, horsys,] and *cancelled between these words* R.
42   ther] *corrected from* thers R.
44   feates] feauties R.

tilte. And then for the chalengeours procedid owt of Westmynstre Halle Sir George Herberd, Sir Rowland, knightes, the Lord
Barneis, the Lord Henry of Bokyngham—in whight harnes   75
armyd, uppon their goodly cursours right weell and plesauntly
trappid and garnysshid in riche maner and fourme—and aftir
theim the Duke of Bokyngham in his pavylion of silke, whight
and grene, beyng iiij square with propir turrettes and pynacles
of curyous werk, set full of red rosys of the Kinges bagges, the   80
which pavylyon was borne and upholdid and also conveyed
with right many of his servantes on foote in jakettes of silke,
blak and red, with many othir of his and the seid lordes,
servantes, and galantes weell horsid, trappid, and hangid with
spancles of goold and bellys, that their apparell, avancyng of   85
their horsis, and demeanour of curyage was great pleasure and
gladnes to the Kynges Grace and to all the beholders of the
hooll Realme of Englond ther beyng present. And thus they
made their araies and rod abought the tilte, doyng their
reverens whan they cam bifore the Kynge till they cam [to]   90
thende next Westmynster Halle, ageyne where they stode upp
and made their pauce and tarians. Eftsones for the contrary
parte the trumpettes blew up the feld oones or twyes in goodly
maner of werre, and anoon cam owte of the Kynges Strete in at
the gate that openyth toward the sentwary for the defendeours   95
Guyllam de la Ryvers in his pavylion in a goodly shippe borne
up with men within, himself rydyng in the myddes; and Sir
John Peche, knight, in his pavylion of silke, rede, borne over
his hed; the Lord William of Devynshire in a red dragon leed
by a gyant and with a great tree in his hond; therl of Essex in a   100
great mountayn of grene with many ragges, treis, herbys,
stones, and marvelous bestes upon the siddes, and on the
highte of the mountayn there was a goodly yonge lady in her
heer pleasauntly beseen for his pavylion; the Lorde Marquyes
in a riche and a costelow pavylyon of cloth of gold, himself   105
alwey rydyng within in harnes. And thus they made ther
passage rownnde abowte the feld, doyng their obedyens and
curtesy to the Kyng, till they cam in like wise to the place of
their entirhaunce, that unto this goodly ryaltie and devyce and
behavor [have] not beseen in like in very longe remembraunce.   110
And inmediatly as they were departid owt of their pavylions,
by the Kinges assignement and the oversight of the Constable
and Juges were stavys brought unto them. And so they chargid

90–1   cam to thende] cam thende R.
110   have not beseen] R omits have; cp. 4/401.

fol.52ᵛand ranne toguyther egerly. And at this furst curse ranne the /
    Duke of Bokyngham and the Lord Merquyes, and the Duke   115
    brake his staf right well and with great sleight and strenght
    upon the Lord Marquyes. And at the secunde curse, the Lord
    Marquyes brake his staf uppon the Duke in like wise. And thus
    the residue of the lordes and knightes ranne `orderly´ togiders,
    and for the moost parte, at every curse other the on staf other   120
    the other—or moost comonly bothe—were goodly and with
    great art and strength brokyn of meny pecys, that such a feld
    and justes ryall so noble and valiauntly doon have not ben sen
    ne hard, the which goodly feates and therof the hooll discrip-
    cion appieryth weell pleynner and more opyn in the bokys of   125
    the haroldes of armys. And in this goodlynes and maner the
    day was concludid honourably.

        The thurde chaptre: of the disguysyng and banket
        in Westmynster Hall.

The Kynges Grace, intendyng to amplifie and encrease the   130
ryaltie of this noble and solempne fest with many and dyvers
and goodly actes of pleasure, lett cause Westmynster Hall—the
which is of great lengeth, bredith, largnes, and right crafty
buyldyng—his wallis to be richely enhangyd with pleasaunt
clothis of Arras, and in his upper part a riall and a great   135
cuppbord to be made and erecte, the which was in lengeth all
the brede of the Chauncery, and hit was vij settes, shelvys, `or´
haunces of hight, furnysshid and fulfillyd with as goodly and
riche treasure of plate as ever cowde lightly be seen, moch
therof golde and all the remnante beyng gilte. In the which   140
halle the Kinges Highnes upone the fryday at nyght aftir this
first Justes Ryall causid to be appreparyd a goodly disguysyng,
to the which himself, the Lord Prince, the Lord of York, the
lordes of Hispayne—with a great company of lordys of Englond, bothe spirituall and temperall, knightes, squyers, and   145
gentilmen awaytyng uppon the King—were resortid and present. The Quene, my Lady the Kinges Moder, the Lady Princes,
with a goodly company of ffresshe ladies and gentilwomen of the courte and realme awayting upon hir had made
to this seid hall their reparell. And in this forsaid place, when   150
the Kyng [and] the Quene hade takyn their noble seates undre
their clothis of estate and every othir nobles were ordred in
their romys wurshipfull and convenient, than began and entrid
this moost goodly and pleasaunt disguysing, conveyed and

shewed `bi´ iij pagentes propir and subtill, of whom the furst   155
was a castell right cunnyngly devysid, sett uppon certayn
whelys and drawen into the seid hall of iiijor great bestis with
cheynys of golde. Two of the first bestes were lyons, oon of
fol.53ʳthem of gold and the othir silver; oon of the othir was an harte /
with gilte hornys, and the secunde of the same was a `ibex´.   160
Within everych of the which iiijor bestes were ij men—oon in
the fore parte and anothir in the hynde parte—secretly hide
and apparellid, no thing seen but their legges, and yet thoes
were disguysid aftir the proporcion and kynde of the bestes
that they were in. And thus this castell was by these iiijor   165
bestes propirly conveyed from the nethir parte of the halle
before the Kynge and the Quene beyng in the uppar parte of
the same. There were within this castell disguysid viij goodly
and fresshe ladies lokyng owt of the wyndowes of the same.
And in the iiijor corners of this castell were iiijor torettes, that   170
is to say, in every square of the castell on, sett and apperyng
above the hight of hit, `in the which of every of thise torrettes
was a litill childe apparellid like´ a mayden, and so all they iiijor
children syngyng full swettly and ermeniosly in all the commyng of the lengeth of the halle till they came bifore the   175
Kinges Mageste, where, whan hit hade commyn, conveyed and
sett himself sumwhat owt of the weye toward the oon sid of the
halle.

   The secunde pagent was a shippe, in like wise sett uppon
whelys without any leders in sight, in right goodly apparell,   180
havyng her mastys, toppys, saylys, her taclyng, and all other
appurtenans necessary unto a semely vessell, as though it hade
been saylyng in the see, and so passid thorugh the halle by his
hooll lengeth till they cam byfore the Kynge sumwhat beside
the castell. At the which tyme the masters of the shippe and   185
their company in their countenans, spechis, and demeanour
usid and behavyd themsilf aftir the maner and guyse of
marynours, and there cast their ankkers sumwhat beside the
seid castell. In the which shipp there was a goodly and a faire
lady, in her apparell like unto the Princes of Hispayne. Owte   190
and `from´ the seid shippe descendid down by a ledder two
weel-beseen and goodly persons callyng themsilf Hope and
Desire, passyng toward the rehersid castell with their baners,
in maner and fourme as ambassadours from [the] Knightes of
the Mownte of Love unto the ladies within the castell, makyng   195

160 ibex] Whight grehounde *has been cancelled and this word substituted in*
right margin R.

great instauns in the behalve of the seid knightes for thentente
to ateigne the favoures of the said ladies present, makyng their
meanys and intretes as wowers and brekers of the mattir of love
betwene the knightes and the ladies. The seid ladies gave their
finall aunswere of uttirly refuse and knowladge of any such   200
company, or that they were ever myndid to thaccomplisshe-
ment of any such requestes, and pleynly denyed ther purpos and
desire. The two seid ambassadoures, therwith takyng great displeasure, shewed the seid ladies that the knightes wolde for
this unkyend refusell make bataill and assault, so and in such   205
wise, them and ther castell, that it shuld be grevous to abyde
there power and malesse.

fol. 53ᵛ   / Incontynent cam in the thirde pagent in liknes of a great
hill, mount, or mountayne, in whom were enclosid viij goodly
knightes with their baners spred and displaied, namyng them-   210
self the Knightes of the Mounte of Love, the which passid
thorugh the seid halle towardes the Kinges grace. And there
they toke their stondyng upon the othir sid of the shipp. And
than thoes two embassadours departid to the knightes beyng
within the mounte, ther mastirs, sheweng them the disdeyn   215
and refusell with the hole circumstauns of the same; so as they,
therwith not beyng content, with moch males and curragyous
myend, alitide from the seid mount with their baners displayed
and hastely spede theim to the rehercyd castell, which they
forthwith asaultid so and in such wise that the ladies, yeldyng   220
themselvys, descendid from the seid castell and submittid them
to the pouer, grace, and will of thoes noble knightes beyng
right freshly disguysid, and the ladies also, iiijor of theim aftir
thenglissh fachyon and thothir iiijor aftir the maner of Hispayne, dauncyd toguyders dyvers and many goodly daunces.   225
And in the tyme of her dauncyng the iij pagentes—the castell,
the shipp, and the mowntayne—remeovyd and departid; the
same wise the disguysers rehersid, as well the knightes as the
ladies, aftir certayn leysour of their solas and disporte, avoydid
and evanyshid ought of the sight and presens. And then cam   230
doun the Lord Prynce and the Lady Cecill and dauncyd two
baas daunces and departid up ageyn, the Lord Prince to the
Kyng and the Lady Cecill to the Quene. Eftsones the Lady
Princes and oon of hir ladies with her in apparell aftir the
Spanyssh guyse cam doun there dauncyng othir two baas   235
daunces and departid ayen bothe up unto the Quene. Thirde
and last cam doun the Duke of York, havyng with him the

203   two] *written over an erasure R.*

Lady Margaret his sister on his hond, and dauncyd two baas
daunces. And aftirward he, perceyvyng himself to be accombred with his clothis, sodenly cast of his gowne and   240
dauncyd in his jaket with the seid Lady Margaret in so goodly
and pleasaunt maner that hit was to the Kyng and Quene right
great and singler pleasure, and so departid ayen, the Duke to
the Kyng and the Lady to the Quene.

This disguysyng ryall thus endid, began the voyde to entir in   245
this maner of a banket excedyng the prayse of any othir usid in
great seasons bifore. At the which voyde cam in v score couple
erls, barons, and knightes, over and beside squyers, havyng
fol.54ʳ colours and / chenys of gold, everych of them thorughowtly
beryng the oon of theim a spice plate thothir a cuppe, beside   250
Yomen of the Gard that folowyd them with pottes of wynne
according to fylle the cuppis. The spyce plates were furnysshid
in the moost bowntuous maner with spices aftir the fourme of a
voyde and the cuppis replenisshed with wynne accordyng,
universally thorughowt the seid halle distributyd. The nombre   255
of the spice plates and cuppis were goodly and marvellous and
yet the more to be wondred, for that the cuppbord was nothyng
towchid but stode complet, garnysshid, and fulfillyd, nott
oonys dimynysshid. Thus this goodly multitude of estates and
gentels, refresshed with the bountuous plentie of spices and   260
wynnes, at their commodite and leysoure, concludyng this
present Fryday, departid to their reaste.

Uppon the Satirday, bycause he was reynye and not clere ne
stable of wethir, the company of nobles—in the Chirch doing
their duetes to Almighti God, in their boures and chambers—   265
made pastans ryght honourably.

The iiijte chaptre: how the Sonday was expendid
with rialtie.

Upon the Sonday ensueng, there was kepte in the Parliament
Chambre a great and a goodly banket, in the which chambre   270
was iiijor burdys covered with clothes for thestates so that they
might sitt at the seid banket. There was also a stage of dyvers
greas and haunces of hight for the cupbord that the plate
shulde stande inn—the which plate for the moost part was

261 leysoure] leyosure R.
267 Sonday was] was cancelled between Sonday and was R.

clene goold and the residue all gilte and non sylver—and was in   275
lengeth from the closett doore to the chymney.

The Kingez Grace began this banket and sate at the side
table next to his owne chambre, the Princes of Hispayne on his
oon hand and the Counties upon his othir. Next the Counties
sate the Prothonotory, and by him a lady of Spayne; then was   280
therl of Oxinford appoyntid in cours next to sitt, and so he did,
and next him sate the Lady Maystres `off Espayne´, then next
her therl of Derby, and by him a lady of Hispayne.

The Quene sate at the table stondyng at the beddis feett—
which was in the upper part of the chambre and the tabill of   285
moost reputacion of all the tables in the chambre—my Lady
the Kinges Modir oon hir woon hand and the Busshop of
Hispayne on her other, my Lady Cecill and my Lady Kateryn
at the same table.

fol.54ᵛ | The Prince began the side borde next Westmynster Halle,   290
my Lady Margaret the Kynges doughtir next him; and next my
Lady Margaret satt the Duches of Norfolk, then next her satt
my Lord of York, a lady of Ispayne on his oon hond and a
lady of Englond on his other, and than therl of Northumberlond betwene two othir like ladies. And annempst my   295
Lord Prince satt therl of Hispayne and a lady of Hispayne next
the seid Erl. And at the nethir ende of this table satt therl of
Surrey and ij bredren of therles of Spayne.

Att the iiijte borde in the lougher parte of the chambre began
ij ladies of Ispayne, on of them before thothir, then the Lady   300
Dawbeney and the Lady Herbert, the oon bifore thothir, and
then a lady of Hispayne, and the Lady Burgeveny, the Lady
Dacre of the Sought, and then all the gentilwomen of
Hispayne. XXXt barons and knightes were assigned to serve
theim, or there abowtes, and non othir did there service but   305
barons and knightes, except that torchis were born by Esquyers
and by non othir. There was v cours of fflesshe to every messe
of mete, and at every cours vij disshes, and aftir that a cours of
frute of v disshes, and than cam in wafers and ipocras. This
banket began at vij of the clok and contynued two hourys, and   310
aftir that therl and his brodre dauncyd ij daunces. Then the
Kyng, the Quene, and all the estates and nobles departid into
Westmynster Hall, where they beheld an interlude till the

282 Lady Maystres off Espayne] *written over erasure* (*probably* Countess of)
at end of line and into right margin (*Hand C*) R.
282 then next] Surrey *cancelled before* then R.
310 of the clok] of the the clok R.

disguysyng cam `in, the which disguising was shewed´ by ij
pagentes. The first was a thinge made like an herber in goodly   315
maner and proporcion, wherin were xij lordes, knightes, and
men of honour disguysid and richely beseen. This herber was
so propirly brought that such tyme as it came bifore the Kynge
it was turnyd rownde abought in the settyng downe of hit, so as
the Kyng, the Quene, and all thestates might see and behold   320
thorughowtly the proporcion therof. And in the settyng downe
of this herber the gate therof was turnyd towardes the Kyng
and the Quene. And than cam owt thes lordes, knightes, and
men of honour so disguysid, and by themselvys dauncyd a
fol.55ʳlonge / space dyvers and many daunces, and stode asidde. And   325
then blew up the trumpettes, and therwith cam in a goodly
pagent made rounde aftir the fachyon of a lanterne, cast owte
with many propir and goodly wyndowes, fenestrid with fyne
lawne, wherin were more than an hundred great lightes, in the
which lanterne were xij goodly ladies disguysid and right   330
rychely beseen in the goodlyest maner and apparell that hath
ben usid. This lanterne was made of so fyn stuf and so many
lightes in hit that these ladies might perfeitly appiere and be
known thorugh the seid lantern. And aftir that this lantern was
brought and pight bifore the Kyng and the Quene, thise xij   335
disguysid ladies cam owte and dauncyd by themselvys in right
goodly maner dyvers and many daunces a great space. And
then coupled the seid disguysid lordes, knightes, and men of
honour with thes xij disguysid ladies, and so dauncid all
toguyders a great space. And in the tyme of ther all so   340
dauncyng, departid therls, barons, and knightes, to the nombre
of thre score or moo, to fetch upp the voyde for the Kyng and
for the Quene, at the which voyde were xxxti or moo stondyng
spice plates all gillte, and the residue were great gilt bollys with
spices. And as for the cupbord, it was in the same place and of   345
the same lengeth and hight that it was on Fryday at nyght. And
aftir this voyde the Kyng and all his lordes, the Quene and all
her ladies departid to their lodgyng abowte mydnyght.

The v chaptre: of the justes in the Monday.

Uppon Monday next folowyng was runnyng and justes at   350
Westmynster, and tho that were chalengeours the first day
were defendours now the ijde day, and tho that were defendours the first day were chalengeours the ijde daie. They all runne
weell and brake many moo stavys than they did the first

day, and the chalengeours cam into the feld with goodly   355
devices, and the defendeours had non othir thinge but their
harneis and armour.

And uppon the Tuesday thes all noble and valiante knightes
of werre—chalengeours ʼandʼ defenders—had respite and reposid themselvys. And the other nobles and estates solacid and   360
dauncid in their boures and chambers all that same day right
goodly and pleasauntly.

fol.55ᵛ   / The vj chapture: of the noble runnynges at the
large with sharp sperys and turney with armyng
swordes.   365

Uppon the Wedenysday, the tilte within Paleis at Westmynster—the which was ordeigned for defence and saulfgard
of their horsis that shuld excercise the feates of werre with their
speris and othir wepyn—was remeovid and takyn awey and the
grounde made all smothe and playn. Where anon ensueng—as   370
son as the Kinges Grace and the Quenys, with their honourabill company of lordes and ladies, were present in their stagis
and tentes to beholde the pleasaunt dedes of armys—
immediatly entrid in, owt of Westmynster Hall, the noble
Duke of Bokyngham, the Lord Henry of Bokyngham his   375
brothir, the Lord Barnars, Sir George Herbert, and Sir
Rowland, knightes, incontynent aftir that the trumpettes hade
blowde unto the feld, the seid Duke in his pavylion of whight
and grene silk, fachyoned aftre the maner of a goodly chapell
with turrettes and pynnacles with propir vanys uppon them,   380
besett with red rosis of the Kynges Armys of Englond, havyng
before hym v yong children of honour in goodly jurnettes in
maner of clokes of cloth of gold, rydyng uppon pleasaunt
cursours, with othir dyvers of galauntes right costely horsid
and arayed. And in such wise made they all their cours abought   385
the feld, doyng their obediens with curtesy before the Kynges
Grace, and so cam ageyn unto their entiraunce, where they
made pauce and stacion as chalengeours in the moost goodly
wise as they did uppon the Thursday bifore rehersid.

Eftson for the contrary partie, the trumppettes blewe upp   390
unto the feld, rydyng ones ʼorʼ twyes abought the place of
werre. And furthwith entrid in at the gate that opynnyth into
the Kynges strete and seyntwary of Westmynster the Lord

393   Westmynster] westmynter R.

Marques, therl of Essex, the Lord William of Devenshire, Sir
fol.56ʳ John Peche, Sir Guyllam de la Ryvers, knyghtes, / in right   395
goodly maner and guyse, with their folowers and servitours to a
goodly nombre uppon bothe the parties so pleasauntly horsid
and dekkyd, moreover so curagyously avaunsyng their horsys
and cursours, that this riall sight of this great multitude of
noble men—bothe on horsbak and on fote—were so pleasurfull   400
and so goodly that unto hit in tymys past have not beseen eny
lyke. Thus thes Marques, Erl, Lord, and Knyghtes cumpassid
the feld with their horsis, makyng their obediens with curtesy
unto the Kynges Grace, and so cam ayen unto their entiraunce,
and there they stode upp as defendours that day. Unto the   405
tyme, by the Kynges Grace and Highnes pleasure and
oversight of the Constable and Juges, were sharp speris
brought by the servitours unto theim. And so furst the Duke
and the Lord Marques runne toguyders egerly and with great
currage, in great jeopardye and feer of their lyvys, and brake   410
dyvers stavis right valiauntly and with great strengthe. And
secundly, therl of Essex and the Lord Henry of Bukkyngham
rane toguyders with like sharp sperys and did full nobly and
lyke hardy knightes, brekyng uppon ich othir dyvers and many
sperys. Aftir that, the Lord William of Devenshire and Sir   415
Rowland ran and did full coryagiously thacte of that featt of
armys with such strength and powre that they brake many and
dyvers staves ˋiche uppon oþer. The residue copled and ranne
iche to othir and nobly brake their stavys. Andˊ with such and
noble wise the uppheld that day. Hough be hit they ranne with   420
sharp sperys, they forsid so lytill themselvys, and so lytill
favour was usid emong theim, that sumtyme bothe the partis of
theim were borne to the grounde, bothe hors and man. Aftir
that thise noble Chalengeours and Defendours hade thus
fol.56ᵛ valiauntly attemptid iche othir in the poyntes of justes and /   425
runnyng with sharp sperys, uppon that they tourneyd with
swordes. Furst the Duke and the Lord Marquyes, and aftir
that therl of Essex and the Dukys brothir, so wortheily and like
hardy knightes faught and ranne toguyder with such might and
violens that sume of their swordes were strekyn owt of their   430
handes, sume hors and man enclyned to therthe. Thus they all
v coples of lordes [and] knightes turned full egre and valiauntly. Their dedis of armys in that feates were worthy great

400   bothe] bote R.   412   Essex] Essexʳ R.
420   the uppheld] written over an erasure R.
432   lordes and knightes turned] lordes knightes turned R.

preise and in memory to be commendid. Inmediatly aftir this
goodly actes they departid the feld. And ffurst the Chalen-   435
geours repaired into Westmynstre Hall, and the defendours
ageyn ought at the gate into the Kynges strete nygh unto the
Sayntwary. In the meane season while thise bothe companyes
of noble waryers and knightes were absent and harnesyng of
themself, there was brought in, into the feld, a certen barrer,   440
the which was sett overthworth the place bifore the Kynges
stage, beyng of mydde highte of a man, made stedfast and ij
railys on ich ende of the berrer, sett upp right and teyed
toguyder in the toppis with cordys. Ensuyng entryd in the
Duke of Bokyngham, the Lord Henry his brother, the Lord   445
Barneis, Sir George Herbet, and Sir Rowland owt of Westmynster Hall in complete harnes, and procedid unto the side
of the berrer, and there did their obediens with curtesy unto
the Kynges Highnes, and sumwhat withdrew them ageyn, and
made their stondyng yet as chalengeours in this thurde acte of   450
this present day. Forthwith appiered in the gate that opyneth
into the Kynges Strete and Sayntwary a goodly shipe with all
maner of taclynges and marinurs in her, the which in the seid
fol.57ʳ appieraunce made a great and an houge noyse with serpentyns /
and othir gunneshote, and so cam goodly conveyed unto   455
thothir side of the berrer, the v rehercyd defendours beyng all
within her in complete harneis, that is to seye, the Lord
Marquyes, therl of Essex, the Lord William of Devenshire, Sir
John Peche, and Guyllam de la Ryvers. And there they
descendid from their ship without obediens, bycause the day   460
was ferre past. Furthwith there were sent unto the Duke and
his brothir and the Lord Marquyes and therl of Essex—beyng
on fote—ich of theim a spere. And soone they approchid
toguyders and faught with thoes speres, and eftsoone turned
the greate endes, and sore and grevously leyed at iche othir a   465
longe season. Aftir that the othir couples in like wise faught
egrely, and meny strokes were betwene theim. And this was the
straungest feat of armys and goodlyest that hath been seen.
Eftsone they all sembled toguyder and faught wondirly, and
hevy buffettes and herde were betwene theim. And in all their   470
such batall was gunneshote still leten ought of the shippe. This
solempne acte endid, they purposid ˋthemˊ to ther departure
and avoydid the feld in like wise as they entryd. And the same
wey the Kinges Grace, Quenys, and all othir nobles of honour

468 straungest] straunge R.
472 purposid them] than cancelled after purposid R.

resortid to their sopers and lodgynges, and thus goodly con-   475
cludid this present Wedenysday with moch joye and pleasure.

The vijth chaptre: of the justes and turney, and
aftir, of the disguysing and voyde ensueng in the
nyght.

Upon the thursday, the morow aftir, were poyntementes and   480
summynes of justis and turney gevyn unto the nobles knightes,
to the beholdyng wherof the Kinges Highnes, Quenys, the
Lord Prince and Princes, and all othir estates had conveyed
fol.57ᵛ theimself into the / forseid feld, beyng in their tentes and stages
redy present. Than the feld was avoydyd, and the Tippid   485
Stavis and othir officers sett the people in ordre full discreatly.
Thexcellent nombre of commons that were sumwhat towchid
and spokyn of in the first day of justes were now also in their
forsaid stages, wyndowes, and batilmentes right plentuffull and
breme. Incontynent the trumpettes of the Chalengier blue upp   490
unto the feld, encompassyng him ones or twies abought on
their horsbak in right pleasaunt maner. And without tariaunce
cam owt of Westmynster Hall for the Chalengeours party a
goodly company of gentilmen and men of honour, right weell
horsid and beseen, avaunsyng their horsis aftir the moost   495
coragious guyse, dekked and garnysshid with spanglis, bellis,
and othir devyces dyvers and aftir [the] most nuest fachion that
hath ben usid. Aftir them there was a goodly chare of cloth of
gold drawyn with foure marvelous bestes: the two furst were
great lyons, oon of them rede and thothir whight, the thirde   500
best a whight hert with gilt hornys, the fourte an ibex, every
oon havyng within them two men, ther legges aloonly apperyng, beyng aftir the colour and simylitude of the beastes that
they were inn. Within this chare there was a faire yong lady,
the which—whan they hade redyn abought the feld doyng their   505
reverens bifore the Kinges Grace—with mutch curtesy was
delyverd into the Kinges stage emonge the faire and beautyfull
company of ladies, there contynuyng unto such tyme as all the
justes and turney was expyred and endid. The v noble men—
the Lord Marquyes, therl, Lord, and knightes—rode all in   510
complete harneis abought the seid chare, two on the oon sid
and two on thothir, and the Lord Marquyes directly behynde.

510   all in] *written over an erasure R.*

And thus they conveyed the rehersid chare unto the place of
fol.58ʳ their enteraunce, there abyding the defendours / commyng in.
So fortunat hath ever oure realme of Englond beholden, that 515
whatsoever chalenge of armys in him by eny maner straungour
or aliaunt have been made, thaunswere therof right laudably
hath been shapyn and founde by summe noble knyght of oure
owne nacion, wherfor unto this Englissh chalenge is pretens by
Englissh knightes right goodly in armys like aunswere and 520
defendaunce, to the which the trumpettes blue upp, rydyng
oonys or twyse abought `the feld´. Incontynent cam in at the
gate that opyneth into the Kinges Strete and sayntwary a
goodly company of gentilmen and of men of honour uppon
their coursours right richely beseen and arayed as it was 525
expressid in the party of the Chalengeours bifore, aftir whom
folowed immediatly the enactirs of the feates of werre and
Defendours in this behalve: furst Sir Rowland, knight; Sir
George Herbert; the Lord Barners; the Lord Henry of
Bokyngham; the Duke of Bokyngham—all on horsbak in 530
complet harnes right pleasauntly, and ther horsis trappyd aftir
full goodly maner. And thus they compassid the feld rounde
abought, and did their obedience bifore the Kinges Highnes
full curtesly, and so resortid to the place of their entiraunce.
Eftsone were ij stavis with cronalles brought unto theim—oon 535
unto the noble Duke of Bokyngham, thothir to the Lord
Marquyes—and annon they chargid and ranne toguyder at the
large without any tilte and brake their stavys right noble ij or iij
course. Aftir that were othir stavys sent unto therl of Essex and
the Lord Henry, the Dukys brothir, and they also chargid and 540
ranne toguyder. And aftir them every othir couple of Chalengeours and Defendours ich unto othir made ther cursys full nobly
and like valiaunt knightes. Sir Richard Gilford, Countroller
of the Kinges Hous, and Sir Nicholas Vaus were ever
for the most party in the feld every day of the justes right 545
fol.58ᵛ goodly beseen, bothe their horsis / and ther rayement, with
great and massy cheynes of golde abought ther nekkes, and by
them the Kynges Grace did sende his myend and messages into
the feld at his goodly pleasure. This noble runyng at the large
thus endid, there were swordes for the turney delyverd unto 550
the Duke of Bokyngham and unto the Lord Marquyes, and

516 chalenge of armys] of *written in different ink and separated from* chalenge
by an erasure R.
539 othir stavys] two *cancelled and surrounded by dots between* othir *and* stavys
R.

they ranne toguyder and turneyd and had many strokes unto
iche othir. And aftir them therl of Essex and the Dukes brothir
did theis like goodly dedys with swordes and tourneid right
nobly. And in the same maner the Lord Barners and the Lord   555
William of Devenshire, Sir Rowland, Sir John Peche, and all
the residue aftir this severall runnynges and tourney ich with
othir—all the v Chalengeours and the v Defendours—turneid
all in the feld at oones, strykyng, rasyng, and lasshyng at iche
other many strokys and longe season. Summe of their swordes   560
were brokyn of ij peces, and summe other their harneis was
hewen of from their body and felle into the feld. By this season,
the day drew fast unto his end, and thise noble knyghtes
purposid theim to their departyng. Then the Lord Marquyes,
therl of Essex, the Lord William of Devenshire, Sir John   565
Peche, Sir Guyllam de la Ryvers conveyed their chare of cloth
of gold, drawen with the `iiij´ rehersid beastes, unto the Kinges
stage, and there receyved their lady ageyn, and so yede oute of
the feld. And in like maner the Duke of Bokyngham, the Lord
Henry his brothir, and all the defendours made their departyng   570
in like wise as they entryd, in moost goodly behavor and usaige.

The same Thursday at nyght Westmynster Hall was causid
by the Kinges Grace to be goodly apreparid. Furst, the wallis
fol.59ʳ therof were hangid with riche / and costlew clothis of Arres of a
great highte, and in the uppar parte orderyd a Clothe of Estate   575
for the Kinges Highnes with cusshons and carpettes and all
othir goodly requysites unto his noble person and estate. The
cuppbord also of vij shelvys and stages of hight, furnysshid and
fulfillid with precious and sumptuous plate of moost pleasaunt
fachion, was erecte and sett, contenuyng all the brede of the   580
Chauncery. The plate therof were great and massy pottes,
flagons, stondyng cuppis, goodly bollys, and peces—for the
moost dele clene gold and all the residue gilte—as it was uppon
the furst Thursday of justes before rehersid and shewyn. Into
this goodly hall and place thus pleasauntly appreparyd the   585
Kinges Grace, the Quenes Grace, the Lord Prince and Princes,
my Lady the Kinges Moder, with all the noble estates as well
of Englond as estraungers of Hispayne were comyn and
resortid for the purpose and entent to beholde a certaigne
disguysing there assigned, the which shortly, aftir cylens and   590
ordre of every person in their rummys convenient, appieryd
and was shewyn aftir this moost proper wise and maner: that is
to sey, in the lougher ende of Westmynster Hall were disclosid

571   usaige] vsange R.

and brought into sight ij mervelous mountes or mounteyns
right cunnyngly practisid and made, the oon of them of colour   595
grene, plantid full of fresshe trees, summe of them like olyffes,
summe oranges, summe laurelles, genaper, vir tres; dyvers and
many faire and pleasaunt erbys, flouris, and frute—that great
delite is—was to beholde. The ijde mountayn was summwhat
more like unto a roche skorgid and brent with the soone and of   600
derker colour, owt of whoes siddes grew and eboylid, as it had
been, ores of sundry metalles—as of gold, of silvere, lede, and
coper—sulphir, and such other dyvers kyndes of stonys—as
cristall, currall, ambir, and othir moo of marvelous kyend and
fol.59ᵛnature—right subtily pictured / and empayntid as ever hath   605
been seen. These bothe mountayns were fastyned and chenyd
toguyder with a goodly chayne of goolde thorughout bothe
their myddis, and thus were subtilly conveyed and drawen
upon whelys prively and unperceyvved unto the tyme they cam
joynly so tyed toguyders unto the Kynges presens beyng in the   610
higher parte of the seid halle. There were settyng upon certayn
steppis and beanchis of the siddis of the first mountayn of
colour grene xij fresshe lordes, knightes, and men of honour,
moost semely and straunge disguysid, makyng great and swete
melody with instrumentes musicall and of moche ermony, as   615
with tabers and taberiens, lutes, harpys, and recorders. And in
the smale hillis uppon the siddys of the redder mounte or roche
were xij like disguysid ladis, and on in the topp arrayed aftir
the maner of the Princes of Hispayne, all they fresshe appareld
ladies and women of honour havyng like instrumentes of   620
musike, as clavycordes, dusymers, clavysymballes, and such
othir. Everych of theim—as well `lordis´ disguysid in their
mountayn as ladies in thers—usid, occupied, and pleayed upon
ther instrumentes all the wey commyng from the lougher end
of Westmynster Hall till they cam bifore the Kyng and the   625
Quenes Highnes and Magestie, so swetly and with such noyse
that in my myend it was the furst such pleasaunt myrthe and
propertie that ever was herd in Englond of longe season. When
the mountayns with this people were pight and groundid bifore
the Kinges sight, then discendid the xij goodly disguysid   630
knightes and men of honour and dauncyd toguyder delyver and
pleasauntly. And eftson the xij ladyes in like maner discendid
from their hilles and coupled with the seid rehercyd lordes, and
so in a semily they all xxiiijti disportid and dauncyd there a

longe season many and dyvers rowndes and new daunces full   635
curyously and with most manerfull cowntenance. In the meane
fol.60ʳ/ season, the `ij´ mountayns departid and evanysshed owt of
presens and sight. Incontynent entrid in the voyde brought by
iiij or v score couple of erlis, barons, knightes, and men of
honour, oon of theim beryng a spyce plate replenysshid with   640
spices, the othir a cupp suyngly thorughout the hole company.
Aftir theim folowed squyers, gentilmen, and Yomen of the
Gard with pottes of wynn to fill the forseid cuppis whansoever
and as oftyn as they were emtid. At this voyde was distribucion
and delyvery of the rewardes and gieftes unto the lordes and   645
knyghtes that hade so manly uphold and mayntayned the noble
dedes in justes and turney the iiijor daies past, aftir rightusnes
and bountuuse curtesy unto everych of them as the brute and
fame went and was knowen of their worthy merites and
deservynges. And furst the Duke hade geven unto him a ryche   650
and precious stone, a diamond of great vertue and price; the
Lord Marques a rewby; the Dukes brothir, therl, and other
lordes and knightes, ich of theim precious stonys and ryngges
of goold moost excellently and aftir `most´ goodly maner as
they were rightuously prasid and commendid by the hondes of   655
the Princes. And thus the Kinges Grace, the Lord Prince and
Princes, with all othir estates bothe of Englond and of Espayne,
refresshed and joyefull, made unto their lodgynges and restes,
ther semyly departyng with excellent merth and gladnes deducyng this goodly daye unto his end.   660

> The viij chaptre: of the Kinges remeovyng from
> Westmynstre and of the goodly nombre of barges
> with him.

This joyefull Thursday folowith a Fryday of buysynes and
labour mengilled also with goodly pleasures and greate rialtie,   665
in whoes fornon the Kinges officers of Houssold imbuysid
themself in all their deligens and pouer to trusse and stuffe ther
fol.60ᵛgreat and huge standardes, coffers, / chestes, clothe sakkes,
with all othir vesselles of conveyaunce, every officer with such
thinges as he hadde in his governaunce and ruele, and this sent   670
forthe both by many cartes and chariattes by land, and also in

652   a rewby] *written over an erasure R.*
666   Houssold imbuysid] *the following words cancelled between* Houssold *and*
imbuysid: as of the tresurey wardrop Napery Vyntry Butry pantry cokery
squyler and skelery with all other offices and Rommys of Necessite *R.*

dyvers botes and wherys by watir, for the Kinges Grace is
remeovyng and departure unto his manoir and lodgyng of
Rychemond. Whethir his Highnes thought now aftir this
solempne pleasure to resorte, with his holl and singuler   675
company of gentils and estatis, as unto his oonly chambre and
closett electe, the bright and shynyng sterre of byldyng, the
mirrour and patourne of all places of delyte, commedite, and
pleasure, there entendyng to fenyssh, conclude, and end the
rialties of this moost excellent of this Prince and Princes   680
mariage and weddyng. For whoes convenient and worshepfull
attendaunce, and thus by watir, the ryall conveyng and company in his seid passage were redy present, by the season that
his Highnes and liege servantes hade dynyd, a great and a goodly
nombre of barges, for the moost partie of every lordes in   685
Englond, bothe spirituall and temperall, cheynyd unto the
bridge of Westmynster, as many as might, and the residue
roweng and skymmyng in the rever and Thamys, awaytyng the
Kynges commyng forth. First for the Citie of London there
was the Mayers barge, the Shrevys barge, and Aldremen,   690
dyvers bargez of and for the Craftes of the Cytie, havyng their
standardes and stremers with their connizansis right weell
dekkyd and replenysshed with worshipfull company of the
citezens. Moreover, there were of lordes temperall, as the Duke
of Bokynghames barge, therl of Oxinford is barge, therl of   695
Derbys barge, therl of Northumberlondes barge, therl of
Shrewesbury is barge, therl of Essex and of Kentes barges,
with meny othir noble lordes barges of the realme, the
Bushoppis of Cantirbury and of Yorkes bargez, the bushop of
fol.61ʳWynchestres barge, and many moo of the spiritualte, / the 700
Kynges barge, the Quenys, the Princes, my Lady the Kinges
Moders, the Duke of Yorkes, with the residue right goodly
covered, payntid, and beseen, unto the nombre of iij score
goodly barges or there aboughtes. Furthwith in the aftirnon,
the Kinges Noble Highnes cam downe to the rehersid bridge of   705
Westmynstre made of tymbre, besett with goodly postes with
lyons and dragons and othir beastes and figuris corven, empayntid, and gilte sett uppon their hightes and toppis, and
there His Grace, with his excellent company of lordes and
estates, entrid into his barge and toke the watir, and every othir 710
lord into their barges, savyng such as gave attendaunce unto

672 for the Kinges Grace] for the the kinges grace R.
691 of and for the] of And soe /// the R.
693–4 of the citezens] of the the citezens R.

the Kinges noble person, `as the Lorde Prince, the Duke off
Yorke, the Duke Bukynham,´ and therl of Oxinford, Great
Chamberleyn of Englond, and othir moo, whoes barges were
freite and fillid with their servantes and attendoures. Thes all   715
great nombre of barges, above and beside wherys, brought and
condute the Kynges Magestie and Highnes—with the moost
goodly and pleasaunt myrthe of trumpettes, clarions,
shalmewes, tabers, recorders, and othir dyvers instrumentes, to
whoes noyse uppon the watir hath not been hard the like—unto   720
his londyng and settyng upp at a village callid Mortlake within
a myle or there abought of the rehersid manoir of Richemond.
There his hors, the Quenes, and othir nobles and estates their
horsis mette with them, and so they very late in the silens of the
hevyng were receyved into the seid Richemond with torche   725
light moost worshipfully to the nombre of `iij´ hundred or moo,
borne and holden by gentilmen and Yomen of his Garde, and
thus were pleasauntly brought into that noble lodgyng, wherin
aftir the receytes and compforte of spyces and wynnys
departid every noble unto his reast ande ease.   730

The ixth chaptre: of the huntyng in the Kinges
parke and of the descripcion of the Place of
Rychemont.

fol.61ᵛUppon the Satirday next foloweng in the aftirnon, / the
Kynges Grace lett make redy his hors, and many othir estates,   735
bothe of Englond and of Hispayne, to waite uppon His
Highnes were redy on their horsbakkes and mulis unto a
goodly company, and so cam forth ought of the gates and
entrid the pleasaunt grene and playne bifore the seid gates.
Aftirward the Kinges Highnes ledde the estraungers into his   740
parke adjoynyng unto the rehersid Manoir of Richemond, and
there causid wanlaces to be made and the dere to be brought
abought, and gave the estraungers fre chace with bowe and

713   and] written over an erasure by scribe C, R.
717   condute the] a word has been erased between these two words, leaving a
space; the final -te of condute has been written over part of this erasure R.
726   iij] interlineated above an erasure, perhaps on R.
735   hors] written over a partly erased word now illegible R.
740–55   The scribe of R has written 740–8 (Aftirward ... pleasure) after 748–55
(And ... beholde), but the reviser has indicated the order adopted here by placing
the letters b, A, and C in the margins at the appropriate points in the text.

hownde. And there therl of Hispayne strake a dere with his
crossebowe, and great slaughter was of veneson by the seid   745
estraungers, and brought unto the quarrey. The flesshe therof
the Kinges Grace distributid and `gave´ unto the Espanyardes
to do therwith ther will and pleasure. And when they were
departyng homward, there were Yemen of the Crowne and of
the Kinges Garde with their bowes and arowes, whom the   750
King causid ffirst severally to shote bifore his Grace and the
Hispanyardes presens, and aftir that to shote all toguyders at
oones, to the nombre of xxiiijti or there aboughtes, that their
sharp lances and great strokes of their bowes was right goodly
to beholde.   755

Aftir that, the Kinges Highnes and the rehersid company of
nobles repaired agayn unto the pleasaunt Place of Richemond
biforseid, of thise `great´ comodities, pleasures, and excellent
goodlynes as heraftir in this pusaunt discripcion shall partly
folowe and appiere. That is to sey, this erthly and secunde   760
paradise of oure region of Englond and, as I credeably suppose,
of all the great parte and circuyte of the worlde, the lantirne
spectacle and the bewtyouse examplere of all propir lodgynges,
the Kinges goodly Manoir of Rychemond is sett and bullid
fol.62^r betwene dyvers / highe and pleasaunt mountayns in a vailey 765
and goodly playnys and feldes, where the moost holsom eyerys
and leigher opteyneth ther course and accesse, founded and
erecte uppon the Thamys sid and fresshe ryver, viij mylys
beyond and from the noble Cytie of London. He is quadrat and
iiijor square, girde and emcommpassid with a strong and   770
mighti breke wall of grete lengthe and curious phacion, which
girdell is goodly barred and besett with towres in his eche
corner and angle and also in his mydde wey, of many grece and
stages of height. Is bocles and opynynges `be´ stronge gates of
duple tymbre and hert of oke stikkyd full of nailys right thikke   775
and crossid with barres of iron. Within this rehersid gates there
is a faire large and brode courte, curraunt, arraisid, and bankyd
in the myddys for `the´ rayne flough, havyng his chanelles and
voydauns to observe and kepe him alweyes from soile and
fowlenes. Uppon ich side of this goodly courte there are galeres   780
with many wyndowes full lightsume and commodious; ought
of thes galeres uppon the brikke wallys be dorys and entiryng
into pleasaunt chambers, ostere, and lodgyng of necessitie for
such lordes and men of honour that waytis or els suys unto the
Kinges Grace or Highnes, as well straungers as of his owne   785

746   estraungers] estaungers *R*.   773   corner] con^r *R*.

liege people and subgettes. Within this uttir space and large
courte there is a lesser curtylage peivyd with fyne frestone or
marbill, in whoes myddill there is a conducte and cestirne of
stone iiijor square, craftily made with goodly sprynges and
cokkys rennyng in his iiijor quartirs beneth, that at the will of   790
the drawers of the watir opynnyth and is closid agayn. In the
upper parte there are lyons and rede dragons and othir goodly
beastes; in the myddes certayn branches of redde rosys, owt of
fol.62ᵛthe which floures and rosys is evermore rennyng / and curse of
clene and moost purest watir into the cesterne beneth. This   795
conduite prophitabill servys the chambers with watir for ther
handes and all othir offices as they nede to resorte. The
pleasaunt halle is uppon the right hand of this curtilage, xij or
xviten greces of highte pavid with goodly tille, whoes rof is of
tymber, not beamyd ne brasid but propir knottes, craftly   800
corven, joyned and shett toguyders with mortes and pynned,
hangyng pendaunt from the sede roff into the grownde and
floure, aftir the moost new invencion and crafte, of the pure
practif of gementri, cast owt with wyndowes glasid right
lightsume and goodly. In the wallys and siddys of this halle   805
betwene the wyndowes bethe pictures of the noble kinges of
this realme in their harnes and robis of goolde, as Brute,
Engest, King William Rufus, Kyng Arthur, King Henry—and
many othir of that name—King Richard, Kyng Edward, and of
thoes names many noble waryours and kinges of this riall   810
realme with their fachons and swordes in their handes, visagid
and appieryng like bold and valiaunt knightes, and so their
dedis and actes in the croniclis right evydently bethe shewen
and declared emonge thes nombre of famous kinges. In the
higher parte, uppon the left hond, is the semely picture and   815
personage of our moost excellent and heyghe Suffrayn now
reignyng uppon us, his liege people, Kyng Henry the VIIth, as
worthy that rumme and place with thoes glorious princes as
eny king that ever reigned in this lond, that with his great
manhode and wisdam hath contynued nobly and victorious   820
unto this now the xviijth yere of his reigne. The wallis of this
pleasaunt halle were hongid with riche clothes of Arres, there
werkys representyng many noble batalles and seages, as of
Jerusalem, Troye, Albe, and many other, that this hole appre-
fol.63ʳparement was most glorious and joyefull to considre and /   825
beholde. In the lefte side of the curtilage, above over other like
grees, is the chapell, weell paved, glasid, and hangyd with cloth
of Arres, the body and the quere with cloth of golde and the
autirs sett with many relikkes, juelles, and full riche plate. In

the wallys of this devoute and pleasaunt chapell is picture of   830
kynges of this realme, of thoes whoes lif and vertue was so
abundaunt that it hath pleasid Almighti God to shew by theim
dyvers and many miracles and be recount as sayntes. Thes be
the sayntes: Saint Edward, Kyng Cadwaleder, Seint Edmond,
and many moo right propirly pictured and beseen. In the right   835
side of the chapell is a goodly and a privy closett for the Kyng,
richely hangid with silke and travasse carpet and cusshons for
his noble Grace; the aultier is also hangid and platid with riche
relikes of gold and precious stone; the rofe is celyd and whight
lymyd and chekeryd with tymber losengewise, payntid with   840
colour of asure, havyng betwene every chekir a rede rose of
golde or a portculles. In the othir sid of the chapell othir by the
like closettes for the Quenys Grace, and the Princes, my Lady
the Kynges Modir, with othir estates and gentilwomen. From
the chapell and closettes extendid goodly passages and   845
galaris—payved, glasid, and poyntid, besett with bagges of
gold, as rosis, portculles, and such othir—unto the Kinges
chambers, the first, the secunde, the thirde enhaungyd all thre
with riche and costely clothes of Arras, celid, whight lymyd,
and chekeryd as the closett was bifore discrivyd, with their   850
goodly bay wyndowes glasid sett owte. Dyvers and many moo
goodly chambers there bethe for the Quenys Grace, the Prince
and Princes, my Lady th⟨e⟩ Kinges Mothir, the Duke of
Yorke and Lady Margaret, and all the Kinges noble kynred
and progeny, pleasaunt dauncyng chambers and secret clos-   855
ettes most richely enhaungid, dekkyd, and beseen. Undre and
fol.63ᵛbeside the halle is sett / and ordred the housis of office—the
pantry, buttry, selary, kechon, and squylery—right poletikly
conveyed, and wisely ther coles and fuell in the yardes without
nyghe unto the seid offices; and in the leeft side of this goodly 860
lodgyng under the Kinges wyndowes, Quenes, and othir
estates, moost faire and pleasaunt gardeyns with ryall knottes
aleyed and herbid—many marvelous beastes, as lyons, dragons,
and such othir of dyvers kynde, properly fachyoned and corved
in the grownde, right well sondid and compassid with lede—   865
with many vynys, sedis, and straunge frute right goodly besett,
kept, and norisshid with motche labour and diligens. In the
lougher end of this gardeyn beth pleasaunt galerys and housis
of pleasure to disporte inn at chesse, tables, dise, cardes, bylys,
bowling aleys, buttes for archers, and goodly tenes plays, as   870
well to use the seid plays and disportes as to behold them so

853   Lady the Kinges] *an inkblot obscures* -he *in* the *R.*

disportyng. The tourys of this excellent place were turrettid
and pynnaclid, the hall, chambers, and other offices coverde
and nobly addressid, and uppon everych of them—bothe
penacle and lover—a vane of the Kinges armys payntid and   875
gilte with riche gold and asure in such excedyng guyse and
maner that ass well the pleasaunt sight of theim as the heryng
in a wyndy day was right marvelous to know and undrestond.
This Place of Richemond is neighburd also with ij most
devoute and vertuous housis of religion, the hous of the holy   880
men and wemen uppon the oon side of the ryver callid Syon
Staous and the hous of the monkes of the chertirhous callid
Shene uppon the other sid of the ryver, in the which monastirs
and places of religion is every houre of the nyght and day made
to Almighti God solempne prayours and peticions. Thus in   885
this noble lodgyng the Kinges Magestie with his company this
Satirday at nyght is entrid aftir his huntyng, and there with
moch myrthe and pleasure he reposith all that season.

fol.64^r   / The xth chaptre: of the disportes on the Sonday; of
the disguysyng and voyde and of the great gieftes of   890
plate and treasure unto the Espaynyardes at ther
departyng.

In the Sunday ensueng: the duetie of the religion of Cristom-
dome is that the service and worship of God shulde `be´ above
all `othir´ thynges worldly especially maynteyned, and so verily   895
it was, aftir the moost excellent solempnite abought the honour
of Almighti God, with prikkyd songe and organs and goodly
seremonys in the quere and aultirs, and thus `was´ the fornoon
expendid holily and with great vertue. In the aftirnon the
Kinges Highnes yede with a right pleasaunt company of gentils   900
and estates thorugh his goodly gardeyns lately rehersid unto his
galery uppon the walles, apreparyd pleasuntly for his Highnes,
and certayn burdes there redy sett: summe with chessis,
summe with tables, byles, dice, cardes, the place of buttes redy
for archers, bowlyng aleys, and othir goodly and pleasaunt   905
disportes for every person as they wolde chose and desire.
Uppon the owtside of the wallis directly undre the wyndowes
were barres and voyde spaces for justes. Also there was sett
uppe and arraysid ij highe and great postes with crochis, these
postes fast sett and dryvyn in the grownd. Over the crochis was   910

895   worldly] wordly R.

a great kabill stretchid stedfastly and drawen with a whele and
stayd uppon bothe the siddes with dyvers cordes so that the
sight of yt was like unto the ryggyng of an hous. Uppon thys
frame and kabill ascendid and went upp an Hispaynyard, the
which shewed there many wonders and delyverous poyntes of   915
tumblyng and dauncyng and othir slayghtes. First, he went
fol.64ᵛupp unto the frame, and a certayn stay in his / hand, to the
nombre of xlti fote, summwhat aslope, and when he cam to the
hight left his stay and went uppon the cabill—sumtyme on
patens, sumtyme with tenes ballys, sumtyme with `feters of`   920
iron, dauncyng with belles, and lepyng many leapys uppon the
seid cabill bothe forward and bakward. He played sumtyme
with a sword and a bukler. Eftson he cast himsilf sodenly from
the rope and hang by the tooes, summtyme by the teethe moost
marvelously, and with grettest sleighte and cunnyng that eny   925
man cowde possibly excercise or do. Aftir thes longe beholdyng
of the delyvernes and poyntes with othir goodly disportes, the
Kynges Grace and noble company entrid agayn thorugh thes
pleasaunt gardeyns his rehersid lodgyng of Richemond unto
evynsong and so unto his soper. Agaynst that His Grace hade   930
supped, the goodly hall was addressid and goodly beseen and a
riall cupbord sett theruppon in a bay wyndow of ix or x stages
and haunces of hight, furnysshid and fullfillid with riche and
goodly plate of gold and of silver and gilte. And in the upper
parte of the hall a cloth of gold, carpettes, and cusshons for the 935
Kinges Noble Mageste, whether, when that His Grace was
cumme and his wilbeloved company of nobles, entrid inn a
pleasaunt disguysing conveyed and shewyd by a glorious trone
or a tabernacle mad like a goodly chapell `fenestred` full of
lightes and brightnes. Within this pagant and tabernacle was   940
anothir stondyng cupbord of riche and costely plate to great
substaunce and quantite. Thes trone and pagant was of ij
storys, in whoes lougher were viij goodly disguysid lordes,
knightes, and men of honour, and in the upper story and
particion viij othir fresshe ladies moost straungely disguisid   945
and aftir moost pleasure`full` maner. Thus when this goodly
werk was approchid unto the Kinges presens and sight—
`dravyn and conveyd uppone whelys by iij woddosys, ij befor
and one behynd, and one eyther `syde` off the sayde trone ij
mermaydes, one off them a man myrmayde thother a woman,   950
the man in harnesse from the wast uppeward, and in every off

942   Thes trone] stre *cancelled between* thes *and* trone R.
949   trone] hone R.

the sayde mermaydes a Chyld off the Chapell syngyng ryght
suetly and with quaint armoney´—descendid thes viij pleasaunt, disguysid, galauntes men of honour, and bifore ther
fol.65ʳcomyng forth / they cast ought many quyk conys, the which   955
ran abought the halle and made very great disporte. Aftir, they
dauncyd dyvers goodly daunces, and furthwith cam doun the
viij disguysid ladies, and in ther apparaunce they lete fle many
whight dowys `and berdis´ that flew abought the hall, and great
laughter and disporte `they made´. Thise lordes and ladies   960
copled toguyder and dauncid a longe season many courtly
roundes and pleasaunt daunces. Aftir that therl of Hispayne
and a lady of the same contreth dauncid two bace daunces and
yed upp ageyn. Aftir this cam in a voyde of goodly spices and
wynn brought by a great nombre of erlis, barons, and knightes   965
to a great company as hit hath ben declared in voydes before.
This present day tharchebushop of Hispayne, the Bushop,
therl, and his brothir made their repastes severally, every oon
of them in their owne chambers and lodgynges, and they had
cupbordes made unto them of the Kinges plate and treasure   970
right goodly and riche—tharchebushop is cupbord to the
somme and value of vj or vij hundrid mark, the bushopis unto
the value of v hundrid, therl is v hundrid, therl is brothir iij
hundrid—the which all plate and treasure the Kinges goodnes
bountuously gaf clerly unto everich of theim, as unto them they   975
were made with most noble wordes and thankes of their great
diligens, labour, and peyne that they hade with his noble
Doughter-in-the-Lawe suffryd and abedyn. And thus was this
moost joyefull day endid and expiryd, and the worthy nobles
departid to their reaste.   980

The xjth chapture: of the departyng of the Hispaynyardes, and of the Prince remeovyng into Wales,
and of his dissease and sekernes.

fol.65ᵛUppon the Monday folowyng, the Hispaynyardes, aftir / that
they had dynnyd, toke ther leve of the Kinges Grace, the   985
Quene, my Lord Prince, my Lady the Kynges Modir, of
dyvers other of the nobles of Englond bothe spirituall and
temperall, toke their levys also of their owne and noble Princes
now of Englond and Hispayne with the moost goodly maner,
behavour, reverens, and obediens, havyng with them many   990

959   and berdis] *added in right margin R.*

honourable lettres and messages from the Kynges Highnes, the
Quene, the Prince, the Princes, unto their Highe Suffrayn of
Hispayne, with many goodly bokys, pictures, and examples of
this moost excellent receyte and fynall conclucion of mariage,
with his hooll commodite solempnities, and apperteynnaunce   995
exhibet and hadde of the behalve of the Realme of Englond in
the premissid matier. And thus the Archebushop of Hispayne
spede him to his havyn and shippyng to Suthampton, therl to
Dover and so to Caleis, and every othir to their moost spedefull
and next departure. To whom the Kinges gracious wisdam of   1000
his provicion singuler committid and delyvered his patentes
enseasid for their liberall and fre pasport thorugh his hooll
realme by every citie, towne, and village without distrobill,
enserchyng, or eny othir vexable demaundes of his liege
people, by whom they thus shuld passe or convey, as well for   1005
their owne persons as for their cariage and assporture of greate
seid giftes, reward, and treasure. Yit was there assignid and
lefte unto the Lady Princes at her desire and the Kinges
pleasure and will a great nombre bothe spirituall and temperall,
and also ladies and gentilwomen of Hispayne to be with her   1010
officers and servantes and to wayte uppon her Grace for
compforte and solas. Nevertheles, as nature, kyend, and maner
fol.66ʳ woll often tyme / be disposid peynfully and with great hevynes
to bere and suffre the departyng of frenship and company—
especially in such wise `and´ maner as thes nobles truely and   1015
[with] m⟨uc⟩h diligens hade usid theimself towardes and
ageynst this their goodly Princes and Mastres wherupon she
was partly annoyd and pensif of their seid myss and absens—
the which assone as the Kinges grace and goodnes hade
apperceyved and knowen, he curtesly lete desire and calle unto   1020
him the Princes and her ladies with dyvers ladies of Englond
and brought them to a lybrary of is, wherin he shewed unto her
many goodly pleasaunt bokes of werkes full delitfull, sage,
mery, and also right cunnyng, bothe in Laten and in Englisse.
Yit over this, to augment and encrease gladdes, mytigat   1025
sorowe, refresshe and compforte the sperites of her, hes
prudent Highnes had ordeigned and provydid there a jueller
with many rynges with precious stonys and houges dimysentes
and juelles of moost goodly fachion—they beyng every oon of

---

997   premissid] pʳmssid R.   1004   or] *written over an erased* and R.
1013   tyme be disposid] be disposyd *cancelled after* tyme *at end of fol. 65ᵛ R.*
1016   with much] *a blot has made one or two words illegible R*; with much
V25.

them of moche riches and treasure—and there desired her to   1030
overse them and beholde them well, and aftir that to chose of
them oon such as likyd her best. And aftir that she had chosen
and electe at her pleasure, for her sake every lady of Hispayne
with her hade their severall eleccions, and the residue was
distributid and geven to the ladies of Englond. And thus with   1035
this pleasures and othir disportes and commodities, she summwhat asslakyd her hevynes and drew herself unto the maner,
guyse, and usages of Englond with her moost dere and lovyng
husbond, the noble Prince Arthur, with her reverent and
wilbeloved ffadir-in-the-lawe, Henry the vijth, by the grace of   1040
God Kyng of Englond and of Fraunce and Lord of Irlond, and
fol.66ᵛElizabeth his noble / Quene and wief, her moder. And whereas
of aunncyent and rightuusse title have laudably `be´ usid and
be accustomed the kynges of this oure noble Realme of
Englond in their ediccions, proclamacions, and of their   1045
dominyons and lymytes of the londes and emper the opyn
expressions to calle and name them Kynges of Englond and of
Fraunce, Lordes of Irlond, and Prince of Wales; therupon to
ther princes and heires of their bodies succedyng and laufully
and procreat they have dyvydid, assigned, and of congruens   1050
impartid to ther seid prince and heires the rehersid principacion, rule, and proventes of the hole contreth and partyse
of Walys, to the mayntenaunce of their houssold and honour;
in the which maner and suffraunce oure present noble Kyng
and Soveraigne Henry the VIJth to his worthy Prince Arthure   1055
hadde clerely the seid londes of Walys remysid and uppyeldon;
which, aftir this accomplement and end of this mariage and
noble solempnities in this boke lately declared—callyng unto
him many and dyvers of the great and well-lernyd persons in
the lawes bothe spirituall and temperall for the entent of good   1060
and sober ruele and guydyng to be kept and observed, dyvers
also gentilmen of the realme for is honour and estate—departid
from the Kinges Highnes is father with his goodly Lady and
wief, the Lady Kateryn of Hispayn, unto the seid contreth of
Walys, governyng the seid contreth moost discretly and aftir   1065
moost and rightuous ordre and wisdam. And there he nobly
contynued, to the great compfort and gladnes of the commons,
uppholdyng and defendyng the pore and rightfull quarelles,
fol.67ʳrepressyng malice and unleafull dispocicion, / amplifieng and

encreasing the lawes and the service of Almighti God, from the   1070
Fest of the Natyvite of Criste in the yer biforeseid unto the
solempne Feste of the Resurrection, at the which season grue
and encreased uppon his body, whethir it were by surfett or by
cause naturall, a lamentable and—ne, the pleasure of God wer
hever to be paciently takyn and suffrid—the moost petifull   1075
disease and sikenes, that with so sore and great violens hedde
batillid and dryven in the singler partise of him inward; that
cruell and fervent enemye of nature, the dedly corupcion, did
uttirly venquysshe and overcome the pure and frendfull blod,
without almaner of phisicall help and remedy. Thus the lyvely   1080
spirites of this noble Prince finally mortified, to oure Realme of
Englond and all Cristente dolour, sorow, and great discomp-
fort. Thus by course and ordre approching thoure and
instaunt of his departure, with the moost hoole and discrete
myend, levyng and comyttyng is cors to the seremonys of the   1085
interment and burylles in therthe, aftir the custome of the
Chirche of God, [he] gave and uppyeldid with the moste
humble devocion his speryte and soule to the pleasure and
hondes of Almighti God.

1082   dolour, sorow,] and *cancelled between* dolour *and* sorow R.

[BOOK 5]

/ The furst chaptre of the vth booke: conteynyng the manour hough the Kinges Grace and Quenys were certified of the dethe of his wil-beloved son.

In the yer of oure Lord God a thousand fyve hundrd and two, the secunde day of Aprill, in the Castell of Ludlowe disseacid   5
Prince Arthure, ffurst begoten son of our Soveraigne Lord King Henry the VIJth the xvijth yer of his reigne. Immediatly aftir whoes dethe Sir Richard Pole, his Chamberleyn, with othir of his counseill, wrott and sent lettres to the Kingez Counsell to Grenewich where His Grace and the Quenes lay,   10
and certified theim of the Princes departyng; which discretly sent for the Kinges goostly fadre, a Frere Observant, to whom they shewed this moost sorowfull and hevy tydynges, and desired him in his best maner to shewe hit to the Kyng; which, in the mornyng the Tuesday then folowyng somewhat bifore   15
the tyme accustomed, knokkyd at the Kinges chambre dore, and whan the Kyng undrestod hit was his confessour, he commaundid to lete him inn, which confessour commaundid all thoes there present to voyde, and aftir due salutacion began to sey: *Si bona de manu dei suscipimus mala autem*   20
quare non sustineamus, and so shewed His Grace that his darrest son was departid to God. And whan His Grace undrestod that sorowfull and hevy tydynges, [he] sent for the Quene, sayng that he and his Quene wolde take the peynfull sorowes toguyders. And aftir that she was commyn and sawe   25
the Kyng hir lord and husband in that naturall and peynfull sorowe—as I harde sey—that `with´ full, great, and constant confortable wordes [she] besought His Grace that `he´ wolde furst, aftir God, remembre the wellith of his owne noble

---

1 fol. 68^r] *the last third of fol. 67^r and all of fol. 67^v are blank R.*
1–3 The furst chaptre ... wil-beloved son.] *om. A.*
8 dethe] dissese *A.*   8–9 with othir of his counseill] *om. A.*
10 Quenes] quene *A.*   12 a Frere Observant] *om. A.*
13 moost sorowfull and hevy] heuy & soroufull *A.*
15 Tuesday then folowyng] tewesday next folowyng *A.*
17 he] *A, om. R.*   18–9 commaundid ... voyde, and] *om. A.*
22 darrest] derist *A.*   23 and hevy] *A,* hevy *R.*
27 with full, great] with great *A.*

person, the compfort of his realme and of hir, and how that my   30
fol.68ᵛLady / his Moder hade never noo moo children but him oonly,
and that God by His Grace hade ever preservyd him and
brought him where that he was, over that howe God had lent
them yet a faire, goodly, and a towardly yong Prince and two
faire Princessis, and over that, God is where He was, and we   35
bothe yonge inough, and that the prudence and wisdam of His
Grace spronge over all Cristendome, so that hit `shulde´ please
him to take this accordyng therunto. Than the Kyng thanked
her of hir good compfort, and aftir that she was departid and
commyn to hir owne chambre, naturall and modirly remem-   40
braunce of that great losse smote hir so sorowfull to the hert
that thoes that were abought her were fayn to send for the
Kyng to compforte her. And than His Grace of true, gentill,
and feithfull love in good hast came and relyved her, and
shewed her howe wise counseill she had geven him bifore, and   45
he for his parte wolde thanke God of his sondes, and wolde she
shulde do in like wise.

The secunde chaptre: hough the cors was buryed
and what ordinaunce was therabowt.

The corps was boulid and weell bamed and sered and con-   50
venyently dressid with spices and othir swete stuf such as thoes
as bare the charge therof cowde purvey and that hit might be
furnysshed of, and was so sufficiently doon that it nedid noo
leed but was chestyd, which cheste was covered with a good
blak clothe cloos sewed to the same with a whight cros and   55
sufficient rynges of iron to the same, and thus leyed in his

32–3   and brought him] om. A.
33   he was] he is A.   33–4   lent them] lent hym A.
34   a faire, goodly, and a towardly yong] A, a faire goodly R.
34–5   and two faire Princessis] A, two faire Princes R.
35   and over that] and how A.   37   spronge] sparng A.   37   please] like A.
40   naturall and modirly] Nature and motherly A.
43–4   gentill, and feithfull] faithfull & Jentyll A.
46   of his sondes] of his handys A.   47   in like wise] the same A.
48–9   chapter title om. A.   50   boulid] bowellyd A.
50   bamed and] A, om. R.   52   as bare] that hade A.
52   purvey ... might] om. A.   53   of] om. A.
54   but was chestyd] but chested A.
55–6   with a whight ... the same] om. A.

chambre undre a table coveryd with riche clothis of goold,
havyng a rich cros over him, and certeyn candilstikkys of silver
fol.69ʳ over him with tapers of wex brennyng, and iiij other / great
candilstikkes of latone with iiijor great tapers contynually   60
brennyng there. And certayn of his almes folkys of Shere
Thursday immediatly before sate there abowte holdyng torchis
bothe nyght and day, and so thus remaynydde unto the Fest of
Seint Georges day at aftirnon, at which season he was remeovyd to the parisshe chirche in maner that foloweth.   65

Furst the haulle was voydid, and there was ordeigned a tabill
with trostilles into the tyme the procession was redy and come
for the corps to remayn on, which was brought from his
chambre thethir, borne by Yomen of his Chambre undre a
riche clothe of blak clothe of goolde with a cros of whight   70
clothe of goolde. And aftir that the three bushoppis had sensid
the corps and cast holywatir, many noble men sett to their
handes: as the Lord Garrard; the Lord John Grey of Dorzett;
Sir Richard Crofte, Styward of his Hous; Sir William Ovedale,
Countroller of the same; Sir John Mortymer; Sir Walter   75
Baskervile; Sir John Harle; Sir Thomas Cornuall; Sir Richard
de la Bere; Sir Thomas Ingilfeld; and other.

Therl of Surrey, principall morener, in his sloppe and
mantell of blak, havyng his mornenyng hode over his hed,
folowed next the corps; than therlles of Shreuesbury and of   80
Kent with sloppis and hodis only; and the Lord Grey Ruthyn
and the Baron of Dodeley; the Lord Powis and Sir Richard
Pole, the Princes Chamberleyn, in like wise.

fol.69ᵛ   / The thirde chaptre: of thaddressyng and ordre of
the canope and baners, and of the berers of theim.   85

The canope `was´ borne over the corps by Mastir Haward,
Mastir Antony Willughby of Broke, Mastir Ratclif of Fitzwa-
tir, Mastir Seint John.

58 havyng] *A, om. R.*   58–60 of silver ... great candilstikkes] *om. A.*
61 And] *A,* And a *R.*   63 thus] this *A.*   63 unto the Fest of] into *A.*
67 the tyme the procession was] the tyme procession was *R,* tyme the
procession were *A.*
70 riche clothe of blak clothe of goolde] riche blake clothe off gold *A.*
71 three] there *R,* iij *A.*   75 Countroller] Comptroller *A.*
76 Harle] Arle *A.*   80 therlles] *A,* therl *R.*
81 and the Lord] The Lord *A.*
83 wise] maners *A.*   83 the Princes] his *A.*
86 the corps] hym *A.*   86 Mastir Haward] Mʳ *[blank in MS]* haward *A.*
                                              84–5 *chapter title om. A.*

At every corner of the canope a baner: furst, a baner of the
Trinyte borne by Thomas Troys; the secunde, a baner of the   90
Patible born by Sir Thomas Blount; the thirde baner of Oure
Lady borne by Thomas Dodley; the fourte baner of Seint
George borne by Edward Hungerford.

Next bifore the corps, a baner of the Princes owne armes,
borne by Sir Griffith vap Sir Ris; on every sid of him, an officer   95
of armes.

Before theim two Spanyardes, of the best belongyng to the
Princes; before them the Purservantes; then `the´ bushoppis,
abbottes, and priours; bifore them the parsone and all the
seculer preistes of that towne; and bifore theim the two ordres   100
of ffreers of that town, havyng the gentilmen bifore them. And
on every side of the procession and so bakward toward the
corps iiijor score pore men in blak mornenyng abites, `beryng´
iiijor score new brennyng torchis besides all the torchis of the
towne. And [it] was conveyed into the quere of the parissh   105
chirch, there where was but a light herse, abowte the which
fol.70ʳ were / ordeigned certayn stolys for moreners coveryd with blak
clothe, which aftirward thofficers of armes toke for their fee.

The iiijte chaptre: of the dirige and solempne
Massis, and of the offeryng at theim.   110

Than began the dirige, and an officer of armes in a highe voyce
began at the quere dore, 'for Prince Arthur soule and all
Cristen soulys, Pater Noster &c'. Than the Bushop of Lincolne

91   thirde baner] iijde a banʳ A.
92   the fourte baner] and the iiijth A Baner A.
97   two Spanyardes, of the best] ij of the best spanyardes of the best A.
98   before them] and so A.   98   then] om. A.
100 that towne; and bifore] the towne byfore A.
100 ordres] A, ordre R.
101 of ffreers of that town] of the freers of the towne A.
101-2   And on every] On evʳy A; A begins a new paragraph with these words.
102 bakward toward] bakwardes towardes A.   103   blak] om. A.
104 new brennyng torchis besides] A, new torchis beside R.
105 the parissh] that parishe A.
107 for moreners] for the morenars A.   108   aftirward] after A.
108 fee] fees A.   109-110   om. A.
110 at theim] a word has been cancelled between these two words in R.
111-2   in a highe voyce began] om. A.   112   dore] om. A.
113 Pater Noster &c.] A, Pater Noster R.   113   Than] om. A.

sange *Placebo*; the Bushoppes of Lincolne, Salisbury, and
Chestre red the thre lessons. And whan the dirige was doone,   115
all the lordes, knightes, officers of armes, and othir gentilmen
accompanyed the seid morenars to the castell. That nyght and
every nyght before and after were ordeynid goodly watchys.

On the morne the Bushop of Chestre song Oure Lady
Masse, which was songe with children and priked songe with   120
orgons. At that Masse noo man offerid but therl of Surrey as
chief morner, and all the oder morners and officers of armes
accompanyd him, and he hade bothe carpet and cusshyn. Sir
William Ovedale, knyght and countroller of the seid Princes
hous, gave him his offeryng, which was a pece of golde of xl d.   125
And alweyes, as often as the seid Erl offrid the Masse penys, a
gentilman of his owen bare his trayne.

Then the ijde masse of the Trinyte `was´ songon by the
Bushop of Salisbury and the quere without organs or children.
And at that Masse therl of Surrey offred a pece of golde of v s.   130
for the Masse peny, accompaned as before.

fol.70ᵛ   / The iijde masse `was´ of Requiem, songen by the Bushop of
Lincolne. At that Masse offred ffurst therl of Surrey a noble for
the Masse peny, accompanyed as bifore rehersid; then therlles
of Shrewisbury and of Kent, but they had noo carpett nor   135
cusshon; then the Lord Grey Ruthyn and the Baron of Dodley;
then the Lord Powys and Sir Richard Pole; then the Lord
Garrard and the Lord John Grey of Dorzet; then thambassatour of Hispayne, called Don Peter de Yeaule, and therl of
Surrey offrid for themself, and then they bare ther owne   140

114   sange] began *A*.   115   the dirige] dirige *A*.
116   officers of armes] *om. A*.
117–8   and every nyght … watchys] *A*, there was ordeigned A goodly watche
R.   120   was songe with] was with *A*.
120–1   children and priked songe with orgons] children prike song & organs
A.   121   noo man offerid] offred no man *A*.   122   chief morner] chieff *A*.
122   officers] thofficers *A*.   124   knyght and] *A*, *om. R*.
124   Princes] *A*, prince *R*.   125   gave] gaue gave *A*.
126–7   as often … his trayne] the said erlles trayne was borne by a gentilman
of his owne *A*.   128   Then the ijde] The ijde *A*.
128   was songon] songon *A*.   130   And] *om. A*.   130   of v s.] *A*, vos *R*.
132   `was´] *om. A*.   133   ffurst] *A*, *om. R*.   135   of Kent] *A*, Kent *R*.
136   Lord Grey Ruthyn] *A*, Lord Ruthyn *R*.
136   Baron of Dodley] lord dodeley *A*.
138   Lord John Grey] lord grey *A*.
138–9   thambassatour] *A*, thambassadours *R*.
139   called] *A*, *om. R*.   140   offrid for themself] for hym selff *A*.
140–1   then they bare ther owne offringes] then he bare his owne offryng *A*.

offringes; aftir them all noble banerettes, bachelers, and noble
people in great nombre; aftir them the bailiffes and all burges
of that towne.

That offeryng doon, Doctor Edenham, amoner and confes-
sour of the seid Prince, seid a noble sermon and toke to his   145
antetyme, *Beati mortui qui in Domino moriuntur*; that
seid and don, he went to the dole and gave every poore man
and woman a grote. At that Masse, thabbot of Shrewsbury was
gospeller, and thabbot of Borey, epistoler, and whan Masse was
doon, the lordes as before went to dyner to the castell. That   150
nyght at Dirige was non of the lordes, but the Bisshop of
Chestre did the devyne service. And on the morne thabbot of
Shrwesbury sang by note the masse of requiem, and at that
masse the Lord Grey offrid a noble for the masse peny in
thabsens of therll off Surrey.   155

The vth chaptre: of the appreparyng of the chare,
horsis, and clothes abought the corps.

fol.71ʳThe riche chare was prepared in maner as / ensuyth: drawyn
with vj horsis, trappid with blak cloth, havyng riche scochyns
of gold betyn on bokeram and iij chariet men in mornyng abite,   160
the baylys of the chare coverd with blak velvet and the siddes
of the same; over the chare a clothe of blak velvet with a cros of
whight clothe of golde.

141   all noble banerettes] all other banerettes *A*.
141–2   noble people] noble men *A*.   142   bailiffes] bayly *A*.
142   burges] the burges *A*.   144   Edenham] Ednham *R*, Ednam *A*.
145   noble] notable *A*.   147   to the dole] to dole *A*.   148   was] *A, om. R.*
149   Borey] borsey *A*.   150   as before] *A, om. R.*
150   went to dyner to the castell] went to the Castell to dyner *A*.
151   at Dirige was] to dirige came *A*.
151–2   the Bisshop of Chestre did] *A*, they did *R; in R, a blank space ⅔ line
long separates* did *from* they.   152   And] *om. A.*
152–5   on the morne ... therll off Surrey] *A*, on the morn the lord of
Shrewsbury offrid A noble for the masse peny in the absence of therl of Surrey,
which masse was song by Note by thabbot of Shrewsbury *R*.
156–7   The vth chaptre ... the corps] *om. A.*
158   The riche] Then the ryche *A*.
158   prepared in maner as ensuyth] ordeynyd as ensuythe *A*.
160   betyn on] beten vppon *A; in A*, wᵗ vj horsys *has been cancelled between*
beten *and* vppon.
161–2   of the chare coverd with blak velvet and the siddes of the same] & the
sides of the chare couerid with blake veluet *A*.

Item, there was ordeiyned an other clothe of fyne blak to cover that clothe from duste and the wethir, with a cros of   165
whight damaske; and in the fowle whether a cered cloth over all the chest, with the corps in the chare covered with riche blake clothe of golde before spokyn of. All the mornars did folowe the chare with mornyng hodes over ther hedes; at every corner of the chare, a baner borne by noble men. Thorugh the townys   170
there and by all the wey, ij noble men went on every sid of the draught horsis with mornyng hodes over their hedis.

Next bifor the fore hors, Sir Griffith vap Sir Ris in mornyng abitt rode on a courser trappid with blak, with a litill scochyn on the coursers forhed (and so hade the fore hors of the   175
draught and noo moo on the forhede) bering the Princes baner. And the bushoppis rode bifore that baner, and other gentilmene byfore theim in good maner.

The vjth captre: of the nombre of torchis and torche beris, and the observans at Ludlowe of dirige and   180
Massys.

In goodly wise there were ordeigned vj^{xx} torch berers, wherof iiij^{xx} bare torchis brennyng thorough Ludlowe and oder townes by the wey and thothir xlti to support them. And when
fol.71^{v}they were in the feld, they were put owte, all / savyng xxiiijti   185
abowte the chare. Thofficers of armes and the sergeantes of armes rode aboute the baner, and so bakward as was the maner.

164   an other clothe] A clothe *A.*
165   that clothe from duste] that oder clothe for the duste *A.*
165   and the wethir] *om. A.*
166–8   in the fowle whether ... before spokyn of] & ou^r all in the foule weder a serid clothe All the chest with the corps in the chare was coueryd with the Riche clothe of gold before spokyn off *A.*
169   chare with mornyng hodes] corps ther hodes *A.*
169–72   at every corner ... over their hedis] *om. A.*
174   with blak] in blake like thodir *A.*
175   the coursers] *A,* that courser *R.*
175–7   (and so hade ... the Bushoppis] beryng the princes baner Item a nother litill scochyn on the fore horsse hede of the draught of the princes armes—Item the bisshops *A.*
179–81   The vjth captre ... and Massys] *om. A.*
182   In goodly wise] *A, om. R.*   183   bare] *om. A.*
183–4   oder townes by the wey] *A, om. R.*
185   savyng xxiiijti] sauyng a xxiiijti *A.*
186   armes and the] *A,* Armes the *R.*   187   aboute] *A, om. R.*
187   as was] & was *RA.*

On Seint Markes day, from Ludlow to Beaudly, `was´ the
foulist, caulde, wyndy, and rayny day and the werst wey that I   190
have seen—ye, and in some place fayne to take oxen to drawe
the chare, so ill was the wey. And as sone as he was in the
chapell of Beaudley there, and sett in the quere there with such
lightes as might be for that rome, the Dirige began. That done,
the lordes and other went to their dyners, for it was a fastyng   195
daye. And on the morn, therl of Surrey offrid at the Masse of
Requiem a noble for the Masse peny in maner as before, at
which Masse season there was a generall dole of pens of ij pens
to every pore man and woman.

The vijth chaptre: of the noble rewardes that every   200
chirche had of scochyns and money wherin the body
did reast.

Item, at every chirch that the corps remaynyd in were well
furnisshid of scochyns of my lordes armes, bothe of metall and
of colours, and every parissh chirche, or religious place, or   205
ordre that mete the corps by the wey with procession and range
their belles hade a noble of gold, iiijor torchis, and vj scochions
of armes. From Beaudley Sir Richard Croft and Sir William
Ovedall, Styward and Countroller of the Princes House, rode
bifore to Worcestre and suffryd no man, malier, nor othir to   210
entre the gate of that citye into the tyme the corps was come.
And then every thyng was ordred as folowith.

Furst ffresshe scochions were sett on the chare and draught
horsis where nedid, and vj^{xx} new torchis delyvered to the vj^{xx}
torche berers at the townes ende. That day was faire, and then   215

189   Markes] Marquis *A*.
189–93   was the foulist ... chapell of Beaudly there] *om. A.*
193   such] *om. A.*   194   that rome] the Rome *A*.
196   And] *A, om. R.*   196   at the Masse] *A*, at masse *R*.
197   a noble for the Masse peny] *A*, a noble *R*.
197–8   at which Masse season] That masse duryng *A*.
200–2   the vijth chaptre ... did reast] *om. A.*
203   Item, at] *om. A.*   204   of scochyns] with scochyns *A*.
204–5   and of colours] *A*, and colours *R*.
205–6   chirche, or religious place, or ordre] chirche religious place or oder
A.   206   by the wey] *A, om. R.*   210–1   to entre] *A*, entre *R*.
211   into the tyme] in to tyme *A*.   211   come] comyn *A*.
213   Furst] *A, om. R.*   214   horsis] horsse *A*.   214   to the vj^{xx}] to vj^{xx} *A*.
215   at the townes ende] *A*, and at the townes ende *R*.
215   That day was faire] that was a faire day *A*.

the gentilmen ij and ij toguyders and all othir as were bifore
ordred. And than the ordres of ffrers evyn there at the townes
ende censid the corps and then procedid to the gate of that
fol.72ʳcitie, at which gate / were the balliffes and the honest men
of that citie on fote alonge a rowe in every side, and in the   220
myddys the Vicar Generall or Chaunceler of the Bisshopp of that
see with a good nombre of seculer chanons in grey amyces with
riche copys, and othir curates, seculer preistes, clerkes, and
children with surpleces in great nombre, and I suppose all the
torchis of the towne, which went on every sid of the strete   225
before the new torchis, which were all as many as might well
stonde from the towne gate to the great chirche gate. The
gentilmen were conveyed thorugh the strete on the left hand
bifore the chirchyarde, at the whiche gate the iij bushoppis in
riche copis censid the corps, and there was takyn owte of the   230
chare and conveyed undre the canope as bifore with baners and
all seremonies as before. And within the chirche yard were
thabbottes and the Priour with his covent all in pontificalibus,
that is to sey, thabbottes of Gloucestre, Evynsham, Chestre,
Shrewesbury, Towkesbury, Hailes, and Borey; the Priour of   235
Worcestre and of Mecoll Malvarn, with their covent all in
pontificalibus; and thus with procession procedid thorough the
quere to the hersse, which hersse was the goodlist and the best
wrought and garnysshed that ever I sawe.

216–7   were bifore ordred] well before ordeynyd *A*.
217   the ordres] *A*, thordre *R*.   217   of ffrers] off the ffreers *A*.
218–9   of that citie, at which gate] *om. A*.
219–20   and the honest men of that citie] with all the honeste men of the same
A.   220   in every] in on euʳy*A*, on *cancelled between* in *and* euʳy *R*.
220–1   and in the myddys] *A*, *om. R*.
221   Bisshopp] *A*, bushoppis *R*.
222   amyces] *A*, amys *R*.   225   of the strete] the strete *A*.
226–7   which were all as many as might well stonde] which all were as many
as myght stond wele *A*.   227   chirche gate] chirchyerd *A*.
228   gentilmen] gentilmen horses *A*.   228   thorugh] *om. A*.
231   the canope as bifore] a canape before *A*.
232   seremonies as before] *A*, thinges *R*.   232   were] *A*, where *R*.
233–4   thabbottes and the Priour ... thabbottes of Gloucestre] thabbottes
off gloucestre *A*.   234   Chestre] *A*, And chestre *R*.
236–7   with their covent all in pontificalibus] *A*, *om. R*.
238   which hersse] *A*, ˋwhichˊ *R*.
238–9   and the best wrought and garnysshed] *om. A*.

The viij chaptre: of the great nombre of lightes and   240
tapers brennyng abought the herse and the nombre
of berers of the armes, with the hole obsequies and
devyne service.

There `was a´ M^{l}xviij lightes, ij great stondardes, a baner of the
Kynges armes, a baner of the Kinges of Spaynes armes, a baner   245
of the Quenes armes, a baner of the Quenes of Spaynes armes,
a baner of the Prince armes, a baner of the Princes armes, ij of
Walis, oon of Kadwalider, a banroll of Normandy, a banrell of
Gien, a banrell of Cornwall, a banrell of Chestre, a banrell of
Pontew, and a C penselles of dyvers bages.   250

fol.72^v / Also the riche valance and the clothe of magestie `was´ well
frenged. Also the hersse was double railid, covered with blake
clothe and also leied undre footte, which aftir was `the´ fees to
the officers of armes.

At that Dirige was ix lessons aftir the custome of that chirche. 255
The furst was rede by thabbott of Tewkisbury, the ijde by
thabbot of Shrewesbury, the thirde by thabbot of Chestre, the
iiijte by thabbot of Evisham, the vth by thabbot of Gloucestre,
the vjth by the Priour of Worcestre, the vijth by the bushop of
Chestre, the viijth by the Bushop of Salisbury, the ixth by the   260
Bushop of Lincolne. And at the magnificat and benedictus, all
that were in pontificalibus did sence the corps at ons; the same
tyme the Vicar Generall with all the seculers sange dirige in
Oure Lady Chapell.

240–3 The viij chaptre ... and devyne service] *om. A.*
244 There was a M^{l}xviij lightes] few lesse then v^{c}lightes *A; in A, these words*
follow immediately after ever I sawe *in line 239 and without break.*
245–6 a baner of the Kinges of Spaynes armes, a baner of the Quenes armes]
a baner off the quenys armes a ban^r of the kyng off Spaynes armes *A.*
246 Quenes] quene *A.*   247 Prince] p^{r}inces *A.*
247–8 ij of Walis, oon of Kadwalider, a banroll of Normandy] a ban^r of
Normandye / ij banrolles of walis a banroll off cadwallader *A.*
251 the riche valance and the clothe] *A,* riche clothe *R.*
251 was] *om. A;* and *cancelled before* well *R.*
252 Also the hersse was double] *A,* and Also double *R.*
253 which aftir] *a cancellation separates these words in R.*
253 the fees] fee *A.*   255 was] were *A.*   258 vth] *A,* v *R.*
259 vjth] *A,* vj *R.*   259 vijth] *A,* vij *R.*   260 viijth] *A,* viij *R.*
260 ixth] *A,* ix *R.*   261 the magnificat] magnificat *A.*
262 at ons] all at onys *A.*

The ixth captre: of the noble and solempne watche   265
in the nyght, and of the Massis and offeringes in the
mornyng bothe of money and also of the delyvery of
the Princes armour of knighthode.

That nyght there was a goodly watche of lordes, knightes,
squyers, gentilmen usshers, officers of armes, yemen, and   270
many othir.

On the morn by viij of the clok were all the morners redi at
Oure Lady Masse, which was songe by the Bushop of Chestre,
and an abbot the gospeller and a priour episteler, at which
Masse therl of Surrey offrid as bifore at Ludlow.   275

The ijde Masse ʻwasʼ of the Trinite, songen by the Bushop of
Salisbury, at which Masse therl of Surrey offrid as bifore, viz, v
s. for the Masse peny. At that Masse, ij abbottes gospeller and
episteler.

fol.73ʳ   / The third Masse ʻwasʼ of requiem, songen by the Busshop   280
of Lincoln, thabbot of Hailes epistoler, and thabbot of Towkis-
bury gospeller. The maner of thoffryng at that Masse, viz:

Furst the carpet and the cosshen were laid, and all the
mourners, noble men, officers, and sergeantes of armes went
bifore hym to thofferyng of that Mas Peny, and so conveied   285
hym ageyn. Then ij of thofficers of armes delyuerid the riche
braudred cote of armes to therls of Shrewisbury and of Kent,
and they and the sergeantes of armis went bifore theym.
Thofficers of armes delyverd the sheld to the Lord Grey
Ruthen and the Lord Dudley; in like wise the swerd, the   290
pomell forwardes, to the Lord Powes; and Sir Richard Polle
after that, the helm with the crest, to the Lord John Grey of
Dorset. And to the said Sir Richard Polle, then Sir John
Mortymer, baneret, Sir Richard de Labere, baneret, Sir
Thomas Cornwaill and Sir Robert Throgmorton, bachilers,   295

265–8   The ixth captre ... of knighthode] *om. A.*
268   of knighthode] and *cancelled before these words R.*   272   viij] vij *A.*
273   Oure Lady] *an* h *has been cancelled before* oure, *and a virgule has been
cancelled between these words R.*   273   songe] songen *A.*
274   the gospeller] gospeller *A.*   274   which] the which *A.*
277   viz] vz *R, om. A.*   280   was of requiem] *om. A.*
282   viz] *om. A.*   283   the cosshen] cusshyn *A.*
285   bifore hym to thofferyng of that Mas Peny] to thofferyng of that masse
peny before hym *A.*   286   of thofficers] Officers *A.*
286–7   riche braudred cote of armes to] *A,* cotearmure enbraudred unto *R.*
291   pomell] *A,* poynt *R.*   291   Polle] Poole *A.*
293   Polle] Poole *A.*   293   then Sir John] Sir John *A.*

conveid the Man of Armys—which was therl of Kildares son
and heir, callid the Lord Garrard, armed with the Princes owne
harneis on a courser richeley trappid with a trappure of velwet
enbrawdred with nedle werk of the Princes armes, with a pollax
in his hand the hed downward—into the myddes of the quere,   300
where thabbot of Tewkisbury, gospeller of that Masse, receyved thoffryng of that horse, and the said Man of Armes alight
fol.73ᵛand was led / with thax in his hand as bifore to the Busshop by
Sir Richard Crofte, Stuard, and Sir William Owdale, Comptroller, and from thens to the vestry. But to have sene the   305
wepinges when thoffering was done, he had a herd hert that
wept not. That done, the iij Erlis went up toguyder and offred
for themself. There went no officer then bifore theym, nor
carpet ne cusshen after theym. The barons, banerettes, and
bachilers, and all men that wold, savyng those of the cite   310
bicause of the siknes that then reigned emonges them, offred in
Our Lady Chapell to the Vicar Generall, who also kept there iij
solempne Massis.

The x chapter: of thoffring of the palles of clothe of
goold which the lordes mourners offred to the corse,   315
and of dole of money to the poure peple.

All thoffringes of money done, the Lord Powes went to the
qwere dore where ij gentilmen husshers delyverd hym a riche
pall of cloth of goold of tissue which he offred to the corse,
where ij officers of armes receyved it and laid it along the   320
corse. The Lord of Dudley in like maner offred a pall, which
the said officers laid over the corse. The Lord Grey Ruthen
offred another, and everych of the iij erlis offred to the corse iij

---

296   Kildares] kyldare *A*.   300   downward] donwardes *A*.
300   into the myddes of the quere] into the myddes *cancelled between* myddes
and of *R*.   305   vestry] Reuestre *A*.
306   wepinges when thoffering] wepyng when thes Offringes *A*.
307   toguyder] to guyders *A*.   308   officer] officers *A*.
310   and all men] all men *A*.   311   them, offred] them they offrid *A*.
312–3   who also kept there iij solempne Massis] ther which kept also iij
masses *A*.   314–6   The x chapter . . . the poure peple] *om. A*.
317   All thoffringes of money done] all thoffryng of the mony doon *A*.
321   in like maner offred a pall] offred a nother in like wise *A*.
322   over the corse] a crosse ouʳ the Corps *A*.

fol.74ʳpallis of the same / cloth of goold—the lowest erl began fyrst—
which `all´ were laid crosse over the corse.   325

That done, began the sermon said by a noble doctour, which
enduring, there was a great generall dole of grotes to every
pour man and woman.

At tyme of Saynt Johns gospell, Sir Griffith vap Sir Rise
Thomas offred to the Decon the riche enbrawdred baner of my   330
lordes armes.

        The xj chapter: of thensencyng of the corse and
        leyng therof into the grownd, with great
        lamentacion and sorow.

That gospell fynesshid, all the forsaid prelates cam and sensid   335
the corse with all the covent stonding withowt thuttermest
barris, singyng dyvers and meny antems. And at every kirielei-
son an officer of armes with an high voice said, 'for Prince
Arthures sowle and all xpen sowlis, Pater noster &c'. That
fynesshid, a minister of the church toke awey the pallis, and   340
then gentilmen toke up the corse and bare it to the grave at the
sowthe end of the high aulter of that cathedrall churche where
were all the dyvyne services. And then the corse with weping
and sore lamentacion was laid in the grave. The orisons said by
the Busshop of Lincoln, also sore weping, he set the crosse over   345
fol.74ᵛthe chest and cast holiwater / and erth theron. His Officer of
Armes, sore weping, toke of his cote of armes and cast it
alonges over the chest, right lamentably. Then to have sen Sir
William Owdale, Comptroller of his Houshold, sore weping
and criyng, toke the staff of his office by bothe endes and over   350

325   which all] all *cancelled before* which R, which A.
325   crosse] a Crosse A.   326   a noble doctour] mʳ doctoʳ [*space*] A.
326–7   which enduring] at which season A.
327   a great generall dole] a gret dole A.
329   tyme of] *om.* A.   329   vap Sir Rise] A, vap Rise R.
330–1   of my lordes armes] *om.* A.
332–4   The xj chapter ... and sorow] *om.* A.
335   That gospell] which gospell A.   337   barris] barriers A.
338   with an high] in a high A.   339   Pater noster &c] A, patʳ nr R.
343   were all the dyvyne services. And then the corse] after all the deuyne
seremonyes & that the corps A; that *cancelled between* then *and* the R.
344   sore lamentacion] piteous lamentacions A.
345   he set] set A.   346   Officer] officers A.
347   sore weping] *om.* A.   347–8   cast it alonges] leid it a long A.
350   endes and over] the endes & on A.

his own hed brake it and cast it into the grave, and in likewise
did Sir Richard Crofte, Stuard of his Howsold, and cast his
staff broken into the grave, and in likewise did the gentilmen
husshers their roddes. It was a pitious sight, who had sene it.

> The xij chapter: of the proclamacions for dettes that   355
> were owyng by the Prince or eny of his servantes,
> and of the contentacion of them.

All thinges there fynesshid, there was ordeynd a great dyner,
and in the morn a proclamacion made openly in that cite, if eny
man cowd shew eny vitailles onpaid in that contre that had be   360
taken by eny of that noble Princes servantes bifore that day,
they shold com and shew it to the late Steward and
Comptroller and Cooferer, and they shold be contentid.

And thus God have mercy on good Prince Arthures sowle.
Amen.   365

---

351   into the grave] to the graue *A*.
351–3   and in likewise did Sir Richard Crofte, Stuard of his Howsold, and
cast his staff] Sir Richard Croft stward of his housse in likewise cast the staff
A.
353–4   and in likewise did the gentilmen husshers their roddes] & the
gentilmen vsshers ther roddes *A*.   354   who had] whose had *A*.
355–7   The xij chapter ... the contentacion of them] *om. A*.
358–9   a great dyner, and in the morn] a notable dyn^r. And on the morne
after *A*.
359–63   in that cite, if eny man ... they shold be contentid] that yff any
vitailles onpayd in that countre had be takyn by any off that noble princes
seruantes before that day they shuld come & shew it to the late stward and
comptroller & Coferrer & they shuld be content *A*.
364   Arthures] Arthur *A*.

APPENDIX
THE TOURNAMENT CHALLENGES AND SCORE CHEQUE

I. The Buckingham Challenge

This edition of the Duke of Buckingham's tournament cartel (cited as *BC* in the Introduction and Commentary) takes College of Arms, MS M. 3, fols. 24ᵛ–26ᵛ as its copy-text. Although a later copy than the other substantive manuscript, Staffordshire County Record Office, MS D.1721/1/1, fols. 425–7, *M3* represents the text of the cartel that actually governed the performance of the tournament (see Introduction, pp. lxxi–ii). Both manuscripts are of relatively equal textual authority, and variants from the Staffordshire MS (*St*) can often be used to correct errors in the College MS (*M3*). All departures from copy-text, as well as all substantive variants from these texts, are duly noted in the textual apparatus. The French translation of the challenge, British Library, MS Additional 46455, fols. 6ʳ–8ᵛ, also has textual value. Whenever the French text can be used to help decide between variants in *St* and *M3*, the French readings are listed in the textual apparatus.

II. The Suffolk Challenge

Only French versions of this text (cited as *SC* in the Introduction and Commentary) have survived. The two manuscripts, both copied in Calais at the same time from a common original, are of relatively equal textual authority. The version preserved in Archives of Simancas, MS P.R. 54–14, fols. 5–8 (*Sp*), however, is marginally freer of manifest error and is the product of a professional scribe; the version preserved in British Library, MS 46455, fols. 4ʳ–6ʳ (*Cal*) is a hasty transcript made by Henry VII's French Secretary at Calais. As a consequence, this edition uses *Sp* as its copy-text and lists all of the *Cal* variants in the textual apparatus.

III. The Score Cheque

Possibly the oldest English jousting cheque extant, the text is found uniquely in *M3*, fol. 25ᵛ. For a discussion of the method of scoring and the meaning of the various marks, see Sydney Anglo, 'Archives of the English Tournament: Score Cheques and Lists', *Journal of the Society of Archivists*, ii (1960–4), 153–62.

THE BUCKINGHAM CHALLENGE

fol. 24^{v} Here aftir ffolowythe the articles off Justys of
Edward Duc off Bokyngham at the mariage off
Prince Arthur. A⁰ 1501. M^{l}ccccc.j.

Please it Your Highnesse to undrestand that apon knowlege
had off the noble mariage purposyd to be solempnised the xiiij   5
daye of Novembre next ensuyuyng, comyng betwen the right
highe and myghti Prince, your derrest sonne and heyre appa-
rant, the Prince off Wales, and the right noble and excellente
Princesse, the Ladie Katherine, doughter unto the right high,
mighty, and excellent Prince and Princesse, the King and the   10
Quene of Spayne; and forasmoche as the noble and laudable
custome of this your triumphant reame have been in tyme
passed, that at suche high festis and dayes of honour, excersice
and faictes of the necessary discipline of armes have been
shewed to thenabeling of Noblenesse and Chivalrie; therfore   15
oon gentilman, your humble subgict, accumpanyed with iiij
other gentilmen, remembring the grete nombre of nobles as
wel of this youre realme as of other reames and cuntreis likly to
be at the said feast disposed and apte to knyghtly actes, and
being moche desirous and encouraged to doo after their powers   20
that may bee to the honour of the said feast, and ferther to
accomplishe thinges that may be agreable to Your Highnesse,
the Quenes Grace, and to the pleasir of the Prince and Princes,
and of al ladies and gentilwomen (the favoir and licence of
Your Grace furst opteigned), and shal put themselfes in devoir   25

1–3 Here aftir ... A⁰ 1501] The Articles of the Chalenge, at the mariage of
prince Arthure, made by Edwarde duke of Buckingham, earle o⟨f⟩ herford
& northampton & perche, lord of thornbery, breknok holderness a⟨nd⟩
knight of the most noble ordre of the gartar & grea⟨t⟩ constable of
eng⟨land⟩ St; no heading, Cal.
5–6 the xiiij daye of Novembre ... comyng] before thende and laste daie of the
moneth of Septembre nowe next ensuing or nere thervpon St; dauant lafin du
moys de septembre prochain venant ou enuiron Cal.
11 forasmoche as] forasmoche and St; pour ce que Cal.
16 iiij] .vj. St; six Cal.
20 their powers] their power St; leurs puissans Cal.
25 in devoir] endeuo^{r} St; en deuoir Cal.

to shewe and execute the excercise of certain faictes of armes
articulerly hereafter ensuyng.

First the said gentilman, that is to sey the Duc of
Bokingham, accompanyed with iiij other gentilmen, for the
causes above specified, bynd themself to be present at suche   30
day and houre after the said mariage and in suche place as by
fol. 25^r Your Highnesse shal be lymitted, horsed and / armed in helme
and sheld as apperteyneth to Justis Roial, to mete with any
suche gentilman straunger or other, being of iiij lynagis,
as shall list to come and present him in the feld, to recountre vj   35
courses without any rest of avauntage or male engynne on any
part, in the presens of Your Grace, your Commissioner,
deputie, or jugge in that partie, alweyes provided that no
personne not being a gentilman of iiij lynagis, any his offre
natwithstanding, be not receyved to do armes but at the libertie   40
of the said v chalengeours.

Also if any gentilman deffendor shal renne and happen to
misse in al six coursis without atteint, that then he so missing
yeld hym at the grace and pleasir of my Ladie Princesse,
whedir he shal that day do ferther armes or nat. And secondly,   45
if he shal fortune to misse in other six courses, then to submitte
hymself and to be at the pleasir and commaundement of the
Quenes Grace of his any further excercise in faict of armes that
day, onlesse that it be demed by the jugis in that caas ordeyned
to be in the defaute of the horsse. And in semblable wise, the   50
seid chalengeours to observe the contentis of this article for
thair part.

Item, if any of the chalengeours or deffendours shoulde
fortune to be disarmed in any pece, that then he submitte
hymself, and for the restitucion therof or nat at furst or   55

---

29 iiij] .vj. *St*; six *Cal.*
35 as shall list] as shall liste *St*; plaira *Cal*; as list *M3*.
40 at the libertie] at liberty *St*; a la liberte *Cal.*
41 v] vij *St*; *numeral om. Cal.*
44 yeld hym] yelde hymself *St*; se Rende *Cal.*
49 onlesse that it be demed] onlesse then yt maie be demed *St*.
50 of the horsse] of the horse *St*; du chal *Cal*; of his horsse *M3*.
50 And in semblable] and semblable *St*; & en semble *Cal.*
51 the contentis] thes contentis *St*; le contenu *Cal.*
52 part] partes *St*; part *Cal.*
53–4 shoulde fortune] *St*; fortunoit *Cal*; shal fortune *M3*.
55–6 furst or second] firste or seconde *St*; primier ou second *Cal*; furst and
second *M3*.

second tyme, if suche caas shal fall, then to be doon at every tyme in maner as it is comprised in the article before rehersed, wiche is at the pleasure and commaundement of the Quene and my Ladie Princesse.

And ferther for the more honnour to be doon as wel unto this   60
feast as to the pleasir of the King and Quenes Grace, the Prince, Princesse, and al ladies and gentilwomen, the said gentilman, accumpanyed with iiij of his said companye, for the better prouses of him and themself in armes, the iijde day next after unto the furst day of justis, by Your Grace as before to be   65
appointed, or at suche day after as it may like Your Grace tassigne, shal after thair powers endevoir them to execute thes articles ffolowing:

First the said gentilman, accompanied with the foure forsaid, shal present themself at suche houre and place as shal like Your   70
Highnesse, horsed and armed in maner of warre as shal best like hym in oisting harneis, to renne with sharp speres or other at the Kinges pleasirs toguider at oons, three to thre, without tilt in open feld, ij courses ageinst every gentilman of iiij linages as above is specified, of what contre so ever he be of, that shal   75
thesaid day assemble in the feld to answere as a contrepart, and so ffolowingly every of them to be answered iij to iij. And if any of the last defendours ther shal be seen to remain unserved the numbre of iij, yet they shal be served at this faict with as many of the chalengeours evenly as be left of the deffendours, as ij to   80
ij, or oon to oon, or in suche wise as shal please the King.

Item, after this faict of armes in maner here expressed, doon, and accomplished, the seid gentilman, with his iiij chalengeours, with sharpp swerdis, the pointes rebated, shal tourney ageinst every of the said deffendours served in the last faict, iij   85
to three and everi to thair contreparti ffollowingly as before, al maner weyes above the sadel, every gentilman to his most

56–7 doon at every tyme] done ‘of’ hym at euery tyme (with *has been cancelled after* done) *St.*   57 the article] the articles *St*; larticle *Cal.*
61–2 the Prince] and the prince *St*; & au plaisir des prince *Cal.*
63 iiij] fyve *St*; cinq *Cal.*   64 prouses] prase *St*; esprouuer *Cal.*
64 themself] themselfes *St.*
65 the furst day] the furste *St*; le premier Jour *Cal.*
68 articles] exercises of armes *St*; pointz et exercises darmes *Cal.*
69 the foure] .v. *St*; cinq *Cal.*
70 themself] hymself *St.*   74 tilt] taill *St*; lice *Cal.*
82 Item, after] Item that after *St*; Item apres *Cal.*
82 maner here expressed] maner expressed *St.*
83 with his iiij] and his fyve *St*; avec sesdict cinq *Cal.*
86 and everi] and every *St*; & chascun *Cal*; or everi *M3*.

avauntage (the foyne of the swerd expresly to be except) after
the due ordre of armes, until the numbre of x strokes be set
and fully striken, moo or lesse, as shall please the King.   90

fol. 26ʳ   / Item, after this exercise of armes so doon, every parties to
light on fote, and therupon al suche pecis of harneis furst
chaunged and taken as in that caas shal be requisite, the seid
gentilman, with the same foure of his companie, and every of
them shal shewe themselfes at the barriers to be ordeined in the   95
place, and the same to kepe and defende ageinst al commers,
with speres oonly prepayred for that entent; that is to wite,
three to iij or oderwise of like numbre on either parties, and the
said chalengeours to answere their contreparties in defending
the said barriers, that every of them shal have striken xij   100
strokes or elles as many moo or lesse as shal please the Kinges
Highnes.

Item, if it happen (as God forbede) that any of the said
chalengeours be hurt or disarmed in suche wise as for that day
he shal no more renne, in this caas it shal be leful that the said   105
gentilman sette suche another in his place as he shal seme good
for to furnyshe the said actis, so that he be one of the same
nombre and companye furst appointed.

Item, the said gentilman, accompanied with thodir gentil-
men of his companie aforesaid, shal do provide and cause to be   110
brought into the feld and place assigned by the Kinges
Highnes, al maner speres and swerdis necessary for thaccomplishment of the said faict of armes, wiche, furst mesured
and assised by the herauldis, the deffendours shal alweyes have
the choyse of the same.   115

Item, if the said gentilman or any of his companye or thair
countreparties shal happenne to slee oder hors in thexecucion
of any thes actes before expressed, that then he geve unto the
partie whose hors shalbe so slayne an oder as good as that was

88 the foyne ... except] *om. St, Cal.*   90 fully] *om. St, Cal.*
90 moo or lesse ... King] *om. Cal.*
91 this] that *St*; celui *Cal.*   94 foure] fyve *St*; cinq *Cal.*
103 if it happen] if it shall happen *St*; sil advient *Cal.*
106 suche another] *St*; tel autre *Cal*; an oder *M3.*
107 for to furnyshe] to furnishe *St.*
107-8 one of the same nombre] *St*; lun des nomber *Cal*; of the nombre *M3.*
109 thodir] other *St*; les autres *Cal.*
110 and cause] or cause *St.*   111 and place] or place *St.*
113-14 mesured and assised] ouersene measured and assised *St*; benes et
mesures *Cal.*   117 oder] others *St*; autre *Cal.*
118 any thes actes] any of thies actes *St.*   118 unto] to *St.*

by indifferent jugement, or elles the silf same horsse wiche he   120
then shal ride upon.

Item, be it acertaigned that the forsaid gentilman in no caas
hath entreprised these faictes of armes nether of presumpcion,
disdayne, malice, or dispite of any gentilman, but that to
thentent that he may the rather therby achieve thacqueintance   125
of noblenesse and of suche noble men wiche therin have had
ure and desire of the⟨ir⟩ knyghtly courages to encrese ther
honour by such exercise, and wherbi allso he shall inowe do
thyng honorable unto the feast agreable unto the Kinges and
the Quenes grace and acceptable unto the pleasur of my said   130
Lord Prince, my Ladie Princesse, and al ladies and
gentilwomen.

Over this, the said gentilman, by the xxxti day of Octobre
next comyng, wol do set in the place to be appointed by the
King for the said justis iiij trees; wherof oon of most price to be   135
a chery tree highest set betwene the two oder trees, wherof the
oon side to be al white and thodir side holy red of colour; and
the two other trees, wherof oon to be a pyneaple tree to be set
in white colour right ageinst the whiet side of the said chery
tree; and the iijd a pere tree to stand of red colour right ageinst   140
the red side of the said chery tree; and thes iij trees to be
environded and accompased with a pale of bothe the said
colours, wherin a gate of like colour to be made and therat to
hang a bucyne or gret horne. And forasmoche as the same
gentilman and his companye chalengeours shall do hang upon   145
the said chery tree every thair shildes to thende thair suffic-
cance of blood for thentreprise of thes faictes of armes may the
more expresly be knowen; that is to wite, suche as wil kepe the
Justis Roial at the furst day shal do hang thair shildis forsaid on
the white side of that chery tree, and those that will put   150

123 these] the St; ces Cal.
125 that he may] St; quil puisse Cal; he may M3.
128 honour] St; honneur Cal; honours M3.
129–30 Kinges and the Quenes grace] kinges highnes and the quenes grace St;
de la bonne grace du Roy & de la Royne Cal.
130 the pleasur of] om. St, Cal.
131 my Ladie] and my lady St; ma dame Cal.
133 xxxti day of Octobre] furste daie of August St; premier Jour daoust Cal.
139 of the said] St; dudict Cal; of the same M3.
143 and therat] and thereon St.   144 same] said St; Icelui Cal.
146 to thende] St; affin que Cal; to thentent M3.
150 of that chery] of the chere St; decelui cerisier Cal.

themself in devoir to exercise the faictes and discipline of armes
the last day of this chalenge shal do hang thair shildis on the
red side of the said chery tree. Therfore within fortnyght after
the said trees shalbe thus sette in place to be assigned for that
entent at the pleasure of the Kinges Highnesse, that every   155
suche gentilman as of his knyghtly courage, now or in the
meane tyme, shalbe disposed tanswere the furst day of Justis
Roial, in token therof do hang his shilde upon the pyneapul
tree being white of colour; and every suche personne as the last
day of this chalenge wil present hymself tanswere unto al suche   160
faictes of armes as that day in the forsaid articles ar purposed
(with Godes helpe) to be doon, do hang his shilde upon the
pere tree couloured red. And over this, that every gentilman
defendour in that silf day that he shal do his name to be entred
and written and his shild to be hanged upon the tree therto   165
appointed, that then he or some other personne for hym blow
audibly in the said bucyne or gret horne, and therof to have
witnesse if suche shalbe required.

Item, that gentilman or gentilmen straungers reseant in
weward parties, being of noble blood and desirous to do faictes   170
of armes at the said fest, and cannot present his or thair shildes
at the tyme appointed, shal be answered by the said chalengeours during the said fest or within xl dayes after, or elles at
suche tyme as shal please the King.

---

151 in devoir to exercise] indevo^r exercyse *St*; en deuoir de exercer *Cal*.
151 and discipline] and dysceplyne *St*; & discipline *Cal*; and the necessary
discipline *M3*.   151 153 of the said] *St*; dudict *Cal*; of the same *M3*.
156 now or in] nowe is or in *St*.   157 of Justis] at Justis *St*.
158 upon the pyneapul] on the Pyneapple *St*.
160 unto al] to all *St*.   161 ar purposed] as purposde *St*.
166 that then he] that he than *St*.
169 that gentilman or] euery gentilman and *St*; que chascun gentilhomme ou
Cal.

THE SUFFOLK CHALLENGE

fol. 5^r Humblement suplieur a Vostre Tres Excellent Grace. Comme
ainsi soit que conclusion de mariage entre tres hault et excellent
prince vostre ainsne filz et hoir apparent le Prince de Gales, et
la tres excellente Princesse Dame Katherine fille des Roy et
Royne dEspaigne, Dieu devant sera sollempnize environ la fin   5
de cest este prouchain ensuivant. Et en tant aussi que a la
sollempnisacion de telles tryumphantes festes il a este ac-
coustume danciennete pour tous gentilz hommes dhonneur soy
metre en devoir de honnourer toutes telles festes pour lhonneur
du Roy leur souverain seigneur et pour son plaisir comme   10
vaillans chevaliers pour acquerir honneur en faiz darmes cest
assavoir les joustes royalles et le tournoy et autres faiz darmes,
pourquoy nous six gentilz hommes de ceste, vostre tres
honourable court, voz serviteurs domestiques—cest assavoir le
Conte de Suffolk, le Conte de Essex, le Seigneur de Haryngton,   15
le Seigneur Guillaume de Devenshire, Jehan Peche, chevalier,
et Guillaume de la Riviere, escuier—humblement suplions a
Vostre Grace nous octroyer licence dacomplir les faiz darmes
comprins en ces presens articles, lesquelz nous avons intencion
faire pour lhonneur de Vostre Grace et de la feste dessusdite et 20
pour nulle autre cause ne intencion. Suplions a Vostre Grace
donner licence et aussi rendre graces a tous les nobles hommes
qui vouldront soubzscrire leurs noms a leur respondre a ces
articles ensuivans. Et quil plaise a Vostre dite Haulteur commander Garretierre et autres voz officiers darmes de publier en   25
ceste vostre tres honnourable court et en autres places ou il
plaira a Vostre Grace cesdits articles ensuivans.

fol. 5^v / i Premierement lesdits six gentilzhommes se presenteront
le cinq^{me} jour aprez la solempnisacion dicelle feste au palais de
Westmonstier, a telle heure que le Roy le commandera, pour   30
respondre a tous gentilz hommes de nom et darmes de quelque
nacion quilz soient, en tel harnoys comme meilleur leur

---

2 ainsi soit] soit *om. Cal.*   4 la tres] la *om. Cal.*
5 Dieu devant sera sollempnize] sera dieu dauant fait et sollemnize *Cal.*
6 de cest este] d[aou]st este (aou *erased*) *Sp*; decesteste *Cal.*
23 a leur] a nous *Cal.*   31 de nom et darmes] de non et et *Cal.*

semblera nul excepte sinon le grant heaulme et lescu, par ainsi
quil soit franc en la selle sans bricquet ou attache; et a courir
huit cours en la lice avec lances a fers esmoulus ou autres   35
poyntes telles quil plaira au Roy commander et ordonner.

ij Item sainsi est quil sourvienne plus de nobles hommes que
ne pourroient courir ce jour que adonc ung autre jour soit
appoincte au plaisir du Roy. Et sainsi est que tous courent leurs
cours accomplis devant que le jour soit expire que adonc ilz   40
puissent de rechief courir autant de cours comme il plaira au
Roy jusques a ce que le jour soit passe et expire.

iij Item que nul homme ce jour estant en harnoys comme dit
est ne soit servy a cheval ou a pie, maiz que chascun voise
querir sa lance a ung escharfault pour ce ordonne et avec icelle   45
courir jusques a ce que elle soit rompue.

iiij Item sil advient que aucun desdits gentilz hommes de
lune et autre partie ou de toutes deux perde ou laisse cheoir sa
lance dedens huit cours il ne la pourra ravoir arriere sinon au
plaisir de la princesse et des dames, excepte se lun ou lautre   50
perdoit sa dite lance en croisant ou en grande attaincte. Et se
fol. 6ʳ elle est ainsi perdue il la pourra / lun ravoir arriere. Et sil pert
sa lance la seconde foiz dedens lesdis huit cours, ne lun ne
lautre ne la pourra avoir arriere, sinon que ce soit par le
commandement de la Royne et au desir des dames. Et sil pert   55
sa lance la tierce foiz dedens les viij cours dessusdits il ne raura
point sa lance sinon que ce soit par le commandement du Roy
et a lespeciale requeste de celui qui ainsi aura perdu sa lance. Et
sil laisse tumber sa lance la iiij[e] foiz dedens lesdits viij cours il
ne la raura point. Et le non acomplissement desdits viij cours   60
sera mis sur lui et en sa faulte excepte que ce soit en croisant ou
grande actainte comme dit est devant.

v Item sil advient que aucun desdits gentilz hommes soit
blece ou desarme, il sera loisible a lun de ses compaignons de
son parti dacomplir ses cours se celui qui est ainsi blece ou   65
desarme le desire par ung officier darmes. Ou autrement le non
acomplissement desdits viij cours sera mis sur lui et en sa
faulte.

vi Item le vij[e] jour aprez ladite feste, les devantdis six gentilz
hommes se presenteront en ladite place a cheval et en harnoys   70

---

33 sinon] si nom *Cal.*   34 attache] actache *Cal.*   36 et ordonner] *om. Cal.*
38 adonc] adont *Cal.*   38 ung autre] unc autre *Cal.*
40 devant] dauant *Cal.*   46 que elle] quelle *Cal.*
52 ravoir] auoir *Cal.*   52 Et sil] Et se Il *Cal.*   54 avoir] Rauoir *Cal.*
55 desir] plaisir *Cal.*   57 sinon] se non *Cal.*   59 laisse] lesse *Cal.*

comme dit est dessus, et chascun deulx ira querir une espee trenchente ou autre espee au lieu assigne telle quil plaira au Roy commander pour rencontrer quelconque autres gentilz hommes de nom et darmes de quelque nacion quilz soient et tournoier ensembles par couples lun de lun coste et lautre de lautre coste jusques a ce que chascun desdits gentilz hommes / fol. 6ᵛ aura frappe xviij coups avecques lesdits espees audessus de la selle par toutes manieres excepte destoc. Et que lun ne mecte main a lautre.

vij Item sil advient que aucun desdits gentilzhommes de lun ou autre party ou de tous deux perde son espee devant que lesdits xviij coups soient accomplis, il ne la pourra ravoir sinon que ce soit au plaisir de la princesse et des dames. Et sil la pert la seconde foiz, il ne la pourra ravoir sinon que ce soit du commandement de la Royne et a la requeste des dames. Et se tous deux ou lun pert son espee la tierce foiz ilz ne les rauront point sinon que ce soit du commandement du Roy et a lespecialle requeste de celui qui ainsi aura perdu son espee.

viij Item ce tournoy finy, chascun desdits six gentilz hommes monte et arme comme dit est dessus ira querir une lance pointue ou autre telle quil plaira au Roy audit lieu appoincte pour rencontrer tous gentilz hommes de nom et darmes qui vouldront venir de quelque nacion quilz soient et courir ensemble trois cours par couples deux dun coste et deux de lautre coste ainsi que le Roy le commandera sans lice avec leurs dites lances jusques a ce que lune soit rompue. Et saucun deulx laisse cheoir ou perde sa lance il ne la pourra ravoir arriere sinon quil donne a son compaignon qui la rencontre ung dyamant incontinent pour le presenter a sa dame. Et se lun ou fol. 7ʳ tous deux perdent leurs lances a ung cours, chaiscun / deulx pourra ravoir sa lance pourveu que lun en requerre lautre pour lamour de sa dame par ung officier darmes et adonc courir de rechief ensembles.

ix Item de toutes les lances et espees ordonnees par le Roy pour ceste cause, les ceulx de dehors auront tousjours le choix.

x Item sil advient dedens lesdits deux jours que aucun deulx blece le cheval de son compaignon soit avec lance ou espee en sa deffaulte, il lui donnera telle piece de harnoys comme celui quil aura rencontre vouldra choisir quant ilz auront fait. Et sil

92 tous gentilz] tous autres gentilz *Cal.*
92 de nom et darmes] de non et armes *Cal.*
94 ensemble] ensembles *Cal.*
105 les ceulx] les *om. Cal.*

94 dun coste] dlun coste *Cal.*
109 quil aura] qui aura *Cal.*

tue le cheval de son compaignon, celui qui le tuera donnera a   110
lautre le cheval sur lequel il est monte ce jour et le luy delivrera
tout incontinent.

xi Item sauceuns gentilz hommes estrangiers de quelque
nacion quilz soient desirans faire faiz darmes a aucune desdits
joustes ou tournoys devantdit ne pourient bonnement y venir   115
aux jours appoinctez que adonc saucun tel vient a quelque
heure dedens quarante jours aprez ladite feste ilz seront receux
par lesdits six gentilz hommes ez faiz dessusdits a toutes heures
quil plaira au Roy leur commander.

xii Item sil advient que aucun desdits six gentilz hommes   120
chalengeurs soit blece devant que les faiz contenus esdits
articles soient acomplis que adonc les autres gentilz hommes de
sa compaignie qui ne seront point blecez jusques au nombre de
ung acomplisse lesdits faiz.

fol. 7ᵛ   / xiij Item celui qui rompra le plus de lances comment elles   125
doivent estre rompues ait le prix.

xiiij Item quiconque frapera trois foiz a la veue et rompe sez
lances ait le prix.

xv Item quiconque frapera lautre par terre avec son coup de
lance ait le prix.   130

xvj Item quiconque frapera lautre ius hors de la selle ou par
terre homme et cheval ait le prix devant celui qui frape trois
foiz a la veue.

xvij Item celui qui frapera trois foiz a la veue ait le prix
devant celui qui rompt le plus de lances.   135

xviij Item celui qui frapera ung cheval avec la lance nait nul
prix.

xix Item celui qui frapera ung autre quant il a son dos
tourne avec une lance ou quant il est desgarny de sa lance nait
nul prix.   140

xx Item celui qui frapera la lice trois foiz nait nul prix.

xxj Item celui qui mectra hors par deux foiz sa piece de teste
nait nul prix.

xxij Item seront ordonnez et appoinctez certains officiers
darmes, desquelz lun se tiendra en court, lautre a Westmon-   145
stier, et le tiers a lestandart en Chep, pour veoir les noms de
telz nobles hommes comme viendront pour respondre ausdits
six gentilz hommes estre mis en escript esdits articles. Soubz

---

115 devantdit] deuantdis *Cal.*   127–8 sez lances] sa lance *Cal.*
131 ius hors de la selle] hors *om. Cal.*   132 devant] dauant *Cal.*
135 devant] dauant *Cal.*   135 rompt] Rompra *Cal.*
148 mis en escript] mis et escrips *Cal.*

fol. 8^r lesquelles seront deux congnoissances cest assavoir / une rose
vermeille et ung rouge dragon. Et celui ou ceulx qui vouldront   150
courir ledit cinq^e jour escrivent leurs noms dessoubz la rose
vermeille. Et celui ou ceulx qui vouldront respondre ledit vij^e
jour escrivent leurs noms soubz le rouge dragon entrecy et le
premier jour daoust prouchain venant. Excepte les estrangiers,
lesquelz auront tousjours loisir a leur plaisir jusques audit jour   155
de mariage et quarante jours aprez. Et aussi chascun desdits
nobles hommes respondans delivreront audit officier darmes
estant a Westmonstier une targe ou escusson de ses armes pour
estre par icelui officier `darmes´ pendu a ung arbre au palais de
Westmonstier ordonne especialement pour ceste cause. Sur   160
lequel seront les armes dudit Seigneur prince et de la princesse
pour lhonneur et mariage desquelz ceste feste sera tenue. Et les
armes desdits six gentilz hommes lesquelz entreprennent ceste
chalenge seront mises audessoubz desdites armes.

xxiij Item sil y a aucune chose en cesdits articles non   165
entendue ceulx qui les vouldront avoir declarez pourront aler
vers lun desdits officiers darmes et ilz leur monstreront plaine-
ment ce quilz leur en demanderont.

153 soubz] dessoubz *Cal.*   162 desquelz] desquelx *Cal.*
166–7 aler vers] aler enuers *Cal.*

THE SCORE CHEQUE

A⁰ 1501

Chalengeurs

The ffurst daye at the Justes Royall

Answerers

The ffurst daye

The Lord Marquis
Thomas

The Lorde
Henry off
Bokyngham

Therll
of Essex

The Lord
Barnesse

The Lord William
of Devon

Sir Rouland
de Veillevill

Sir John Peche

Mᵈ Sir George Herbert was hurt

Guillam de la
Rivere

Charles Brandon

Phillipp Cronier

Dedo de Azeveido

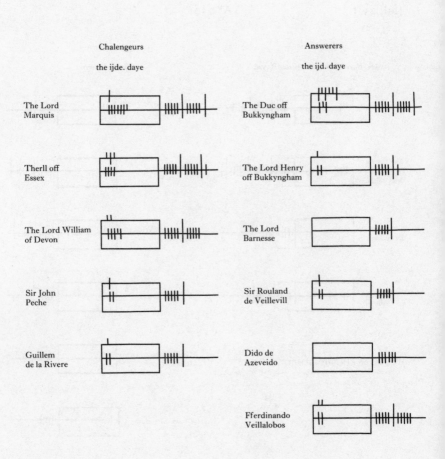

Chalengeurs

the ijde. daye

Answerers

the ijd. daye

The Lord
Marquis

The Duc off
Bukkyngham

Therll off
Essex

The Lord Henry
off Bukkyngham

The Lord William
of Devon

The Lord
Barnesse

Sir John
Peche

Sir Rouland
de Veillevill

Guillem
de la Rivere

Dido de
Azeveido

Fferdinando
Veillalobos

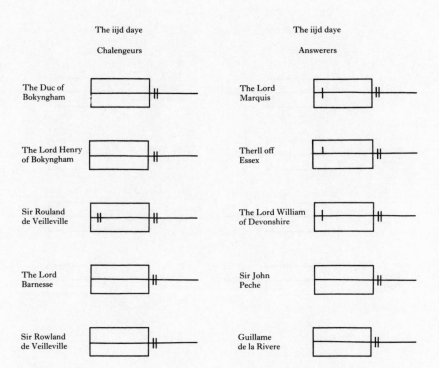

The iijd daye

Chalengeurs

The Duc of
Bokyngham

The Lord Henry
of Bokyngham

Sir Rouland
de Veilleville

The Lord
Barnesse

Sir Rowland
de Veilleville

The iijd daye

Answerers

The Lord
Marquis

Therll off
Essex

The Lord William
of Devonshire

Sir John
Peche

Guillame
de la Rivere

The Lord
Marquis

The Duc
of Bokyngham

Therll of
Essex

The Lord
Henry

The Lord William
of Devonshir

Sir Rowland
de Veilleville

Sir John
Peche

The Lord
Barnesse

COMMENTARY

Prologue

6 *Microcosmus*: Although not as familiar as the cosmic form of the analogy, geographical microcosms are frequently encountered in the Middle Ages and Renaissance. Cf. *Cursor Mundi*, ed. R. Morris, EETS, os lix, 1874, reprtd. 1961, 36–9; Sir Walter Raleigh, *The History of the World*, I.ii.5.

24–7 Cf. Boethius, *De consolatione philosophiae*, II, met. viii.

26–31 For the tripartite division of the earth see Isidore of Seville, *Etymologiarum*, XIV, ii, and Bartholomaeus Anglicus, *De proprietatibus rerum*, trans. John Trevisa, gen. ed. M.C. Seymour (Oxford, 1975), xv, 1.

38–40 *Saynt Austyne named thies people ... nominacion*: A garbled allusion to Bede's story about St Gregory the Great, who inquired about the identity of some fair-complexioned youths that he saw in the slave-market one day. When told they were Angles, he replied, 'non Angli, sed angeli'. Later, upon becoming Pope, he sent St Augustine to convert the English to Christianity (*Ecclesiatical History*, II, i). The story was frequently retold in the Middle Ages (e.g., the *Legenda Aurea*), but St Augustine is never elsewhere credited with being the first to name the English 'angels'.

44–6 *The preceptes of God*: The great commandment, Matthew 22:36–9.

55–6 *Affermyng peax ... necessarie*: An awkward parataxis. The 'sawes and vedutes', not the 'many noble princes', are affirming peace.

64–9 A frequently-cited example of the vanity of ambition. See, for example, Gower, *Confessio Amantis*, iii, 2439–2480, and Shakespeare, *Hamlet*, V.i.135–203

91–2 *This pusant and litle tretes*: By *pusant* the author probably means some form of Fr. *pusil* ('very little') rather than Fr. *puissant* ('powerful', 'mighty'). Cp. 4/759, 'this pusaunt discripcion'. His habitual use of paired, synonymous adjectives throughout the *Receyt* further points in this direction.

Book I

10–2 *Gardie and companye … order and condute*: The author concludes his sentence with a series of clauses modifying *gardie and companye*. They are a company of nobles of that country, they are *lymyted* (appointed) and assigned *to her assistentes* (to her assistance), and they have been appointed that they themselves should order and conduct the journey.

12–6 *Thympacient wiendes … ladie and princesse*: A good example of the writer's habitual practice of interrupting his syntax with qualifying clauses. The author wants to contrast the hopeful expectations of the Princess' voyage to England with its nearly disastrous outcome, so he inserts *fatally ordynate and predestynate* immediately after his mention of *the bifore-desired passage of the said Princesse to the coostes of Englond*. This adjectival phrase interrupts, however, what is in effect a compound prepositional complement, since he means to stress that the passage of the Princess' gifts and dowry, as well as of the Princess herself, were endangered by the storm.

16–24 The Spanish fleet left Corunna on 17 August; four days later a storm overtook it, driving the ships back to the Spanish coast at Laredo. They remained there for nearly a month, refitting lost rigging and topmasts and repairing leaks. They reembarked on 27 September, this time under the guidance of Stephen Brett, a Devonshire pilot sent out by Henry VII to look for the Spaniards. Cf. G.A. Bergenroth, *Calendar of State Papers, Spanish* (London, 1862), i, 246, 258, 261–2, and G. Mattingly, *Catherine of Aragon* (Boston, 1941), 21–2.

21–4 *That unto the rulers … they shold retourne their course*: The confused syntax here results from the curious use of *unto* and from the interruption of the verbal phrase (*was … expediently thought*). The author apparently construes his verb, *was thought*, as a passive, but, oddly, he uses the prep. *unto*, in place of *by*, to identify the agents of the verb: it was thought by the rulers and crafty mariners. Although neither *MED* nor *OED* records *unto* in this sense, the various dative uses of the preposition may have suggested this usage. At the same time, the author also interrupts the verbal phrase by inserting a clause to suggest an unselfish purpose for the sailors' thoughts of returning to their harbours: *moost to thenfreight persones to be savegardid* (i.e., most of all, that the passengers might be safeguarded).

28–9 *They arryved at Plymmouthe ... the west*: The ships were expected at Southampton, which port Queen Isabella considered 'the safest harbour in England' (Bergenroth, *Calendar of State Papers, Spanish*, i, 254). The ships arrived instead at Plymouth, probably because they were under the navigational guidance of Stephen Brett, a Devonshire pilot (above, 1/16–24n). As a consequence, the King had no one on hand to meet the Princess when she arrived on 2 October, and he was faced with the formidable task of moving the machinery of the Princess' reception from Southampton to Devonshire and of arranging her journey, stage by stage, from the West Country to London. See G. Kipling, *The Triumph of Honour* (The Hague, 1977), 174.

46–51 The King received news of the Princess' arrival on 4 October. The Privy Council immediately met to consider the arrangements for the Princess' journey to London. As its first action, the Council dispatched Sir Robert Willoughby, Lord Broke, to meet the Princess at Exeter on 17 October; he was to be accompanied by a retinue of four heralds, four sergeants at arms, twelve palfreys, and a litter (B.L. MS Cotton Vespasian C. XIV, 95^v). The writer's information here obviously derives from hearsay or some form of Council minutes rather than from first-hand observation.

51–9 The Privy Council directed 'my lord Tresourer', Thomas Howard, Earl of Surrey, to meet the Princess Katharine at Amesbury on 25 October. He was to be accompanied by the Duchess of Norfolk (Elizabeth Talbot, widow of John Mowbray, 4th Duke of Norfolk), her ladies in waiting, and a number of bishops, abbots, lords, and knights (B.L. MS Cotton Vespasian C. XIV, 96). They were then to accompany the Princess and attend upon her for the remainder of her journey.

60ff. The Privy Council minutes make no provision for the King's visit to the Princess at the palace of the Bishop of Bath and Wells in Dogmersfeld. She was to be the guest of the Bishop, who had joined the party at Amesbury, on 5 and 6 November (B.L. MS Cotton Vespasian C. XIV, 97^r). The writer's circumstantial account of the King's movements contrasts sharply with his vague references to the Princess' journey and suggests that he may have been a member of the King's retinue.

78 *Myddell eires*: According to a widely-cited theory of Aristotle (*Meteorologica*, I. iii–iv), clouds could only form in the middle stratum of the atmosphere between the two main strata of the atmosphere, a hot-dry 'exhalation' ('fire') which fills the space between the Celestial Sphere and the tops of the highest mountains, and a cold-moist 'exhalation' ('air') which extends from the surface of the earth to the hot-dry stratum. Heat reflected from the earth prevents clouds being formed close to the earth, while the air beyond the tops of the mountains is carried round with the motions of the Celestial Sphere, similarly preventing cloud formation. Cf. Bartholomaeus Anglicus, *De prop. rerum*, xi. 4: 'A cloude is impressioun imade in þe eyre of many vapoures gadred into one body in þe myddel region of þe eyr, iþickened togedres by cooldnesse of place'.

80 *Esthampsted*: Prince Arthur was apparently staying at the royal manor in Easthampstead, a residence often used for hunting parties in the Windsor forest. Cf. *Victoria County History, Berkshire* (London, 1906–24), iii, 77–9.

80–86 The 'wise sawes' would include 'the subject's love is the king's lifeguard', based ultimately upon Seneca, *De Clementia*, I.xix.6. Cf. F.P. Wilson, *Oxford Dictionary of English Proverbs*, 3rd edn. (Oxford, 1970), 783. The writer seems to have a particular form of that proverb in mind: 'Opes regum, corda subditorum' (source untraced, but adoped c. 1810 as the motto of the Austrian Order of Leopold); Queen Elizabeth's remark—'we come ... for that which in right is our owne, the hearts and true allegiance of our subjects, which are the greatest riches of a kingdome'—also recalls the same form of the proverb (Holinshed, *Chronicles* (London, 1807), iv, 378). See also Peele's *Device of the Pageant Borne Before Wolstan Dixie* (ed. D.H. Horne, *Life and Minor Works of George Peele* (New Haven and London, 1952), 211), ll. 72–75, for another version of the same proverb.

140 *And ensueyng*: Neither *OED* nor *MED* notes *ensuing* in the adverbial sense here adopted. *Ensueyng* might therefore possibly be construed as a pr. part. conjoined to *to be present*. If so, the writer would mean that Prince Arthur was known to be present and that he was also known to be ensuing (i.e., following the King, or on his way to meet the Princess). This somewhat strained alternative reading is unnecessary, however, because the author elsewhere uses *ensueyng* in this adverbial sense (meaning *next, subsequently*). Moreover, he is particularly fond of beginning independent clauses with *and*. At 3/299–302 we find an almost exact parallel to the sense here adopted: *And ensueng the Lord Prince, and His Grace, and nobles ... departid to his seid arrayed chambre and bedde*. Cf. also 2/665, 4/370, and 4/444 for other clearly adverbial usages.

144–46 *They were by deputies contractid*: In August 1497 Arthur and Katharine were formally betrothed at Woodstock, the Spanish ambassador, De Puebla, standing as proxy for Katharine. The couple was then married by proxy at Bewdley on 19 May

1499, when Katharine reached marriageable age, with De Puebla again taking Katharine's part in the exchange of vows. This ceremony was repeated once again the following year, when Arthur had reached his fourteenth year. Cf. W. Busch, *England Under the Tudors: Henry VII* (London, 1895), 122–41. *Their either othre presens*: each other's presence.

146–7 *The which semly ensurans, ... honorably endid, ...*: The seemly betrothal, having been honourably concluded according to expectations ...

150 *Their mynstrelles*: See 2/675–6n.

161ff. The Privy Council minutes directed the Duke of Buckingham to meet the Princess 'betwix Chertesey and Croydon at the fote of Banstede downe' and details the names of those who should attend him (B.L. MS Cotton Vespasian C. XIV, 97). Instead of heading for Croydon after leaving Chertsey, as originally intended however, the procession apparently followed the Thames to Kingston, and the Duke met the Princess somewhat north of the planned rendezvous.

169 *That vyllage*: Presumably Kingston-Upon-Thames. According to the Privy Council minutes, the Princess was to stop over at the Archbishop of Canterbury's Palace at Croydon for two days before travelling on to Lambeth. At this point in the minutes, however, the dating of the various stages in the planned journey has become badly confused; because the scribe has given the same date to two different events (she was to be at both Dogmersfeld and Chertsey on 6 October; cf. B.L. MS Cotton Vespasian C. XIV, 97^r), the procession found itself a day behind schedule. When it was realized that a stop at Croydon would have delayed the Princess' arrival in Lambeth, leaving her too little time to rest and prepare for her entry into London on 12 October, a stopover in Kingston was substituted.

175–6 *The to her ... assigned*: The assistants of the realm of England assigned to her by our Sovereign.

192 *Paris Gardeyn*: A manor house, formerly the property of John de Paris (temp. Richard II).

194 *Baynardes Castell*: According to Stowe (*Survey of London*, ed. H. Morley (London, 1890), 94), Henry VII 'new built this house' in 1501, 'not embattled, or so strongly fortified castle like, but far more beautiful and commodious for the entertainment of any prince or great estate'. It was evidently part of Henry's extensive rebuilding and refurbishing programme, designed to project an image of royal magnificence, leading up to the marriage of Arthur and Katharine. The reconstruction of Richmond Palace, after the fire of 1497, is the most obvious example of this plan (see 4/756–888 and nn.), but as the writer's comments make clear, Henry intended Baynard's Castle to be yet another showpiece for his Spanish guests.

198–202 *Where to his noble ... Princes of Hispayne*: This long clause, which refers back to *Baynardes Castell*, describes the matters which were brought before the King in formal audience (*to his noble and prudent audiens ... hade ther recourse*) at that venue. These three categories of matters are detailed in the three adjectival clauses at the end of the sentence: matters befitting the King's own honour and rights, matters pertaining to the comfort and justice of the realm at large, and, in particular, matters concerning the receiving (*endutyng*) of the Princess Katharine.

208–9 *The stedfast, sure, and secret chambre of Englond*: An allusion to the commonplace description of London as 'the King's Chamber'; cf. Lydgate, 'King Henry VI's Triumphal Entry into London' (in *Minor Poems*, ed. H.N. MacCracken, EETS os cxcii, 1934; reprtd. 1961, 632): 'your moste notable Citee off London, othir wyse called youre Chaumbre'.

239ff. According to Polydore Vergil, Henry instituted a personal bodyguard of about two hundred men on the day of his coronation; 'in this he imitated the French kings so that he might thereafter be better protected from treachery' (*Anglica Historia 1485–1537*, ed. and trans. D. Hay, Camden Series, lxxiv (London, 1950), 7). If the writer is correct in estimating their number at three hundred, Henry must have considerably augmented them for this occasion. They appear here for the first time in Tudor green-and-white livery (cf. 2/318–9n.).

255–6 *All thinges leied aparte ... ther manour*: The members of each guild, dressed in distinctive liveries and hoods, attend the Princess in separate groups. The writer uses *manour* for *craft guild* here in the sense that the guildsmen in their liveries are like the liveried retainers of a lord.

Book II

14–23 This list of the 'right semely company' assigned by the King to attend the Princess on her formal entry into London differs considerably from the one specified in the Privy Council orders: B.L. MS Cotton Vespasian C. XIV, 98^v–99^r.

28 For the Bridge Gate see Stowe, *Survey*, 88.

31 A tabernacle was a canopied structure, such as a tomb, shrine, statuary niche, or roodloft. Its distinguishing features were a booth-shaped recess topped by a 'tabernacle-work' canopy of ornamental carved work or tracery. Cf. *OED* 'Tabernacle', sb., 4a, b, c and 9. For such tabernacle-work canopies as the framework for pageantry, see the *Beauchamp Pageants* (B.L. MS Cotton Julius E. IV), 1^r–2^v, 6^v–7^r, 9^r, 10, 12^r–13^r, 14, 16^v–17^r, 20^r, 21–24^r, 25^r, 26^r–7^r (ed. V. Dillon and W.H. St John Hope (London, 1914)). Cf. Lydgate's description of a pageant at Cornhill in 1432: 'a tabernacle off moste magnyficence' (*Minor Poems*, 638). As a convention of manuscript painting, 'tabernacle' describes the niche-shaped opening surrounded by ornamental borders commonly encountered in Flemish illuminations.

34 St Katharine holds a toothed wheel, her usual symbol in medieval representations. The Emperor Maximinus had commanded that she be torn apart upon such a wheel because of her uncompromising profession of Christian faith. An angel, however, destroyed the wheel at Katharine's prayer as it was about to harm her. Cf. *Golden Legend*. She appears here as Katharine's patron saint.

36 St Ursula's 'great multitude of virgyns' serve as her identifying symbol. According to legend, Ursula was a 5th century British princess who went on pilgrimage to Rome with 11,000 virgins; all were massacred by the Huns at Cologne. She appears here as a specifically British saint, and one, moreover, plausibly of King Arthur's 'lynage' (2/99).

40–2 A Garter, emblazoned with the motto of the Order ('Honi soit qui mal y pense'), surrounds a Lancastrian red rose rather than a Tudor union rose. The heraldic badge thus signals the Lancastrian theme of this pageant. As St Ursula points out, Katharine's descent from John of Gaunt has created a common bond between the Princess and the Saint: they both 'comon owt of oon cuntrye' (2/92–8 and n.).

48–50 The Three Ostrich Feathers was the badge of Arthur, Prince of Wales, while the portcullis was a Beaufort badge. As a supporter of the royal arms, the Rampant Lion had been an English royal beast since the 12th century; his colour was usually gold. Cf. H.S. London, *Royal Beasts* (East Knoyle, 1956), 9–15. Red ('red gold') was an acceptably 'royal' alternative, however, and cheaper to paint.

51–2 The carved and gilded timber refers to the tabernacle-work framing of the pageant stages.

58–9 'Let it not be painful to leave your native dwellings, Katharine; foreign kingships will give more splendour to you'.

72 Katharine was in fact named after her great-grandmother, Katharine of Lancaster. Cf. Mattingly, *Catherine of Aragon*, 6.

74 St Katharine is apparently still thinking of Katharine's baptism, where she was chosen to be the Princess' patron (2/67–73) (i.e., by being given the saint's name). Her claim to have helped the Princess 'to Crist your first make' conflates two familiar Pauline images: baptism incorporated the recipient into the Body of Christ (1 Cor. 12:13ff) and marriage signifies the sacramental and nuptial union of Christ and His Church (Eph. 5:23). These images are brought together in the Sarum *Ordo Sponsalium* (*Missale Sarum*, ed. F.H. Dickinson (Oxford, 1861–83), 837*–40*).

90–1 'May you be happy and auspicious for my Britons, Katharine, for you will be another evening star to them'.

92–8 St Ursula refers to Katharine's descent from John of Gaunt through both of her maternal grandparents. Her grandmother, Isabel of Portugal, was the great-granddaughter of John of Gaunt and Blanche of Lancaster, while her grandfather, John II of Castile, was the grandson of John of Gaunt and Constance of Castile. St Ursula, however, does not herself claim Lancastrian heritage, only that she comes from the noble blood of 'this land of Lancastre' (i.e., England).

99–100 St Ursula, according to Geoffrey of Monmouth, was the daughter of Dionotus, Duke of Cornwall and King of Britain under the Emperor Maximianus. Ursula's claim that Arthur came out of her lineage and that she is 'nere kynne' (2/107) to him depends only upon their common British nationality and royal status.

104–5 By 'Arthure' Ursula means 'Arcturus', the medieval name for Ursa Major: '*Arthurus* is a signe imade of seuene sterris ... comounliche iclepid in englische "Cherlemaynes Wayne" ... *Arthurus* ... is propirliche a sterre iset bihinde þe taile of þe signe þat hatte *Vrsa Maior* ... And þerfore al þat constellacioun *Arthurus* haþ þat name of þat sterre, as Isidir seiþ' (Bartholomaeus Anglicus, *De prop. rerum*, viii. 23). This usage was especially prevalent because it was endorsed by the Book of Job (9:9, 37:32) and Gregory the Great's *Moralia*; see Anglo, *Spectacle*, 62.

107–10 The association of St Ursula with Ursa Minor is apparently the poet's own invention.

110–2 Ursula means that Cynosura, not 'Arthure', gives comfort to travellers by night. Cynosura is properly the North Star, which 'lediþ in þe see men þat sailiþ and haueþ schipcraft' (Bartholomaeus Anglicus, *De prop. rerum*, viii. 22). It thus guides travellers as Ursula guides Katharine.

113–4 The description of Prince Arthur as a second King Arthur was one of the major themes of early Tudor political propaganda, thus Bernard André: 'Haec est illa dies qua Arturi saecula magni / Effigiem pueri sub imagine cernere claram / Nostra queant' (J. Gairdner, ed., *Memorials of King Henry the Seventh*, Rolls Series x (London, 1858), 45; cf. also lx–lxi). See Kipling, *Triumph of Honour*, 85; also S. Anglo, 'The *British History* in Early Tudor Propaganda', *Bull. John Rylands Library*, xliv (1961), 17–48, who overlooks the Arthurian symbolism of these very pageants.

129 *A foundacione off stone*: Probably the Great Conduit in Gracechurch Street, which had only recently been constructed (in 1491, according to Stowe, *Survey*, 49). The pipes to the new conduit only began to be laid in 1494 (C.L. Kingsford, *Chronicles of London* (Oxford, 1905), 200). Another London Chronicle (*The Great Chronicle of London*, ed. A.H. Thomas and I.D. Thornley (London, 1938), 299), merely places the pageant opposite the Falcon (Inn?), but the new conduit was probably the only place in Gracechurch Street where one could find a ready-made foundation of stone three or four feet high with water courses running out of it. The conduit served as the central anchor of the pageant castle; two 'wynges' (2/182) extended the castle from the conduit completely across the street 'into menys wyndowes and stallis' on either side (2/163). Two large portcullises in the wings allowed the procession to pass through the pageant and ride past the conduit (2/162–4).

137–44 *Certeyn bagges*: A crowned Union Rose, a crowned Garter, a Fleur-de-lis (referring to the English claim to the throne of France), and a crowned Beaufort portcullis. Only the crowned Garter badge is unusual. Apparently consisting of three Garters surrounding a central crown, the whole in turn topped by a crown, it probably referred to the three Tudor princes (Henry VII, Arthur, Henry) who were members of the Order.

145 *Clowdes with beamys of golde*: Henry VII's sunburst badge; cf. A.C. Fox-Davies, *Complete Guide to Heraldry* (New York, 1909), 468–9.

146 *Whight hertes*: Originally Richard II's badge, it was claimed by the Yorkist faction in the War of the Roses and assumed by the Tudors, who apparently 'regarded it as a royal beast like the swan and antelope' (London, *Royal Beasts*, 57). *Pekokkes*: untraced as a Tudor royal badge.

147–60 Because the 'foundacione off stone' (conduit) occupied the middle of the pageant castle, this gate could not be located at street level, like the two in the wings, but had to be built atop the conduit structure. Together, these three portcullises form the most symbolically distinctive feature of Castle Policy, so much so that the writer calls it 'this pagent of the Castell of Portcullys' (2/273). The entire structure thus imitates a Tudor heraldic badge, the Beaufort (*beau fortresse*) Portcullis; its Lancastrian associations are emphasized by the use of red roses to cover the joints of the portcullis. Such symbolic castles, as G.R. Kernodle points out (*From Art to Theatre* (Chicago, 1944), 78), conventionally served as symbols of realms; this one clearly represents Tudor England (hence the Tudor badges in the battlements and the royal arms displayed just above the central portcullis), and the miraculous opening of the Beaufort gates to receive the Princess (2/186–8) neatly symbolizes a manifest triumph of Tudor diplomatic policy.

156 Owen Tudor took the red dragon emblem as a token of his supposed descent from Cadwalader, the last British king. The dragon recalls King Vortigern's prophetic vision of a struggle between a red dragon (representing the British) and a white dragon (representing the Saxons). The white dragon, though initially successful, is finally defeated by the red; hence the prophecy that a British king, one of the seed of Cadwalader, would one day again wear the crown of Britain. Wishing to be seen as the fulfiller of this prophecy, Henry VII fought the battle of Bosworth Field beneath the red dragon banner and subsequently took that beast for one of his heraldic supporters. Cf. Anglo, *Spectacle*, 44–5 and London, *Royal Beasts*, 43–6.

157 Originally one of Edward III's royal beasts, the white greyhound became a Tudor heraldic emblem when Henry VI granted it to his half brother, Edmund Tudor, upon the latter's creation as Earl of Richmond. Upon Henry VII's accession, it was conventionally paired with the Red Dragon as a supporter of the royal arms, as here. Cf. London, *Royal Beasts*, 39–41.

160–1 The civic chronicles describe Policy as 'a man arayd lyke a Senatour' (*Great Chronicle*, 299; Kingsford, *Chronicles*, 237), an identity better suited to his position as a 'governoure' who has his 'singler ihe' trained 'to the comonweall' (2/197, 206) than a knight. Probably the writer confuses Policy with Noblesse, whom he also describes as a knight (2/173–4 and n.).

173–5 The writer's descriptions of Noblesse and Virtue differ considerably from those of the civic chronicles. Possibly both are describing Noblesse correctly. Our writer makes him a knight with 'an hedepece' (helmet?); the *Great Chronicle* describes him merely as 'most Richely apparaylyd' (299). Perhaps both refer to a well-dressed nobleman carrying a helmet as a symbol of his status much as St Katharine carries her wheel. But our writer is certainly mistaken in describing Virtue as a bishop. The *Great Chronicle* identifies her more correctly as 'a vyrgyn Representyng vertu Rygth goodly apparaylid' (300), a characterization amply seconded by Noblesse, who repeatedly refers to her as female (2/232–6). Since the writer probably did not see the performance of this pageant, he may well be supplying traditional characterizations for the speakers. As T.W. Craik points out, virtues in the English interlude are normally represented by men dressed in the robes of holy orders (*The Tudor Interlude* (Leicester, 1958), 54). The devisor of this pageant, however, was thinking more of French than of English characterizations, a point made abundantly clear when our writer mistakenly renders Noblesse's French name in its English form, 'Noblenes'. The choice of Noblesse and Virtue as interlocutors, in fact, depends upon Jean Molinet's *Le Trosne d'honneur*, where they lament the death of Duke Philip the Good before being allowed a vision of him in heaven. In that poem, Dame Vertu is similar to the pageant character, Virtue: 'une dame de hault pris, avironee d'extreme clarté simple toutefois de maintien et d'abis, mais tres richement aornée et couronee de couronne estofee de diverses pierres precieuses' (*Faictz et Dictz*, ed. N. Dupire, SATF (Paris, 1936), i, 44). The devisor does transform Molinet's Dame Noblesse, however, into a man.

184–5 'This sound castle is for virtue, not for nobility, but without me no entrance lies open in this place'. Cf. 2/785–99 below.

188 *The bright sterre of Spayne, Hesperus*: According to Isidore of Seville, Spain (Hesperia) took its name from the star Hesperus (*Etymologiarum*, XIV, iv, 28). Thus Katharine's 'native star' miraculously opens the gates of the castle for the Princess, facilitating her ascent. At the same time, of course, Katharine herself is the 'bright sterre of Spayne' who, by approaching the pageant, 'shines' upon the gates and causes them to open.

193–203 Policy, as his name suggests, seeks in Katharine the proper public virtues which will render her 'apte to have auctoryte within thys realme'. The *de vera nobilitate* argument of these three speeches must consequently appear in the context of Katharine's role as a future queen. As R. Kelso points out, 'a man may practice the private virtues all his life and still not be worthy of nobility, for virtue that is private is restricted in its influence, while that virtue that is suitable for ennobling, is public, conferring benefits on the whole state ... Virtue then which is profitable to one's country is sufficient cause for ennoblement, in fact the only true cause and test' ('Sixteenth Century Definitions of the Gentleman in England', *JEGP*, xxiv (1925), 378). Policy thus finds in the Princess 'tokenes of vertue and nobles, / Two thynges to the comonweall necessary'.

209–10 *Si virtus ... habent*: 'If virtue is wanting, wealth, birth, and even power have nothing except the name of nobility'.

212–3 In most treatments of the *de vera nobilitate* theme, virtue leads to honour and thus confers nobility. Here, however, noblesse and virtue are equally necessary prerequisites for achieving honour. Noblesse examines Katharine primarily to determine that she 'be come of noble blode' (2/220) before Virtue discovers within her a 'very dispocicion naturall' to the Cardinal Virtues (2/253–4). Noblesse is primarily interested in Katharine's ability to rule; as a future queen, she must have noble stature in order to rule effectively. But in order to rule wisely, she will need virtue as well. Consequently, he passes her on to Virtue for further instruction.

c224 *Theoryke*: Theological. While some senses of 'theoric' can mean 'contemplative' (cf. *OED* 'Theoric', a.²), the word here is probably an error for 'theologik'. The poet is making the conventional distinction between the Four Cardinal and Three Theological Virtues (cf. *OED* 'Theological', a., 1 and refs). Cp. 2/761–4 where the description of Pageant Five also distinguishes conventionally between 'the vij vertues, the iij Theologik and iiij Cardinalles'.

225–31 A common humanist application of the *de vera nobilitate* doctrine. Cf. Kelso, 382: 'much of the insistence on virtue is intended not to comfort the lowly born but to admonish the well born who seem generally to have prided themselves on birth to the neglect of virtue'.

227–8 *The noble ... Be applied of their right propertie*: The noble must devote themselves to their right property. Cf. *OED*, 'apply', v. 13 and citation: 'Of here beaute sumwhat too say I will applye my wittes all'.

241–2 Si tibi virtutem ... Nobilitata nimis: 'If you will gain virtue alone for yourself, although the rest may be lacking, you will be exceedingly noble' (?); *nobilitata* is almost certainly the correct reading, since the Cotton Vitellius A XVI scribe corrects from *Nobilitate* to that reading, in agreement with G. One would expect, however, either *nobilis* or perhaps *nobilitatis*.

254 *Everych Vertue Cardinall*: As W.O. Harris points out, the Cardinal Virtues had come 'to be thought of as the kingly virtues, the proper means of training rulers and of honoring them, as well as the standard for judging their conduct' (*Skelton's Magnyfycence and the Cardinal Virtue Tradition* (Chapel Hill, North Carolina, 1965), 145). Virtue is thus more interested in examining Katharine for the Cardinal than the Theological Virtues, for the former are specifically appropriate to the ruler.

257 *Dispocicion*: A pun; the word is used both in its general sense as a statement of one's characteristic inclinations and in its technical sense in terms of astrological influence. Cf. *MED*, 'disposicioun', n., 5, 6; *OED*, 'Disposition', sb., 5, 7. Katharine will thus be helped to Honour because her spouse, Arthur, is inclined to virtue as she is (cf. 'a very dispocicion naturall', 2/253), but her journey will also be facilitated because the disposition of 'Arthur' (= Arcturus) is especially favourable to it (cf. 'King Alfons ... of your fate the dispocicion can telle' 2/266–8).

275 *Enjoynyd to the condute*: This conduit was a castellated structure originally built in the midst of Cornhill Street in 1282 as a prison for 'night-walkers and other suspicious persons'. It was then called the Tun because it was built 'somewhat in fashion of a tun standing on one end'. In 1401, the prison was converted to a cistern for water conveyed there by pipes from Tyburne, but a timber cage, stocks, and a pillory were built atop the structure for the continuing accommodation of prisoners. Cf. Stowe, *Survey* 199–201. Because it was designed as a building rather than a conduit, it stood much higher than the other London conduits; consequently, the pageant was attached to the conduit rather than built atop it, as at the Gracechurch St. conduit (cf. 2/129n.), which was apparently only three to four feet high.

277–81 *Havyng in his forefrunte iij great pylours ... havyng two portcullys in the seid forefronte of yelowe*: G. Wickham (*Early English Stages*, i (London, 1959), Pl. xvii) groups the three pillars in the middle of the castle façade and locates the two portcullises at the sides. Probably, however, the three pillars framed the two portcullises, the two green ones at the ends of the façade ('on every sid j') and the red one between the two gates ('and in the myddis oon pelour of red marbill empayntid').

286 *Many dyvers bagges*: Cf. 2/137–44n.

297 *Within this pagent*: the writer describes a large, booth-shaped recess in the 'forefrunte' of the pageant containing a bench, three actors, and a 'volvell' attached to the ceiling of the recess; in effect, it is another 'tabernacle' (cf. 2/31n) which allows the viewer to see both the exterior and interior of a structure simultaneously.

307 *Such persones*: The civic chronicles explain that King Alfonso, Job, and Boethius were chosen for this pageant because they 'were Reputid ffor iij the most cunnyng as Alphons astronomer Job dyvyne & Boecius phylyzofyr' (cf. 2/471). To-gether with the Archangel Raphael, the four actors represent the four possible ways of knowing: angelic revelation, astrological prognostication, philosophical inquiry, and religious faith. Cf. Kipling, *Triumph of Honour*, 92.

308–9 *A blew spere of the mone especiall with othir planettes and sterrys in their curse and ordre*: The civic chronicler identifies this astronomical device more precisely as 'the zodyak wyth the xij sygnys In a volvell' (*Great Chronicle*, 301). A 'volvell' (sometimes called a 'lunarie' or 'nocturnal') is a very common astrological device used to ascertain the rising and setting of the sun and moon and to determine the appropriate astrological signs corresponding to the rising and setting of the sun and moon. A sort of two-dimensional planetarium related to an astrolabe, it is com-posed of a series of circles of graduated sizes, usually made out of vellum or paper, fastened together at the centre so that all could turn on a common axis. Generally, the largest circle is calibrated to show the twenty-four hours of the day. On top of this, a slightly smaller circle is calibrated to show the twelve months of the year and the twelve signs of the zodiac. Over this is fastened another circle with a projecting indicator, identified by a symbol representing the sun; this circle too was calibrated for the twenty-nine and one-half day lunar cycle. Finally, another circle with a projecting indicator lay on top of this, identified by a symbol representing the moon. Thus, it was possible to set the indicators for the age of the moon and the day of the month and then rotate the outer circle to bring the hour of the day to the sun indicator. Then, by reading a series of extra calibrations on the zodiac circle, one could find the times of the rising and setting of the sun and moon, and in what sign of the zodiac they would rise and set. Cf. the fifteenth-century 'Rewle of the Volvelle', quoted in A. Dyce, ed., *Poetical Works of John Skelton* (London, 1843), ii, 336, from Bodleian Library, Ashmolean MS. 191, 199. See also for illustrations, New York, Metropolitan Museum of Art, *The Secular Spirit* (New York, 1975), cat. no. 200, and *Horizon*, v (1963), 2. The pageant volvell was apparently set to show 'the encreace & wane of the mone wyth many othir conclucions of astronomy' (*Great Chronicle*, 301), as is appropriate to 'this Pagent of the Mone' (2/320–1). It would of course be possible to add yet other calibrations and other indicators to show the rising and setting of Hesperus and the position of Arcturus, and the comments of the various speakers seem to suggest that this indeed had been done.

313 *Above this blewe spere*: Raphael occupies another niche or 'tabernacle' placed just above the volvell. As he points out in his speech, archangels move the spheres of heaven; hence, his position just above the volvell symbolizes his role as the instrument of divine revelation through astronomy. Raphael, in other words, is supposed to be understood as responsible for the motions of the sphere of the moon which are traced by the volvell on which he stands.

318–9 *Chekiryd with whight and grene*: White and Green were Henry VII's livery colours, perhaps taken from the attributed arms of King Arthur (a white cross on a green field). They were to become the dominant colours of Tudor royal pageantry. The *Justes of the Moneths of May and June* (1507), for example, features a hawthorn tree bearing 'a shield of white and green, which colours be most comfortable and pleasant for all seasons' (Kipling, *Triumph of Honour*, 134), and the Duke of Buckingham, acting as Challenger in the wedding tournament, chooses to enter the tilt in a white and green pavilion decorated with royal badges, although his own servants wear black and red Buckingham livery (cf. 1/167–8, 4/82–3).

320–2 Traditionally, the moon (*Luna*) was regarded as female while the sun, which enclosed it in its sphere (*Sol*), was considered to be male; hence the 'appropriateness' of the moon to the Princess' destiny and of the sun to Arthur's (2/513–5). For the moon's femininity, see Pliny, *Natural History*, 2, 104. Milton (*Paradise Lost*, viii, 94–152) evidently makes use of this tradition.

324 *Raphaell*: The civic chronicles report that Raphael had 'goldyn & glyteryng wyngis & ffedyrs of many & sundry colours' (*Great Chronicle*, 301). The wings of angels often appear as golden, glittering, and full of multi-coloured feathers in contemporary paintings. See, for example, the Van Eyck *Ghent*

Altarpiece and the Annunciation scene in the *Hours of Mary of Burgundy*, which is surrounded by a border of peacock feathers (Bodleian Library, MS. Douce 219–220, 97ᵛ–98).

327–43 Medieval commentary traditionally assigned to archangels the offices of instructing men and inspiring prophets. Cf. Bartholomaeus Anglicus, *De prop. rerum*, ii. 17.

346–7 Raphael's claim that archangels move 'these orbes and speeres' of heaven derives, ultimately, from Plato, who thought that the motions of the planets were due to 'Intelligences' which moved them in their spheres (*Republic* 616E–618D). Christian neo-Platonists developed these abstract 'Intelligences' into angels who guard the planetary spheres. Raphael thus presides over the 'sphere of the moon' in this pageant. Moreover, he is one of seven angels always standing in God's presence, a number corresponding to the seven planets of the Ptolemaic cosmos. We are probably to understand by Raphael's position above the volvell that he is the ultimate source of the motions of the moon; if, as Raphael says, all knowledge comes ultimately from angels, then the insights of the wise men below the volvell, derived from the motions of the moon, must constitute the angels' declaration of the 'hevenly mysteres to man' (2/333). In himself, Raphael comprehends perfectly the meaning of this marriage; the wise men below him comprehend only partially, each according to his particular gift of understanding.

348–9 *On of the seven*: Tobias 12:15; see also Luke 1:19, Apoc. 8:2, and 1 Enoch 20:1–3. Raphael's 'especiall charge' is inferred from Tobias 6:16–22; cf. Milton, *Paradise Lost*, V, 221–3.

357–8 Raphael required Tobias to remain continent for three days after his marriage to Sara, remaining in the bridal chamber with her but giving himself 'to nothing else but to prayers with her'. Only when the third night had passed might he 'take the virgin with the fear of the Lord, moved rather for love of children than for lust'. In this way only might he distinguish himself from those 'who in such manner receive matrimony, as to shut out God from themselves, and from their mind, and to give themselves to their lust' (Cf. Tobias, 6:14–22, 8:1–9).

361 *Figure*: Horoscope. Cf. *MED*, 'figure', n., 7; *OED*, 'Figure', sb., 14. Anglo ('London Pageants', 73–5) misconstrues this word to mean 'image' and then speculates that Alfonso and Job must have originally appeared in the fourth pageant, where there does appear an image or representation of Arthur. In fact, Raphael merely introduces the figure or horoscope of Arthur which Alfonso constructs for the Princess based upon his reading of the volvell above his head. When Alfonso finishes, Job again refers to the same horoscope: 'Alfons hath shewed you the hevenly bodies ... and of your spouse a figure' (2/427–8). Cf. Webster, *Duchess of Malfi*, II.ii.84–5: 'I'll presently / Go set a figure for's nativity'.

362 *Gabriell*: perhaps because he is not paying attention to the substance of the text he is copying, the author here confuses the archangels Raphael and Gabriel in this brief connective passage.

363 *Alfons*: Alfonso X, The Wise, King of Castile (1252–84). A patron of learning particularly interested in Astronomy, he directed compilation of the Alfonsine Tables by a group of eminent Arabian, Christian, and Jewish astronomers. He also composed the *Instrumentes*, a treatise upon astrological instruments. As King of Castile, he was an ancestor of the Princess Katharine (hence 'Doughtir Kateryn', 2/367).

374–80 These lines constitute Alfonso's astrological 'figure' for the wedding, which he explains in the balance of his speech. It consists of the Sun entering Sagittarius while Arcturus is entering into conjunction with Hesperus. Indeed, the sun entered the sign of Sagittarius early in the morning of 13 November 1501, and the wedding of Arthur and Katharine (the conjunction of Arcturus and Hesperus) took place under the sign of Sagittarius on the fourteenth. On the dating, see Anglo, *Spectacle*, 72 n. 1. Since the date of the wedding could not have been fixed until after Katharine's arrival in England on 2 October 1501, these lines— and consequently Alfonso's speech—must have been composed only shortly before the performance.

375 A triplicity, or trigon, is technically a combination of three signs of the zodiac distant 120 degrees from one another. There are four such triplicities, each assigned to one of the four elements. Sagittarius, as Alfonso says (2/397), is in the 'triplicite of the Lyon' (Aries, Leo, and Sagittarius) to which is assigned the element fire (hence the 'firy circumferens and bande', 2/385). Cf. Bartholomaeus Anglicus, *De prop. rerum*, viii. 9.

389 *Ye, Lady, bere the bagge of Sagittary*: Katharine, born on 16 December, was in fact a Capricorn; in the late fifteenth century the sun entered Capricorn about the twelfth of December.

389–94 *The bagge of Sagittary*: Apparently a reference to the story that King Stephen assumed a sagittary as his arms because he successfully invaded England and claimed the throne in 1135 when Sagittarius was in the ascendant and because the battle was clinched by his archers (hence Alfonso's reference to victory over enemies). Stephen did arrive in England under the sign of the Sagittary—Henry I died on December 1135 and Stephen had

himself crowned by Christmas—but there is little historical
support for a battle of any kind, much less one won by archers.
Nicholas Upton, a fifteenth-century heraldic authority, gives
Stephen's attributed arms as three sagittaries while other writers
give him only one. See Anglo, *Spectacle*, 72 n. 2 and R. Dennys,
The Heraldic Imagination (London, 1975), 119.

395–6 An obscure allusion. Prince Arthur, born on 20
September 1486, was in fact a Libra, not a Sagittarius. A later
sixteenth-century tradition, however, closely associated Prince
Arthur with archery. T. Roberts, *The English Bowman* (London,
1801), 86 says that Prince Arthur 'became so expert in the use of
the long-bow, that a good archer was honoured by being stiled
Prince Arthur'. An Elizabethan archery society, which apparently
traced its origin to the reign of Henry VII, took the name 'Prince
Arthur's Round Table' and met yearly for a festive shooting
match, each member taking the persona of one of King Arthur's
knights. C.B. Millican thinks it was called '*Prince* Arthur's Round
Table' because of 'the association of archery with Arthur, Prince
of Wales' ('Spenser and the Arthurian Legend', *RES*, vi (1930),
169 and n. 5). Perhaps the association of Arthur with archery
accounts in some way for this reference to his Sagittarian birth?

397 Just as Alfonso associates the Sagittarius with England
(2/382–3), so he stresses that identification further by emphasiz-
ing the Leonine triplicity of which Sagittarius is a part (cf.
2/375n); the Lion is the British royal ensign.

398–401 Sagittarius is the Day House of Jupiter; this particular astrological conjunction is an omen of great estate. Cf.
Bartholomaeus Anglicus, *De prop. rerum*, viii. 9.

406–8 *As your self may se here evidently*: Apparently Alfonso
directs Katharine's attention to a symbol for Arcturus figured
prominently upon the volvell. At 2/411 he will direct her attention
to a symbol for Hesperus upon another dial of the volvell.

420–6 *Anothir astronomy*: Alfonso, an 'astronomer', had found
astrological significance in the disposition of stars and planets;
Job, like his Biblical exemplar, is compelled to look beyond the
cosmos to its Prime Mover (cf. Job, 38:1–33). Job's 'other'
astronomy thus consists of asking why God made this particular
arrangement of heavenly bodies, and his answer takes the form of
an anagogical 'figure' rather than Alfonso's astrological one. In
his astronomy, the stars illumine heavenly mysteries rather than
foretell earthly fortunes; his speech, as a consequence, reduces
Alfonso's horoscope, point by point, into a series of anagogical
metaphors.

425–6 Cf. Hawes, *Pastime of Pleasure*, ll. 2724–30:

Thus god hymselfe is chyef astronomyer
That made all thynge accordynge to his wyll
The sonne the mone and euery lytell sterre
To a good intente and for no maner of yll
Wythouten vayne he dyde all thynge fulfyll
As astronomy doth make apparaunce
By reason he weyed all thynges in balaunce.

434 *The Sonne of Justice*: Sol Justitiae, a conventional epithet
for Christ; cf. Rabanus Maurus (*Allegoriae*, in Migne, *Pat. Lat.*,
cxii, 1057–8) and Gregory the Great (*Moralia*, in Migne, *Pat.
Lat.*, lxxvi, 30–1). The phrase, Job's anagogical metaphor for
the sun in Alfonso's horoscope, is particularly appropriate to
Prince Arthur, who was born at the equinox when the sun was
entering Libra, the sign of Justice, and who will appear in the
next pageant wearing the Pauline spiritual armour of Justice while
riding a stellar chariot through the sphere of the sun. See also
Anglo, *Spectacle*, 81–2 for another interpretation.

435–6 As Boethius (*De consolatione philosophiae*, I, met. v)
observes, Hesperus shines brightly at sunset, but its light dims at
sunrise (when it is called 'Lucifer'). Job's anagogical interpretation for Hesperus, then, also contrasts the star's brightness at
nightfall with its dimness at dawn, and declares that the star's
dimming or 'death' in the west is comforting, for the star's 'dying'
heralds the rising of the 'Sun of Justice'. Accordingly, in the next
passage, Hesperus will dim before the rise of the Sun of Justice in
the form of Arthur riding in his seven-starred chariot. See
Kipling, *Triumph of Honour*, 89. See also Anglo, *Spectacle*, 80–1,
for discussion of Christian Resurrection symbolism in these lines.

437–8 *The Lyon of Juda*: Job's anagogical metaphor for what
Alfonso calls the triplicity of the Lion. It is another conventional
epithet for Christ, who sprang from the tribe of Judah, and who,
by his own might, was resurrected from the dead. A number of
astrological illustrations, of which Albrecht Dürer's is the most
famous, depict the sun as ruler of the planets and astride a lion.
The poet could also have drawn upon Pierre Bersuire, *Repertorium moral* (Nuremberg, 1489), s.v. 'Sol Justitiae' for this potent
combination of symbols. Petrus Apianus, *Cosmographicus liber*
(Landshut, 1524), xix^r, startlingly reproduces Job's vision by
placing the Sun of Justice and his Lion within the zodiac dial of a
volvell. See also Rabanus Maurus, *Allegoriae*, in Migne, *Pat.
Lat.*, cxii, 983; cf. Apoc. 5:5, Gen. 49:9, Prov. 30:30, 2 Esdras
12:31–2, and Anglo, *Spectacle*, 80.

439–40 Job takes his anagogical interpretation of the seven
stars of Arcturus, appropriately, from Gregory the Great,

Moralia, in Migne, *Pat. Lat.*, lxxvi, 515–19. See Anglo, 'London Pageants', 59–61, for a full discussion.

448–9 The *Great Chronicle* reports that the Princess rode on toward St Paul's without waiting to hear 'Boecius' speak because 'the day soo ffast passyd'. The actor, however, delivered his speech nevertheless. *Great Chronicle*, 304–5.

465 *Bodies spereycall*: Macrobius describes stars as both 'spherical solids' and as the stellar bodies of souls (*Commentary on the Dream of Scipio*, tr. W.H. Stahl (New York, 1952), 142–8).

487–8 *A skochon of whight with Seint Georges crosse and a red swerd*: The civic arms of London.

493–5 *Laudate dominum de celis … laudate eum in excellis*: Ps. 148:1–2. The angels appropriately praise the Father of Heaven with excerpts from this most 'astronomical' psalm in which those in the heavens and the high places, the angels, the sun, and the moon are all invited to praise their Creator.

496 *Te deum* …: These angelic scriptures are excerpted from the *Te Deum Laudamus*, a hymn conventionally sung at Sunday Matins before the New Testament lesson. The third and fourth lines ('Tibi omnes angeli Tibi celi et universae potestates / Tibi cherubim et serpahim incessabili voce proclamant') appropriately imagine the various orders of angels singing praises to the Father, as in the pageant.

496–500 The 'chare' is not a chair (hence 'golden throne', as in Anglo, *Spectacle*, 78), but rather a car or chariot, here specifically a *triga* (three-horse chariot) as identified in the Latin distich. Cf. *MED*, 'char', n., 1–3; *OED*, 'char', sb.², 1. Consequently, the four 'great sterres like iiij wheles runyng very swyftly' serve as the wheels of the chariot. The pageant thus represents the constellation Arcturus (Ursa Major) in its conventional guise as a chariot or wain (e.g., Charles' Wain). So conceived, the constellation was thought to be a triga; four of the seven stars became the wheels of the chariot while the other three marked the positions of the three horses along the thill or shaft. For such a representation, see Petrus Apianus, *Quadrans Apiana astronomicis* (Ingolstadt, 1532), G2ᵛ. In the pageant, the three 'armyd knightes' (2/508; the *Great Chronicle*, 305, calls them three 'childyr clene armyd') probably represent the other three stars of the constellation, especially since they turn the great cosmic wheel and thus apparently 'move' the chariot through the heavens.

In England, the constellation Ursa Major/Arcturus was often known as 'Arthur's Wain', and poets from Lydgate to Jonson to Sir John Davies imagined that King Arthur was 'translated to a starre' in the constellation Arcturus. Cf. Lydgate, *Fall of Princes*,

viii. 3095–3108; Jonson, *Works*, ed. Herford and Simpson (Oxford, 1925–52), vii, 325; Davies, *Poems*, ed. R. Krueger (Oxford, 1975), 231–2; Kipling, *Triumph of Honour*, 82–8. Probably the civic chronicler is thinking of 'Arthur's Chariot' in this sense when he refers to 'Arthure clene Armed in his Golden chare' and further to 'the chare of Arthur' (*C*, 191ᵛ) in describing this star-chariot. The image in the 'chare' thus represents both King Arthur and Prince Arthur in order to suggest that the Prince is a second King Arthur; this was one of the main themes of early Tudor political propaganda (Kipling, *Triumph of Honour*, 83–5). See also the note to 2/520–1 below.

Katharine sees Arcturus for the first time in human form when she reaches the sphere of the sun. According to both Macrobius and Boethius, the soul ascending from earth to heaven resumes its stellar body in the sphere of the sun (*De consolatione philosophiae*, IV, met. I; *Commentary on the Dream of Scipio*, 133–5). In Chaucer's translation, the soul is 'i-maked a knight of the clear star' in the sphere of the sun (*Works*, ed. F.N. Robinson (Boston, 1957), 359), a phrase that might account for Arthur's appearance 'armyd at all pesis' (*Great Chronicle*, 305) in 'the sperituall Armour of Justice' (2/525).

500 According to the Ptolemaic model of the universe, the spheres of the cosmos turned about the earth. The hub of this pageant wheel, as a consequence, had 'the centour of erthe' painted upon it. Cf. Boethius' description of the cosmos as a 'wheel that beareth the stars' (*De consolatione philosophiae*, tr. Chaucer, *Works*, 326) and his reference to 'the stars of Arctour' that are 'i-turned nigh to the sovereign centre or point (*that is to say, i-turned nigh to the sovereign pool of the firmament*)' (tr. Chaucer, *Works*, 367).

500–3 According to the London chronicles, the background or 'brede' of the wheel represented 'a celestiall place' or 'an heven, wheryn was paynted the xij signes' (Kingsford, *Chronicles*, 244; *Great Chronicle*, 305). As this description makes clear, however, the constellations represented included more than just the zodiac. In addition to the zodiacal constellations Leo ('sume lyons'), Pisces ('sume fisshis'), Taurus ('bullis'), Virgo ('virgyns'), Gemini ('nakyd men'), and Ares ('ramys'), the description also specifies Ursa Minor ('berys'), Pegasus ('hors'), and Serpens ('wormys'). These two-dimensional constellation pictures thus served as a background for the three-dimensional presentation of Arthur in the Wain. Perhaps the zodiacal constellations appeared on the rim of the wheel while the others filled the background?

504–7 *Bokys of astronomy, havyng lynys . . . aftir the aspectes . . . unto othir*: The particular 'lines' referred to here do not connect stars together so as to form the outlines of constellations (*berys, lyons, marmaydes, bullis*, etc.); rather they connect the various signs of the zodiac so as to identify their planetary 'aspects' (sextile, quartile, triune). Hence the *lynys* are *deducte* from one sign to another according to (*aftir*) their aspects, meaning that they trace the courses of the various planetary aspects (cf. *OED* 'Deduce', v.). An 'aspect' describes the relationship between a planet in any given ascendant sign to two other signs of the zodiac, either the two signs 60 degrees to either side (sextile), or the two signs 90 degrees to either side (quartile), or the two signs 120 degrees to either side (triune). Sometimes, as Bartholomaeus Anglicus points out (*De prop. rerum*, viii. 9), 'opposition' and 'conjunction' are also referred to as 'aspects', but this is an incorrect usage. For a 'volvell' with the zodiac constellations connected by aspect lines, see *The Secular Spirit*, cat. no 200. In the previous pageant, Alfonso comments at length upon one such relationship: Jupiter ascendant in Sagittarius and in triune aspect toward Aries and Leo (the triplicity of Leo); cf. 2/375n.

508 *Iij armyd knightes*: As in Hans Burgkmair's 'wheel chariot' woodcut for the *Triumph of Maximilian I*, the three 'armyd knightes' turn the wheel by attempting to climb the 'vice' or circular stair notched into the inside of the wheel. Three in number, they probably represent the three other stars of the 'Golden Triga'. By turning the wheel, they propel the chariot, and hence serve, in a manner, as the stellar draught-horses to Arthur's Wain. Cf. Anglo, *Spectacle*, 78; Kipling, *Triumph of Honour*, 86–7.

513–5 This pageant visualizes the 'figure' or horoscope promised by Gabriel and explained by Alfonso and Job in the previous pageant. The pageant thus depicts the Sun/son in Arcturus. As Job foretold, Katharine sees the Prince in the form of 'the Sonne of Justice, therthe illumyneng', and he rides in his Chare, 'Arthure, illumyneng iche cost / With vij bright sterrys, vij yeftes of the Holy Gost' (2/434, 439–40).

According to Bernard André, Prince Arthur's natal horoscope in fact amounted to 'the Sun in Arcturus': 'Orta enim Arcturi stella, quae secundum genetliacos xij. calend. Octobris oritur Arturus quoque princeps natus est' (J. Gairdner, *Memorials*, 41). The meaning of this horoscope depends upon the double meaning of *orta*, meaning both 'born' and 'descended'. First of all, this rather platonic horoscope asserts that both Prince Arthur and the star Arcturus were 'born' at the same time. This assertion

depends upon the coincidence of the Prince's birth with the
autumnal equinox, a date which has been gauged since classical
times by the rising of Arcturus just at dawn on that day (cf.
Isidore of Seville, *Etymologiarum*, III.71). In this way, the birth
of Prince Arthur coincided with the figurative yearly 'birth' of
Arcturus. Secondly, the horoscope declares the Prince to be
'descended' from the star Arcturus, a statement which refers to
the supposed 'translation' of King Arthur to the star Arcturus (cf.
n. to 2/496–500 above). The coincident 'birth' of Prince and star
thus portends the rebirth of King Arthur in the Tudor prince.
For these reasons, as Fronesis (see following note) tells Katharine,
the pageant represents both an 'expresse ymage' of Arthur as a
reborn King Arthur and a 'fygure certayne' which declares the
'fatall dispocicion and desteny' of the Prince according to his
horoscope, the sun in Arcturus.

516 The author does not identify the speaker, but both civic
chronicles report that 'certayn personys' sat beneath the wheel,
'among the which oon beyng namyd Fronesis utterid the pre-
pocicion here undyr ffoluyng' (*Great Chronicle*, 305); the description thus allows either a male or female speaker. Anglo would
identify Fronesis (ad. L. Phronesis, Understanding) with *acumen
sapientiae*, which Gregory the Great sees as characterizing the
rays of the Sun in his *Moralia in Job* (*Spectacle*, 83–4). Given the
rarity of *Phronesis* (as opposed to *Sapientia* or *Sophia*) in Latin,
such a strained reading seems unlikely. Phronesis, however, was
well known to the Middle Ages in one particular context. In
Martianus Capella's *De nuptiis* (ii, 114), she appears as the
mother of Philologia who helps to prepare her daughter for an
ascent through the spheres of the cosmos to the Temple of
Jupiter. Since Fronesis serves here as an advisor to Katharine
who is undertaking a similar journey, it seems probable that the
speaker's name was deliberately chosen to recall the *De nuptiis*.
Cf. Kipling, *Triumph of Honour*, 90–5.

517–8 'The golden chariot of Arthur always is turned about
the motionless pole and not immersed in the Hesperian waters'.
Based loosely upon Boethius, *De consolatione philosophiae*, IV,
met. v, 1–6. Cf. Chaucer's translation (in *Works*, 367). *Hesperiis*:
both G and C agree on the mac. nom. sing. suffix, *-ius*, but *aquis*
requires a fem. abl. pl. ('the Hesperian waters') unless the poet
misconstrued Hesperius to be a 4th decl. gen. sing. noun ('the
waters of Hesperius'). Since he elsewhere (2/91) uses the conventional form, *Hysperus*, such a misconstruction seems unlikely
here. St Gregory the Great also attaches great significance to the

fact that Arcturus never sets (*Moralia*, in Migne, lxxvi, 515–19); cf. Anglo, 'London Pageants', 60.

520–1 Britain is properly the land of King Arthur; here the poet deliberately encourages this conventional association before continuing, 'your spouse most bounteous' in order to suggest once again that the Prince is another King Arthur.

525 For the spiritual armour of Justice, cf. 2 Cor. 6:7; Isaiah 59:17; Eph. 6:13–17; Anglo, *Spectacle*, 84–5. Hawes provides his protagonists with this spiritual armour in both *The Example of Virtue* (ll. 1387–1401) and *The Pastyme of Pleasure* (ll. 3375–81).

526 *The prophete*: Cf. Isaiah 32:17–19; Jer. 22:3–4.

544 Like three of the other pageant stations, the Standard was one of the City conduits, but unlike them it was a frequent place of executions as well. Cf. Stowe, *Survey*, 260.

547–51 Evidently sculptured or painted figures, these four 'sage personys' wear the long robes and hats emblematic of prophets in medieval art and drama. Cf. the 'company of prophets' who greeted Henry V in 1415 'with venerable white hair, in tunicles and golden copes, their heads wrapped and turbaned with gold and crimson' (F. Taylor and J. Roskell, *Gesta Henrici Quinti* (Oxford, 1975), 107). Cf. also T.W. Craik, *The Tudor Interlude*, 53–4 and S.M. Newton, *Renaissance Theatre Costume* (London, 1975), 90–2, 143–4.

554–9 The details of this pageant, consisting of the Throne of God surrounded by hierarchies of angels and golden candlesticks, derives from Apoc. 1:12–16, 4:1–10, 5:1–8. For similar representations, see W. Kurth, *Complete Woodcuts of Albrecht Dürer* (New York, 1963), figs. 107–08 and C. Sterling and C. Schaefer, *The Hours of Etienne Chevalier* (New York, 1971), Pl. 27. In 1392, Richard II encountered a similar pageant at the Little Conduit in Chepe, but without the golden candlesticks: 'a throne completely surrounded by three circles of angels . . . Above them was sitting a youth representing God himself: a light beaming like the sun shines upon him. His face is fiery and his garments snowy-white; he sits above the celestial hierarchies' (Richard Maydiston, *Concordia: Facta Inter Regem Riccardum II et Civitatem Londonie*, ll. 322–30; tr. C.R. Smith, diss. Princeton 1972, 201). Anglo, 'London Pageants', points out that 'almost every illuminated apocalypse manuscript would have included a vision of the seven-fold symbolization of the Universal Church with God the Father, seated on the throne of heaven, presiding over the cosmos', and he lists some ten such MSS (87 & n.85).

556–7 According to the *Great Chronicle*, the 'personage Representyng the ffadyr of hevyn' was 'all ffourmyd of Gold'

(306). In the medieval drama, God, Christ, and the angels conventionally wore gilt masks or gilt face painting, presumably to portray divine radiance. In this case, however, the gilding was particularly appropriate since the pageant itself was founded upon Apoc. 1:12–16 where St John envisions the Son of man whose 'face was as the sun shineth in his power'. Cf. M. Twycross and S. Carpenter, 'Masks in Medieval English Theatre', *Medieval English Theatre*, 3 (1981), 96–105.

570 Cf. Apoc. 1:8, 1:17, 22:13. The Father appropriately begins his speech with the first words St John hears the Lord God say.

570–6 As St Augustine explains (*City of God*, XIV, 22), the Lord created male and female, with bodies of different sexes, for the explicit purpose of engendering offspring and so increasing, multiplying, and replenishing the earth. In this way, the marriage of Adam and Eve in Paradise becomes the figure or type of all Christian marriages, particularly since, as the *Sarum Missal* explains, the institution of marriage, alone of all the Lord's blessings bestowed upon Adam and Eve, has not been taken away either as a punishment for original sin or as a consequence of the deluge. Cf. Dickinson, 840*; Matthew 19:4–6.

577–8 These lines perhaps reflect Apoc. 21:3: 'Ecce tabernaculum Dei cum hominibus, et habitabit cum eis. Et ipsi populus eius erunt et ipse Deus cum eis erit eorum Deus'; cf. Anglo, 'London Pageants', 81.

579–83 In the *Moralia*, St Gregory the Great identifies the seven stars of the constellation Arcturus with the seven golden candlesticks of Apoc. 1:20. The stars thus symbolize the Universal Catholic Church: 'Quid namque Arcturi nomine, qui in coeli axe constitutus, septem stellarum radiis fulget, nisi Ecclesia universalis exprimitur, quae in Joannis Apocalypsi per septem Ecclesias septemque candelabra figuratur'. He then adds that the constellation's seven stars also represent the Spirit of Sevenfold Grace: 'Quae dum dona in se septiformis gratiae Spiritus continet, claritate summae virtutis irradians, quasi ab axe veritatis lucet' (Migne, *Pat. Lat.* lxxv, 865–6). Cf. Anglo, 'London Pageants', 59–60. The latter may account for the Father's equation of the lights of the candles/stars with various virtues.

592–7 Cf. Deut. 28:1–14; both *sustennce* (R) and *substance* (G, C) are possible renderings of the Latin *fructus*.

599–600 'Beautiful virgin, Henry VII summons you, the bride, from the farthest lands so that you may marry Arthur'. I follow Kingsford's emendation (*Chronicles*, 246) of *extremis* for *extremus*.

607 A popular metaphor for the Incarnation. Cf. Caxton's
Royal Book (London, 1484), a translation of the *Somme le Roi*:
'Ysaye the prophete sawe in spyrite the gloryouse espowsaylles
that were made in the bely of the blessyd vyrgyn marye whan the
blessyd sone of god espoused her / and toke in hyr our blood and
our flesshe / our humanyte and our nature' (ch. lxxxvj).

608–14 Cf. Matthew 22:1–14. The wedding service itself
popularized the conventional identification of marriage as a
'mystery' which signified the sacramental and nuptial union
between Christ and the Church: 'Deus, qui tam excellenti
mysterio conjugalem copulam consecrasti, ut Christi et Ecclesiae
sacramentum prae signares in foedere nuptiarum' (Dickinson,
840*).

621 *Moost Cristen kyng*: A formal title bestowed by a pope.
The title is accompanied by the insignia of a sword and cap of
maintenance. Henry had a sword and cap of maintenance from
both Innocent VIII (1489) and Alexander VI (1496) and would
receive another from Julius II in 1506.

622 Prelacy's likening of Henry VII to the Father of Heaven
pointedly takes advantage of the fact that the King stood watching
the procession, 'in very opyn sight' of the people, from a house
just opposite this pageant (below, 2/633–640). Perhaps, as Anglo
suggests, the features of the Father were made to resemble those
of Henry VII ('London Pageants', 81).

633 The civic chronicles identify the 'marchauntes chambre'
as the house of 'william Geffrey, habyrdassher' (*Great Chronicle*,
306; Kingsford, *Chronicles*, 245).

650 *The*: They.

666–9 Essex and his retainers wear the ostrich-feather badge
of the Prince of Wales.

675–6 Henry VII's household account books show that a
considerable number of musicians and minstrels travelled with
Katharine to London. Henry rewarded the Princess' 'styl-
mynstrels' (shawm players) and the Princess' trumpet players
(these would have included sackbut players) on 4 December 1501;
he also rewarded the nine trumpets of Spain (4 December 1501),
two Spanish minstrels (7 January 1502), and 'My Lady Princess
mynstrells' (20 May 1502) as well as the Earl of Spain's trumpets
(i.e., the Count of Cabra) on 4 December 1501. P.R.O. E
101/415/3.

681–2 The Privy Council, by the Queen's commandment, had
provided a rich litter, a palfrey with a 'pillion', and a richly-
garnished chare for the Princess' entry into London. Her appearance upon a mule, despite all these elaborate provisions, suggests

some last-minute deference to Spanish custom or to the Princess'
wishes. See *The traduction & mariage of the princesse* (London,
[1500]), 3, and B.L. MS Cotton Vespasian C. XIV, 97ᵛ, 98ᵛ.

685–91 Katharine apparently wore both a coif, a close-fitting
undercap tied beneath the chin, and a hat. Although the former is
usually designed to cover the hair entirely, here it has been
adapted to allow her hair to hang down about her shoulders, a
sign of her status as an unmarried woman. Her maids of honour
(below, 2/704–7) wear the same headdresses, while Doña Elvira
wears her hair completely covered, as befits a matron (below,
2/707–11).

720–5 This 'hors-lytter richely beseen' was apparently the one
specifically prepared, by the Queen's commandment, for the
Princess' use upon her entry into the city. The Queen's command
also accounts for the appearance here of the three 'maydynes of
honour', who were to 'folowe next to the sayde lytter' as
'henxmen in side sadillis & hurnes all of one sute' (*Traduction*,
3ʳ). An illustration of such a litter appears in College of Arms,
MS M. 6, 41ᵛ (*Heralds' Commemorative Exhibition 1484–1934*
(London, 1936), Pl. xii).

725–9 According to the Queen's command, 'a faire Palfrey
with a pylion richely arraied and led in hond for the said
pryncesse' was to follow next to the Maids of Honour (*Traduction*, 3ᵛ). Such a 'palfrey of honor' with a 'pylion' follows
immediately after the Queen's litter in College of Arms, MS M. 6,
41ᵛ (*Heralds' Commemorative Exhibition*, Pl. xii).

729–44 The Queen also commanded that 19 palfreys 'all in a
suyt be ordeined for suche ladies as shalbe appoynted to folow
next unto the pillion' and ordered that five chares 'diversely
appareilled' follow next after; one of these was to be 'richely
garnysshed for the saide pryncesse' while the other four were
reserved for 'suche ladyes as shalbe appointed to folow'. Finally,
an undetermined number of other chares was to be provided if
they could be found. The writer's description shows that these
commands were carefully followed. See *Traduction*, 3ᵛ (mis-
printing 'xi palfreis' for 'xix palfreis') and B.L. MS Cotton
Vespasian C. XIV, 97ᵛ.

744–5 Sir Thomas More provides a less circumspect description of the plainness of the Spanish escort: 'Except for three, or at
the most four, of them, they were just too much to look at:
hunchbacked, undersized, barefoot Pygmies from Ethiopia. If
you had been there, you would have thought they were refugees
from hell' (E.F. Rogers, *St Thomas More: Selected Letters* (New
Haven, 1961), 2).

755–6 For the Little Conduit, built in 1442, see Stowe, *Survey*, 48.

757–73 In its main features, this pageant follows the decription of the Throne in Jean Molinet's *Le Trosne d'honneur*: 'la noble dame Vertu le presenta devant Honneur, duquel la face resplendissoit comme le soleil, car il estoit glorifié en son precieux trosne, auquel il avoit fait preparer deux chaÿeres richement aornees de fin or, l'une a dextre, l'autre a senestre; et allors que Honneur aperchut cestre tres haulte et excellente fleur de noblesse, le grand duc d'Occident, il fist convocquier et appeller tous les bienheurés du celestiel empire, et en leur presence, le assist a sa dextre et luy donna sceptre et couronne de laurier'. In order to reach this throne, it was necessary to pass the nine spheres of the cosmos, where there were nine virtues and nine worthies, before reaching the Throne itself, set above the cosmos among the stars. So Katharine must ascend the 'great peier of steires' with a virtue 'dwelling' on each step to reach her Throne of Honour (cf. 2/792–8). Cf. *Faictz et dictz*, I, 56, 45, 46; Kipling, *Triumph of Honour*, 75–9.

785–91 Cf. Plutarch, *Marcellus*, 28; Cicero, *De Natura Deorum*, 2. 23. 61; Anglo, 'London Pageants', 83. The interconnected temples of Virtue and Honour, already a commonplace allusion in the Late Middle Ages, became a staple of the emblem books; cf. Picinelli, *Mundus Symbolicus* (Cologne, 1694), ii, 79.

792–8 The stair or ladder of virtues was a medieval commonplace (cf. Augustine, *Confessions*, xiii. 9; Hilton, *Scale of Perfection*; R. Tuve, *Allegorical Imagery* (Princeton, 1966), 87–9). A pageant was devoted to this subject during Margaret of Anjou's London civic triumph (1445): 'From vertu to vertu men shall vp ascende / Then shall God be seyn in the Mount Sion', citing Psalm 83:8 (G. Kipling, 'London Pageants for Margaret of Anjou', *Medieval English Theatre*, iv (1982), 23). Molinet also adapts the same commonplace in *Le Trosne d'honneur* by visualizing the nine spheres of the cosmos as the steps of such a *scala perfectionis*, each sphere presided over by a Virtue and a Worthy. Given these precedents, in a pageant already indebted to Molinet, it seems unlikely that the devisor would have derived his imagery from a far more tenuous version of the same commonplace: Job 31:37 as interpreted by Gregory the Great (Anglo, *Spectacle*, 91).

812 *The Recordar*: Sir Robert Sheffield's Latin oration, on behalf of the City, in praise of Katharine's 'adventus' is preserved in P.R.O. SC 1, vol. 51, 214. The MS, however, is considerably faded and damaged.

813–6 *Moch treasoure* ...: The City traditionally gave a gift of 500 marks to those it honoured with a civic triumph. For the City's threat to reduce the amount of its gift because of a dispute over the 'seventh pageant', see below, 3/216n.

820–9 For the identity of the bishops and abbots who were to meet Katharine *in pontificalibus* and conduct her to the high altar of St Paul's for 'such Cerymonyes as in suche case is accustumed', see the Privy Council order, B.L. MS Cotton Vespasian C XIV, 99ᵛ. The same order also provides for her to be taken directly from St Paul's to a chamber in the Bishop of London's Palace where she might rest 'oon day at the leest before the day of her mariage & more as the case shall require' to recover from 'her long travaill & labour'.

832 *Paleis of Derham*: Durham House in the Strand, the London residence of the Bishop of Durham.

838–51 *No marvell ... Almyghti God*: This very long and pompous sentence is based upon a very simple thought: that the royal entry turned out so well is evidence of God's pleasure in the marriage of Arthur and Katharine. There are two main parts to the sentence. In the first part, the author observes, somewhat abstractly, that it is no marvel that the royal entry (*that matter*) was brought (*deducid*) and led (*conveied*) to such a happy conclusion (*theffectes of felicitie*), which effects [both] Mediating Grace and lawful purpose actuate (*meovith*; cf. *OED* 'Move', v.). He then interrupts his thought with a series of clauses meant to illustrate, in the abstract, the two-fold actions of Mediating Grace: first, it moves people to begin such great matters (*ffirst to ther incepcions and begynnyng*), then it assists the participants in carrying out these same great matters with 'great influens of strength and vertu'. He further interrupts this illustration with a parenthetical observation: Proof or demonstration (*thexperyence*, cf. *OED*, 'experience', sb.) sufficient to judge Almighty God content and pleased with this marriage might be obvious (*evident*) and confirmed (*aproperyd*; see following n.) in [the outcome of] this present day. The author then begins (*notwithstandyng the wonderfull preyse of the people* ...) the second main part of his sentence. This constitutes a circumstantial account of the *experyence* (proof) that confirms God's pleasure in the marriage. He thus points out that notwithstanding the royal entry's many inherent dangers for the crowds watching the show (such as the press of the crowd, trampling by horses, and falls from high places), yet no such accident occurred at all, praise be to Almighty God.

841–2 *Evident and aproperyd*: By *aproperyd* the author apparently means 'confirmed' (hence a synonym for *evident* in the adjectival doublet), a form of *approbate/approbated/approbation* based upon a substitution of unvoiced *p* for voiced *b*. See also 2/504, *aropered and namyd*.

855–7 *Their messages … commaundement*: A confusing parataxis. The writer interrupts the main verbal phrase, *to intrete of and uppon*, with an enumeration of the *messages, embasshions, and singler titles* of the King of Spain's commandments which form the bases of the entreaties. *Singler titles of their Lord Soverayne of their realme his commaundement*: the several articles (lit. 'headings', subjects) of the King of Spain's commandment. These 'titles' are enumerated below ('thies singler articles of her [the Princess'] conveyaunce', 2/876–91).

860 *Agreable*: Agreeably.

875–91 *Everych poynt and circumstaunce of their commyssion*: These are the *singler titles* of the King of Spain's commandments referred to above (2/856–7). These commandments apparently governed the Princess' journey from her departure through her wedding. They covered such diverse matters as: 1) the forms of attendance required of the Princess' servants; 2) instructions to avoid particular countries and coasts should the ships be blown off course in a storm; and 3) arrangements to safeguard the Princess' person and (particularly) to preserve her virginity. The point of this entreaty is to have the King certify that they have faithfully carried out the various articles of this commandment and to be released formally from any further responsibility over the Princess' welfare. For one of the difficulties that the Princess' 'guiders and safe-conductors' encountered in carrying out their sovereign's commandment, see above, 1/87–113.

899–918 Despite the writer's assurance that the Princess herself initiated this visit, she in fact was following one of the Privy Council plans. See B.L. MS Cotton Vespasian C. XIV, 100f. The writer, however, does not report the presence of the Duchess of Norfolk, who was to call upon the Princess and accompany her to Baynard's Castle.

918 *Honourable*: Honourably.

Book III

10 *Ffurst thauter with their plates*: *Their* apparently does not refer to *auter* but instead refers to the indefinite 'they' who are identified with St Paul's and who thus possess the plates, jewels, and relics.

11–3 *With copys and vestmentes ... of full great valoure*: The author modifies *copys and vestmentes* with three, relatively parallel, adjectival phrases: *in their suetes* (the copes and vestments are made in matching sets), *honourably to the mynystres abehovabill* (they are honourably befitting to the ministers who wear them), and *of full great valoure* (they are of very great worth). The confusion occurs in the second of these phrases because the author divides the adjective from its adverbial modifier by inserting the prepositional phrase between.

13–4 *The quere also enhaungyd with clothis of aras*: The Privy Council charged Giles Daubeney, the Lord Chamberlain, with the responsibility of seeing that 'the Church of paules be hanged with Aras soo high that the lowest parte therof be vij or viij fote from the ground' (B.L. MS Cotton Vespasian C. XIV, 101).

15–26 A 'haulte place' was built in the nave of St Paul's next to the Consistory. In essence an elevated platform covered with red cloth, it served as a stage upon which the wedding ceremony could take place and be viewed by a standing congregation. In addition, a railed passageway, five feet high, was built from the choir door to the 'hault place' 'soo as therby growe noon Impedyment to the sight of the people' when the Princess made her entrance into the church. A traditional structure, it was 'deuised to be made like vnto the haulte place at the Cristenyng of the kinges Childern' (B.L. MS Cotton Vespasian C. XIV, 100ʳ). Cf. *Great Chronicle*, 310, and, for a diagram of such a traditional 'hault place', Leland, *Collectanea* (London, 1774), v, 340.

26 *In objecte annempst this place*: Cf. *OED* ppl. a. 1.b, quoting Wyatt (1541): 'The other stands object Against the same'. *Objecte* is always (as in the Wyatt citation) a ppl. a. (ad. Lat. *objectus*, thrown), but the presence of the prep. *in* here suggests that the writer may conceive *objecte* as a noun (cp. *in opposition*). In essence, the phrase is an example of the writer's habitual use of intensifiers; it is perhaps best construed as meaning *directly* *opposite this place*, the phrase *in objecte* forming an intensifying parallel to *annempste*.

33 *Costely and riche clothis of Arras*: For Henry VII's patronage of tapestry-weaving, see G. Kipling, 'Henry VII and the Origins of Tudor Patronage', in *Patronage in the Renaissance*, ed. G.F. Lytle and S. Orgel (Princeton, 1981), 137–46. In particular, Henry owned a Passion set, woven by Pasquel Grenier of Tournai, which he hung in the chapel at Calais when he met the Archduke Philip of Burgundy in 1500. This may have been one of the sets hung in St Paul's. Cf. Kipling, *Triumph of Honour*, 61 and n. 31 and below, 4/821–6n.

59 *O si me inveniat*: Although Luke 2:26 alludes to Simeon's successful prayer 'that he should not see death, before he had seen the Christ of the Lord', the words of Simeon's prayer derive from one of St Augustine's sermons which was widely read as a homily for the Feast of the Purification: 'Symeon ille senex diu vixerat ... et audierat responsum, quod non esset visurus mortem: nisi prius vidisset Christum. Intelligite, fratres, quantum desiderium habebant antiqui sancti videre Christum. Sciebant illum esse venturum: et omnes qui pie vivebant quotidie in orationibus suis dicebant, O si me hic inveniat illa nativitas. O si, quod credo in scripturis Dei, videam oculis meis' (*Breviarium Sarum*, ed. F. Procter and C. Wordsworth (Cambridge, 1886), iii, 133–4).

60 *Aron is rode*: Cf. Numbers 17:1–11. The miraculous flowering of Aaron's rod in the night served as one of the 'commonest Old Testament prefigurations of the virgin birth of the Messiah' in Christian iconography (G. Schiller, *Iconography of Christian Art* (London, 1971), i, 21, 54).

69–70 The poet confuses the Circumcision with the Purification as the occasion on which Simeon saw Jesus.

71 *This noble songe*: The *Nunc dimittis* or 'Canticle of Simeon', based upon Luke 2:29–32. Lines 73–77 are an approximate translation of this canticle, which was regularly sung at Compline and Vespers.

78ff. At this point, the poem embarks upon an extensive parallel between Christ's presentation in the temple and the marriage of Arthur and Katharine at St Paul's. Just as Simeon embraces the Christ child 'with mooche joy and gladdnes' (3/71), so the day of the marriage is one 'of pleasure, joye, and gladnes above many othir' (3/82). The two dates, 1 January and 14 November, thus stand as comparable Presentations in the Temple, a point made in the final lines of the poem, which characterize the witnesses to the wedding as so many 'Simeons' who had 'well taryed' to see this moment.

80 *Allege him for his pere*: The poet means that the wedding day is the 'peer' or equal of Christ's circumcision in pleasure, joy, and gladness.

95–7 *Duetie and serymonyes of annourement ... service of thonour temperall*: Apparently the author is distinguishing between the worship due to God (*annourement*; cf. *OED* 'Anoure', v., ad. OF *anorer*) and the reverence due to high estate (*thonour temperall*).

97–8 *As it is premisid, apprepared in is solempnites*: The writer refers to the preparations described just above in chapter 1. Cf. *OED*, 'Premise', v.

111–2 *The Kinges Wardrope*: The King's Wardrobe lay just off Carter Lane, which ran along the wall of St Paul's, just outside the south gate of the Cathedral. The Wardrobe contained storehouses, workshops, and a dwelling suitable for royal visits to the City, as in this case. The Privy Council originally planned for Arthur to arrive a day or two before the wedding and stay in the Bishop of Salisbury's Palace, but altered this plan to the Wardrobe because of its convenience to the south door of St Paul's, where the Prince was to arrive for his wedding. Cf. B.L. MS Cotton Vespasian C. XIV, 100^v.

116–8 The Privy Council minutes make no provision for the Prince to change into his wedding clothes in the Bishop of London's Palace.

121ff. For the Privy Council directive prescribing the Princess' entry into St Paul's through the West Door attended by the Duke of York (the future Henry VIII), see B.L. MS Cotton Vespasian C. XIV, 100^v.

131–2 *Xviij mooe bushoppes and honourabill abbottes*: The Privy Council directed only eight bishops and six abbots to attend the Archbishop of Canterbury in the marriage ceremony (B.L. MS Cotton Vespasian C. XIV, 100^v). The author of the *Great Chronicle*, however, counted nineteen 'Bysshoppys & abbottys than mytrid' in attendance (310).

156ff. *A coyf of whight silk ...*: The author is apparently describing an 'Anne of Brittany cap', then very fashionable and named for the contemporary French queen who popularized it. It comprised two parts: a white coif edged with a fluted ruffle was first fitted closely to the head. Over this was worn an outer cap which had a relatively wide band over the fore part of the head and reached to the shoulders. This band, usually lined with a rich fabric of contrasting colour, was often edged with jewels (as was Katharine's) when worn by women of wealth and station. Apparently the jewelled band of Katharine's outer cap has been modified into a kind of bridal veil. Cf. B. Payne, *History of Costume* (New York, 1965), 249–50, 292–3.

163–4 *Certayn rownde hopys . . . aftir their countray maner*: The verdugeo, a system of rigid hoops designed to spread and display the fabric of a woman's skirt, first appeared in the court of Castile about 1470. It was the ancestor of the farthingale. At this period, however, the hoops were attached to the outside of the gown, and might consist either of plain wooden hoops or of hoops covered with fabric contrasting in colour with the gown. The fashion spread rapidly through Castile and Aragon, but was only just becoming fashionable in France and Italy at the time of the wedding, hence the author's (correct) characterization of the hoops as particularly Spanish. Cf. Payne, *History of Costume*, 259 and F. Boucher, *20,000 Years of Fashion* (New York, [1967]), 204.

177–8 [   ] *houre and more*: The *Great Chronicle* reports that the entire ceremony 'endurid well upon ij howrys or more', but specifically includes in its reckoning the formal reading of the marriage contracts at the West Door: 'ovyr the Sacrementall office, there were Rad sundry Instrumentys & othyr wrytyngys the whych axid a long leysour' (310). For the *Receyt*'s version of the earlier ceremony at the West Door, cf. 3/130–42.

182–5 Trumpeters and other minstrels, under the direction of Sir Thomas Lovell, Yeoman Usher of the King's Chamber, were positioned over the West Door of the Cathedral and charged to 'blow contynuelly' from the time that the Princess emerged from the Bishop of London's Palace until she reached the 'hault place', and again when she returned from the Cathedral to the Bishop's Palace after the ceremony. B.L. MS Cotton Vespasian C. XIV, 101^v, 102^v.

216ff. *The vij pagent*: The construction of this pageant occasioned a good deal of friction between city and court. In the second version of the Privy Council minutes, Sir Charles Somerset was asked to provide a traditional English wine fountain, 'a solemn conduit well and pompously devised for to run divers sorts of good wines' to be placed 'somewhat besides the said great west door' of St Paul's (College of Arms, MS 1st M. 13, 8^v–9^r). At this point, the elaboration of a fountain into a pageant had never entered the Council's deliberations. Hardly more than a bit of consolatory liberality, the fountain was meant to dispense wine to the multitude while the courtiers banqueted in the Bishop of London's palace after the wedding. Sometime in the summer of 1501, however, after the City's own plans for the reception of the Princess were far advanced, Sir Reginald Bray decided to turn the fountain into a pageant and bill the city for the costs. The outraged civic council responded by threatening to deduct this additional expense from the traditional gift of 500 marks which it had intended to present to Katharine during her royal entry (Corporation of London, *Repertory*, i, 87ʳ). Faced with this ultimatum, the court withdrew its demand for payment, and 'in þe Ende, sir Reynold Bray & othir of the kyngis counsayll had of the Chambyrlayn ffor the charge of the same [pageant] C li.' (*Great Chronicle*, 310). Payments to carpenters for this pageant totalled £24, and a payment of £100 to John Atkinson, the court's accountant and purchasing agent, probably can be identified with the one mentioned in the *Great Chronicle* (P.R.O. E 101/415/3, 3 Nov. 1501 and 7 Jan. 1502). Together, these two sums nicely substantiate Wickham's estimate of an average cost of £120 for each outdoor pageant (*Early English Stages*, i, 289).

217-22 The jewel-studded mountain burgeoning with precious ores became one of Henry VII's favourite dynastic emblems: the Rich Mount of England. A kind of heraldic pun, the emblem plays upon the name of Henry's earldom (Richmond = Rich Mount) to depict the King as a source of Princely Magnificence. The emblem held particular significance at the time of the wedding, for Henry had rushed through the rebuilding of Sheen Palace (destroyed by fire in 1497) in time to entertain the wedding party there, and he had named it 'Richmond'. Inevitably, his subjects saw the new palace as a Rich Mount as well; cf. *Great Chronicle*, 295; J. Leland, *Cygnea Cantio* (London, 1658), 5; Bernard André, in Gairdner, *Memorials*, 108. The emblem was still serving as a viable Tudor dynastic symbol early in Henry VIII's reign. A Rich Mount pageant appeared at the King's Christmas revels in 1512-13 (Hall, *Chronicle* (London, 1550), 22).

222-41 The *Great Chronicle* describes this pageant as 'a Towyr wheruppon stood iij Imagis whereof eyþir of theym was lyke a kyng and beyng armyd ech of theym bare a scochun of Sundry armys, whereof the middylmest Representid kyng arthur beryng In his Scochun þe armys of Bretayn' (310). If the chronicler is right in identifying the middle king specifically as Arthur (as seems likely) instead of a merely symbolic 'King of Englond', then the pageant is probably based upon some variant of the Three Christian Worthies theme. The 'King of Fraunce' would then be Charlemagne, while some Spanish worthy—perhaps El Cid, Alfonso the Wise, or conceivably even Amadis—has replaced Godfrey of Boulogne as the third Worthy. The meaning of the pageant, whatever the specific identities of the Kings, is clear, however: the marriage of Arthur and Katharine

unites three wellsprings of English royal greatness (French,
British, and Spanish) upon the Rich Mount of England (see
Kipling, *Triumph of Honour*, 97–100). The kings are identified
heraldically; the white hart (albeit winged) had been a French
royal device since the time of Charles VI and the greyhound is
almost as old. More to the point, both of these French heraldic
animals had been assimilated into English royal usage (most
notably by Richard II and Edward III respectively), thus
heraldically illustrating the theme of the pageant. The English
Red Dragon is of course a Tudor (hence 'British') royal emblem
(above, 2/156n.), while the Castle and Lion emblems borne by the
King of Spain represent Castile and Leon. The trees also burgeon
with French fleurs-de-lis, English Lancastrian roses, and Spanish
oranges.

241–5 The pageant still incorporates the 'solemn conduit, well
and pompously devised for to run divers sorts of good wines'
which the Privy Council directed to be placed 'somewhat beside
the great West door of the church, in the South side thereof' so
that it might 'run continually all that day [of the wedding] and
part of the pipes to run till midnight following' (*M*, 8ᵛ–9ʳ).

249ff. The arrangements for this banquet were entrusted to
Giles Daubeney, the Lord Chamberlain. For the Privy Council
directives, see B.L. MS Cotton Vespasian C. XIV, 102ᵛ–103ʳ.

253–4 *A stondyng cuppbord with plate of clene gold ... plentie*:
The first of many cupboards full of gold and silver dishes which
were a central feature of all the court banquets. Ostentatiously
displayed at each court feast, they constitute the most pervasive
symbol of Henry's liberality. This one alone, according to the
Great Chronicle, held over £12,000 in goldware, evidently purchased for this occasion (312). Moreover, a new cupboard
appeared at each new feast, and even when the tables were fully
set, as the author later points out, 'the cuppbord was nothyng
towchid but stode complet, garnysshid, and fulfillyd, nott oonys
dimynysshid' (4/257–9). Indeed, many of the dishes were given
away in yet another show of courtly liberality. These cupboards,
in short, served to demonstrate that the magnificence of the royal
estate committed to the celebration of the festival was apparently
boundless, a point made by the Scots humanist, Walter Ogilvie,
who attended some of these banquets and singled out these
cupboards for particular admiration: 'Why should I mention the
sideboards on which stood precious gold and silver ware of every
kind? You might have seen jewel-encrusted goblets, dishes of
purest gold, and whatever finery goldsmiths and engravers or
even the famous Mentor knew how to devise, in great and

unbelievable abundance, not to mention the other countless banquet dishes displayed in other places. All these fine things were virtually beyond counting' (National Library of Scotland, MS Advocates 33.2.24, 26–7, my translation). For an illustration of such a cupboard, see Kernodle, *From Art to Theatre*, 96.

263–71 The *Great Chronicle* adds that the wedding dinner consisted of three courses with 12 dishes served at the first course, 15 at the second, and 18 at the third (311).

304–7 The 'congruent usages and custom' described here for blessing the nuptial bed, the sleeping chamber, and the newly married couple in the bed form integral parts of the wedding service as prescribed in the *Sarum Missal* (Dickinson, 844*–5*).

307–9 *Than furst refresshid ... their singler departure*: Because the subject of the verb *were* has been omitted, it is not entirely clear whether the bride and groom or the attendant nobles are being required and admonished to their departures after first being refreshed with wine and spices. Since the ceremony described in the *Sarum Missal* concludes with the priest's formal dismissal of the bride and groom, the former reading is at least possible (*His peractis, aspergat eos sacerdos aqua benedicta; et sic discedat et dimittat eos in pace.* Dickinson, 845*). The latter reading, however, seems more likely since the priest requires and admonishes [them] to their *singler* (i.e., separate) *departure*(s).

335 *Of honour*: I.e., in order to do the Spaniards honour.

338 *The Couldeherber*: One of the most important and imposing town houses or 'inns' which served as the London residences of important churchmen, nobles, and wealthy citizens. Most recently, Richard III had given it to the College of Arms as a permanent home on the occasion of their incorporation in 1484. Less than a year later, however, Henry VII cancelled both the heralds' incorporation and the grant of Coldharbour, which he gave to his mother, Margaret Beaufort, for life. Cf. C.L. Kingsford, 'Historical Notes on Mediaeval London Houses', *London Topographical Record*, x (1916), 94–100.

348 *His lodgyng*: the Coldharbour.

360ff. *Of the offeryng ... at the Chirche of Powlys*: This ceremony is not foreseen in the Privy Council plans. The *Great Chronicle* (312) includes a brief report of this incident.

381–6 *In this ordre ... the Kinges person*: This passage is badly muddled and quite possibly textually corrupt. The writer has been describing the various groups of nobles riding in procession. These groups are generally ordered in a hierarchical sequence, beginning with the lowest ranks of nobility and rising to the highest. Hence, the procession begins with the esquires; followed by the knights, lords, and barons; then various members of the higher nobility, both English and Spanish, riding two by two (Bishop of Spain and Archbishop of York; Earl of Shrewsbury and Earl of Spain; Archbishop of Canterbury and Archbishop of Spain). At this point, the writer attempts to describe those marching in procession just before the King (*In this ordre toward the Kinge*). These should be the *lordes officers of the lond* (i.e., the Great Officers of State): Steward (Lord Willoughby de Broke), Lord High Constable of England (the Earl of Derby), Earl Marshall (Prince Henry, Duke of York), and Great Chamberlain of England (the Earl of Oxford). Of these, Lord Willoughby de Broke seems to have been generally absent from the wedding festival, possibly because of illness (although he did travel to Devonshire to meet the Princess, he was reported ill when the second version of the Privy Council minutes was drawn up in the Spring of 1501, and he died in August 1502). The other three are listed in this passage. By virtue of their offices, they belong in this procession *mediatly before His Grace* (immediately before the King). Prince Henry and the Earl of Derby ride side by side—Henry to the right, Derby to the left—and they are followed in turn by the Earl of Oxford, who rides alone (possibly because Lord Willoughby de Broke, who should accompany him, is missing), but on the right side of the procession, *sumwhat nere to the Kinges person*. The writer, however, has apparently transposed the offices held by Prince Henry and the Earl of Derby; Henry, the Earl Marshal, is called *Cunstable of England* and Derby, the Constable, is called *Marshall*. Elsewhere, however, the author gives Derby his proper title: *Constable of the seid Realme* (4/53).

396–7 *With chenes and colours of golde*: Cf. *Great Chronicle* (312): 'Thys day sir Nycholas Vaus ... ware a coler of Essis which weyed as the Goldsmyth þᵗ made It Reportyd viij C li. of noblys'.

404ff. The Privy Council minutes (B.L. MS Cotton Vespasian C. XIV, 103) planned the Princess' departure from London to Westminster on the third day after the wedding (i.e., Wednesday, rather than Tuesday). She was supposed to travel from the Bishop's Palace to Baynard's Castle accompanied by the same litter, nobles, and servants who accompanied her on her entry into London. The *Great Chronicle* (312) confirms the *Receyt*'s report and adds that the party rowed from Paul's Wharf.

418ff. Contrary to this somewhat idealistic report of the 'right weell dekkyd and arayed' barges, the *Great Chronicle* points out that the Mercers were fined ten pounds by the Mayor and Aldermen because their barge 'was not garnysshid and apparaylid accordyng unto theyr worshyp, nor soo well as othyr, which were of lasse auctoryte' (312). For the various Privy Council provisions for barges, see B.L. MS Cotton Vespasian C. XIV, 103^v, 94^v.

427–34 *Knightes of the Bathe ... to the nombre of lviij*: The names of 58 'knyghtes of the bathe made at the mariage of the prince arthur' appear in *Writhe's Book of Knights* (B.L. MS. Additional 46354, 198ff.), although Sir Robert Throgmorton appears twice. A slightly different list of 58 names appears in B.L. MS Cotton Claudius C. III, 47^r–54^r, in essence a copy of *Writhe's Book*, but supplemented and corrected from other sources. Ordinarily, knighthood was conferred on individual knights in a simple dubbing ceremony. But such ceremonial occasions as coronations or royal marriages called for a more lengthy and elaborate ceremony. On such occasions, knighthood would be conferred upon a number of candidates at the same time, and the ceremony would include a symbolic purification by bathing. Such knights had been known since the early fifteenth century as 'Knights of the Bath'. See Sir A. Wagner, *Heralds of England* (London, 1967), 145, 357, and Plates xxxii–iv for discussion of this point and for contemporary illustrations of the ceremonial.

445–6 *And that shuld be for them nedfull*: And everything else that they should need [for the ceremony].

452 *Xviij moo knightes*: According to *Writhe's Book of Knights*, Henry dubbed not eighteen but twenty-five 'knights of the carpet ... at the said marriage' in addition to the fifty-eight Knights of the Bath (24^r). Since heralds were professionally involved in this event, the error here, together with the author's vagueness about the status of the 'additional' knights, again suggests that the author was not himself a herald.

Book IV

5ff. *The great and large voyde space bifore Westmenstir Halle*:
The 'outer ward' of the Palace of Westminster, an area now
known as the 'New Palace Yard'. The tilt ran east–west along the
north front of the Palace from the Water Gate at the river to the
gate leading to the Abbey. Such an east–west axis, as Wickham
points out, ensured 'that the combatants should not have to fight
with the sun in their eyes' (*Early English Stages*, i, 37). For a
description of the area as it was known in the Late Middle Ages,
together with sixteenth-century drawings of the area, see H.M.
Colvin, gen. ed., *The History of the King's Works*, 6 vols.
(London, 1963–82), i, 540, 546–7, and Plates 24, 36B. The Privy
Council assigned Sir Richard Guildford the responsibility for
overseeing these arrangements (B.L. MSS Cotton Vespasian C.
XIV, 94^r and Harley 69, 43^v).

10 *The sentwary*: Westminster Abbey. A gate at the west end
of the 'outer ward' led directly to the Abbey.

12 *A goodly tre*: For this Tree of Chivalry, which stood at the
north-east corner of the Palace Yard (where it was always in view
of the royal box located on the south side of the yard), see the
Introduction (above, xxvi–viii) and the tournament challenges
(BC/133–68, SC/144–64).

19 *A stage*: Wickham points out that the best seats at a
tournament 'face north, that is, away from the sun. These were
invariably reserved for the Court. Opposite, facing into the sun,
would sit the civic dignitaries'. The arrangement of the lists
described here, Wickham observes, was 'standardized in shape
and size in the reign of Richard II ... and enforced throughout
the fifteenth and early sixteenth centuries' (*Early English Stages*,
i, 34–8).

31 *The Chekyr Chambir*: The Exchequer Chamber, attached to
the west side of the Palace, fronted on the Palace Yard. Cf.
Colvin, *History of the King's Works*, i, 540.

78ff. *His pavylion*: The *Great Chronicle* gives a quite similar
description of the Duke's pageant car (which it calls 'a Chapell'),
but adds a few details overlooked by the author of the *Receyt*.
When the Duke emerged from his 'Chapell', he wore 'an
excedyng bush of Ostrich ffedyrs upon his helmet' while his horse
trapper was decorated with the Princess' heraldic emblems, four

'grete castellys made of Goldsmythis werk'. These emblems identified him as the royal couple's 'Chieff Chalengeour' in the tournament that day, a point underscored when he 'cawsid the said Bush of ffedyrs to be takyn ffrom his hede pese and to be presentid unto the kyngis Tent' (*Great Chronicle*, 313).

95ff. *The defendeours*: The *Great Chronicle*'s report of these pageant cars is far less reliable than that of the *Receyt*, although it often contributes additional detail. The chronicler thus fails to recognize Sir John Peche (whom it calls 'a Gentylman unknowyn'), and it combines Devonshire's red dragon pageant together with Essex's mountain pageant to produce a single, impossibly ponderous and complex pageant car: 'And ffowyrtly cam In therle of Essex all closid In a mountayn wyth a woodhous precedyng and beryng a Sere Tre In his nek, and In his Rygth hand a lyne of white & Grene sylk that was ffastenyd abowth a Rede dragunnys nekke whych drewe the said mountayn, and upon the Topp of the said mountayn was sett a vyrgyn In hir here Rycchely apparaylyd and an unycorn lyyng his hede In hyr lapp'. The chronicler does, however, recall Guillaume de la Rivers' punning pageant car rather more graphically than does the *Receyt*: 'a Shypp Crossaylid and the nethir partys thereof hangid wyth peyntid cloth colourid lyke unto the watyr' (313).

103–4 *In her heer*: The 'goodly yonge lady' wears her hair hanging down about her shoulders rather than tied up and covered, an emblem of her status as an unmarried woman. Cf. 2/685–91 and n.

111 *As they were departid owt of their pavylions*: The *Great Chronicle* reports that each of the defenders emerged from his pageant car in a distinctively-coloured suit of armour: the Marquis in coal-black armour with a helmet of cloth of gold paled with black, Devonshire in gilt armour, Guillaume de la Rivers in blood-red armour, Essex in 'Brygth armour uncolourid', and the unidentified Sir John Peche likewise in uncoloured armour (313–14).

113ff. Although the *Receyt*'s account of the pageant cars was more accurate than that of the civic chronicler, its account of the first day's joust is far less accurate. The *Great Chronicle*, for example, points out that the Duke and Marquis missed one another entirely on their first course and that the Earl of Essex, 'because his hors was not apt ffor to cope', lost on points to his opposite number, the Lord Henry of Buckingham. It further gives a colourful account of the surprise entry into the lists of a Spanish knight 'wythowth any apparayll of hym sylf or of his hors whoos armour was not dygth to the Sale'. In three courses, the

Duke broke two spears upon the Spanish knight while the Spaniard broke but one upon the Duke, 'which lytyll was allowid ffor It was brokyn w^t crossyng' (314). The accuracy of the chronicler's version is generally supported by the score cheque (appendix, 109), where the Spaniard is identified as Dedo de Azeveido and his score is marked as a single spear broken on his opponent's body.

154ff. *This moost goodly and pleasaunt disguysing*: The first of William Cornish's three disguisings, this show allegorizes the royal courtship and marriage in terms of the moralized *Roman de la Rose* imagery popular at the time. Cornish's central incident, the storming of the castle of love, has a long history both in England and on the Continent. Here, however, Cornish reverses the usual symbolic meaning of the motif (the assault of male lust upon feminine chastity, leading to the triumph of virtue and submission of the knights) and allows the knights to win. In his version, the English knights—types of Prince Arthur—represent the virtues of love, while the Spanish ladies—types of Princess Katharine—represent romantic indifference. For the tradition of the castle-storming game, see R.S. Loomis, 'The Allegorical Siege', *Am. Jour. of Arch.*, 2d. Ser., xxiii (1919), 255–69. For a discussion of the meaning of the disguising, see Kipling, *Triumph of Honour*, 103–05. For Cornish's authorship, see the Introduction, above, xxiii.

155–78. *The furst was a castell*: The pageant is a heraldic symbol for Spain. The castle itself represents Castile, and the four beasts are Spanish rather than English. Hence the (by English standards) unusual silver lion—which was, in fact, the usual colour of the lion as a symbol of Leon in the Spanish royal arms—and the Spanish ibex instead of the more common English antelope.

263–6 The author confusingly separates the subject of his sentence (*the company of nobles*) from its predicate (*made pastans*) with a series of qualifying clauses. Here the interrupting clauses refer to the places where the nobles 'made pastans' (in the Church and in their own chambers) because the weather did not permit them to do so outdoors.

313 *An interlude*: The King's Players, led by John English, almost certainly performed this interlude. Except for a payment to an anonymous group of 'pleyers' for a Twelfth-Night performance, only 'John Englishe the pleyer' and 'The Kinges pleyers' are named in the court account books during this period. See the several payments, representing several different performances, disbursed on 7 and 8 January 1502, P.R.O. E101/415/3, printed in

S. Anglo, 'Court Festivals of Henry VII', *Bull. John Rylands
Library*, xliii (1960–1), 38.

314ff. *Ij pagentes ... an herber ... a lanterne*: Both the arbour
and the 'lantern' (actually a palace of fame) are conventional
allegorical settings in courtly love poetry. In particular, this
pairing of arbour and lantern pageants strongly recalls the setting
and situation of Lydgate's *Complaint of the Black Knight* and
Temple of Glass, two poems almost always paired in manuscript.
As in Lydgate's poem, lonely knights exclusively populate the
arbour while ladies inhabit the 'lantern'. The disguising uses
these conventional settings to portray the love of Arthur and
Katharine as the sort of heroic passion enshrined in the *Temple of
Glass*. Apparently, the 'lantern' pageant pleased the King particularly well, for it appears again a few weeks later in a disguising to
celebrate the betrothal of Princess Margaret to James IV of
Scotland (Leland, *Collectanea*, iv, 203). For a full discusson of
these matters, see Kipling, *Triumph of Honour*, 105–9. For the
identification of John English as the devisor of these pageants, see
above, xxiii.

319–22 *The settyng downe of hit*: All of the other disguising
pageants seem to have been 'sett uppon certayn whelys' and rolled
into the hall (see 4/156ff., 4/608ff., and 4/948ff.). These arbour
and lantern pageants, however, seem to have been carried into the
hall and 'set down' (cp. also *this lantern was brought and pight
bifore the Kyng and the Quene*, 4/334–5). Possibly the twelve lords
and twelve ladies carried their respective pageants into the hall
before emerging from them to perform their dances. This contrast
between manhandled pageants on this occasion and wheeled
pageants on the other three occasions also points to the likelihood
that one designer devised this disguising while another was
responsible for the other three. See the Introduction above,
xxiii.

323ff. *Thes lordes ... by themselvys dauncyd a longe space*: The
pattern of dancing in this disguising symbolically represents the
courtship and marriage of the Prince and Princess. At first the
men and women dance separately to dramatize their loneliness;
then the two groups dance together in a matrimonial concord.

350–7 The civic chronicler's report is equally brief and
laconic, although he does report that the Marquis of Dorset 'brak
moost speris and to hym was allowid the honour of that daye'
(*Great Chronicle*, 315). The score cheque, above 109, supports
this conclusion.

377–85 *Incontynent aftir that ... horsid and arayed*: The author
marshals a single adverbial clause (*incontynent aftir that the*

trumpettes hade blowde unto the feld) and a series of adjectival
clauses (*the seid Duke in his pavylion . . . horsid and arayed*) at the
end of his sentence in an attempt to clarify the syntax of a
sentence already overloaded with qualifiers. The adverbial
clause refers back to the main verbal phrase (*immediatly entrid
in*) while the series of adjectival clauses refers back to one
element (*the noble Duke of Bokyngham*) of the compound
subject. He arranges his clauses (adverbial first, then adjectival)
to mirror the inverted syntactical order of the sentence (verb
first, then subject).

407 *Sharp speris*: For the relevant ordinance governing the tilt
in open field with sharp spears, to be run on the second day of
Buckingham's challenge (i.e., the third day of the combined
tournament), see BC/69–81. A. Young points out that virtually all
Tudor and Jacobean tournaments were fought with rebated
(blunted) weapons, but the temptation to try sharp weapons
remained great because their very danger offered a supreme test
of courage. This was one of the very few Tudor tournaments to
allow sharp weapons; even the articles of combat for the Field of
Cloth of Gold prohibited them. *Tudor and Jacobean Tournaments*
(London, 1987), 14.

422–3 *Bothe the partis of theim were borne to the grounde, bothe
hors and man*: Something of an exaggeration. The *Great Chronicle*
reports that only 'oon of the deffendours was ovyrturnyd hors &
man' on this occasion, 'which was Reportid to be sir Rowland that
hadd the ffalle, & my lord henry that gave hym the Strype, But
some Reportid othirwyse' (315).

426–7 *They tourneyd with swordes*: For the relevant ordinance,
see BC/82–90.

432 *Turned*: Tourneyed.

440ff. *A certen barrer*: For the ordinance governing foot
combat with sharp spears at the barrier, see BC/91–102. See S.
Anglo, *The Great Tournament Roll of Westminster* (Oxford, 1968),
43–4 for a discussion of this form of tourney.

464–5 *And eftsoone turned the greate endes*: And soon after
tourneyed with the butts, or larger ends, of the spears. Cf. the
barriers contest at the Field of Cloth of Gold, where the knights
'fought first with punchion spears, i.e. spears with sharp points
. . . When the spears were broken, the combatants cudgelled each
other with the stumps, giving heavy two-handed blows and then
hurling the fragments at one another'. J.G. Russell, *The Field of
Cloth of Gold* (London, 1969), 140.

498ff. *A goodly chare*: Neither the tournament challenge nor
the civic chronicles mentions this chivalric playacting.

499–504 *Foure marvelous bestes ... they were inn*: Evidently the same four 'beasts' who drew the castle pageant into Westminster Hall on the previous Friday evening (above, 4/153–68). Again, a team of peculiarly Spanish heraldic beasts is appropriate since the lady in the chariot obviously serves as a representation of the Princess Katharine.

515 *Beholden*: Endured, remained, stood. Cf. *OED* 'Hold', v. The *be-* prefix is merely emphatic.

519 *This Englissh chalenge is pretens*: The 'pretence' (i.e., the formal assertion of the worthiness of the cause or occasion) of this English challenge. Cf. *OED* 'pretence', sb., 1, 2. See also BC/1–27 and SC/1–27. *Is* functions in this phrase as the sign of the genitive rather than as a verb.

535ff. The tournament challenge (SC/69–103) called for a tourney with swords followed by a tilt without a barrier on this day. According to both the *Receyt* and the *Great Chronicle*, these events were performed in the opposite order.

544 *Sir Nicholas Vaus*: The civic chronicler describes the somewhat startling costume of Vaux, whom he mistakenly thinks to be one of the 'deffendours'. Vaux 'was apparaylid afftir the Guyse of a Turk or Sarasyn wyth a white Rolle of ffyne lynyn cloth abowth his hede the endys hangyng pendaunt wyse, and syttyng upon a styrryng horse w^t short styropys that his knees were evyn with the horsis nekk, In soo much that when hys hors Ran men mygth see a large Span heygth atwene hys body & sadyll / which Sadyll was verray lowe behynd & fflat, Soo that men marvaylid how he mygth sytt so suyr concyderyng the corage & styrryng of his hors' (314). Both costume and saddle-gear were obviously unsuited to the tourney, but served Sir Nicholas well in his role as one of the King's messengers, 'right goodly beseen, bothe their horsis and ther rayement' as described in the *Receyt* (4/545–6).

552–3 *They ... had many strokes unto iche othir*: The relevant tournament ordinance prescribes for the tourney an exchange of eighteen blows for each knight (SC/80–3). According to the civic chronicler, however, the tournament judges, led by the Lord Treasurer (the Earl of Surrey), determined that each bout of the tourney on this day should last only until each participant had delivered twelve strokes. However, 'they lykyd theyr Game soo well that they wold not dyssevyr tyll they were fforcid by the marchall & his servauntis' (*Great Chronicle*, 315).

594ff. *Ij mervelous mountes or mounteyns*: The two chained mountains represent England and Spain linked by matrimonial and political union. The green mountain, planted with a variety of herbs, flowers, and fruits, represents Britain, while the sun-scorched rock studded with minerals and gems seems to represent Spain. So, too, the musical harmony produced by the twenty-four disguisers reflects the matrimonial and political concord achieved in the Anglo-Spanish marriage. Walter Ogilvie apparently remembered this disguising as the most impressive of the four: 'Domus lignee faberrime facte una cum montibus ligeis veris nativisque simillimis. Ade[o] ars ingeniosa naturamque imitari conatur. Intra regiam aulam subito cum maxima admiratione repserunt, ex quibus paulautim nymphe ad dearum effigiem formate progrediuntur. Cantantur cantica voce pene angelica sic noctum flammis et canticis funalia canticaque angelica facile vicerunt' (National Library of Scotland, MS Advocates 33.2.24, 36). For identification of William Cornish as devisor, see Introduction, above xxiii. For discussion of this disguising, see Kipling, *Triumph of Honour*, 109–11.

634 *In a semily*: In a group. H's emendation, *in a semily sort*, imagines *semily* to be an adjective. The word, however, is a legitimate variant of the noun, *sembly* (cf. *OED* 'sembly', sb., 1, 2, and forms).

650–6 These jewels were apparently acquired by the Marquis of Dorset and paid for by the King. On 4 Dec. 1501, Henry paid £20 'to thomas Grey for a point diamount & an Emeraild' and 40 Marks 'for a Rose of Rubions crouned with a diamount' (P.R.O. E 101/415/3).

661ff. Even the most recent version of the Privy Council orders, which dates from 4–8 October 1501, contains no provision for a move from Westminster to Richmond. The Palace, formerly called Sheen and destroyed by fire in 1497, was being rushed to completion for the wedding. Probably a move to Richmond was anticipated, at least provisionally, by the end of August. By that date, plans for the disguisings had expanded from one to four, and John English had been drafted to help William Cornish in their construction. By 3 November, when both men received their payments for the full set of four disguisings, including the Richmond disguising, plans for the move must have been well established. In early October, the Council probably was not yet certain that Richmond, still undergoing reconstruction, was ready to house a state festival; a month later, it clearly was. This visit of the Spanish guests to Richmond thus marks the formal inauguration of the new palace. For the importance of the palace in establishing a symbolic identity for the Tudor dynasty, see above 3/217–22n. and Kipling, *Triumph of Honour*, 3–8. For dating, see the Introduction, above, xxii–iii.

687, 705–6 The 'bridge of Westmynster' was a landing stage, not a bridge in the modern sense. The Privy Council minutes provided for the 'amendment' of the Bridge as well as the 'renewal' and 'new painting' of the 'kinges Beestes and armes' on the Bridge (B.L. MS Cotton Vespasian C. XIV, 103ᵛ).

756ff. This description of Richmond Palace should be compared with Anthony van den Wyngaerde's drawings (Ashmolean Museum, frequently reproduced), done in 1562. The details of the drawing closely agree.

770–1 *A strong and mighti breke wall*: The use of brick at Richmond marks an important development in Tudor architecture. G. Webb points out that 'the use of brick at Richmond and especially Hampton Court, where no expense is likely to have been spared, is the culmination of a long process by which this material became a way of building valued for its own qualities ... the example of Germany and the Low Countries was strong' (*Architecture in Britain: the Middle Ages* (Harmondsworth, 1956), 204). In particular, the architects seem to have had such Lowlands chateaux as the Palace Gruuthuse (where Edward IV spent his brief exile) in mind. In its stone inner buildings and brick outer walls, Richmond thus stands as a transitional experiment, somewhere between the traditional freestone palace (Westminster, for example) and the quintessentially 'Tudor' building of red brick (Hampton Court or Nonesuch).

790 *Rennyng in his iiijor quartirs beneth*: As the author makes clear a few lines later, the water flows from water-cocks (which are probably mounted on a central shaft rising from the middle of the cistern) down into a square-shaped reservoir. That the water runs into the cistern's 'iiijor quartirs' implies that the water-cocks are accessible from each of the four sides.

799–804 *Whoes rof is of tymber ... practif of gementri*: The compiler is apparently describing a hammer-beam roof similar in construction to those of the great halls at Eltham Palace (c. 1479–80) and Hampton Court (c. 1530–35). Thus he notices that the roof is not merely beamed and braced (as in a box-framed roof with horizontal tie-beams) but arch-braced. He particularly notices the ornamental 'knottes' which cover the triple mortise-and-tenon joints where the upper arch, hammer-beam, and curved brace meet at the inside end of the hammer-beams. His eye travels down the upper arch, to the hammer-beam joint, from which the knots seem to 'hang pendant', then down the curve of the hammer-beam support to the wall and into the ground. Cf. M. Wood, *The English Mediaeval House* (London, 1965), 313–21 and Plates xlvii–viii. J. Harvey, *English Medieval Architects*

(London, 1954), 184, suggests that this roof was the work of
Thomas Mauncy, who was appointed the King's Chief Carpenter
by 1496.

806ff. As H.M. Colvin and J. Summerson point out, the
'pictures' described here are probably sculpted figures, not
paintings. (For this usage, cf. *OED* 'Picture', sb., 2d.) The
Parliamentary Survey of 1649 thus reports that the Hall was then
'adorned with eleven statues, in the sides thereof'. See Colvin,
History of the King's Works, iv, 227, and W.H. Hart, 'The
Parliamentary Surveys of Richmond, Wimbledon, and Nonesuch', *Surrey Archaeological Collections*, v (1871), 77. It is, of
course, possible that wall paintings were later replaced by statues,
but the author's description of Henry VII's likeness as a 'picture
and personage' tends to suggest statuary as well. The statues of
former English kings lining the walls of the Great Hall focus upon
a single statue of Henry VII, which was placed at the 'higher
parte' of the hall (i.e., over the place where the king would
customarily sit). This decoration scheme thus anticipates the later
arrangement of portraits focusing upon Holbein's fresco of Henry
VIII in the Whitehall Privy Chamber (see R. Strong, *Holbein and
Henry VIII* (London, 1967), 52–4 and Plate 50). Unlike the
Whitehall decoration scheme, however, these statues are not
arranged genealogically; these are not Henry's ancestors so much
as kingly types of 'bold and valiaunt knightes' (4/812). All are
English kings who have achieved fame as conquerors, from
Hengist, King of Kent, and Arthur, to Richard the Lionhearted
and Edward III. Probably, however, the writer mistakenly
identifies William the Conqueror as 'King William Rufus'. These
statues attempt, in short, to portray the victor of Bosworth as a
bold, chivalric conqueror. Consequently, instead of orbs, scep-
tres, or dynastic symbols—emblems of justice and authority—
they hold falchions and swords. Similarly, the tapestries hanging
beneath these portraits (cf. 4/821–6n.) are also devoted exclusively
to images of chivalric conquest.

821–6 Henry VII, as did Edward IV, extensively admired the
work of Pasquier Grenier of Tournai, weaver to the court of
Burgundy and the greatest tapissier of his time. These three sets
of tapestries—*The Siege of Jerusalem, The Destruction of Troy*,
and *The Siege of Mount Alba*—all Grenier's work, testify to the
king's high regard for the Burgundian tapissier. Henry inherited
the *Siege of Jerusalem* set (along with two other Grenier designs)
from the collection of Edward IV. Upon Henry's accession, the
new king promptly granted Grenier safe conduct and protection
for the selling of his tapestries in England. In 1488, Henry

purchased the eleven-piece *Destruction of Troy* set from Grenier. A duplicate of a set originally woven for Charles the Bold and presented to the Burgundian Duke by the merchants of Franc-de-Bruges in 1472, it became the centrepiece of Henry's own collection. He not only hung it in his new great hall at Richmond, but he also took it to Calais in 1500 to lend magnificence to his celebrated meeting with the Archduke Philip. Cf. Kipling, *Triumph of Honour*, 41, 61; W.G. Thomson, *History of Tapestry* (London, 1930), 110, 146, 151; W. Campbell, *Materials for a History of the Reign of Henry VII* (London, 1873–7), ii, 280–1; C.L. Scofield, *Edward IV* (London, 1923), i, 459–60; J.G. Nichols, *Chronicle of Calais* (London, 1846), 50.

826–7 *Above over other like grees*: Even higher than the height of the hall, which is 'xij or xvjten greces of highte' (cf. 4/798–9).

829–35 Like the 'pictures' in the Great Hall, these are probably statues rather than paintings (see note to 4/806ff above). These statues have also been chosen as kingly prototypes of Henry VII. Instead of 'noble warriors', however, these are all saintly kings: Edward the Confessor, Edmund, and Cadwalader (who was presumably included both for his Arthurian connections and because he renounced worldly preoccupations at the end of his life in obedience to an angelic voice). Cf. Geoffrey of Monmouth, *Historia Regum Britanniae*, xii, 17–18. The 'other' statues would almost certainly have included one of Henry VI, whose canonization Henry VII actively promoted.

842–4 *In the othir sid ... gentilwomen*: Apparently the writer means that in the other side of the chapel were other similar ('like') closets for the Queen, Princess, Lady Margaret, and other court gentlewomen.

845–6 *Goodly passages and galaris*: Another architectural innovation at Richmond was the extensive use of covered galleries which permitted passage from one side of the palace to the other without having to cross the open courtyard.

850–1 *With their goodly bay wyndowes glasid sett owte*: Probably the author means that the glass panes for the bay windows had been 'set out' into their frames for the occasion. As in many houses of the time, such glass windows were still designed as moveable luxuries, temporarily secured in their rectangular casements by iron bars or bolts while the owner was in residence. When the owner departed, the glass was removed and the shutters closed over the empty casements. See Wood, *English Mediaeval House*, 358.

868–9 *Galerys and housis of pleasure*: Another architectural innovation. Richmond's long, covered gallery surrounding ornamental gardens (detailed in the Wyngaerde drawings) repeats a familiar feature of Franco-Burgundian palaces. See Sir J. Summerson, *Architecture in Britain, 1530–1830* (Harmondsworth, 1953), 3, 11 n. 1.

879–85 Syon was an abbey of Bridgettines, a double order of nuns and religious men. Founded at Twickenham by Henry V in 1415, it was moved to Syon in 1431. The men and women each had their own conventual buildings separately enclosed. Their two chapels were under the same roof and took the form of a double chancel, each with its separate stalls. A gate connected the two, but this was unlocked only when the clergy said mass at the altar of the sisters' chapel. The clerical brothers served the community as chaplains, the lay brothers as sextons and labourers, but the order remained essentially a nunnery under the governance of an Abbess. Sheen was a house of Observant Friars. Henry VII established the house in 1499 as part of the rebuilding programme of Richmond Palace. See also below, 5/12 and n. D. Knowles and R. Hadcock, *Medieval Religious Houses* (London, 1971), 202, 231; *The Myrroure of oure Ladye*, ed. J.H. Blunt, EETS es 19 (London, 1873), xi–xxiii.

938ff. *A glorious trone or a tabernacle mad like a goodly chapell*: The writer seems to be describing a two-storey structure consisting of two large chambers, one atop the other, each built in the manner of an archbishop's or king's stall, enclosed on three sides and canopied with ornamental carving known as 'tabernacle-work' (cf. *OED*, 'Tabernacle', sb., 9). Like English's lantern pageant, this two-storey throne is 'fenestred full of lightes and brightnes'—i.e., the three enclosed sides are windowed to ensure that the disguisers can be seen from all sides. For a discussion of this pageant as a Throne of English Royalty, its glittering brightness and beauty reminiscent of Richmond Palace (whose name was 'Sheen', meaning 'brightness' and 'beauty'), see Kipling, *Triumph of Honour*, 111–14.

953 *Quaint armoney*: A textual crux. In squeezing these words into the margin, the reviser crowds his letters and uses an abbreviation he does not use elsewhere. The adjective describing 'armoney' is thus composed of two letters, q and t, connected by an expansion symbol. I adopt the Harley 69 reading here. Conceivably, however, the q can be read as a c and long r crowded together, in which case the word might be better expanded as 'crost' (*i.e.*, 'crossed'). In that case, the writer would be describing the effect of vocal parts which 'cross' one another in contrasting rising and falling patterns. MS Vincent 25, 41^r, apparently frustrated in attempting to construe this word, reads 'muche armony'.

955–9 *They cast ought many quyk conys ... they lete fle many whight dowys and berdis*: Both doves and coneys are emblems of Venus representing, respectively, sexual and spiritual love. Together, the rabbits and doves thus represent the two sides of perfect love, which has been achieved by the wedding of Arthur and Katharine. For further explanation, see Kipling, *Triumph of Honour*, 113–4.

1022–4 *A lybrary of is*: Henry established the first royal library at Richmond and appointed a Burgundian librarian, Quentin Poulet of Lille, to supervise his collection. Poulet brought a number of scribes and illuminators into the royal service; together, they produced a number of elegant illuminated manuscripts in addition to purchasing others—both manuscript and printed—from abroad. See Kipling, *Triumph of Honour*, 41–52 and R. Strong, 'From Manuscript to Miniature', in *The English Miniature* (New Haven, 1981), 25ff.

1027–32 In the months preceding the wedding, Henry extensively patronized a 'jeweller of Flanders' from whom he purchased jewels amounting to £76/10/0, perhaps in anticipation of this largesse (P.R.O. E 101/415/3, 20 August and 20–21 September 1501).

1075–6 *The moost petifull disease and sikenes*: Mattingly speculates that Arthur died of the sweating sickness, which 'was abroad in the West that spring' and 'came in March to Ludlow', where the Princess also seems to have been stricken (*Catherine of Aragon*, 48). The *Receyt* itself confirms that 'the siknes ... then reigned' in the vicinity of Worcester, at least (5/311), and the conspicuous absence of Katharine at any of the many funeral ceremonies suggests that she may have been too ill to attend.

Book V

8–9 *Sir Richard Pole ... with othir of his counseill*: Polydore Vergil reports that the following constituted Prince Arthur's Council (The Council of the Marches of Wales): Sir Richard Pole, Sir David Philips, Sir William Uvedale, Sir Richard Croft, Peter Newton, Henry Vernon, Thomas Englefield, John Waleston, Henry Marin, Dr William Smith (Bishop of Lincoln and the Lord President of the Council), and Dr Charles Booth. Cf. *Anglica Historia*, 120–1.

12 The Friars Observant were established in a monastery adjoining Greenwich palace by Edward IV in 1481. They were highly regarded by Henry VII, who confirmed the order at Greenwich in 1485 and added five more houses during his reign at Canterbury, Newark, Newcastle Upon Tyne, Richmond, and Southampton. The establishment of a convent of Friars Observant attached to Henry's new palace at Richmond (above, 4/879–85 and n.), probably modelled on the similar arrangement at Greenwich, demonstrates the King's attitude. See Knowles and Hadcock, *Medieval Religious Houses*, 230–1.

15 *The Tuesday then folowyng*: Presumably, the narrator means the Tuesday following Arthur's death (which occurred on Saturday, 2 April). This interview therefore took place on 5 April, allowing only two days for the messenger to reach Greenwich from Ludlow. On Friday the eighth of April, according to the *Great Chronicle*, a solemn Dirige was sung for Arthur's soul in every parish Church in London, followed by a Requiem mass on Saturday the ninth (318).

20–1 *Si bona ... sustineamus*: Job 2:10. 'If we have received good things at the hand of God, why should we not receive evil?'

50–4 Cf. the ordinances to be observed for the interment of a king, which were apparently codified for the funeral of Edward IV. After the body had lain in state for 'the space of ij days and more if the weder will it suffre', the embalmer was to 'take hym away, and bowell hym and then eftsones bame hym, wrappe hym in raynes well trameled in cordies of silke, then in tartryne trameled, then lede hym and coffre hym' (College of Arms, MS I. 7, 7, printed in J. Gairdner, ed., *Letters and Papers of Richard III and Henry VII* (London, 1861), 3. Cf. also College of Arms, MS I. 3, 7ʳ and B.L. MS Stowe 688, 89). The description here suggests either that Prince Arthur's body did not lie in State before being embalmed and 'chestyd', or that the narrator arrived after the lying-in-state.

61–2 *His almes folkys of Shere Thursday*: Apparently Prince Arthur had followed the royal custom of choosing twelve poor men on Maundy Thursday, washing their feet, and distributing alms to them.

64–118 These lines describe the events of Saturday, 23 April, comprising the transfer of Arthur's coffin from the Great Hall at Ludlow to the Parish Church, where the singing of a Dirige closed the day.

70–1 *A riche clothe . . .*: Cp. the similar 'riche and a large clothe of gold with a crosse of white clothe of gold above' which covered Edward IV's coffin as it was borne into Westminster Abbey (Gairdner, *Letters and Papers*, 5).

89–93 *At every corner . . . a baner*: According to a MS 'manner of burienge great Person', four banners are to stand at the four corners of the hearse: The Trinity, Our Lady, St George, and the deceased's patron saint (*Archaeologia*, i (1770), 347). Edward IV's banners thus included a banner of St Edward (Gairdner, *Letters and Papers*, 5). Since Arthur was not named for a saint, however, a 'baner of the Patible' replaced the saint's banner. The court painter, John Fligh, received 33s. 4d. for painting Prince Arthur's four banners. P.R.O. LC 2/1, 29^v.

119–52 *On the morne*: Sunday, 24 April. The events of the day comprised three funeral masses and a Dirige. This order of ceremony, which is repeated at Worcester, follows that of Edward IV's funeral. In both cases three solemn masses ('the first of Our Lady, the ij^{de} of the Trinitie, the third of requiem') invariably are sung in order by bishops, and the day is closed with the saying of the Dirige and with 'watches'. This order continued for eight days during Edward IV's funeral. Gairdner, *Letters and Papers*, 4–5.

146 *Beati mortui . . . moriuntur*: Blessed are the dead who die in the Lord (Apoc. 14:13), one of the two texts prescribed to be read as the Epistle during the daily Office of the Dead in the *Sarum Missal*.

152ff. *On the morne*: Monday, 25 April (St Mark's Day—see 5/189). The day primarily was given to the transfer of Arthur's body from Ludlow to Bewdley, with a Requiem mass before leaving Ludlow and a Dirige after reaching Bewdley.

158 *The riche chare*: According to the ordinances to be observed for the interment of a king, the body was to be carried in 'a chair opon, with lightes, baners, accompanyed with lordys and

estates as the counsaill can best devyse, havyng the horse of that
chair traped with dyvers trapers, or els with blacke trapers with
scochons richely beten, and his officers of armes abowt hym in his
cottes of arms'. Unlike a King's funeral carriage, however, Prince
Arthur's 'chare' was not decorated with an image of the deceased
with sceptre and crown. Gairdner, *Letters and Papers*, 3–4. The
decoration of Prince Arthur's funeral carriage was entrusted to
the King's Painter, John Serle, and to other prominent court
painters, including John Brown (who was to become Henry
VIII's King's Painter in 1511) and John Fligh. Their labours
consisted primarily of painting coats of arms and the banners
described at 5/73–6. P.R.O. LC 2/1, 29ᵛ. For the artists, see E.
Auerbach, *Tudor Artists* (London, 1954), 144, 163, 185.

162–3 *Over the chare a clothe ... golde*: Edward IV's funeral
'chare' was similarly covered with 'blacke velvet, having above
that a blacke clothe of gold, with a white crosse of gold'
(Gairdner, *Letters and Papers*, 7).

196ff. *On the morn*: Tuesday, 26 April. At this point the
narrator breaks off his day-by-day circumstantial account of the
cortege's progress from Ludlow to Worcester. His vague references to 'every chirch that the corps remaynyd in' (5/203) and to the
various churches, religious places, and orders that met the
procession along the way contrast sharply with his usual recounting of minutiae. He does stress, however, that Sir Richard Croft
and Sir William Uvedale left the cortege at Bewdley and rode on
ahead to make preparations for its reception at Worcester
(5/208ff). When he next resumes his detailed account of the
procession (5/213), the narrator in fact describes the results of
those very preparations. Taken together these circumstances
suggest that the narrator left the cortege after Requiem mass on
Tuesday morning, accompanied Croft and Uvedale to Worcester,
and could not give more than a vague account of the cortege's
progress between those two points.

215 *That day was faire*: Since several days have apparently
passed between the cortege's departure from Bewdley and its
arrival in Worcester, the date cannot be fixed with certainty from
context. Mr R.R. Stratton, Assistant Librarian, Worcester Cathedral Library, very kindly searched for the precise date in the
records both at the Cathedral and at the County Record Office
without success. However, the narrator does tell us that the
procession arrived in Worcester on the day before the funeral. At
this time, it was usual to arrange such ceremonies as the marriage
of Arthur and Katharine and the Prince's funeral at Ludlow on
Sundays 'for the more solempnyte' (*Traduction*, 3ᵛ). If such a

consideration dictated the scheduling of the funeral and burial at Worcester Cathedral for Sunday, May first, then the cortege arrived in the city on Saturday, 30 April, on the fifth day after leaving Bewdley.

221–2 *The Vicar Generall*: The Bishop of Worcester, Silvester de Giglis, was an Italian whom Henry VII had appointed to the see as a benefice. He apparently never visited Worcester, but remained at Rome where he served Henry as a diplomatic agent at the Curia. The actual administration of the see was put into the hands of a Vicar General, Dr Thomas Wodyngton, who performed the duties of a bishop without enjoying the perquisites of a bishop's rank. This arrangement produced odd cosequences at Arthur's funeral. Since Arthur was to be buried in Worcester Cathedral, the Bishop would normally take precedence in officiating at the ceremony. Because the see was in the hands of a Vicar General, however, virtually all the visiting clerics took precedence over Wodyngton, who was relegated to a relatively minor role.

244–50 John Fligh painted the banners of the King and Queen of Spain and the King and Queen of England, but the King's Painter, John Serle, received £40 for painting the rest, including a banner of 'tharmes of Brute' and 'oon of tharmes of Irlonde' which the narrator fails to mention. P.R.O. LC 2/1, 30^v.

251 *The clothe of magestie*: This featured 'a grete ymage of our lord Jesus cryste sitting vppon the Raynbowe ... with divers writtinges in the same'. John Gayner received 53s. 4d. for painting it. P.R.O. LC 2/1, 31^r.

282ff. *The maner of thoffryng*: The ceremonial of offering at the final Requiem mass the 'riche braudred cote of armes', the shield, the sword, the helm with the crest, and the Man of Arms follows the pattern established at the funeral of Edward IV (Gairdner, *Letters and Papers*, 9). R.E. Giesey traces the use of a Man of Arms to the funeral of Bertrand du Guesclin in 1389, where 'four knights, completely equipped with the armour' of du Guesclin, took part in the ceremony 'as if they were demonstrating the presence of his body'. By means of the Man of Arms, 'the deceased was impersonated in order to allow him to take part in the offering at his own funeral' (*The Royal Funeral Ceremony in Renaissance France*, Travaux d'humanisme et Renaissance xxxvii (Geneva, 1960), 90–91).

283–5 *All the mourners ... went bifore hym*: The narrator omits the name of the noble appointed to offer the mass penny.

292 *The helm with the crest*: Not an actual helmet, but an oversize, gilded helmet with an intricately carved crest made expressly to be carried in the funeral procession. See B.L. MS

Add. 35324, 36ᵛ, for a contemporary painting of Queen Elizabeth's 'great helm' as carried in her funeral procession (colour
plate in R. Marks and A. Payne, *British Heraldry* (London, 1978),
86–7). Prince Arthur's symbolic helmet was made by Vincent, the
King's Armourer, gilded, and decorated by one of the noted
artisans of the time, Richard Rowhanger. The latter received, for
example, 30s. for 'carving & painting of a lion crowned' for the
helmet's crest. P.R.O. LC 2/1, 30ʳ. For Rowhanger, cf. Auerbach,
Tudor Artists, 7–9, 183–4.

318–9 *A riche pall of cloth of goold*: Cp. the narrative of
Edward IV's funeral: 'Incontynent that done, the lordes offred
certein clothes of gold to the corps, everyche after his degre or
estat' (Gairdner, *Letters and Papers*, 10).

326 *A noble doctour*: Perhaps Dr Charles Booth, a member of
Prince Arthur's Council. The other doctors in attendance (Smith,
Ednaham, and Wodyngton) have all been elsewhere identified in
their roles, respectively, as Bishop of Lincoln, Prince's Almoner,
and Vicar General.

329 *Saynt Johns gospell*: The Sarum Requiem mass prescribes
John 2:21–7.

341–2 *The grave at the sowthe end of the high aulter of that
cathedrall churche*: A tomb and chantry chapel were erected over
the Prince's grave in 1504. Cf. E.F. Strange, *The Cathedral
Church of Worcester* (London, 1900), 60.

346–54 *His Officer of Armes ... who had sene it*: According to
Roger Machado's description of Edward IV's funeral, the Officers of the Household (Steward, Controller, Chamberlain, Treasurer) throw their staves 'into the grave of the king in token of
being men without a master, and out of their offices'. For the
same reason, the heralds throw their coats of arms into the grave,
but they then immediately don new tabards as a sign that they are
now servants of the new king (Gairdner, *Letters and Papers*, xvii).
Among the five heralds attendant, only Thomas Wriothesley,
Wallingford Pursuivant to Prince Arthur, performs this symbolic
ceremony here. Unlike a royal herald, he does not put on a new
tabard; he does not automatically become a herald to another
prince. Rather, he has become a man without a master like the
other household officers.

The Buckingham Challenge

4–27 The opening section of this cartel is closely modelled upon the corresponding section of a challenge drawn up for the royal wedding tournament of 1477, an occasion which offered an obvious precedent for the celebrations of 1501. The 1477 challenge was preserved in the 'Office Book' of William Ballard, March King of Arms in Edward IV's reign; this book was bought from Ballard's widow by John Writhe, Garter King of Arms, in 1490 (Wagner, *Heralds and Heraldry*, 108). For a discussion of these points, leading to an identification of Writhe as the author of the 1501 challenge, see the Introduction, above xxvii–viii.

28–59 These articles establish the familiar rules for the 'Jousts Royal', the most popular form of the Tudor tournament. They are distinguished from the other forms of tournament to be run on other days by the use of specially designed tournament armour (hence, the reference to 'helme and shield' at BC/32–3; cp. the Suffolk challenge, SC/33, 'le grant heaulme et lescu'), blunted spears, and a barrier to separate the horses. Since Tiptoft's Ordinances continued to serve throughout the Tudor period as a kind of standard reference to the detailed rules of the Jousts Royal, these articles need only establish the ground rules particular to this joust (e.g., the social qualifications necessary, the number of courses to be run, and so on). For Tiptoft's Ordinances, see SC/125n. and Anglo, *Tournament Roll*, 108–9.

36 *Rest of avauntage*: The English name for a combination lance-rest and queue; 'This last is a horizontal bar projecting backwards under the arm and terminating at the rear in a hook under which the butt-end of the heavy lance can be lodged' (C. Blair, *European Armour* (London, 1958), 161 and n., Fig. 271). Although frequently used in continental tournaments, they were often prohibited in English tournaments of the period, as in the cartels for the 1477 and 1511 jousts at Westminster (Harley 69, 1ᵛ; Anglo, *Tournament Roll*, 110).

64–5 *The iijde day next after* ...: In fact, the events described in the following articles took place on Wednesday, 24 November, the sixth day after the first day of the tournament. It was, however, the third day of the combined Buckingham–Dorset tournament.

69ff. The article calls for a particularly dangerous form of the joust, running at large. Indeed, the specifications of the contest deliberately increase the risk of injury: the knights are to use sharp rather than blunt spears; they wear common 'oisting harneis' (military armour) rather than armour especially designed to protect the knight against the particular dangers of the tilt; and they run against one another in groups without a tilt or barrier. As S. Anglo points out, the use of a tilt to separate the knights 'was clearly precautionary: it would prevent the horses from colliding; it would help the warrior to keep a straight course; and, by increasing the angle of incidence between lance head and on-coming knight, it would ensure that the lance would snap rather than pierce the armour' (Anglo, *Tournament Roll*, 41–2). Never-theless, the Suffolk challenge also prescribes a similar event (SC/89–103). The score cheque shows that the knights minimized the danger by running only the minimum number of courses prescribed in the respective articles. Thus they ran only two courses each on the third day (the number specified in the Buckingham challenge, BC/74) and only three courses each on the fourth day (the number specified in the Suffolk challenge, SC/94).

82ff. This article provides for a tourney on horseback. The number of knights and the number of strokes might vary in such contests—here they are to fight three to three and exchange ten strokes each, but in the Suffolk challenge they are to fight by couples and exchange eighteen blows each (SC/69ff.)—but other-wise the tourney was a fixed and popular event in the late-medieval tournament. See Anglo, *Tournament Roll*, 42–3.

88 *The foyne ... except*: This prohibition against thrusting with the point of the sword (cp. Suffolk challenge, SC/78) was usual in English tournaments as a safety precaution, although a few tournaments specifically did allow the stroke. Cf. Anglo, *Tournament Roll*, 43 and n. 4.

91ff. This article provides for a form of combat later to be known as the 'barriers' in which groups of knights fought one another over a barrier or tilt. It was to become very popular, the subject of much allegorical development in the later-sixteenth and early-seventeenth centuries, but at this time it is only a minor event in the tournament; barriers appear only infrequently before the sixteenth century. Cf. R.C. Clephan, *The Tournament* (Lon-don, 1919), 41, 105; E. Welsford, *The Court Masque* (Cambridge, 1927), 113, 143, 151, 188.

116–21 'Provision against the wounding or killing of horses occurs constantly in European articles of challenge from the latter half of the fifteenth century' (Anglo, *Tournament Roll*, 44 n. 2). This provision is, in fact, a version of one of Tiptoft's ordinances. Cp. SC/106ff., a similar provision.

133ff. For a discussion of these proposed Trees of Chivalry, which differ in some important respects from both the one proposed in the Suffolk challenge (SC/156–64) and the actual tree as described by the author of the *Receyt*, see the Introduction, above xxvi–viii.

The Suffolk Challenge

5–6 *Environ la fin de cest este prouchain ensuivant*: In late May, 1500, when this challenge was originally proclaimed, the royal wedding was expected to occur 'in the monethe of August or of Septembre next comyng', according to the original version of the Privy Council orders (*Traduction*, 2ʳ).

28–68 As in the first articles of the Buckingham challenge, these first five articles establish the rules for the 'Jousts Royal'. Unlike the Buckingham challenge, however, the compiler of the challenge has seen fit to include, at the end of the challenge (SC/125ff.), a version of Tiptoft's Ordinances, probably because the challenge is being proclaimed to a group of Burgundian knights who would not be automatically familiar with them, as would their English counterparts.

29 *Le cinq^me jour ...*: In fact, the events described in these first five articles took place on Monday, 22 November, eight days after the wedding.

34 *Sans bricquet ou attache*: Apparently a prohibition against straps and attachments that might help steady the rider in the saddle or grip the lance. Cp. the cartel for the Westminster Tournament of 1511: 'thise iiij knightes shall present theym self in the ffeld ... in harneys for the Tylte withoute tache or brecket ... fraude, diceyt, or any other malengyne' (Anglo, *Tournament Roll*, 110; see also 44). Cf. *OED* 'Tache', sb.², 1.

69 *Le vij^e jour ...*: The events described in the following three articles in fact took place on Thursday, 25 November, eleven days after the marriage.

69–79 For the differences between Buckingham's version of the tourney on horseback and the version outlined in these two articles, see BC/82ff., n.

89ff. This provision for 'running at large' generally parallels that of the Buckingham challenge, except for its romantic provision for buying back a dropped lance with a 'diamond' to be presented to the opponent's lady. Cp. BC/69ff.

125ff. Articles xiij–xxj are quite literal translations of the ordinances devvised in 1466 by John Tiptoft, Earl of Worcester, to govern Jousts Royal. For the English text (taken from College of Arms, MS M. 6, 56–7), see Anglo, *Tournament Roll*, 108–9. In drawing up these French versions, however, the herald has omitted those ordinances dealing with striking 'coronall to coronall' and those ordinances dealing with the finer points of judging whether broken spears should be allowed or disallowed in scoring.

144–64 This ceremony has apparently been adopted from a similar provision in the challenge for the royal wedding tournament of 1477. According to both challenges, copies of the tournament articles were to be posted in nearly the same three places: at the gate of the King's Palace, at the Standard in Chepe, upon London Bridge (1477); at the court, at Westminster, at the Standard in Chepe (1500). Each copy was to be presided over by heralds. Each copy would have a set of symbolic 'congnoissances' affixed to them which represented the various days of the tournament. In each case, the knights are required to choose the days in which they will answer the challenge by subscribing their names beneath the appropriate symbol. For the 1477 challenge, see College of Arms, MS M. 3, 8^v; B.L. MS Harley 69, 1^v. Buckingham's challenge intended to achieve the same choice by having the knights hang their shields upon one of two Trees of Chivalry representative of the two days of challenge (BC/153–68).

GLOSSARY

THIS glossary is intended primarily to explain words and senses now unfamiliar, to elucidate special contextual meanings, and to identify words that may seem orthographically disguised. As a rule, no more than two occurrences of a given word in a particular sense are listed. References to the Duke of Buckingham's tournament challenge are identified by BC; otherwise all other references are to the *Receyt*.

a *v.* have [worn-down form of the modal auxiliary] 3/449.

abedyn *pp.* endured, sustained 4/978.

abehovabill *a.* befitting, proper to 3/12–13.

abite *n.* religious habit 5/160, **abites** *n. pl.* 5/103.

abyding *pr. p.* awaiting 4/514.

accombred *ppl. a.* encumbered 4/239–40.

accompased *ppl. a.* surrounded, encircled BC/142.

accomplement *n.* achievement 4/1057.

accordyng *adv.* accordingly 4/254.

acertaigned *pp.* made certain BC/122.

achewe *v.* achieve 2/381.

addresse *n.* the action of making ready; *made* ∼ made ready 2/862.

addressid *ppl. a.* prepared, provided 4/18, 4/24; *pp.* 4/931.

addressyng *n.* decoration, furnishing, arrayment 3/246; **addressid** *pp.* arrayed 4/874.

advertised *pp. let all theym ... to be in that mattier* ∼ let them all voice their opinions upon that matter 1/100–1.

ageynst *prep.* in anticipation of 2/355; *prep.* towards, with respect to 4/1017.

agoodly *a.* comely, fair, handsome [*goodly* + *a-* as an intensifying prefix] 2/817.

agreable *adv.* agreeably 2/860.

aleyed *pp.* laid out 4/863.

aliaunt *n.* alien, foreigner 4/517.

alight, alitide *pa. t.* alighted, jumped lightly down 4/218, 5/302.

allevyat *pp.* relieved, released from 3/317.

almon *n.* almond 3/60.

aloonly *adv.* only, solely 4/502.

amoner *n.* almoner, official distributor of alms 5/144.

amyces *n. pl.* fur-lined hoods or hooded capes 5/222.

amyte *n.* friendship, friendliness 2/94.

annempst(e) *prep.* in respect of 1/109; *prep.* over against, close to 3/237; *prep.* opposite to, facing 3/26, 3/170; *prep.* alongside, against 4/25.

annoied *pp.* interfered with 1/67.

annon *adv.* at once, instantly 4/537.

annourement *n.* worship 3/95–6.

annowrement *n.* ornament, decoration 3/251.

antems *n. pl.* anthems 5/337.

antetyme *n.* antetheme, text prefixed to a sermon as theme 5/146.

aperteyned *pp.* pertained, belonged to 2/888; **apperteynyng** *pr. p.* belonging, suitable, befitting 1/199, 3/8.

apon *prep.* upon BC/4.

apparament *n.* preparation 3/289.

apparament *n.* decoration, furnishing 3/246.

apparantly *adv.* manifestly Pro/58, 1/221.

apparaunce, apparens n. appearance 4/32, 4/958.

apparell n. rigging of a ship 4/180.

apparement n. ceremony 3/409.

apperceyve v. perceive, observe 3/30; **apperceyved** pp. 4/1020.

apperteynnaunce n. everything naturally belonging to or suitable to 4/995.

appetitis n. dispositions 1/178.

applied pp. devoted; *Be ~ of their right propertie* must devote themselves to their rightful attributes 2/228.

appreparement n. preparation 4/824–5; **appreparyng** pr. p. preparing 3/270–1, 5/156; **apprepared, -yd** ppl. a. prepared 3/98, 3/278, 4/142, 4/585.

approximate a. next to, in the proximity of 2/376.

appulles n. pl. apples 3/236.

appurtenans n. appurtenance, adjunct, accessory 4/182.

apropered, -yd pp. designated 2/504; pp. confirmed 2/841–2 (see note).

araide ppl. a. arrayed, made ready, embellished 1/197.

arais, arraies n. pl. arrays, dispositions 3/374, 4/3.

armoney, ermony n. harmony 4/615, 4/953; **armoneously, ermeniosly** adv. 2/558, 4/174.

armyng swordes n. pl. military swords, as opposed to swords specifically designed for the tourney 4/364–5.

armyns n. pl. ermin furs 2/765.

armys n. pl. coats of arms 2/771.

a(r)raysid, arreysid pp. raised up 1/267, 3/16–7, 4/8, 4/909.

arrerid pa. t. reared up 1/21.

aslope a. inclined, slanting 4/918.

aspectes n. pl. the relationship between a planet in an ascendant sign to two other zodiacal signs (see 2/504–7n.) 2/506.

asserteyned pp. informed, made certain 1/126, 1/189.

assised pp. measured BC/114.

asslakyd pa. t. decreased, diminished 4/1037.

asspire v. reach, attain 3/64.

assporture n. removal, carrying away 4/1006.

astately adv. stately 3/250.

ateigne v. attain 4/197.

atteint n. attaint, a hit in tilting BC/43.

attendancis, -daunces n. pl. services, actions of waiting upon 1/40, 1/225.

aunncyent a. ancient 4/1043.

austerall a. southern 2/313.

auter, autier, aultier n. altar 3/6, 3/10, 3/200.

avaunsyng pr. p. advancing 2/669.

avoided, avoyded, -yd pa. t. departed, withdrew 4/229; pp. voided, freed, removed from office 1/111; made empty, cleared 4/485.

awaytyng pr. p. waiting; *unto them ~* waiting upon them 1/213.

ayders n. pl. helpers, supporters 1/253.

baas daunces, bace daunces n. pl. formal dances in slow time 4/235–6, 4/238–9, 4/963.

bagges n. pl. badges 2/137, 2/159.

bamed pp. embalmed 5/50.

banket n. banquet 4/128, 4/272.

banrell, -roll n. a long, narrow flag or streamer 5/248, 5/249.

barrer, berrer n. barrier 4/440, 4/443, 4/448.

barris n. pl. barriers 5/337.

basones n. pl. basins 2/814.

baylys n. pl. bails, half hoops for supporting the cover of a wagon 5/161.

baynes n. pl. baths 3/428, 3/453.

be prep. by, by means of 1/143, 2/207.

beanch(e) n. bench 2/297, 2/299.

behalve, bihalve n. behalf, matter, case, aspect, respect; *for that ~* for that purpose 2/861; *in this ~* in this case 4/528; *on her ~* on her behalf 1/159; *in every maner ~* in all respects 1/174; **behalvys, behavys** n. pl. *in all ~* in all respects 3/6; *of all other ~* of all other matters 2/474–5.

beholden pp. endured, stood, remained [the *be-* prefix here

merely serves as an intensifier]
4/515.

berdis *n. pl.* birds 4/959.

beris *n. pl.* bearers 5/180.

berys *n. pl.* bears 2/501.

beseen *pp.* equipped, arrayed 4/495,
4/835; seen to, arranged 4/931.

beseeng *n.* fashion, array 3/148.

best *n.* beast 4/501; **bestes** *n. pl.* 4/499.

besy *a.* busy 2/876.

beten *ppl. a.* beaten 1/244.

bethe *v.* (*pr. ind. pl.*) are 4/806.

bewtyouse *a.* beauteous, beautiful
4/763.

bildid, bullid, byllid, -yd *pp.* built
2/127, 3/16, 3/218, 4/20, 4/764.

blason *n.* blazon, heraldic achievement
2/391.

blew(e) *a.* blue 2/308, 2/313.

blode *n.* blood Pro/11.

bocles *n. pl.* armoured gates 4/774.

body *n.* nave 4/828.

bokeram *n.* buckram 5/160.

bolles *n. pl.* round knobs 2/555.

bollys *n. pl.* bowls 4/344, 4/582.

borderers *n. pl.* people living in a
district bordering upon another
1/34.

boriall a. boreal, northern 2/313.

boulid *pp.* disemboweled 5/50.

boures *n. pl.* dwellings, abodes 4/265,
4/361.

bowes *n. pl.* boughs 3/63.

brasid *ppl. a.* braced 4/800.

braudred *ppl. a.* embroidered 5/287.

brede *n.* breadth 2/126, 2/507.

bredes *n. pl.* breads 3/207.

brekers *n. pl.* messengers, bringers of
news, introducers 4/198.

breme *a.* numerous 3/191, 4/490.

brent *ppl. a.* burnt 4/600.

brodre, brothir *n.* brother 4/311,
4/428.

brute *n.* renown, fame 4/648.

bucyne *n.* type of trumpet (ad. OF
buisine) BC/144, BC/167.

burde *n.* board, table 3/256; **burdes,
burdys** *n. pl.* 3/255, 3/278,
4/271.

burgenyth *v.* burgeon Pro/17.

burges *n. pl.* burgesses, magistrates of
the town 5/142.

busteous *a.* coarse in texture 2/744.

buttes *n. pl.* shooting targets 4/870,
4/904.

byles, -ys *n. pl.* billiards 4/869, 4/904.

byse *n.* a pigment made from smalt,
either blue byse or (more probably here) green byse 2/52.

cape-a-pe *adv.* armed from head to
foot 2/160–1.

capeten *n.* captain 2/161.

celebrate *ppl. a.* celebrated 3/201.

celid, -yd *ppl. a.* provided with a
ceiling by lining the inner side
of the roof 4/839, 4/849.

ceptour *n.* sceptre 2/769.

cercenet *n.* sarcemet, a fine, soft silk
material 2/667.

cered *ppl. a.* rendered waterproof with
wax 5/166.

certified *pp.* made certain of, informed 5/3; **sertefyed** *pa. t.*
informed 3/294.

cesterne, -irne *n.* cistern 4/788,
4/795.

chanons *n. pl.* canons 5/222.

chapiter, chaptre, captre, -ure *n.*
chapter 1/1, 1/30, 1/114, 1/155,
2/123, 2/751, 5/179.

chare *n.* cart, waggon 2/497–8, 5/156.

charge *n.* commission, responsibility
5/52; **charges** *n. pl.* 3/429.

chariet *n.* cart, waggon 5/160; **chariattes** *n. pl.* 4/671.

chekyr *n.* checker, pattern of small
squares 2/300; **chekirs, -yrs** *n.
pl.* 2/299, 2/301, 2/305; **chekeryd, chekiryd** *pp.* 2/318,
4/840.

chertirhous *n.* charterhouse, a Car-
thusian monastery 4/882.

chestyd *pp.* placed in a chest 5/54.

cheynes *n. pl.* chains 2/143.

clavycordes *n. pl.* an early keyboard
instrument, predecessor of the
piano 4/621.

clavysymballes *n. pl.* harpsichords
4/621.

clene *a.* pure 4/583.

clothis *n. pl.* sails 1/18.

cokkys, *n. pl.* water-cocks, spouts
4/790.

coles *n. pl.* coals 4/859.

colours *n. pl.* collars 3/396.

colours *n. pl.* a coloured device, badge, heraldic emblem 5/205.

comers *n. pl.* visitors 1/260.

commedite *n.* commodity 4/678.

commennde *v.* entrust 2/344.

comment *n.* expository treatise, commentary 3/43; **commentes** *n. pl.* 3/36.

commodious *a.* conveniently spacious 4/781.

commodite *ppl. a.* well-arranged [ad L. *commodat-*, ppl. stem of *commodare*] 4/995.

commyn, comyn *pp.* come 2/3, 4/176, 5/25, 5/40.

compassid *pa. t.* circled, made a circuit of 4/532.

conducte *n.* conduit 3/242, 4/788.

condute *v.* escort 1/12; **condutid** *pa. t.* 1/171; **condute** *pp.* 2/824.

condutes *n. pl.* conductors, escorters 1/263.

congruens *n.* congruence, agreement 4/1050.

congruent *a.* suitable, proper 3/304.

conizansis, connizansis, conysances *n. pl.* cognizances, distinguishing crests or marks 1/220, 2/320, 4/692.

conservature *n.* preserver, custodian 2/527; **conservatours** *n. pl.* 1/252–3.

constory *n.* consistory 3/27.

contentacion *n.* the action of contenting or satisfying 5/357.

contentis *n. pl.* contents BC/51.

contrepart(i) *n.* opponent BC/76, BC/86; **co(u)ntreparties** *n. pl.* BC/99, BC/117.

contreth *n.* country 1/29, 1/123; **contrethis** *n. pl.* 1/143.

convenient *a.* suitable, appropriate 2/27.

convenyences *n. pl.* correspondences 2/460.

conveyed *pp.* arranged 4/859.

conys *n. pl.* coneys, rabbits 4/955.

cooferer *n.* an officer in the Royal Household of England next under Controller 5/363.

coostes, -is *n. pl.* coasts 1/12, 1/14, 2/878; **costes** *n. pl.* points of the compass, quarters 2/312.

cope *n.* vault 3/86.

copled *pp.* engaged as opponents in a joust 4/418.

copys *n. pl.* copes, ecclesiastical vestments 3/11, 5/223.

coriouse *a.* curious, intricate 2/669; **coryously** *adv.* 2/562.

cors *n.* corpse 4/1085, 5/48.

corven, -yn *ppl. a.* carved 2/51, 4/801.

costes see **coostes**.

costlew, -elow *a.* costly 4/105, 4/574; **costeously** *adv.* 2/513.

cours(e), curse *n.* course, order, series 2/137; ∼ *of time* progression of time 2/852–3; *in* ... ∼ in order, in turn 2/309, 3/147–8; *in* ∼ *next* next in order 4/281; *n.* course, path of movement 4/385.

courteyns *n. pl.* curtains 2/46.

covenably *adv.* suitably, appropriately 1/136.

cowde *pa. t.* could 4/139.

cowplid *pp.* coupled (in marriage) Pro/82.

credeably *adv.* credibly 4/761.

cristente *a.* christian 4/1082.

crochis *n. pl.* poles with forked tops used as supports 4/909.

cronalles *n. pl.* heads of lances ending in three or four short spreading points 4/535.

cronell *n.* coronal, coronet 2/769.

cumpassid *pa. t.* made a circuit of 4/402.

currages *n. pl.* carriages, bearings, appearances 1/265.

currall *n.* coral 3/221, 4/604.

curraunt *a.* flowing 2/131.

curraunt *a.* inclined, sloping 4/777.

curse *n.* see **cours(e)**.

curse *n.* channel 2/130; *n.* running, flow of water 4/794; *n.* course, division of a meal 3/262; *n.* the rush together of the combatants at a tilt 4/114, 4/117; **cursys** *n. pl.* 4/542.

cursers, -iours, -ours *n. pl.* coursers, horses 1/79, 1/263, 2/668, 2/846, 4/41–2, 4/525.

curtilage, curtylage *n.* small courtyard 4/787, 4/798, 4/826.

curyage *n.* courage 4/86.

curyous *a.* exquisitely prepared 3/264.
cylens *n.* silence 4/590.
Cynosura *n.* Cynosura, the northern constellation of Ursa Minor 2/110.

darrest *superl.* dearest 5/22.
debonayre *a.* gracious 2/232.
deducte *ppl. a.* traced, drawn 2/505.
deducyng *pr. p.* bringing 4/659–60; **deducid** *pp.* brought 2/839.
defaute *n.* default, want, defect BC/50.
defendaunce *n.* defence 4/521.
dele *n.* part; *for the moost* ~ for the most part 4/582–3.
delecates *n. pl.* delicacies 3/264, 3/282.
delyver *adv.* lightly, nimbly 4/631; **delyverous** *a.* 4/915; **delyvernes** *n.* quickness, agility 4/927.
demeanour, demeanure *n.* behaviour, conduct 1/189, 2/752.
dener *n.* dinner 3/283, 3/336.
depnes *n.* depth 3/241.
deposid *pa. t.* took off 1/138.
deserviant *pr. p.* ministering with zeal 3/45.
desire *v.* invite 4/1020.
devoir *n.* endeavour; *put themself(es) in* ~ to do what they can, to endeavour BC/25, BC/151.
devyce *n.* arrangement, contrivance, invention 4/109.
dimitt *v.* dismiss 3/75.
dimysentes *n. pl.* diamonds 4/1028.
discrivyd, discryvyn *pp.* described 3/155, 3/391.
dispocicion, -sycion *n.* situation of a planet in a horoscope 2/268, 2/322, 2/515; *n.* inclination 2/253; *n.* temperament 2/257; **dispocicions** *n. pl.* 2/260.
disporte *n.* diversion, entertainment 4/229; **disportes** *n. pl.* 1/152, 2/915.
disseacid *pa. t.* deceased 5/5.
dissease *n.* disease 4/983.
distrobill *n.* disturbance 4/1003; **distroublyng** *vbl. n.* disturbance 4/43; **distrobled** *pa. t.* disturbed 1/19–20.
domified *ppl. a.* the planets located in their respective houses 2/398.

dowys *n. pl.* doves 4/959.
dredfull *a.* inspiring dread, awesome 2/890.
duetie *n.* duty 3/95; **duetes** *n. pl.* 4/265.
duple *a.* double, twofold 4/775.
dusymers *n. pl.* dulcimers 4/621.
dystingued *ppl. a.* distinguished; ~ *in* divided into 2/224.

eboylid *pa. t.* boiled, bubbled out 4/601.
ediccions *n. pl.* edicts, commands 4/1045.
edified *pp.* built 2/125.
effucion *n.* outpouring, utterance 3/306.
eftsone(s) *adv.* soon after 2/650, 3/298, 4/92.
egge *n.* edge 2/168, 3/62.
egre *adv.* eagerly 4/432.
eires, eyerys *n. pl.* air, atmosphere 1/27, 1/78, 4/766.
electe *pp.* chosen, picked out 2/269, 4/1033; **eleccions** *ppl. a.* choices 4/1034.
emcommpassid, encompased, -sid *ppl. a.* encircled 1/197, 4/13, 4/770; **encompassyng** *pr. p.* making a circuit around 4/491.
empayntid, enpayntid, -yd *pp.* painted 2/48, 2/50, 4/605, 4/707–8.
emper *n.* empire 4/1046.
empoyntid *pp.* appointed, furnished, equipped 2/512.
emtid *pp.* emptied 4/644.
enbasshions *n. pl.* ambassadorial missions Pro/84; *n. pl.* messages conveyed by an ambassador 2/856.
encharge *v.* enjoin or commission a person to do something 3/432.
enchesion *n.* reason, cause Pro/26, 1/68.
enclyned *pa. t.* was disposed towards 2/893; *pa. t.* fell down, went down 4/431.
encompanyed, -yd, -ed *pp.* accompanied 1/226, 3/109, 3/122, 3/172.
encrese *n.* progress, advancement 1/68.
endevoir *v.* endeavour, exert BC/67.

endutyng *n.* inducting, introducing or bringing into 1/201.

eneth *adv.* scarcely 1/215.

enfreight *a.* freighted, transported 1/22.

engynne *n.* contrivance *male* ∼ illegal appliance, (fig.) trickery BC/36.

enhaunced *pa. t.* lifted up, raised up 1/19; **enhauncid, -sid** *ppl. a.* elevated 2/298, 3/22.

enhaunged, -id, -yd *pp.* hung 3/13, 3/339, 4/856.

enhight *pp.* elevated [form of **enhaunced**? cp. 3/22] 3/15.

enjoynyd *ppl. a.* joined, attached 2/275.

ennormly *adv.* immorally, criminally 2/882.

ennouryd *pp.* ornamented, decorated 3/6.

ensealid *pp.* affixed with seals 3/141; *opynly declared* ∼ publicly announced that seals had been affixed to 3/139–40.

enseasid *ppl. a.* put in possession; *his patentes* ∼ patents that he endowed them with 4/1002.

ensencyng *pr. p.* censing, incensing 5/332.

enserche *n.* inquiry, search 1/105; **enserchyng** *vbl. n.* 4/1004.

enservyd *pp.* served 3/345.

enspeciall, especiall *adv.* especially, particularly 2/308, 3/273.

ensured *pa. t.* assured 1/91.

ensurans *n.* betrothal 1/146; **ensured** *pp.* betrothed 1/146.

ensuyth *v.* (*pr. 3 sg.*) follows 5/158; **ensuyd** *pa. t.* followed 1/52; **enseyng, ensueng, -yng** *adv.* subsequently, next 1/140, 2/665, 3/299; **ensueng** *a.* following, next 4/893.

entendid *pp.* intended 4/16.

entendyng *pr. p.* attending, waiting upon 1/272.

enterpretacion *n.* interpretation 1/142.

entre *n.* entry 2/67; **entres** *n.* arrival, entrance 1/33, 2/8.

entre *v.* enter 2/216; **entride** *pp.* entered 1/205.

ermony, ermeniosly see **armoney.**

erthe *n.* earth 2/500.

espyre *v.* aspire 2/262.

estraungers *n. pl.* aliens, foreigners 4/588, 4/743.

estriche *n.* ostrich 2/48, 2/305.

evanyshid *pp.* vanished, disappeared from view 4/230.

even *adv.* exactly, precisely 2/401.

evencristen *n. pl.* fellow christians Pro/46.

ever *a.* every 3/252.

everych *pron.* everyone 2/457; *a.* each and every; *the* ∼ *poynt* each and every point 2/875.

examplere *n.* exemplar 4/763.

excheweng *vbl. n.* exclusion 4/40.

excludid *pp.* relieved, exempted from (an obligation) 1/111.

exonerat *pp.* relieved from 2/889.

expedicion *n.* the action of helping forward or accomplishing 3/294.

expellid *pp.* expelled, driven away 1/77.

expendid *pp.* spent 4/267.

expresse *a.* exact 2/361, 2/522.

eyerys see **eires.**

fachion, -yon *n.* fashion, manner 4/327, 4/580; **fachyoned** *pp.* 4/379.

fachons *n. pl.* falchions, a type of broad, curved sword 4/811.

faict *n.* feat, deed BC/48, BC/79; **faictes** *n. pl.* BC/14, BC/26.

fane *n.* metal plate resembling a flag or banner bearing a coat of arms 2/172; **fanys** *n. pl.* 2/166, 2/179; see **vane.**

fatall *a.* fated 2/515; **fatally** *adv.* fatefully 1/15.

fayn *a.* false, feigned Pro/95.

fayne *a.* necessitated, *in some place* ∼ *to take oxen* in some place(s) it was necessary to take oxen 5/191.

feithe *n.* faith 2/581.

fenestrid *ppl. a.* having windows; ∼ *with fyne lawne* furnished with windows of fine lawn 4/328–9.

ferme *a.* firm 2/529.

figure *n.* a horoscope 2/361, 2/428.

figured *ppl. a.* represented emblematically 2/576.

floure *n.* floor 2/32, 2/35; **flours, -es** *n. pl.* 2/31, 2/38.

floure de luce, flowrd luce *n.* fleur-de-lis, an emblem resembling a lily or an iris 2/142, 2/153; **floures de luces** *n. pl.* 2/293.

former *a.* foremost 2/480, 2/500.

fornoon *n.* forenoon, morning 3/414.

forsid *pa. t.* regarded, had care for 4/421.

fouldyng *pr. p.* folding; ∿ *stole* folding stool 2/696.

foyne *n.* a thrust with the point of a sword BC/88.

freite *ppl. a.* freighted, laden 4/715.

frestone *n.* freestone, a fine-grained sandstone or limestone 2/134, 2/276.

fulfilled, -yd *ppl. a.* filled full 4/258, 4/579.

fully *adv.* in a full manner or degree, completely 1/161.

gainct *n.* jointure Pro/3.

galaris, galeres *n. pl.* galleries 4/780, 4/782, 4/846.

gardie *n.* guard 1/10.

garnysshid *ppl. a.* decorated, ornamented, furnished 1/196, 4/21, 4/77, 4/258.

gasynges *vbl. n.* gazings 3/102.

geat *n.* jet 3/220.

gementri *n.* geometry, spec. the art of measuring or planning associated with architecture 4/804.

genaper *n.* juniper 4/597.

gest *n.* substance, pith Pro/93.

gestes *n. pl.* notable deeds as recounted in a history 3/35.

gevyng *pr. p.* giving 2/112.

girde *ppl. a.* girded, surrounded 4/770.

girdell *n.* that which surrounds (here, the brick wall) 4/772.

gladdes *n.* joy, gladness 4/1025.

glasid *ppl. a.* glazed 4/804, 4/827.

goo *ppl. a.* gone 2/784.

goolde *n.* gold 4/807.

goostly *a.* spiritual; ∿ *fadre* confessor 5/12.

gouvernay *n.* governance 1/110.

grante *n.* bestowal of privileges, right, or possession 2/870.

gres *n.* step, stair 3/129; **greas, grece(s), -ses** *n. pl.* 4/26, 4/773;

n. pl. steps in a direct line of descent used as a unit of measurement 3/15, 3/22; *n. pl.* degrees, steps in ascent, here specifically the stepped shelves in a cupboard 4/273.

grotes *n. pl.* small coins worth about four pence 5/327.

grounde *n.* the main surface or first coating of colour, serving as background for other colours or designs 2/145.

groundid *pp.* set down 4/629.

guerdon *n.* reward 2/628.

guyders *n. pl.* guiders 2/854.

habunde *v.* to abound, to overflow, to be plentiful 2/468; **habundaunt** *a.* abundant 3/283.

harbage *v.* lodge 1/73.

harde *pa. t.* heard 2/808; **hard** *pp.* 3/371.

harnes *n.* armour 3/239; **harnessid** *ppl. a.* armed, in armour 3/233.

haunces *n. pl.* shelves 4/138, 4/273.

hawberts *n. pl.* halberds 1/246.

hedepece *n.* headpiece, helmet 2/173.

heer *n.* hair 4/104.

height, hight *n.* top 2/139, 2/141, 2/143.

herber *n.* flower garden, arbour 4/315, 4/317.

herde *a.* hard 4/470.

here *pron.* her 3/330.

hever *adv.* ever 4/1075.

hevyng *n.* evening 4/725.

heyghe *a.* high 4/816.

hight(e) *n.* stature 2/132, 2/147.

hode *n.* hood 5/79; **hodis, -es, -ys** *n. pl.* 1/256, 5/81, 5/172.

holde *n.* holding, property 1/214.

hole, hoole, hooll *a.* whole 1/20, 1/200, 2/283, 2/289, 2/837; **holy** *adv.* wholly BC/137.

holys *n. pl.* saints 3/115.

honorate *a.* full of honour 1/43.

honourable *adv.* honourably 2/918.

hopys *n. pl.* hoops 3/163.

hors-litter, -lytter *n.* horse-litter, a litter carried between two horses, one in front and the other behind 2/720, 2/721.

hough *adv.* how 3/313.

howge *a.* huge 2/649.

husshers *n. pl.* ushers 5/318.

ihe, yee *n.* eye 2/197, 4/62.
imbuysid *pa. t.* busied, occupied 4/666.
implied *pa. t.* declared or set forth in writing 3/142.
incepcion *n.* inception, beginning 1/97; **incepcions** *n. pl.* 2/840.
incontynente *adv.* immediately 2/827.
inducyng *vbl. n.* reception 2/12.
induyd *pp.* dressed, clothed 3/118.
inowe *adv.* enough, sufficiently BC/128.
instauns *n.* appeal, suit 4/196.
intentes *n. pl.* designs, plans, projects 2/845.
intentifly *adv.* completely, fully 1/61.
intrete *v.* deal with a subject 2/855.
intretes *n. pl.* entreaties, supplications 4/198.
ipocras *n.* wine flavoured with spices 4/309.
iwisse *adv.* certainly, truly 2/63.

jobardie *n.* jeopardy, danger 1/264; **jeopardies** *n. pl.* 1/3, 1/39, 2/847.
journeis *n. pl.* movements, passages 1/26.
joynly *adv.* joined, tied together 4/610.
juge *v.* judge 2/842.
juges *n. pl.* judges 4/113.
jurnettes *n. pl.* a kind of cassock or cloak 4/382.
justes *n. pl.* jousts Pro/99, 4/1.

kabill *n.* cable 4/914.
kechon *n.* kitchen 4/858.
kerchiers *n. pl.* cloths to cover the head 2/710.
knet *pp.* knitted 2/441.
knottes *n. pl.* flower-beds laid out in intricate designs 4/862.
kowd *pa. t.* could Pro/63.

ladde *pp.* led 2/213.
lantirne *a.* light-giving 4/762.
large *n.*; *at the* ∼ in general, all at once 4/537–8.
lase *n.* lace 2/686.

lates *a.* lattice 3/28.
latone *n.* a mixed metal of a yellow colour 5/60.
lawne *n.* a type of fine linen 4/329.
leafull, lefull *a.* right, lawful 1/83, 2/840.
lede, leed *n.* lead (the mineral) 4/602, 5/54.
leders *n. pl.* haulers, here people who manhandle a pageant into place 4/180.
ledid *ppl. a.* leaded, covered with lead sheets 2/176.
ledis *n. pl.* leads, sheets or strips of lead used to cover a roof 2/644.
leed *pp.* led 2/824, 4/99; *n.* see **lede**.
leigher *n.* soil, loam 4/767.
lete, lett *pa. t.* caused 2/860; ∼ *desire and calle* caused to be invited and called 4/1020.
leves *n. pl.* hinged doors 2/148.
levy *n.* raised walkway 3/16, 3/21.
levys *n. pl.* leaves 4/12.
levys *n. pl.* departures, farewells 4/988.
leysour(e) *n.* leisure 4/229, 4/261.
light *v.* alight, dismount BC/92.
lightsume *a.* bright, well lighted 4/781, 4/805.
limyt, lymytt *pa. t.* appointed, assigned 3/299–300 text n., 3/306; **lymyted, lymitted** *pp.* appointed 1/11, BC/32.
linages, lynagis *n. pl.* lineages, ancestry BC/34, BC/74.
litche *a.* like, similar to 3/161.
losengewise *adv.* in a lozenge pattern 4/840.
lougher, lower *a.* subordinate 1/237, 2/32, 2/176.
lover *n.* a domed turret 4/875.

ma(i)stres *n.* mistress Pro/57, 3/288, 3/292.
make *n.* mate 2/74.
male engynne *n.* fraud, deceit, guile BC/36.
males, -esse *n.* malice 4/207, 4/217.
malier *n.* four wheeled dray 5/210.
manerfull *a.* becoming, gracious 4/636.
mantill *n.* rampart, breastwork 2/283.
marmaydes *n. pl.* mermaids 2/502.
marynours *n. pl.* mariners 4/188.
maydynes *n. pl.* maidens 2/722.

meane *a.* intermediate in time; *in the* ～ *season* in the meantime 3/398.

meanys *n. pl.* laments, complaints 4/198.

meas, messe *n.* a table set for a 'mess' or small group of people eating together 3/259; serving of food, course of dishes in a banquet 4/307.

mede *n.* recompense, reward 2/628.

mediat *a.* mediating; *the which* ～ *grace* by the action of mediating grace 2/839.

mediatly *adv.* immediately (either a scribal error or a clipped form) 3/382.

mengilled *pp.* mingled 4/665.

mete *a.* suitable, proper 2/103, 2/394.

mete *pa. t.* met 5/206.

metropoliton *n.* an archbishop or other bishop having authority over the bishops in a province (ad Lat. *metropolita, -ae* bishop of a chief city) 1/229.

mighteryd *ppl. a.* mitered 3/132.

mirrour *n.* pattern, exemplar 4/678.

monastirs *n. pl.* monasteries 4/883.

mone *n.* moon Pro/23, 2/308.

monysshe *v.* admonish, exhort, remind 3/352; **monisshid** *pp.* 3/309.

moo *a., adv., pron.* more 1/235 and *passim.*

morenars *n. pl.* mourners 5/117; **morenyng, mornyng** *pr. p.* mourning 5/79, 5/160.

mortes *n. pl.* mortices, cavities or holes in which a structure is fitted so as to form a joint 4/801.

mortified *pa. t.* progressed toward death 4/1081.

mountenans *n.* amount 3/395.

myddes *n.* middle, midst 3/234, 3/241.

mydweyes *n. pl.* middle portions of the streets 1/262.

myend *n.* thought, opinion 2/364; **myendes** *n. pl.*; *their good* ～ their good wishes 2/819-20.

mytigat *v.* mitigate, lessen 4/1025.

neithir *conj.* nor 1/217.

nethir *a.* lower; ～ *ende* lower end 4/297.

note *n.* record, account Pro/1.

nyghtid *pa. t.* spent the night 1/186.

nyghyngys *n.* nearness, proximity 3/19.

obediens *n.* obeisance, a gesture of reverence 4/403, 4/448.

objecte *ppl. a.?* (see n.) opposite, over against; *in* ～ *annempst this place* directly opposite this place 3/26.

obsequens *n. pl.* acts of compliance, courtsey 3/203.

occupie *v.* employ oneself in 2/869.

oder *a.* other 5/122.

oderwise *adv.* otherwise, alternatively BC/98.

oisting *ppl. a.* military BC/72.

olyffes *n. pl.* olives 4/596.

onlesse *prep.* unless BC/49.

oppresed *pa. t.* pressed down by force 1/18.

opteigne, -eygne *v.* obtain 2/327, 2/380; **opteigned** *pa. t.* 2/392; *pp.* BC/25.

or *adv.* before 1/161; *prep.* ere, before 2/782; *conj.* before 2/798; **or ever** *adv. phr.* even before 1/161.

ordinat *a.* orderly 2/653.

ordinaunce *n.* regulation, management 5/49.

ordynate *a.* ordained, destined, appointed 1/15.

ostere, ostrie *n.* hostelry, lodgings 1/215, 4/783.

oþer *a.* other 4/418.

ought *adv.* out 4/230, 4/437.

oultragious *a.* violent, furious 1/18.

over *adv.* in addition to, besides 3/414.

oversight *n.* supervision, management 4/407.

overthworth *prep.* opposite 4/441.

owre *n.* hour 1/139; **owres** *n. pl.* 1/119.

pale *n.* a stake fence 3/243, 4/14.

pall *n.* a cloth spread over a hearse or tomb 5/319, 5/321; **palles, -is** *n. pl.* 5/314, 5/324, 5/340.

pament *n.* pavement 3/15.

parage *n.* lineage, descent 2/463.

pardurable *a.* permanent, everlasting 2/61.

parleyaunce *n.* conversation 3/349.

partid *pp.* imparted, given 3/139.

parties, -ise, -yse *n. pl.* parts Pro/14, 4/1052, 4/1077.

party *n.* part; *for the most* ~ for the most part 4/545.

pastans *n.* pastime, recreation 4/266.

patens *n. pl.* wooden-soled footwear designed primarily to elevate the feet above muck and mud 4/920.

patentes *n. pl.* letters from the sovereign conferring a right or privilege 4/1001.

patible *n.* a cross 5/91.

patourne *n.* pattern, exemplar 4/678.

pauce *n.* pause 4/92, 4/388.

peivyd *pp.* paved 4/787.

pekokkes *n. pl.* peacocks 2/146.

pelour *n.* pillar 2/278, 2/290; **pelers, -ours, pilours** *n. pl.* 2/279, 2/758, 2/759.

penselles *n. pl.* small pennants or streamers 5/250.

peracte *pp.* performed, accomplished 3/178.

perduryd *pp.* endured, lasted 3/177.

pere *n.* pear BC/140, BC/163.

pere *n.* peer, equal 3/80.

perfight *a.* perfect 2/330, 2/361.

perisshid *pa. t.* destroyed, killed 3/62.

persid *pp.* pierced 2/189.

perused *pp.* spoken 1/134.

pesyblenes *n.* peacebleness Pro/60.

phacion *n.* fashion 4/771.

pictour, -ure *n.* depiction 2/38; *n.* depicture 3/38; *n.* depiction, specifically, a statue 4/815, 4/830; **pictures** *n. pl.* 4/806; **pictured** *ppl. a.* depicted in sculpture, sculpted 4/835.

pight *pp.* set, placed 4/335, 4/629.

pilyon *n.* a woman's light saddle, a pillion 2/726.

place *n.* manor house 4/732, 4/757.

playnes *n. pl.* plains 1/90.

plays *n. pl.*; *tenes* ~ tennis-courts 4/870.

plightes *n. pl.* plaits, folds 3/161.

polesye, pollici *n.* policy 1/254, 2/183, 2/194.

poletikly *adv.* expediently, wisely 4/858.

pontificalibus *n. pl.* [Lat. *abl. pl.* of *pontificalis*, pontifical] official robes; *in* ~ in pontificals, in the vestments proper to the wearer's ecclesiastical dignity 5/233, 5/262.

portculleis, -es, -ys *n.* a grating made to slide up and down the gateway of a fortified town 2/122, 2/150, 2/163; *n.* the figure of a portcullis as an heraldic badge 2/49, 2/142, 2/144, 4/842.

poudrid *ppl. a.* powdered, dressed with powder 2/765.

pouer *n.* power 4/667.

poyntementes *n. pl.* appointments, equipment 4/480.

poyntes *n. pl.* feats 4/927; ~ *of justes* feats of jousting 4/425; *n. pl.* particular details or characteristics 2/643.

poyntid *ppl. a.* appointed, furnished, equipped 2/553, 4/846.

poysye *n.* motto or short inscription 2/41.

practif *n.* workmanship 3/39, 4/804.

practisid *ppl. a.* executed, wrought 4/595.

predestynate *ppl. a.* fated 1/15.

prefixed *ppl. a.* appointed, settled on beforehand 1/5, 3/364.

premisid, premissid *pp.* stated previously, aforesaid 3/97, 4/997.

presentes *n. pl.*; *the* ~ *there* those people present there 2/566.

pretens *n.* an assertion of right or title 4/519.

pretermisid *pp.* omitted 3/94.

preyse *n.* press, crowd, throng 2/845.

priked (-kyd) songe *n.* a descant or counterpoint accompanying a simple melody 4/897, 5/120.

principacion *n.* position and dignity of a prince 4/1051-2.

procreate *ppl. a.* begotten 2/398.

propertie *n.* quality, attribute 2/228.

propond *pp.* offered Pro/79.

prouses *n.* prowess, valour BC/64.

proventes *n. pl.* jurisdiction 4/1052.

purvey *v.* make provision for 1/48, 1/73; **purveyed** *pp.* provided 4/24.

pusant, -aunt *a.* very little (see Pro/91n.) Pro/91, 4/759.

pusauns, puysauns *n.* a number, crowd (of people) 3/99, 3/394, 4/61.

pyneaple, pyneapul *n.* pine-cone; ∼ *tree* pine-tree BC/138, BC/158.

pynned *pp.* fit into mortises with tenons 4/801.

quadrat *n.* an instrument used for measuring altitudes and distances 2/489; *a.* square or rectangular 4/769.

quarrey *n.* collection or heap of deer killed at hunting 4/746.

quere *n.* choir (body of people) 2/823; *n.* choir (place in the church) 3/6, 3/13.

queremen *n. pl.* choirmen 1/233.

queresters *n. pl.* choir-boys 1/233.

quyshons *n. pl.* cushions 2/731.

qweke *a.* quick, vivid 2/652.

ragge *n.* coarse or rough stone 2/177; **ragges** *n. pl.* 3/220, 4/101.

rasyng *pr. p.* cutting, slashing 4/559.

ray *n.* line, rank 2/806; **raise, raies** *n. pl.* 2/2, 2/26, 2/477, 2/543.

reame *n.* realm BC/12.

rebated *ppl. a.* blunted, dulled BC/84.

recerved *pp.* reserved 2/770.

receyt(e) *n.* reception Pro/2, 4/994; **receytes** *n. pl.* 4/729.

recount *pp.* regarded, considered 4/833.

recountre *v.* [ad F. *renconter*] to meet in battle BC/35.

redyn *pp.* ridden 3/449, 4/505.

regalee *n.* royal prerogative 2/229.

rehersid *ppl. a.* aforementioned 1/209, 1/272.

relik(k)es *n. pl.* relics 4/829, 4/839.

remyge *n.* outfit of oars, oarage [ad Lat. *remigium*] 1/20.

remysid *pp.* remitted 4/1056.

renne *v.* run at tilting BC/105.

rennyng *a.* flowing 4/790, 4/794.

repaire *v.* go 1/36.

reparell *n.* the act of returning or going to a place 4/150; **repairellys** *n. pl.* 3/365.

reseant *n.* resident, dwelling BC/169.

resorte *n.* assemblage, throng 1/216, 3/101.

resortid *pp.* came 4/589; *were* ∼ had come to 4/146; *pa. t.* went 4/475.

respited *pp.* granted respite; *convenyent leisure to her* ∼ suitable respite having been granted to her 1/132.

revoked *pp.* repealed, rescinded Pro/43.

reylys *n. pl.* rails 3/18.

reynye *a.* rainy 4/263.

riall *a.* royal 3/1, 3/214; **rialtie** *n.* royal pomp or splendour 3/449, 3/457.

rodeloftes *n. pl.* a loft or gallery forming the head of a rood-screen 2/32, 3/192.

rof(f) *n.* roof 4/799, 4/802.

rollys, roullys *n. pl.* cloth bands or fillets 2/284, 2/286.

rum(e), rumme *n.* space 2/661; *n.* position 4/818; *n.* place 2/27; **romys, rummys** *n. pl.* 4/153, 4/591.

rybbe *n.* timber, rafter, purlin 2/758.

ryggyng *n.*; ∼ *of an hous* the ridge or roof of a building 4/913.

sage *a.* wise 4/1023.

sakbotes *n. pl.* a type of bass trumpet with a slide for altering the pitch 2/675.

satisfyeng *vbl. n.* contenting, answering, fulfilling of a request 2/897.

saulfgard *n.* safeguard 4/367.

say *n.* assay, trial 3/299; *n.* a cloth of fine texture resembling serge, sometimes partly of silk 3/18, 3/23.

secret *a.* private; ∼ *chambre* privy chamber 1/208.

sedis *n. pl.* seeds 4/866.

seied *pp.* said 2/119.

seieng *pr. p.* saying 2/364.

sekernes *n.* sickness 4/983.

selary *n.* cellar 4/858.

semblaunce *n.* likeness 2/538, 2/585; **semblable, semblaunt** *a.* like, similar 2/550, BC/50.

semble, semily *n.* an assembly, gathering of people 3/370, 4/634; **sembled** *pa. t.* assembled 4/469.

sement *n.* cement 2/136.

semly, -ely, -yly *a.* becoming, of pleasing appearance 2/11, 3/112, 4/659, 4/815.

semys *n. pl.* seams 2/135.

sence *v.* incense, pass incense over 5/262; **sensid** *pa. t.* 5/335.

sentwary *n.* sanctuary 4/10, 4/95.

sered *pp.* wrapped in grave-clothes (cerements), shrouded 5/50.

serpentyns *n. pl.* cannons 4/454.

sertefyed *pa. t.* see **certified**.

serymonyes *n. pl.* ceremonies 3/95.

sett *ppl. a.* fixed, placed 2/807.

settes *n. pl.* places where things are set, shelves 4/137.

severally *adv.* separately 4/968.

shalmewes *n. pl.* medieval musical instrument of the oboe class 2/675, 3/183.

sherevys *n. pl.* sherriffs 1/252.

shett *pp.* joined, fixed together 4/801.

shote *v.* shoot 4/751, 4/752.

showghtes *n. pl.* shouts 3/194.

signe *n.* constellation 2/104.

signifiour *n.* significator, in astrology, a planet which especially signifies a person in a horoscope 2/374, 2/377.

silf *n.* self; ∼ *same* identical, same BC/120.

singuler, singler *a.* separate, individual Pro/100, 2/882.

sith(e) *conj.* since, because 1/108, 2/585.

skochon *n.* escutcheon, a shield or shield-like surface on which a coat of arms is displayed 2/487; **skochons, scochyns, -ions** *n. pl.* 3/240, 5/204, 5/207, 5/213.

skorgid *ppl. a.* scorched 4/600.

skymmyng *pr. p.* sailing with a light or easy motion 4/688.

sleight(e) *n.* skill, dexterity 4/116, 4/925; **slayghtes** *n. pl.* feats of dexterity 4/916.

sloppe *n.* loose jacket, tunic 5/78; **sloppis** *n. pl.* 5/81.

sofreynge, suffrayn(g) *n.* sovereign Pro/4, Pro/74, 4/816.

sokettes *n. pl.* sockets 1/19.

sondes *n. pl.* God's dispensation or ordinance 5/46.

sondid *ppl. a.* covered with sand 1/262, 4/6, 4/865.

sone *adv.* soon 1/105.

songen, -on *pp.* sung 5/128, 5/132.

soone *n.* sun 4/600.

soper, souper *n.* supper 1/148, 4/930.

sought *n.* south 4/303.

souped, supped *pp.* supped 1/148, 4/931.

spancles, spanglis *n. pl.* spangles, pieces of metal sewn on a fabric for decoration 4/85, 4/496.

spedefull *a.* speedy, quick 4/999.

spere *n.* sphere Pro/22, 2/407; **speeres** *n. pl.* 2/347; **spereycall** *a.* spherical 2/465.

sporys *n. pl.* spurs 3/445.

spronge *pp.* spread, extended (of fame) 5/37.

spryneth *v.* springs 3/60.

squylery *n.* scullery 4/858.

stacion *n.* a halt, a stand 4/388.

stages *n. pl.* levels of scaffolding 4/37; *n.* shelves 4/578, 4/932.

staous *n.* alms-house 4/882.

stappe *n.* step 2/793.

stavis, -ys *n. pl.* rungs on a chair 2/697, 2/735.

stay *n.* pole 4/917, 4/919.

stedfastly *adv.* firmly, fixed securely 4/911.

steiers *n. pl.* stairs 2/760, 2/761, 4/26.

stole *n.* stool 2/696.

stolys *n. pl.* a type of long robe 5/107.

stondyng *vbl. n.* standing-place, station, standing-room 4/32; **standynges** *vbl. n. pl.* 2/847.

strake *pa. t.* struck 4/744; **strekyn, striken** *pp.* struck 1/78, 4/430.

straunge *a.* alien, unusual 2/247; **straungers** *n. pl.* aliens, foreigners 2/677; **straungest** *supl.* most exceptional, most wonderful 4/468.

streite *a.* strict; ∼ *injunction* strict commandment 1/92.

stroke *n.* blow 2/850; **strokes** *n. pl.* bowshots 4/754.

stryve *n.* strife Pro/53.

styrop *n.* stirrup 2/736; **stiroppis** *n. pl.* 2/737.

suberbys *n. pl.* suburbs 1/217.

subtilties *n. pl.* sugary ornamental desserts 3/270.

suerly *adv.* surely 2/215.

suertie *n.* security, bond 2/880.

suetes *n. pl.* sets of church vestments intended to be worn together at the same time 3/12.

suetly *adv.* sweetly 4/953.

suffraunce *n.* sanction, consent 4/1054.

suffreyn *n.* sovereign 1/223.

summynes *n.* summons 4/481.

surfett *n.* surfeit, the morbid condition caused by excessive eating or drinking 4/1073.

sustentacion *n.* supporting of life Pro/34.

suyngly *adv.* subsequently, in due sequence 4/641.

suys *v.* (*pr. 3 sg.*) petitions 4/784.

taberiens *n. pl.* taborins, a type of drum narrower and longer than a tabor 4/616.

tabernacle *n.* a canopied niche or recess in a wall or pillar to contain an image 2/31, 2/39; *n.* an ornate structure in a pageant 4/939, 4/940.

tables *n.* backgammon 4/869, 4/904.

taclyng *n.* tackle, a ship's rigging 4/181; **taclynges** *n. pl.* 4/453.

Tamys *n.* the Thames 1/195.

tarians, tariaunce *n.* tarriance, delay 4/92, 4/492.

tenes ballys *n. pl.* tennis balls 4/920.

teyed *pp.* tied 4/443.

the *pron.* they 2/650, 4/420.

theologik *a.* theological 2/762.

theoryke *a.* theological (evidently an error for 'theologik'; see n.) 2/224.

thethir *adv.* thither, to a particular place 5/69.

tho *pron.* those 4/351, 4/352.

titles *n. pl.* headings, subjects 2/856.

tofore *adv.* before 1/144; *prep.* 3/391, 3/407.

torettes, torrettes *n. pl.* turrets 4/170, 4/172.

tother *pron.* other (of two); *the* ~ the other (of two) 2/481.

tourys *n. pl.* towers 4/872.

toward *a.* auspicious 2/259.

towardly *a.* promising, apt to learn, well-disposed, dutiful, tractable 5/34.

towchid *pp.* touched upon, referred to 4/487.

trappure *n.* a covering put over the saddle or harness of a horse 5/298; **trapped, -id** *ppl. a.* adorned with trappings 2/668, 2/682, 4/77, 5/159.

travasse carpet *n.* a curtain drawn across a room 4/837.

trayne *n.* train, the trailing part of a robe 5/127.

treatable *a.* agreeable, easily handled 2/233.

triplicite *n.* a combination of three signs of the zodiac, each being a third part of a circle distant from the other two 2/397.

trone *n.* throne 2/338, 2/553.

trostilles *n. pl.* trestles 5/67.

trowe *v.* trust, believe 3/59.

trusse *v.* pack up 4/667.

turned *pa. t.* tourneyed 4/432.

turneis *n. pl.* tournaments 3/38.

tylte, tilte *n.* the tilt 4/7, 4/10, 4/40, 4/366.

tyrangill *n.* triangle 2/489.

ubertly *adv.* abundantly, copiously 3/245.

unche *n.* inch 2/561.

upholdid *pp.* upheld 4/81.

uppyeldid *pa. t.* delivered up, surrendered 4/1087; **uppyeldon** *pp.* 4/1056.

ure *n.* practice, custom, habit BC/127.

uttir *a.* exterior, outer 4/786; **uttermest** *superl.* outermost 5/336.

vailey *n.* valley 4/765.

valance *n.* a type of thin woven fabric 5/251.

vale *pp.* veiled Pro/36.

valoure *n.* worth, value, importance, worthiness 3/13.

vane *n.* metal plate resembling a flag or banner bearing a coat of arms 2/50; **vanys** *n. pl.* 2/40, 4/380; see **fane**.

varnesshid *pp.* adorned, embellished Pro/32.

vaute *n.* vault 3/27.

venquysshid *pa. t.* vanquished 2/437.

verdutes *n. pl.* verdicts, opinions Pro/55, 2/869.

vesture *n.* garments 3/117.

vexable *a.* troublesome, vexing 4/1004.

viand *n.* provisions, victuals 1/49, 3/269.

vir tres *n. pl.* fir trees 4/597.

visagid *a.* having the visage of a specific kind 4/811.

voydans, -auns *n.* drainage 2/130, 4/779.

voyde *v.* leave 5/19.

voyde *a.* open, empty 2/279, 4/5, 4/908; *n.* opening 2/136.

voyde *n.* a parting meal, usually with wine and spices 4/245, 4/247.

voydid *pp.* emptied out 5/66; *ppl. a.* having portions cut away 2/281.

vyrond *ppl. a.* encircled 2/283.

wanlaces *n. pl.* appointed stations in hunting 4/742.

warnyd *pp.* advised, given notice of 2/902, 3/440.

waryers *n. pl.* warriors 4/439.

wayters *n. pl.* servants 1/263.

weies *n. pl.* ways, thoroughfares 1/248.

welle *n.* spring, source 2/267.

wellith *n.* welfare 5/29.

were *pa. t.* wore 3/155.

werre *n.* war 4/36, 4/44; **werrys** *n. pl.* 4/65.

wethir, whether *n.* weather 5/165, 5/166.

weward *a.* wayward, distant BC/170.

weye *n.* passage 3/15.

wherys *n. pl.* light rowing boats 4/672, 4/716.

whether, -ir *rel. adv.* whither, to which place 4/674, 4/936.

whoes, whois *poss. pron.* whose Pro/90, 1/27.

wiendes *n. pl.* winds 1/3, 1/12.

wight lymyd *ppl. a.* whitewashed 4/839–40, 4/849.

withinforth *adv.* everywhere within 1/196.

without *prep.* despite 4/1080.

woddosys *n. pl.* wild men 4/948.

wolde *pp.* would 3/330.

woon *n.* one 4/287.

wott *v.* know 2/781.

wowers *n. pl.* wooers, suitors 4/198.

wrought *pa. t.* tossed, seethed, moved violently 1/21.

yed(e) *pa. t.* went 4/568, 4/900, 4/964.

yee see **ihe**.

yeftes *n. pl.* gifts 2/440.

yoven *pp.* given Pro/3.

BIOGRAPHICAL INDEX

THIS index to the persons mentioned in the text lists all occurrences of names or titles except for Arthur, Henry VII, and Katharine of Aragon, who are mentioned too frequently to be usefully indexed. Names appear primarily under official titles, except where the text itself gives personal names. Thomas Grey, 2nd Marquis of Dorset, thus appears under 'Dorset', but Sir Walter Baskerville appears under 'Baskerville'. Cross-references are given in confusing instances. Except in unusual circumstances, persons identified in this index will not also be identified in the Commentary. BC and SC identify references to the texts, respectively, of the Duke of Buckingham's tournament challenge and of the Earl of Suffolk's tournament challenge. Otherwise, all references are to the text of the *Receyt*.

Brittany to join Henry; fought at Bosworth. Admiral of the Fleet and Knight of the Garter, 1/46.

Buckingham (Bokyngham, Bukynham), Edward Stafford, 3rd Duke (1478–1521). Son of the 2nd Duke of Buckingham and Katharine Woodville, aunt of Henry VII's queen. Accompanied Henry VII to Calais in May 1500 where a French version of his Challenge was proclaimed. With the defection of Suffolk in August 1501, he became the highest ranking and most prestigious nobleman in England except for immediate members of the royal family—hence his role as the formal 'challenger', in the place of Arthur and Katharine, at the wedding tournament, 1/163, 2/17, 2/671–2, 2/674, 2/746–7, 2/832–3, 3/387–8, 4/70, 4/78, 4/115ff., 4/375ff., 4/427, 4/445, 4/530, 4/536, 4/551, 4/569, 4/650, 4/694ff., 4/713, BC/2, BC/28–9.

Buckingham (Bokyngham), Lord Henry. See **Stafford, Lord Henry.**

Bury (Burie, Borey) St Edmund's, Abbot of. William Codenham from 1497–c. 1511, 3/133, 5/149, 5/235.

Cabra, Countess of. Wife of Diego Fernandez de Cordoba, Count of Cabra, 3/260, 3/287–8, 3/292, 4/279.

Cabra, Diego Fernandez de Cordoba, Count of (therl of Spain), 1/122, 1/128, 2/679, 3/126, 3/210, 3/259–60, 3/334, 3/379, 4/296, 4/744, 4/962, 4/968, 4/998.

Canterbury (Cantirbury), Archbishop of. Henry Deane (d. 1503). Appointed archbishop in April 1501. Helped negotiate the marriage of Henry's daughter, Margaret, and James IV of Scotland. Officiated at Arthur and Katharine's marriage, 1/228, 2/822, 2/830–1, 3/130–1, 3/172, 3/202, 3/380, 4/699.

Cecil, Lady. 3rd daughter of Edward IV, sister to Henry's queen. Favoured by Henry after her difficulties with Richard III, 3/126, 4/231, 4/233, 4/288.

Chester, Abbot of. John Birchenshaw from 1492–1537, 5/234, 5/257.

Chester, Bishop of (actually the Bishop of Coventry and Lichfield who presided over the Archdiocese of Chester). John Arundell (d. 1503) from 1497–1502, 5/71, 5/115, 5/119, 5/151–2, 5/177, 5/229, 5/259–60, 5/273.

Chamberlain, Lord. See **Daubeney, Giles, 1st Baron.**

Chapel Royal, Dean of. Geoffrey Simeon (d. 1508) from 1491; Dean of Lincoln from 1506, 1/232.

Constable, Lord High, of England. See **Derby, Thomas Stanley, 1st Earl.**

Cornwall (Cornuall), Sir Thomas, 5/76, 5/294–5.

Courtney, Lord William (d. 1509). Son and heir to Edward, Earl of Devonshire. At this time William was in high favour at Court as the husband of Katharine, the Queen's sister. Imprisoned after the Queen's death in 1503. Freed in 1509, but he died before his title was officially restored to him in 1511, 4/99, 4/394ff., 4/402, 4/415, 4/458, 4/510, 4/555–6, 4/565, SC/16.

Crofte (Crofts), Sir Richard. Steward of Prince Arthur's House, 5/74, 5/208, 5/304, 5/352, 5/362.

Dacre, Lady Anne of the South. Daughter of Humphrey Bourchier, who was an illegitimate son of Lord Berners, 4/302–3.

Daubeney (Dawbeney), Lady Elizabeth. Daughter of George Neville, 3rd Baron Bergavenny. First wife of Lord Daubeney, 4/300–1.

Daubeney, Giles, 1st Baron Daubeney and Lord Chamberlain (d. 1508). Served Edward IV and was an early supporter of Richmond. A military commander and an ambassador, helped to make the first treaty of marriage between Arthur and Katharine, 2/635, 2/648.

Dean of the Chapel Royal. See **Chapel Royal, Dean of**.

Deane, Henry. See **Canterbury, Archbishop of**.

De Fonseca, Alonzo. See **Santiago, Archbishop of**.

Derby (Darby), Thomas Stanley (1435–1504), 1st Earl. Served under Henry VI, Edward IV, and Richard III. Married Lady Margaret Beaufort, Henry VII's mother, c. 1482. K.G. c. 1483. Supposedly betrayed Richard by setting his crown on Henry's head at Bosworth. Godfather to Prince Arthur and Lord High Constable, 2/634, 2/647, 3/347–8, 3/384, 4/53, 4/283, 4/695–6.

Devonshire (Devenshire), Lord William. See **Courtney, William**.

Dorset (Dorzet), Lord of. See **Marquis**.

Dudley (Dodley), Lord Edward Sutton (c. 1459–1531/2). K.B. 1487, K.G. 1509, 5/82, 5/136, 5/290, 5/321.

Dudley (Dodley), Thomas, 5/92.

Durham (Derham), Bishop of. Probably William Sever or Senhouse (d. 1505), 2/822–3, 2/832.

Earl of Spain. See **Cabra, Count of**.

Edenham, Doctor. John Ednaham, Arthur's almoner and confessor, treasurer of St Paul's from 1509 (d. 1515), 5/144.

Elizabeth (of York), Queen of England (1465–1503). Daughter of Edward IV and Elizabeth Woodville. Married Henry VII in January 1486, 1/188, 1/203, 2/636–7, 2/900, 2/903, 2/914, 3/29, 3/165, 3/412, 3/416, 4/24ff., 4/45ff., 4/147ff., 4/233ff., 4/284, 4/312ff., 4/371, 4/474, 4/482, 4/586, 4/701, 4/723, 4/843, 4/852, 4/861, 4/986, 4/992, 4/1042, 5/10ff., 5/246, BC/23, BC/48, BC/58, BC/130.

Essex, Henry Bourchier, 2nd Earl (d. 1539). Son of William Bourchier, grandson of Henry Bourchier, the 1st Earl. Nephew of Queen Elizabeth through his mother, Anne Woodville. A Privy Councillor to Henry VII, 2/18, 2/666, 3/388, 4/100ff., 4/394ff., 4/412, 4/428, 4/458ff., 4/510, 4/539, 4/553ff., 4/565, 4/697, SC/15.

Evesham, Abbot of. Probably Thomas Newbolt, 5/234, 5/258.

Exeter, Bishop of. Probably Richard Redmayn (trans. to Ely Sept. 1501) but may be John Arundel who succeeded Redmayn at Exeter in Feb. 1501/2, 1/231.

Ferdinand (Phardinand), King, also Ferdinand II of Aragon and V of Castile and Leon (1452–1516). Son of John II of Aragon, he married his cousin, Isabella of Castile, in 1469. Encouraged expansionist policies and united the Spanish kingdoms into a nation, Pro/3, Pro/87, 1/2, 1/6–7, 1/99, 2/856–7, 4/992–3, 5/245, BC/10–11, SC/4–5.

Fitzgerald, Lord Gerald (Garrard) (1487–1534). Son and heir to the 8th Earl of Kildare. In England as a hostage for his father's loyalty from 1497–1503. His stepmother was Elizabeth St John, first cousin to Henry VII. He succeeded his father as the 9th Earl of Kildare in 1513. Man of Arms at Arthur's funeral, 5/73, 5/137–8, 5/296–7, 5/302.

Fitzgerald, Gerald. See **Kildare, Gerald Fitzgerald, 8th Earl**.

Fitzjames, Richard. See **Rochester, Bishop of**.

Garrard, Lord. See **Fitzgerald, Lord Gerald**.

Garretierre. John Wrythe (d. 1504). Garter King of Arms from 1478. Officiated at the funeral of Edward IV and the coronations of Richard III and Henry VII, SC/25.

Gloucester, Abbot of. Thomas Branch, 5/234, 5/258.

Great Malvern (Mecoll Malvarn), Prior of. Maculin Ledbury, from c.
1497–1507, 5/236.

Grey, George. See **Kent, George Grey, 2nd Earl**.

Grey, Lord John of Dorset (Dorzet). Youngest son of Thomas Grey, 2nd
Marquis of Dorset. Later involved in Wyatt's rebellion; died 1569, 5/73,
5/138, 5/292–3.

Grey, Lord John of Powis (d. 1504), 5/82, 5/137, 5/291, 5/317.

Grey, Lord Thomas. See **Marquis**.

Griffith ap Sir Rhys (d. 1521). Son of Sir Rhys ap Thomas. K.B. 1501, a
companion of Prince Arthur. Present at the Field of Cloth of Gold, 5/95,
5/173, 5/329–30.

Guildford (Gilford), Lady Joan (d. 1536?). 2nd wife of Sir Richard Guildford
and sister of Nicholas Vaux, 1st Lord Vaux of Harrowdan, 1/153.

Guildford (Gilford), Sir Richard (1455?–1506). Privy Councillor, fought at
Blackheath, 1497; Sergeant of the King's Armory, Controller of the King's
Household, 4/543.

Hailes, Abbot of. Thomas Stafford, 5/235, 5/281.

Harle (Arle), Sir John, 5/76.

Haryngton, Le Seigneur de. See **Marquis**.

Henry VIII, King of England (1491–1547). Made Duke of York in 1494 and
Prince of Wales in 1503. Second son of Henry VII and his wife, Queen
Elizabeth of York. Became king in 1509, 2/16–7, 2/682, 2/831, 2/871, 3/125,
3/209–10, 3/383, 4/51, 4/143, 4/237ff., 4/293, 4/702ff., 4/853–4, 5/34.

Herbert, Sir George. Knighted at Battle of Stoke-on-Trent (1487). Possibly a
son of Sir William Herbert, Earl of Pembroke, Henry VII's former
guardian, 4/74, 4/376, 4/446, 4/528–9.

Herbert, Lady. Wife of Sir George Herbert, 4/301.

Howard (Haward), Master (canopy bearer at Arthur's funeral). Probably
one of the sons of Thomas Howard, perhaps Sir Edward Howard
(1477–1513), 5/86.

Hungerford, Edward. Probably Edward Hastings, Lord Hungerford, 5/93.

Inglefield (Ingilfield), Sir Thomas. K.B. 1501, 5/77.

Isabella, Queen of Castile (1451–1504). Daughter of John II of Castile. Married
Ferdinand of Aragon. Mother of Katharine. Patron of Columbus, 1/2,
5/246, BC/10–11, SC/4–5.

Katharine, Lady (1479–1527). Sister to Elizabeth of York and Lady Cecil.
Daughter of Edward IV. Wife of William Courtenay of Devonshire, 4/288.

Kent, George Grey, 12th Earl (d. 1503). Succeeded his father, the 11th Earl, in
1489. Fought for Henry VII at Stoke and Blackheath. First married Anne
Woodville, sister of Edward IV's queen and then later Catherine Herbert,
daughter of the Earl of Pembroke, 1/163–4, 2/18, 2/674, 3/389, 4/697, 5/81,
5/135, 5/287.

Kildare, Gerald Fitzgerald (Fitzmaurice), 8th Earl (d. 1513). Lord Deputy of
Ireland in the closing years of Edward IV's reign. Supported Simnel but
was pardoned by Henry VII. Attainted by the Irish Parliament in 1494 on
the charge of aiding Warbeck and sent to the Tower, but he was pardoned
by Henry in 1496 and reappointed Lord Deputy, 5/296.

King's Mother (Moder). See **Beaufort, Lady Margaret**.

Labere, Sir Richard de, 5/76–7, 5/294.

Lady Mistress (Mastres, Maystres) to Princess Katharine. Her Duenna, Doña Elvira Manuel, wife of Don Pedro Manrique, Katharine's Major Domo, 3/288, 3/292, 4/282.

Lincoln, Bishop of. William Smith (d. 1513/14), Lord President of Prince Arthur's Council, 5/71, 5/113, 5/114, 5/132–3, 5/177, 5/229, 5/261, 5/280–1, 5/303, 5/345.

London, Mayor of. Sir John Shaw (d. 1503). Knighted on Bosworth Field and made a Bannaret by Henry VII at the battle of Blackheath, 1/252, 2/654, 2/811, 3/415, 3/418, 4/34, 4/58, 4/690.

Lord Chamberlain. See Daubeney, Giles.

Majorca, Bishop of. Antonio De Rojas, 1/122, 2/680, 3/258, 3/334, 3/377–8, 4/287–8, 4/967.

Margaret, Princess (1489–1541). Eldest daughter of Henry VII. Married James IV of Scotland in 1503 and became Queen of Scotland, 2/637, 4/46, 4/238ff., 4/291, 4/854, 5/35.

Marquis (Marquyes, Merquyes), Lord. Lord Thomas Grey, 2nd Marquis of Dorset (1477–1530). Known as Lord Harrington until he succeeded his father, Thomas Grey, 1st Marquis of Dorset, on September 20, 1501. K.G. Sept. 22, 1501. Especially active during Henry VIII's reign, promoting the King's divorce and Wolsey's impeachment, 4/70, 4/104–5, 4/115ff., 4/393ff., 4/402, 4/427, 4/457ff., 4/510, 4/512, 4/536–7, 4/551, 4/564, 4/652, SC/15.

Mary, Princess (1496–1533). Third daughter of Henry VII. Married Louis XII of France in 1514. After he died in 1515 she married Charles Brandon, Duke of Suffolk, 2/638, 4/47, 5/35.

Mecoll Malvarn, Prior of. See Great Malvern.

Mortimer (Mortymer), Sir John, 5/75, 5/293–4.

Norfolk (Norffolke), Duchess of. Elizabeth Talbot (d. 1507), the daughter of John Talbot, 1st Earl of Shrewsbury; she was the widow of John De Mowbray (1444–75/6), 4th Duke of Norfolk, 1/54, 3/259, 3/287, 3/292, 4/292.

Northumberland (Northumblond), Henry Algernon Percy, 5th Earl (1478–1527). Son of Henry, the 4th Earl. He succeeded his father in 1489. Made K.B. when Arthur was created Prince of Wales in 1489, 2/17, 2/670–1, 2/748, 2/833, 3/388, 4/53–4, 4/294–5, 4/696.

Officer at Arms to Prince Arthur. Sir Thomas Wriothesley (or Wrythe). Wallingford Pursuivant from 1489–1505; Garter King of Arms from 1505 until his death in 1521, 5/346–7.

Owedale, Sir William. See Uvedale, Sir William.

Oxford (Oxinford), John de Vere, 13th Earl (1443–1513). Son of John de Vere, the 12th Earl, and Elizabeth Howard. His father was executed for his commitment to the Lancastrian cause. He served as Captain-General at Bosworth and also fought at Stoke and Blackheath. Hereditary Great Chamberlain of England, 2/634, 2/647, 3/106–7, 3/285, 3/294, 3/327, 3/384–5, 3/430–1, 4/52, 4/281, 4/402, 4/652, 4/695, 4/713.

Peche, Sir John, 4/98, 4/394–5, 4/402, 4/458–9, 4/556, 4/565–6, SC/16.

Pole (Polle), Sir Richard. Prince Arthur's Chamberlain (d. 1504). K.G. 1499. His mother was the half-sister of Margaret Beaufort, Henry VII's mother, 5/8, 5/82–3, 5/137, 5/291, 5/293.

Powis (Powes, Powys), Lord. See **Grey, Lord John of Powis**.
Protonotary (Prothonotory) of Spain. See **Ayala**.

Queen's Grace. See **Elizabeth (of York), Queen of England**.

Radcliffe (Ratclif), Master. Probably Robert Radcliffe, s. and h. of John Radcliffe, the 9th Lord Fitzwalter. Although his father was attainted for treason and beheaded in 1496, Robert managed to obtain a reversal of the attainder and become the 10th Lord Fitzwalter in 1595. K.B. 1509, K.G. 1524. He became Viscount Fitzwalter, 1525, and Earl of Surrey, 1529, 5/87-8.

Recorder of London. Robert Sheffield (d. 1518). Knighted after the Battle of Stoke-on-Trent, 1487. Speaker of the House of Commons in 1510 and 1512, 2/657.

Rivers (Ryvers, Riviere), Guylliam de la (d. before 1507). Master of the King's Hawks, 4/96, 4/395, 4/459, 4/566, SC/17.

Rochester, Bishop of. Richard Fitzjames (d. 1522) from 1497-1503, 1/231-2, 2/897.

Rome, Legate of. Probably Gaspar Ponce, a Spaniard, master in theology, archdeacon of Majorca, protonotary of the Pope. Administrator for the indulgence of the Jubilee, Ponce was in England 1500-2, but was not formally designated as a legate, 2/683.

Rowland, Sir. See **Veleville, Sir Rowland de**.
Ruthall, Thomas. See **Secretary to Henry VII**.
Ruthyn (Ruthen), Lord Richard Grey (d. 1520/21). Son of George Grey, 2nd Earl of Kent. He succeeded his father as the 3rd Earl in 1503. Attended Henry VIII at the Field of Cloth of Gold, 1520, 5/81, 5/136, 5/289-90, 5/322.

St John, Master. Probably Sir John St John, Lady Margaret's nephew. Son of the Earl of Kildare by his second wife, 5/88.

Salisbury (Sausbury), Bishop of. Edward Audley (d. 1524) from 1501, 1/231, 5/71, 5/114, 5/129, 5/177, 5/229, 5/260, 5/276-7.

Santiago, Archbishop of. Alonzo de Fonseca, 1/121, 1/127, 2/679, 3/334, 3/380-1, 4/967, 4/997.

Savage, Thomas. See **York, Archbishop of**.
Secretary to Henry VII. Thomas Ruthall (d. 1523). Bishop of Durham, 1509. He continued on as Henry VIII's secretary and Keeper of the Privy Seal, 1/234.

Sherriffs (Shrevys) of London. Laurence Ailmer (later Mayor) and Henry Hede, 2/657, 2/811, 4/35, 4/690.

Shrewsbury, Abbot of. Probably Richard Lye (d. 1512), 5/148, 5/152-3, 5/235, 5/257.

Shrewsbury (Shrowesbury, Shreuesbury), George Talbot, 4th Earl, also Earl of Waterford (1468-1538). Son of the 3rd Earl. He fought for Henry at Stoke-on-Trent and was made K.G., 1487. Later he served Henry VIII, attending the Field of Cloth of Gold in 1520, 2/634-5, 2/647-8, 3/107-8, 3/378-9, 4/54, 4/696-7, 5/80, 5/134-5, 5/287.

Simeon, Geoffrey. See **Dean of the Chapel Royal**.
Smith, William. See **Lincoln, Bishop of**.
Spain, Archbishop of. See **Santiago**.
Spain, Bishop of. See **Majorca**.
Spain, Earl of. See **Cabra**.

Spain, Protonotary of. See **Ayala, Don Pedro de**.

Stafford, Edward. See **Buckingham, Edward Stafford, 3rd Duke**.

Stafford, Lord Henry (1479?-1523). Son of Henry Stafford, 2nd Duke of Buckingham, and Katharine, the sister of Henry's queen. Younger brother of Edward Stafford, the 3rd Duke of Buckingham. Later Henry became the 5th Earl of Wiltshire, 1/164, 2/18-9, 4/75, 4/375-6, 4/412, 4/428, 4/445, 4/462, 4/529-30, 4/540, 4/553, 4/569-70, 4/652.

Stanley, Sir George. See **Strange, Sir George Stanley, Lord**.

Stanley, Thomas. See **Derby, Thomas Stanley, 1st Earl**.

Strange, Sir George Stanley, Lord (1460?-1503). Son of Thomas Stanley, the 1st Earl of Derby. Married Joan, daughter of Lord Strange. K.G. 1487, a Privy Councillor to Henry VII, 2/19.

Suche, Lord. See **Zouche, Lord John la**.

Suffolk, le Conte de. Edmund de la Pole (1472?-1513), the Earl of Suffolk. 2nd son of John de la Pole, 2nd Duke of Suffolk, and Elizabeth, sister of Edward IV. Accompanied Henry VII to Calais in May 1500, where he issued the French challenge. Always suspect because of his Yorkist connections, he fled to the Emperor Maximilian in the Tyrol in August 1501. His place as chief challenger in the tournament was subsequently taken by the Marquis of Dorset, SC/15.

Surrey, Thomas Howard, Earl of (1443-1524). Son of Sir John Howard, 1st Duke of Norfolk. Served Edward IV and Richard III, fighting on the Yorkist side at Bosworth. Imprisoned by Henry VII but released in 1489. Lieutenant General of the North, Councillor and Lord High Treasurer 1501-2. Created Duke of Norfolk, 1514, 1/51, 2/18, 4/54, 4/297-8, 5/78, 5/121, 5/126, 5/130, 5/133, 5/139-40, 5/155, 5/196, 5/275, 5/277.

Talbot, George. See **Shrewsbury, George Talbot, 4th Earl**.

Tewkesbury (Tewkisbury), Abbot of. Richard Chelternam (d. 1509), 5/235, 5/256, 5/281-2, 5/301.

Throgmorton, Sir Robert. K.B. 1501, 5/295.

Troys, Thomas (d. before 1509), 5/90.

Uvedale (Ovedall, Owedale), Sir William. Controller of Arthur's household, 5/74, 5/123-4, 5/208-9, 5/304, 5/38-9, 5/363.

Vaux (Vaus), Lord Nicholas of Harrowden (d. 1523). Courtier and soldier, a favourite of Henry VII, he fought at Stoke-on-Trent, 1487, and at Blackheath, 4/544.

Veleville, Sir Rowland de (d. 1535). Native of Brittany, a servant to Henry VII. Knighted in 1497 after the battle of Blackheath, 4/74, 4/376-7, 4/415-6, 4/446, 4/528, 4/556.

Vicar General or Chancellor of the Bishop of Worcester. See **Worcester, Vicar General of**.

Willoughby (Willughby), Master Antony, 5/87.

Willoughby, Sir Robert. See **Broke, Sir Robert Willoughby, 1st Baron**.

Willoughby (Willughby), Lord William (d. 1526). Son of Christopher Willoughby *de jure* Lord Willoughby, 2/20.

Winchester, Bishop of. Richard Foxe (1448?-1528). After studying at Oxford and Cambridge, continued studies at Paris, where he joined Henry VII's cause. After Bosworth, he became Henry's principal secretary of state and Lord Privy Seal. One of Henry VII's most reliable ministers of state. Held in succession bishoprics of Exeter, Bath and Wells, Durham, and Winchester. According to Bacon, he presided over the wedding festivities, 4/699–700.

Worcester, Prior of. Thomas Mildenham (d. 1507), 5/235–6, 5/259.

Worcester, Vicar General of. Thomas Wodyngton (Woodington), LL.D. (d. 1522), from 1487–1503, 5/221, 5/263, 5/312.

Yeaule, Don Peter de. See **Ayala, Don Pedro de**.

York, Archbishop of. Thomas Savage (d. 1507). Active in Henry VII's service, 1/229–30, 2/14–5, 3/378, 4/699.

York, Dean of. Geoffrey Blythe (d. 1530). Bishop of Coventry and Lichfield after 1503. Often employed by Henry VII, 2/15.

York, Duke of. See **Henry VIII, King of England**.

Zouche (Suche), Lord John la (1459–1525/6). Fought for Richard III at Bosworth, captured and attainted. Full dignities restored in 1495. Took part in French campaign, 1492; attended Henry VII to Calais, 1500, 2/20.

SELECT BIBLIOGRAPHY

A. Manuscripts

Edinburgh, National Library of Scotland, MS Advocates 33.2.24.

London, British Library, Add. MS 45131.

London, British Library, Cotton MS Vespasian C. XIV.

London, British Library, Cotton MS Vitellius A. XVI.

London, British Library, Cotton MS Vitellius C. XI.

London, British Library, MS Egerton 2642.

London, British Library, MS Harley 69.

London, Corporation of London Record Office, Journals, X.

London, Corporation of London Record Office, *Rental of the Bridge House.*

London, College of Arms, MS I. 3.

London, College of Arms, MS I. 9.

London, College of Arms, MS M. 3.

London, College of Arms, MS M. 6.

London, College of Arms, MS 1st M. 13.

London, College of Arms, MS Vincent 25.

London, Guildhall Library, MS 3313.

London, Public Record Office, E. 101/415/3.

London, Public Record Office, LC 2/1.

Oxford, Bodleian Library, MS Tanner 85.

Simancas, Archivo General, MS P.R. 54–14.

Stafford, Staffordshire County Record Office, MS D 1721/1/1.

B. Books

Anglo, Sydney, 'The *British History* in Early Tudor Propaganda', *Bulletin of the John Rylands Library*, xliv (1961), 17–48.

——, *The Great Tournament Roll of Westminister*, Oxford, 1968.

——, 'The London Pageants for the Reception of Katharine of Aragon: November 1501', *Journal of the Warburg and Courtald Institutes*, xxvi (1963), 53–89.

——, *Spectacle, Pageantry, and Early Tudor Policy*, Oxford, 1969.

Apianus, Petrus, *Cosmographicus liber*, Landshut, 1524.

——, *Quadrans Apiana astronomicis*, Ingolstadt, 1532.

Bartholomaeus Anglicus, *De Proprietatibus Rerum*, trans. John Trevisa, gen. ed. M.C. Seymour, Oxford, 1975.

Beauchamp Pageants, ed. Viscount Dillon and W.H. St John Hope, London, 1914.

Bersuire, Pierre, *Repertorium morale*, Nuremberg, 1489.

Boucher, François Léon Louis, *20,000 Years of Fashion*, New York, [1967].

Breviarum Sarum, ed. F. Procter and C. Wordsworth, Cambridge, 1886.

Briquet, C.M., *Les filigranes*, ed. A. Stevenson, 4 vols., Amsterdam, 1968.

Busch, Wilhelm, *England Under the Tudors: Henry VII*, London, 1895.

Calendar of State Papers, Spanish, I, ed. G.A. Bergenroth, London, 1862. *Supplement to I and II*, ed. G.A. Bergenroth, London, 1868.

Campbell, Louise, and Steer, Francis, *A Catalogue of Manuscripts in the College of Arms Collections*, foreword by Sir Anthony Wagner, index and biographical notes by Robert Yorke, i, London, 1988.

Campbell, William, *Materials for a History of Henry VII*, Rolls Series lx, London, 1873–7.

The Chronicles of Calais, ed. John Gough Nichols, Camden Society, xxxv, London, 1846.

Colvin, H.M., gen. ed., *The History of the King's Works*, i, London, 1963.

Craik, T.W., *The Tudor Interlude*, Leicester, 1958.

Cursor Mundi, ed. R. Morris, EETS, Original Series, lix, London, 1874 (reprinted in 1961).

Davies, John, *Poems*, ed. Robert Krueger, Oxford, 1975.

Dennys, Rodney, *The Heraldic Imagination*, London, 1975.

Fox-Davies, A.C., *Complete Guide to Heraldry*, New York, 1909.

Godfrey, Walter H., *The College of Arms*, assisted by Sir Anthony Wagner, London, 1963.

The Great Chronicle of London, ed. A.H. Thomas and I.D. Thornley, London, 1938.

Hall, Edward, *The Union of the Two Noble Families of Lancaster and York*, London, 1550 (reprinted Scholar Press, 1970).

Harris, W.O., *Skelton's Magnyfycence and the Cardinal Virtue Tradition*, Chapel Hill, North Carolina, 1965.

Harvey, John, *English Medieval Architects*, London, 1954.

Hawes, Stephen, *The Example of Virtue*, in *The Minor Poems*, ed. Florence Gluck and Alice Morgan, EETS, Original Series, cclxxi, London, 1974.

——, *The Pastime of Pleasure*, ed. William Edward Mead, EETS, Original Series, clxxiii, London, 1928 (reprinted 1971).

Heralds' Commemorative Exhibition 1484–1934, London, 1936.

Holinshed, Raphaell, *Chronicles of England, Scotland, and Ireland*, iv, London, 1807.

Jonson, Ben, *Works*, ed. C.H. Herford and Percy Simpson, Oxford, 1925–52.

Justes of the Moneths of May and June, in *Remains of the Early Popular Poetry of England*, ed. W.C. Hazlitt, London, 1866.

Kelso, Ruth, 'Sixteenth Century Definitions of the Gentleman in England', *Journal of English and Germanic Philology*, xxiv (1925), 370–82.

Kernodle, G.R., *From Art to Theatre*, Chicago, 1944.

Kingsford, Charles L., ed., *Chronicles of London*, Oxford, 1905.

——, 'Historical Notes on Mediaeval London Houses', *London Topo-graphical Record*, x (1916), 94–100.

Kipling, Gordon, 'Henry VII and the Origins of Tudor Patronage', in *Patronage in the Renaissance*, ed. G.F. Lytle and S. Orgel, Princeton, 1981.

——, 'London Pageants for Margaret of Anjou', *Medieval English Theatre*, iv (1982), 5–27.

——, 'The Queen of May's Joust at Kennington and the Justes of the Moneths of May and June', *Notes and Queries*, ccxxix (1984), 158–62.

——, *The Triumph of Honour*, The Hague, 1977.

Knowles, David, and Hadcock, R., *Medieval Religious Houses*, London, 1971.

Kurth, Willy, *Complete Woodcuts of Albrecht Dürer*, New York, 1963.

Leland, John, *Collectanea*, ed. T. Hearne, 6 vols., London, 1774.

——, *Cygnea Cantio*, London, 1658.

London, H. Stanford, *Royal Beasts*, East Knoyle, 1956.

Loomis, R.S., 'The Allegorical Siege', *American Journal of Archaeology*, 2d Series, xxiii (1919), 255–69.

Lydgate, John, *Minor Poems*, ed. H.N. MacCracken, EETS, Original Series, cxcii, London, 1924 (reprinted in 1961).

The Master of Mary of Burgundy, ed. J.J.G. Alexander, New York, 1970.

Mattingly, Garrett, *Catharine of Aragon*, Boston, 1941.

Maydiston, Richard, *Concordia: Facta Inter Regem Riccardum II et Civitatem Londonie*, trans. C.R. Smith, unpublished dissertation, Princeton, 1972.

Memorials of King Henry the Seventh, ed. James Gairdner, Rolls Series x, London, 1858.

Millican, C.B., 'Spenser and Arthurian Legend', *RES* vi (1930), 167–74.

Missale Sarum, ed. F.H. Dickinson, Oxford, 1861–3.

Molinet, Jean, *Faictz et dictz de Jean Molinet*, ed. N. Dupire, Paris, 1936–9.

More, St Thomas, *St Thomas More: Selected Letters*, ed. Elizabeth Frances Rogers, New Haven, 1961.

The Myrroure of oure Ladye, ed. J.H. Blunt, EETS, Extra Series, xix, 1873.

Newton, Stella M., *Renaissance Theatre Costume*, London, 1975.

New York Metropolitan Museum of Art, *The Secular Spirit*, New York, 1975.

Payne, Blanche, *History of Costume*, New York, [1965].

Picinelli, Filippo, *Mundus Symbolicus*, Cologne, 1694.

Polydore Vergil, *Anglica Historia 1487–1537*, ed. and trans. D. Hay, Camden Series lxxiv, London, 1950.

Roberts, Thomas, *The English bowman, or tracts on archery: to which is added the second part of 'The bowman's glory'*, London, 1801.

Schiller, Gertrud, *Iconography of Christian Art*, 2 vols., London, 1971.

Scofield, C.L., *Edward IV*, London, 1923.

Stowe, John, *Survey of London*, ed. H. Morley, London, 1890.

Thomson, W.G., *History of Tapestry*, London, 1930.

The traduction & mariage of the princesse, London, [1500].

Twycross, Meg, and Carpenter, S., 'Masks in Medieval English Theatre', *Medieval English Theatre*, iii (1981), 96–105.

Wagner, Anthony Richard, *Heralds and Heraldry in the Middle Ages*, 2d ed., London, 1956.

Wagner, Sir Anthony, *Heralds of England: a History of the Office and College of Arms*, London, 1967.

——, *The Records and Collections of the College of Arms*, London, 1952.

Wickham, Glynne, *Early English Stages: 1300 to 1660*, i, London, 1959.

Wilson, F.P., *Oxford Dictionary of English Proverbs*, 3rd edn., Oxford, 1970.

Wood, Margaret, *The English Medieval House*, London, 1965.

Young, Alan, *Tudor and Jacobean Tournaments*, London, 1987.